HOW THE WEST

WAS LOST

How the West Was Lost

The Transformation of Kentucky from Daniel Boone to Henry Clay

Stephen Aron

The Johns Hopkins University Press
Baltimore and London

© 1996 The Johns Hopkins University Press
All rights reserved. Published 1996
Printed in the United States of America on acid-free paper
05 04 03 02 01 00 99 98 97 96   5 4 3 2 1

The Johns Hopkins University Press
2715 North Charles Street
Baltimore, Maryland 21218-4319
The Johns Hopkins Press Ltd., London

Library of Congress Cataloging-in-Publication Data will be found
at the end of this book.
A catalog record for this book is available from the British Library.

ISBN 0-8018-5296-x

For Amy

CONTENTS

ACKNOWLEDGMENTS

BILL JORDAN HAS TEASED ME for years about my sense of direction and has rarely missed an opportunity to question what a book about Kentucky has to do with the history of the American West. Overhearing one such razzing, an innocent bystander asked me if my book was really *only* about Kentucky. At that moment, another spectator, Matt Dennis, not so innocently injected that the text was in fact concerned with only a *part* of Kentucky. Needless to say, there was much laughter at my expense, especially since I could not deny Matt's charge. This book is not about all of Kentucky; it focuses almost entirely on the transformations of the Bluegrass and Green River regions. And yet I hope when Bill (and other readers) finish this book they will agree that its concerns amplify far beyond Kentucky, that this story is a significant chapter in the history of "how the West was lost."

I take this opportunity to thank Bill and Matt. The former's teasing prompted me to rethink the direction of my project. The latter's reading helped me bring it to conclusion.

I have a long list of other people and institutions to thank, but there is at least one unknown individual who deserves an anti-acknowledgment. I doubt that person will ever read this, but to the thief who stole my notecards from the trunk of my car outside of the Gene Autry Museum: &#$% you!

Having exorcised that demon, I return to the more pleasant task of expressing gratitude. In reading other acknowledgments, I've noticed that the most common means of doing this is through the language of credit and debt. Considering, though, that this book explores the alternatives to market relations that existed across the Ohio Valley frontier, it seems inappropriate to fall back on market metaphors. Nor does this formula explain much about how I came to this study of Kentucky.

Well before this project reached the starting gate, I had already benefited from the training given me by many talented teachers. Back on the (undergraduate) farm, Robert Gross taught me my first steps. In graduate school at the University of California, Gunther Barth broke me of bad writing habits, Paula Fass pushed me to push harder, Jim Kettner opened up colonial America for me, and Charlie Sellers guided me to the dissertation post. As important in readying the dissertation were the insights of Louis Hutchins, Lizzie Reis, Nina Silber, John Torpey, Anita Tien, and Sharon Ullman.

It has not been the smoothest ride from dissertation to book. Coming out of the gate and coming to Princeton sent my book on a course I had not anticipated. Going back east I got west—or, more accurately, I bolted off in pursuit of the intercultural history of the trans-Appalachian frontier. That I had the chance to follow an unexpected track attests to the freedom afforded by the Princeton history department. That I found my way at all shows how valuable was the feedback I received from so many folks at and about Princeton. The counsel of Jeremy Adelman, Kathy Brown, Alfred Bush, Ignacio Gallup-Díaz, Shel Garon, Evan Haefeli, Judith Hunter, Michael Jiménez, Walter Johnson, Steve Kantrowitz, Karen Merrill, Geoff Plank, Chris Rasmussen, Dan Rodgers, Marla Stone, Sean Wilentz, and Henry Yu were much appreciated. Nat Sheidley belongs on this list and merits another mention for his dedication as a research assistant. Dirk Hartog, I trust, will see what a difference he made to the introduction to this book. John Murrin, I hope, will see how much my errand into the wilderness gained from teaching with him.

On the trip from dissertation to book, I got great jockeying from commentators across the country. Drew Cayton, Kathy Conzen, Bill Cronon, Greg Dowd, Ellen Eslinger, Christine Heyrman, Patricia Limerick, Stuart Marks, James Merrell, Liz Perkins, Sandra Van Burkleo, and Richard White generously critiqued portions of the manuscript. Kathryn Preyer and Alan Taylor read and incisively commented on the whole dissertation; Lowell Harrison and Mac Rohrbough ably did the same for subsequent drafts. Johnny Faragher read both dissertation and final manuscript. What's more, he shared his research, his advice, and his encouragement, all of which was a boon[e] in moving this book from the start to the stretch.

The finish line would be nowhere in sight but for the assistance that I received from librarians in California, Illinois, Ohio, New Jersey, Virginia, Washington, D.C., and, of course, Kentucky. For anyone seeking a place to do historical research, I cannot recommend Kentucky highly enough. That reflects the years of cheerful assistance given me by archivists at the University of Kentucky, the Filson Club, the Kentucky Historical Society, and Western Kentucky University. Nancy Baird, James

Holmberg, William Marshall, and their entire staffs brought me everything I asked for—and more. Tom Appleton deserves here to be singled out. Without his aid and friendship, there would yet be no book—and I would be no colonel.

Robert Brugger, my editor at Johns Hopkins University Press, was enthusiastic about this book when it was just a dissertation and continued to be through the years he waited patiently for the author to deliver the manuscript. That he is still enthusiastic as the book goes to press has given me an enormous boost. So has the skillful copyediting provided by Marie Blanchard and the map making of Bill Nelson.

Liberal financial support from a number of institutions staked this project. The Berkeley Fellowship for Graduate Study sustained me at the University of California and the Robert Middlekauff Fellowship from the Huntington Library funded my research at that magnificent archive. The Princeton University Committee on Research in the Humanities and Social Sciences provided three separate awards for which I am deeply indebted.

I've lapsed, I concede, into the language of the market. That's acceptable when recognizing financial benefactors. It's certainly not suitable for the last round of acknowledgments, to family members. The contributions of Nicole, Tom, and Marilyn Aron cannot possibly be reckoned on any economistic ledger. Nor can those of my brother Paul, who could have gone to graduate school and written his own dissertation/book; I'm glad, though, he decided instead to improve this one through his superb editorial judgments. My son, Daniel Henry, was born when this project was well under way and was saddled with a name that reflects his father's immersion in it. While Daniel did not speed the book down the stretch, he was always (well, almost always) the most delightful of handicaps.

Finally, I come to Amy Green, to whom the book is lovingly dedicated. When I wrote the acknowledgments to my dissertation, I noted that I could have written the thesis without her, "but it wouldn't have been any fun." Five years later, that remains even more true. Indeed, from the day we met and through all the bumps in the making of this book, I have always felt like I was living in the winner's circle.

HOW THE WEST

WAS LOST

Introduction

BOOK TITLES CAN BE TRICKY THINGS. Take this one; its main title may call to mind a particular time and place that we associate with the historical "West." But this book is not about that West. Instead, its focus is on what used to be called "the New West," which, to make matters more confusing, was older than what has come to be called "the Old West." Its subtitle may seem equally deceptive, for while this book treats Daniel Boone and Henry Clay as emblematic figures, it is not a dual biography. The emphasis is on the transformation of their worlds and not on the specific course of their lives.[1]

Daniel Boone (1735–1820) and Henry Clay (1777–1852) inhabited very different, yet not so different, worlds. This book is about that paradox. Focused on the years in which the lives of the two most famous Kentuckians overlapped, this study sorts cultural conflicts and confluences to explain how the world of Daniel Boone gave way to that of Henry Clay. This transformation "from Boone to Clay" encompassed the initial American conquest, colonization, and consolidation of the trans-Appalachian West (the New West) and comprised a seminal chapter in the westward expansion of the United States.

The disparities between the worlds of Boone and Clay seem much more obvious than the similarities. Daniel Boone was eighteenth-century America's archetypal backwoodsman. He spent much of his life in or near Indian country, and the proximity rubbed off. Like the Indian men with whom he mingled, Boone lived in a hunter's world. His happiest times were passed tracking game, living off the land, and enjoying the crude shelter of the Kentucky forest. This was not the Kentucky of Henry Clay. In the early nineteenth century, Clay emerged as the new republic's foremost spokesman for commercial and manufacturing development. Putting his money where his political mouth was, he built a showplace plantation on the outskirts of Lexington and invested in mercantile and industrial enterprises in the city. The opulence and bustle of Lexington, then the economic capital of the trans-Appalachian West, presented a glaring contrast to the wilderness through which Daniel Boone hunted. "No where in America," noted the author of an 1818 guidebook, "has the almost instantaneous change, from an uncultivated waste to the elegances of civilization, been so striking" as in the vicinity of Henry Clay's home.[2]

By the old orthodoxy, most notably articulated by Frederick Jackson Turner, the differences between the worlds of Daniel Boone and Henry Clay made all the difference. For Turner, the transition from Boone to Clay was a synecdoche for the "winning of the West." He depicted a "procession of [ever higher] civilization[s] marching single file." The progress that commenced with Boone, the conqueror of Indians and colonizer of trans-Appalachian lands, culminated with Clay, whose personal and political economy consolidated what Turner considered the highest stage of "civilization." And then, in Turner's sketch of American westward expansion, the cavalcade into Kentucky repeated itself across the continent.[3]

While this book shares Turner's view of the significance of Kentucky, it departs from his tidy "triumphalism." What happened in Kentucky mattered. In important ways, the transformation from Boone to Clay prefigured the ensuing conquest, colonization, and consolidation of that vast domain stretching from the Appalachians to the Pacific which nineteenth-century Americans referred to as the "Great West." But in Kentucky and across the Great West, the processes of conquest, colonization, and consolidation overlapped; they did not unfold in an orderly parade. Nor was the ejection of Indian peoples, the resettlement of expropriated lands, and the construction of a new political and economic order a cause for uncritical celebration. Indeed, in recent years revisionist historians have recast Turner's progressive procession as a gloomy litany of peoples dislodged, cultures disturbed, lands despoiled, and dreams destroyed.[4]

As the title suggests, this book emphasizes ways of life vanished and worlds unmade, but it is not a history of paradise lost. The history of how the West was lost demands more than mere inversions. The passage of Kentucky from the world of Boone to that of Clay was no simple morality play in which wily plutocrats swindled ingenuous common folk, though pioneers and their descendants sometimes saw history that way. Kentucky's transformation from hunting ground to commercialized landscape featured many casualties, but the roles of victim and villain were imperfectly cast. Daniel Boone and fellow pioneer possessors were hardly the "injured innocents" they professed to be. Ohio Valley Indians, who suffered terrible injuries, more obviously fit the part, but it trivializes their history to reduce them to victimized innocents.[5]

It also obscures the messier dynamic that occurred when peoples came together and their different ways collided, and thus deprives the frontier of its proper significance in American history. As used by contemporaries of Boone and Clay, "frontier" identified the periphery of Anglo-American colonization. At the same time, the term referred to the contested territory between "Indian country" and "backcountry." Thanks largely to Frederick Jackson Turner, the frontier of Boone's day acquired a grander historical significance, though the word shed its association with international and intercultural relations. Now, however, historians have stripped the frontier of the providential veneer that Turner assigned it and have recovered its former meaning as perimeter and intersection. Daniel Boone's frontier was not a virgin land but a borderland, a crossroads where Indian and European cultures collided, yet also surprisingly coincided.[6]

A few of Daniel Boone's compatriots crossed what was a still fluid frontier; others, like Boone himself, straddled the cultural border between Indian country and backcountry. But competition, first for game and then for land, drove Indians and pioneers apart. Conquest of Indian country eroded the middle ground that Boone occupied. As the cultural gap between Indian and backcountry widened, the contrast between the worlds of Daniel Boone and Henry Clay narrowed.

Expanding the historical horizon resolves the paradox of worlds different and not so different. Viewed exclusively through the experiences of white men, the worlds of Daniel Boone and Henry Clay may appear at opposite poles. A broader panorama allows us to see what cultural alternatives lay across the frontier and beyond the relatively constricted spectrum from Boone to Clay.

Bringing Rebecca Boone and Lucretia Clay into the picture also shrinks the distance between their husbands' worlds. For Daniel Boone and his pioneer brethren, the dream of settling what they called a "good poor man's country" spurred the colonization of Kentucky. Rebecca Boone and her pioneer sisters, however, understood that a good poor man's country was not the same as a good poor woman's country; indeed, the former was often antithetical to the latter. Through the consolidation of Henry Clay's Kentucky, the worldly ambitions of white men, though by no means all the same, remained distinct from the increasingly other-worldly aspirations of women.

Writing the history of Kentucky from the world of Daniel Boone to that of Henry Clay requires looking beyond the lives of these men; writing the history of how the West was lost requires looking beyond what happened. It demands suspension of the sense of inevitability that inspired histories of how the West was won. Accordingly, this book seeks to explain what did not happen: the preservation of indigenous fauna and flora, the coalescence or at least continued coexistence of Ohio Indian and backcountry hunters, the protection of pioneer homesteading privileges, the equal distribution or redistribution of land, the perpetuation of customary common rights, the democratization of legal and political systems, the abolition of slavery, the confederation of free and unfree laborers, the implementation of an agrarian political economy, the arrival of the millenium.

None of these things came to pass. Henry Clay's Kentucky displaced hunters and held no place for Indians. The proliferation of tenancy, itinerant wage labor, and slavery denied men the independence they wanted and marked Kentucky as a broken promised land. For women, dependence was a given, and the transformations of *this* world offered little hope. Instead, women and some men too looked for salvation in a world away from Boone's and Clay's.

The chapters that follow describe what the transition from "Boone to Clay" meant for the peoples of the trans-Appalachian West. Not a history of paradise lost, this is a book about possibilities lost.

ONE *The Meeting of Hunters*

AROUND SUNSET ON DECEMBER 22, 1769, while hunting near the Kentucky River, Daniel Boone met Will Emery. This meeting of hunters, one from the backcountry, the other from Indian country, was also a meeting of worlds, for the ways of backcountry and Indian hunters were converging geographically and culturally. But as paths crossed, the co-existence of backcountry and Indian country, never too secure, became less so.

Seven and a half months earlier, Daniel Boone, along with five other men and about a dozen horses, had left the Yadkin Valley of North Carolina to hunt deer in the Appalachian Mountains and in the mysterious region beyond. Boone's party included his brother-in-law John Stewart and the trader John Findley. Guided by Findley through the Cumberland Gap, the group split up to begin their more serious pursuit of deer-skins. Together Boone and Stewart ranged widely across the eastern and central parts of Kentucky—until a party of Shawnees surprised the two backcountry hunters. Leading the Indian band was Will Emery or, as he referred to himself in pidgin English, "Captain Will."

The encounter between Boone's party and Emery's was one of a number between "long hunters" from the "Greater Pennsylvania" backcountry and Indians from the Ohio Valley in the game-rich country known as "Kentucke." Beginning early in the 1760s, backcountry men commenced fall and winter hunts that took them across the Appalachians for several months or more at a time. Skirting Cherokee country, long hunters passed through the Cumberland Gap, then headed into an area where no currently occupied Indian towns were located. But Indians from adjacent territories, primarily from villages north of the Ohio River, actively hunted these same lands.[1]

When Ohio Indians—principally Shawnees and Delawares, but including a polyglot mixture of peoples—ran into white poachers, the impact reverberated across the Ohio River, across the Appalachian Mountains, and even across the Atlantic Ocean. Lives and livelihoods were most directly at stake for mingling hunters, but the prospects of relations in Indian country and backcountry hinged as well on the outcome of meetings. Anxiety also gripped colonial elites and imperial administrators who realized that the future of the British Empire was being shaped by the intersection of hunters on the Appalachian frontier.

I

By all testimony, Kentucky was a hunting ground without rival in the third quarter of the eighteenth century. The profusion of game in the territory south of the Ohio River and west of the Cumberland Mountains amazed European explorers, traders, soldiers, surveyors, and settlers. Dr. Thomas Walker, sent in 1750 to spy western lands for the Loyal Company of Virginia, was astonished by the number of animals inhabiting the western slopes of the Appalachians. "We killed in the Journey 13 Buffaloes, 8 Elks, 53 Bears, 20 Deer, 4 Wild Geese, about 150 Turkeys, besides small game," Walker enumerated in his journal. And, he exulted, "we might have killed three times as much meat, if we had wanted it." In the years after Walker's expedition, Kentucky added to its reputation as an unparalleled hunting ground. A collection of game the like of Kentucky, remarked one astounded trader, "is not to be seen in any part of the known World." There, claimed another, "Buffalo, Elk, and Bear were . . . rolling fat, and weary for the rifle shot." And "turkeys so numerous it might be said they appeared but one flock, universally scattered in the woods." [2]

These testimonials did not explain how this extraordinary hunting land came to be, nor did they provide much information about the Indian peoples who hunted there and shaped the landscape. Whites attributed the exuberance of eighteenth-century Kentucky's animal census first to providence and then to the absence of occupants. Why Indians hunted but did not reside in the region puzzled European attestants, who knew little of the history and culture of the Indian peoples of the Ohio Valley. They knew even less about the strategies adopted by Ohio Indians to deal with Europeans like themselves.

Why such rich lands were empty of Indian villages has puzzled historians too. Archaeological artifacts certify the continuous presence of Indian peoples on the south side of the Ohio River for over ten thousand years prior to the arrival of Europeans. When French explorers first penetrated the Ohio Valley in the late seventeenth century, they found dozens of hamlets on the south side of the river, which their maps labeled as Chaouanon (Shawnee) towns. As late as 1736, a French census listed 200 Shawnee men at the village of Eskippathiki on the eastern edge of the Bluegrass region of central Kentucky. The Shawnees, however, were by then a scattered people, and Eskippathiki stood alone. Although John Findley probably visited Eskippathiki on his trading rounds during the 1750s, residents had abandoned the town by the time Findley brought Daniel Boone through the Cumberland Gap.[3]

The desettlement of Kentucky began a century before Daniel Boone or any other Anglo-American hunters crossed the Appalachians. It resulted from a series of invasions of the middle Ohio River valley by Iroquois warriors in the 1670s and 1680s. Pitting Iroquois against Ohio villagers, these wars were not an incidental prologue to the later confrontations of Europeans and Indians in the Ohio Valley. Demographic and economic factors, closely tied to European colonialism, spurred the Iroquois' invasions of the Ohio Valley. Iroquois population had fallen catastrophically as a result of epidemic diseases of European origin and endemic warfare (made more deadly by the introduction of European firearms). To relieve grief and replenish numbers, the Iroquois had long raided neighboring peoples in search of captives for torture and adoption. But the incursions into the Ohio Country were of an expanded scale and to a new end; these were more "beaver wars" than "mourning wars." To control Ohio Valley hunting and trapping grounds, the Iroquois depopulated much of the Ohio Country, including the Shawnee towns in Kentucky. Shawnees dispersed in small contingents into Alabama, Georgia, the Carolinas, and, later, Pennsylvania.[4]

The repopulation of the Ohio Country occurred gradually during the first half of the eighteenth century. Seeking refuge from white encroachments and defying the Iroquois' hegemonic pretenses, several hundred Shawnees, along with other Pennsylvania Indian peoples, began trickling back into the Ohio Country around 1715. Returnees located villages along the lower Scioto River. Shawnee in name, these resettled towns included an assortment of ethnic groups: Pennsylvania Indians heading west to escape Anglo-American encirclement and Illinois Indians moving east to position themselves between French and British trading orbits. By the 1760s, "Shawnee" and other Ohio Indian villages also boasted numbers of people of European or partial European descent. Multilingualism was the rule—witness the adoption of English name and rank by Will Emery. At Chillicothe, the largest Shawnee town, residents typically spoke three or more languages.[5]

An influx of Anglo-American traders, captives, and renegades brought English words and English ways into the multiethnic villages of Ohio Indian country. As part of their incorporation into Indian communities, backcountry-born captives learned to live and think as Indians. But adopted captives, as well as other "white Indians," also introduced colonial food ways, fashions, and furnishings. At the aptly named Newcomer's Town in 1772, missionary David McClure found traditional bark longhouses adjacent to backcountry-style log cabins. The home of the Delaware prophet Neolin, with its stone cellar, staircase, stone chimney, fireplace, closets, and apartments, reminded McClure of "an english dwelling." [6]

While the blending of peoples and material cultures gave villages a new look, Ohio Indians retained an older sense of who they were and how they lived. For men, that meant they were hunters. Ohio Indian men hunted intermittently the year round, but the most concentrated pursuit of game occurred in fall and winter. Unlike brief spring and summer excursions, winter hunts extended over weeks and months and involved travel over long distances. It was these longer hunts that brought men from across the Ohio River and from Appalachian valleys into Kentucky. Although returning Shawnees resettled north of the Ohio, they maintained seasonal claims to Kentucky lands.

Custody of this vast "unoccupied" territory south of the Ohio River was shared, if not always peacefully. From south and north, Indian villagers joined Shawnees as hunters of Kentucky. In the eighteenth century, frequent skirmishes between longtime northern and southern enemies occurred on the geographic middle ground that was Kentucky. Unlike Iroquois expansion of the previous century, these Indian-Indian conflicts were generally small-scale clashes, part of the rounds of retaliatory violence by which woodland Indian men revenged their slain kin and demonstrated their own courage. [7]

Hunting and warring were the measure of manhood among Ohio Indians. Skill in providing meat for relations roused Ohio Indian men as did no other action, except perhaps skill and stoicism in combat or captivity. Young men took these roles most seriously, taking enormous pride in their exploits in warfare and in the game that they provided for their families, especially for elders who could no longer hunt. [8]

Winter hunting trips were not exclusively male sojourns, however. Whole families participated on longer hunting journeys. Women packed necessities and carried belongings from villages to mobile winter hunting camps. There they cut wood, hauled water, dressed game, prepared food, as well as watched over children. This was essential and valued work, yet to Anglo-Americans hardly the source of pride that hunting was for males.

During the peak of the hunting season, Ohio villages were virtually deserted. With the coming of spring, hunters and their families returned. In spring and summer, the tending of crops and the gathering of wild plants became the primary subsistence activities. Women assumed control of the cultivation of beans, squash, pumpkins, sweet potatoes, and especially corn. With that leading role came a dignity that Europeans rarely appreciated.[9]

Indeed, Europeans saw only drudgery and took this division of labor by sex and season as proof of Indian savagery. Anglo-American observers fixated on "the humiliating condition" of Ohio Indian women, who were treated more "as slaves than as companions." By contrast, male hunters lounged about, "it being thought disgraceful for an Indian [man] to labor."[10]

A few astute Europeans offered a more nuanced reading of the labor, gender, and subsistence systems of Ohio Indians. The more observant allowed that hunting entailed considerable skill and exertion, even as it involved extended periods of inactivity. "The morning and evening," elaborated the Moravian missionary John Heckewelder, "are the precious hours for the hunter. They lose nothing by sleeping in the middle of the day." Along with other perceptive students of Indian ways, Heckewelder also attributed the midday idleness of hunters to their unwillingness to work harder to secure undesired surpluses.[11]

The absence of an acquisitive ethic lightened women's work as well, though Europeans rarely noticed and never fully comprehended this. Because Ohio Indians safeguarded their subsistence by combining products of forest and farm, because intercropping of corn, beans, and other plants reduced the depletion of soil, and because Indian mothers bore fewer children than their backcountry counterparts, Indian women found that an acre or two met a family's needs. Nor did they labor alone in the fields. In addition to sharing work with female relations and children, they received timely assistance from adult men, who did not simply sleep away the spring and summer.[12]

Still, certain things a man did not do, as captive James Smith discovered. Taken from western Pennslyvania in 1755, Smith spent five years in Ohio Indian country. Shortly after his adoption, he ventured out to assist his female relations in the fields, winning their applause for his efforts. But when he returned to the village, "the old men" scolded Smith for "hoe[ing] corn like a squaw." Smith learned his lesson about gender roles well. "They never had occasion to reprove me for anything like this again, as I never was extremely fond of work."[13]

In most years, the products of fields figured more prominently than the products of forests in the diets of Indians; nonetheless, European experts consistently devalued Indian farming and Indian farmers. Instead of extolling the security and balance of the Indians' mixed subsistence system, European theorists labeled Ohio peoples as hunters, pure and simple. That designation represented the lowest stage of social evolution and provided a well-worn rationale for Anglo-American conquest and colonization. By ignoring Indian cultivation and then equating improvement exclusively with cultivation, Europeans voided Indian claims to Kentucky.[14]

Not only did Indians cultivate what they needed in the Ohio Country, but Indian improvements did much to enhance Kentucky's status as a hunter's paradise. It was the torch and not the hoe, however, that modified this land. Throughout the woodlands of North America, Indian peoples periodically burned the forests to clear out underbrush and stimulate the growth of new grasses. This, they hoped, would better nourish large herbivores and make prey less elusive. In what is now southwestern Kentucky, the effects of Indian-set fires were most dramatically displayed, as meadows succeeded forests as the landscape's dominant feature. Trained to assess the quality of soil on the basis of the number and types of trees it supported, eighteenth-century European scouts disparaged these prairies as worthless "barrens." But their accounts of abundant game unwittingly attested to the achievements of Indian firemen.[15]

Woodland Indian beliefs also contributed to the abundance of game. Because they regarded animals as their close kin, Ohio Indians limited their hunting. Specific rites varied from one village to another, but across the woodlands Indians shared a rich ceremonialism by which they conveyed reverence for their prey and for the powerful animal "manitous" that were the spiritual guardians of nonhuman "nations." Conducted alongside the preparations for hunting, the pursuit of game, and the disposition of carcasses, elaborate rituals allowed hunters to retain the favor of powerful forces. Failure to perform the ceremonies, or to behave properly before, during, and after the hunt, would sever the bonds between hunter and prey. Bad times would surely follow for the hunter who killed more meat than his family and his fellow villagers needed.[16]

Reciprocity governed relations with human as well as animal kin. Custom, for example, dictated that when a Delaware hunter killed a deer in the presence of a fellow villager, the animal was given to the companion. Shawnees followed a similar protocol, presenting their gift with the remark: "I enliven you as a man." No bargain was struck; the recipient provided nothing in return—though as in other societies where the rules of the market did not obtain, the benefactor expected similar respect should the situation ever be reversed.[17]

Hunters enlivened entire villages through the redistribution of wild meat. Among the Shawnees, observed one American soldier in 1786, "when any of their young men or hunters would kill meat, it was . . . laid down by the chiefs, one of whom cut it into as many shares" as there were "fires" (as there were households in the village). Thus, "no one lived better than another, but all fared alike."[18]

The Indian hunters' commitment to the commonweal left a deep impression on white men and women who got a close look at Ohio village worlds. During the 1750s, the Ohio Indians who captured and adopted James Smith divided wild meat, whether plentiful or scarce, "according to the strictest rules of justice." A quarter century later, captive Jonathan Alder waxed even more enthusiastically about his adopted Shawnee kin's devotion to mutual well-being. His admiration peaked after he injured his back and could not hunt. Throughout his prolonged convalescence, he was carried on a litter. Yet his cousins "refrained from murmuring, and did not seem, in the least, to regret the necessity of carrying me; on the contrary, they . . . treated me, all the time, with the utmost kindness and tenderness, and permitted me to share in the full benefit of the hunt, the same as if I had done my share of the hunting."[19]

The reflections of Smith and Alder imply a continuity in the exchange relations of Ohio Indian hunters; in fact, the third quarter of the eighteenth century brought deep and unsettling changes to the character of exchange within Ohio villages and between Indians and Europeans. The expulsion of the French after the Seven Years' War and the subsequent incursions of backcountry hunters unmade the world that Ohio Indians had known.

The departure of the French deprived Ohio Indians of the cocreators of what Richard White has called "the middle ground," the fragile yet unique common world between Indian men and women and French men in the Great Lakes Country. For the Shawnees, Delawares, and other refugees from Pennsylvania, the French connection was never as binding as for Great Lakes Indians. Returnees to the Ohio Country had attempted to create a middle ground of their own, a location between and apart from French and British domains. From their towns on the Scioto, Shawnees were well positioned to attract both French and British traders but be subject to neither colonial regime.[20]

Unhappy with the Shawnees' independence, a French minister disparaged the Scioto settlements as "a sort of republic with a fairly large number of bad characters of various nations." Fearful of driving Ohio Indians closer to the English, the French tolerated the situation. In fact, they catered to "republicans" by adhering to Ohio Indian expectations about the conduct of intersocietal trade. For the French, this meant placing symbolic and diplomatic considerations above the bottom line. Even as administrators complained about the expense of giving presents, French authorities usually understood that without gifts there could be no friendship, and without friendship there could be neither trade nor military alliance. Friendship was conditional, however. During the Seven Years' War, Ohio Indians attacked English backcountry settlements, but they were ambiguous allies of the French. Rather than French victory, Ohio Indians fought to preserve the balance of power and the balance of trade that preserved their independence.[21]

British victory shattered the Ohio Indians' middle ground and brought vindictive trade policies. During the war, British authorities grew increasingly suspicious of Ohio Indians. One administrator insisted that "the Indians must be Taught to Fear Us and then they'l act Like Fr[ien]ds." Such was the opinion of Lord Jeffrey Amherst, the British military commander in North America. After conquering New France, Amherst was not inclined to conciliate independent and, to his mind, indolent Ohio Indians. Ignoring the counsel of more experienced advisors, Amherst ordered an end to gift giving. Henceforth, trade would be carried out on a strictly commercial basis. Indian hunters would be paid for the skins they exchanged and not rewarded for their unreliable "friendship."[22]

Amherst's efforts won few friends in the Ohio Valley; to the contrary, his attempt to dictate the terms of trade inspired an insurrection that spread across trans-Appalachian Indian country. It spread into the backcountry when Ohio Indian warriors struck British posts and raided western settlements across a broad front. But a trade embargo, a military counteroffensive, and a smallpox outbreak defeated the Indian uprising, which while it enlisted warriors from many villages, remained a decentralized undertaking.

All was not lost, however. The fury of the Indians taught influential administrators how unreconciled Ohio Indians were to their new status as subjects of George III. It prompted the executors of the fur trade to soften their line about the character of exchange. When Anglo-American traders returned to the Ohio Valley, they allowed Indians to set the protocol for trade. Simultaneously, British policymakers hardened their line against the expansion of backcountry settlements. Henceforth, Indian country and backcountry were to be separated at the crest of the Appalachians.

Unfortunately for Ohio Indians, the line did not hold. During the mid and late 1760s, backcountry settlers by the hundreds and then the thousands established farmsteads on the Indian side of the Appalachians. Penetrating even further into Indian country were scores of white hunters, who began to make regular fall and winter hunts into Kentucky. While Indians recognized the threat that long hunters posed, they arrived at no consensus about how to deal with the poachers and with the broader problems of backcountry expansion. Killing poachers and terrorizing backcountry settlers appealed to many, especially to young men, whose place as hunters was most threatened by competition in Kentucky. The experience of the last war weighed more heavily on older and more sober-minded men and women. In village, intertribal, and international councils, they voiced hope for a peaceful solution, one which would get trespassing hunters to respect Indian rights. Ultimately the success of that strategy depended on the collaboration of British colonial authorities who claimed to govern both backcountry and Ohio Indian country.

II

For English and Anglo-American gentlemen charged with preserving peace and trade with Indians and establishing order over the backcountry, the meetings of hunters exposed the limits of their governance. Sympathetic as some officials were to Indian pleas, they lacked the means and often the will to repress backcountry hunters. That failure strengthened militant voices among Ohio Indians. Even Indians of a more accommodating bent proved troublingly independent. Unable either to restrain backcountry hunters or to dictate to Indian hunters, colonial officials watched the Appalachian frontier again become a war zone.

The problem, it seemed to many gentry authorities, was that backcountry settlers in general, and "hunters" in particular, too closely resembled the Indian peoples whose lands they invaded. According to well-heeled travelers, primitive ways prevailed along a wide arc from the interior of Pennsylvania to the uplands of South Carolina. They especially proliferated where hunting lured inhabitants from civilizing pursuits. In the Carolina uplands that were the southern flank of Greater Pennsylvania in the 1760s, the Anglican minister Charles Woodmason confronted a "people of abandon'd Morals and profligate Principles, the lowest Pack of Wretches my eyes ever saw." Emissaries for church and king recoiled from the near-savage "white Indians" who peopled the backcountry. Residents of the upper Ohio Valley, reported Thomas Gage, the British military commander for North America in 1772, "differ[ed] little from Indians in their manner of life." They dressed like Indians (or were "half-naked"), comported themselves like Indians, and indiscriminately consorted with one another like Indians. Backcountry settlers, agreed Sir William Johnson, supervisor of Britain's relations with northern Indians, were "a lawless set of people as fond of independency as" Indians, "and more regardless of government, owing to ignorance, prejudice, democratical principles and their remote situation."[23]

More disturbing, backcountry people, like adjacent Indian villagers, displayed little respect for their "betters" and no enthusiasm for the schemes of improvers and uplifters. The effrontery of backcountry residents appalled Woodmason and other gentlemen who expected their inferiors to behave deferentially. Woodmason typically preached to drunken and hostile audiences, while other Christian missionaries found backcountry inhabitants as indifferent as Indians. Agricultural reformers, too, floundered in campaigns to promote more efficient use of the land. A Quaker improver, William Logan, who urged Carolina farmers to work and live more religiously, reluctantly conceded that "they seem to Chuse their Old way as being less trouble." Indeed, echoed Woodmason, "they delight in their present, low, lazy, sluttish, heathenish, hellish Life, and seem not desirous of changing it."[24]

Gentry commentators blamed hunting for the shared deficiencies of backcountry and Indian country. According to the theory of human developmental history that reigned in the Age of Enlightenment, when backcountry whites hunted, they reverted to the lowest mode of subsistence. True, gentlemen on both sides of the Atlantic hunted too. But they went after game for sport, not subsistence, and thus escaped being stigmatized as white Indians. By contrast, backcountry hunting supposedly underwrote the indigence, indolence, and insolence of inland settlers. Hunting signified the confluence of backcountry and Indian ways of life, while at the same time it caused conflict between frontier peoples.[25]

In addition to encouraging degeneracy and triggering violence, hunting by backcountry settlers challenged established authority. British poaching laws prohibited the laboring portion of the population from engaging in the aristocratic sports of hunting, fishing, and fowling, thus denying the vast majority of Britons an alternative means of contributing to the subsistence of their households—alternative, that is, to the tenant farming and agricultural day labor that enriched the owners of great estates. Liberty of hunting, in contrast, cost British-American landlords a prominent badge of aristocratic privilege and loosened their control over the laboring population. Beneath genteel expressions of contempt for the impoverishment and immorality of backcountry life lurked gentlemen's resentment of the ease with which ill-mannered backcountry hunters lived, and of the democratization of leisure that went hand in hand with the democratization of hunting. In no other place, sniffed William Byrd II, did men "live with less labor than" in the backcountry of Virginia and North Carolina.[26]

In the backcountry, as in Indian country, women suffered by the division of leisure and labor—or so gentlemen contended. Backcountry women lived in the rudest conditions, and they also did the hardest work. While men "played" at hunting and amused themselves in a variety of rough and tumble contests, women toiled. Men made "their Wives rise out of their Beds early in the Morning, at the same time that they Lye and Snore, till the Sun has run one third of his course, and disperst all the unwholesome Damps," charged Byrd.[27]

In perpetuating the view of male pioneers as lazy and improvident, the gentry downplayed the ingenuity of hunters, Indian and white. These authors also demonstrated their unfamiliarity with the intensive labors needed to carve a pioneer farmstead out of the forest. But the exaggeration of backcountry indolence served gentry purposes: it helped to justify the holding of slaves (for where hunting provided necessities, only coercion stemmed man's "natural" inclination to idleness), and it enhanced the value of lands held for speculation. In their promotional tracts, speculators publicized the remarkable possibilities of hunting and fishing in the newly opened lands of North America. How better to attract buyers and tenants to the enormous tracts granted well-connected gentlemen than with promises of unrestricted hunting and leisurely living? The Edenic fabrications manufactured by the agents of land speculators worked. To these mythic poor man's (back)countries, which combined incredibly fruitful soil with the "spontaneous productions of nature" (meaning the abundance of fish and game), came tens of thousands of pioneers.[28]

Hunting, then, left men of wealth and power divided. As rulers, they blamed hunting for the disorderliness of new settlements and for the rage of Indians. There was "but one remedy" against the evils associated with hunting, avowed J. Hector St. Jean de Crèvecoeur, and that was to just say no. "As long as we keep ourselves busy tilling the earth, there is no fear of any of us becoming wild; it is the chase and the food it procures that have this strange effect." Simply banning hunting, however, threatened the profits that great landlords and speculators derived from the reputation of the backcountry as a land of freedom and abundance. More frightening to authorities, prohibition risked exposing their irrelevance. The king's proclamation of 1763 established a boundary across which white hunters were not to go. But almost immediately North American administrators recognized that such edicts were unenforceable.[29]

Despite the outcry against troublesome hunters, colonial game laws never duplicated the repressive "bloody code" that awed English poachers. Though Virginia planters aspired to the standing of English lords, they did so without the latter's crucial monopoly on hunting. Beginning in the seventeenth century, Virginia lawmakers enacted a group of statutes that established deer hunting seasons in Virginia. The game laws of colonial Virginia, however, always exempted the residents of "frontier" counties from seasonal restrictions on taking venison. And while English laws made illegal hunting a capital offense, Virginia poachers faced only fines and whippings.[30]

In the Carolinas, lawmakers took a harder line. Anticipating Crève-coeur's prescription, a North Carolina statute of 1745 narrowed the privilege of hunting to residents of the colony who cultivated at least 5,000 hills of corn. To repress vagrant hunters, who were accused of wasting wildlife, murdering livestock, and promoting disorder, the North Carolina assembly in 1766 doubled the corn-planting requirement and introduced a 100-acre property qualification. As in Virginia, however, penalties were too light and enforcement too lax to restrain illegal hunters.[31]

In South Carolina, extralegal operations put more teeth into anti-hunter crusades. Linking banditry and hunting, planters and yeoman farmers combined in the 1760s to rid the backcountry of disorderly persons who lived by stealing and killing deer. Self-styled "Regulators," eschewing due process, sought to make the South Carolina backcountry safe for "respectable" cultivators. These vigilantes ousted reprobate hunters from the more settled districts of the South Carolina upcountry.[32]

Still, neither legal nor extralegal measures had much effect on the sparsely populated borderlands of backcountry and Indian country. Contemptuous of officials and their injunctions, increasing numbers of backcountry men congregated each autumn at the headwaters of the Holston River to make long hunts across the Appalachians. Colonial authorities could do little in the face of the brazen defiance of long hunters; they had neither the money nor the manpower to police thousands of square miles of frontier.[33]

Admitting that backcountry people "are not to be confined by any boundaries or limits," Sir William Johnson attempted to defuse conflict by convincing Indians to withdraw from contested territory. An opponent of Amherst's punitive policies, Johnson had influential friends among northern Indians, whose interests he earnestly wished to protect. But Johnson was also deeply interested in the acquisition of land to enrich himself and his friends. At Fort Stanwix in November 1768, he persuaded an assembly of more than three thousand Indians, principally members of the Iroquois confederacy, to cede their claims to lands south of the Ohio River and east of the mouth of the Great Kanawha. Almost completely absent from the council were representatives of the Shawnees and Delawares, whose villages lay closest to the lands in question. Johnson knew that Ohio Indians had their own interest in the ceded lands, but he let himself believe that the Shawnees and Delawares were dependents of the Iroquois and that his negotiating partners had a right of conquest to Ohio Valley lands. His ambition to open new lands for Anglo-American hunting, settlement, and *speculation* outweighed his sympathies for underrepresented peoples.[34]

Not surprisingly, the treaty won few friends in the Ohio Country, and militant opposition to British policies soon reemerged. Resentment ran especially high in Shawnee country. At Chillicothe, enraged hunters denounced the pretensions of the Iroquois in making a pact about which the Shawnees had not been consulted and to which they had not consented. Adding insult to injury, the British made no allowance for gifts to Ohio Indians and failed to insist that the Iroquois share theirs. Along the Scioto, talk of war once again dominated village councils.[35]

What really alarmed officials of the British Indian Department was word that disenchanted Ohio Indians were putting together a confederacy. Reports that Shawnee emissaries had in 1769 traveled across Indian country disturbed colonial leaders. So did news of a well-attended conclave at Chillicothe in which preparations for a united front against the Fort Stanwix Treaty and against further Anglo-American expansion were discussed. In August 1770, Amherst's successor, Lieutenant-General Gage, pronounced the possibility of an Indian confederacy "a very dangerous event." Gage's staff, who knew how localistic Indians were in their attachments and how deep-seated were the enmities between northern and southern Indians, assured him that the scheme was "impractical." In October, however, Gage fretted that the congress held on the Scioto "has had more effect than our Indian officers thought possible."[36]

To thwart a potential confederacy, British officials worked to isolate militants. It was a time-tested strategy, and it succeeded again in the Ohio Country in the early 1770s. British officials detached southeastern, Great

Lakes, and many Ohio Indians from the envisioned confederacy. Great Lakes Indians agreed that Kentucky was too distant to defend. South of Kentucky, colonial officers negotiated two treaties with the Chero-kees which kept them from joining with the Shawnees. Even in Shawnee towns, advocates of peace remained roughly equal in number to proponents of war.[37]

More conciliatory Shawnees did not simply resign themselves to the loss of Kentucky. While militants strove in the long term for a grand alliance to roll back the backcountry, and in the meantime killed trespassing hunters, opponents of an immediate war continued to appeal to British officials for comprehensive protection from aggressive "Virgini-ans," a label that Ohio Indians attached to Carolinians as well. They also sidestepped British mediators and tried to reach a piecemeal understanding directly with backcountry "long knives." [38]

It was against this background that Will Emery met Daniel Boone. Once his men restrained Boone and Stewart, Captain Will began his interrogation. Ascertaining the location of the "station camp" at which Boone and Stewart had deposited their skins, Emery impounded the pair's peltry and equipment, including their cherished Pennsylvania rifles. But instead of executing the poachers as English magistrates might have ordered, Emery released them after seven days' captivity. He also pre-sented Boone and Stewart with two pairs of moccasins, a doeskin, a little French gun, and a small amount of powder and shot. By this "trade," Emery afforded the released captives a means to survive on their return to the backcountry. By sparing them, he tried to avoid the cycle of retalia-tion by which the kin of hunters on both sides of the frontier avenged the killing of one of their own. Like English justices who selectively forgave convicted poachers, Emery hoped his mercy would be properly appreci-ated and his message that Kentucky was off limits to white hunters would be relayed across the backcountry. Before parting, he warned Boone and Stewart that the "wasps and yellow jackets" would "surely sting" them if they poached in Indian country again.[39]

Emery's mercy was not unique. Indeed, several other meetings of hunters followed a similar script. Long hunters were warned not to take pelts from animals in Indian country, and their skins and supplies were confiscated. But like Boone, they received guns and shot to keep them alive, and sometimes even advice about where to find "plenty [of meat] to kill to go home." In effect, Ohio Indians treated backcountry hunters much as did the laws of Virginia. Just as Virginia statutes permitted "fron-tier" hunters to take meat out of season, so Ohio Indians differentiated

Daniel Boone. Oil sketch attributed to Chester Harding (c. 1820). Courtesy of the Filson Club Historical Society.

between hunting for food, which they condoned, and killing for skins, which they condemned.[40]

Years later Boone allowed that Emery had treated him "in the most friendly manner"; at the time, however, he and Stewart were infuriated by what they regarded as the theft of their property. Ignoring Emery's advice, the pardoned men resolved to reclaim what they had lost and resumed their pursuit of skins. Stewart's recidivism eventually cost him his life. Boone narrowly escaped to hunt another day.[41]

Showing like disdain for the Indians' merciful justice, other long hunters did not go home as instructed. Their incorrigibility interfered with Indian peacekeeping efforts. And yet the search for accommodation continued. Among the Shawnees, the most influential proponent of peaceful compromise was Cornstalk, a chief of the Mequashake band of the loose-knit Shawnee confederacy. In June 1773, Cornstalk endorsed a plan offered by Captain Thomas Bullitt, a surveyor from Virginia, to share the lands south of the Ohio River. Bullitt was on his way down the Ohio to examine sites for a proposed settlement in Kentucky when he detoured up the Scioto and appeared unexpectedly at Cornstalk's village. The unannounced arrival violated diplomatic etiquette and got the meeting off to a rocky start. But after Bullitt pledged that the farmers who settled on the other side of the Ohio "shall have no objections to your hunting or trapping," Cornstalk replied that he found "nothing bad" in the arrangement. So long as Bullitt took "proper care that we shall not be disturbed in our hunting," Cornstalk promised to advise "our young men to be friendly, kind and peaceable to you." [42]

Cornstalk's vow suggests how far some Ohio Indians were willing to go to avoid war. He did not, of course, speak for all Ohio Indians. His advice was widely ignored, and his influence waned once Bullitt and his party immediately violated the spirit of the accord. Bullitt's purpose was surveying, but his companies' journals indicate as much interest in hunting as in staking lands. Like long hunters, Bullitt and his men recognized no exclusive Indian rights to Kentucky and did nothing to promote sharing. [43]

The poisoning of frontier relations intensified in the spring of 1774 after a group of backcountry ruffians murdered thirteen Shawnee and Mingo Indians. Though Cornstalk and other Shawnee accommodationists still opposed going it alone against the British Empire, they could not stop relatives of the victims from exacting revenge on thirteen backcountry settlers. Retaliation soon escalated into general warfare. Cornstalk was drawn in. So was Governor Dunmore of Virginia, whose superiors in London had not then wanted to fight a war with any or all Ohio Indians. The war ended, or more accurately abated, in October 1774, when 1,100 Virginia militiamen under the authority of Governor Dunmore narrowly defeated 300 Shawnee warriors under Cornstalk at the Battle of Point Pleasant. By the "Terms of Our Reconciliation," Shawnees yielded their hunting rights in Kentucky, and Dunmore pledged to respect the Ohio River as a firm boundary between Indian country and backcountry. [44]

The Anglo-Virginians' show of strength at Point Pleasant was an admission of weakness by the rulers of British America, a sign of how tenuous King George's authority was in the Greater Pennsylvania backcountry and Ohio Indian country. Although the Earl of Dunmore led the Virginia forces and delighted in an outcome that made Kentucky safe for land speculation, he did not command the situation. Indian countries and backcountries, conceded Virginia's last royal governor, were "equally ungovernable," for both were populated by obdurate hunters.[45]

III

Stages of social evolution, neatly demarcated by mode of subsistence in Enlightenment texts, blurred on the Appalachian frontier. Just as the annual cycle of Ohio Indians mixed male-led hunting and female-dominated horticulture, so the subsistence system of backcountry settlers came to rest on a dual-gendered effort. Only in combination with herding, farming, and gathering could hunting (and fishing) furnish interior families with their dietary needs. As game became an increasingly important component of this subsistence system, backcountry and Indian worlds converged. In backcountry, as in Indian country, hunting became an arena in which to demonstrate manhood and mutuality. Yet men and women did not live on wild meat only. Nor did the hunting which made backcountry and Indian men similar make them the same.[46]

Hunting expanded along with the Greater Pennsylvania backcountry. In the first years after Daniel Boone's father arrived in Pennsylvania in 1713, hunting contributed little to the immigrant family's table. Boone's ancestors were Quakers from the south of England, but they were not in this respect different from the thousands of German Pietists and Anglo (or Scots)-Irish Presbyterians who joined them in the Pennsylvania backcountry. Previously prohibited from hunting, newcomers developed their skills gradually. With each move beyond the perimeters of previous white occupancy, the capacity of inhabitants to subsist by hunting had increased. So had the importance of wild meat to the diets of borderers. Memory of harsh game laws faded. Toleration for outside regulations, by Indians or colonial officials, diminished. By the time white settlement pushed into the mountain valleys of southwestern Virginia and northwestern North Carolina, hunting had become a critical part of backcountry life.[47]

Learning to hunt was one of many adjustments that emigrants to the Greater Pennsylvania backcountry made. While the peoples of the backcountry imported a variety of subsistence traditions, all faced a seasoning period in which old ways were adapted to new conditions. Moving to a country where arable land was relatively available but manpower was in short supply mandated a shift from intensive to extensive agricultural practices. Before the change could take place, labor-saving methods had to be adapted. Europeans from deforested regions, however, lacked folk knowledge about clearing woodlands. They did not know how to use fire or girdle trees as Indians did, nor how to plant corn about the deadened snags to break down the soil for future ploughing. The cultivation of "Indian corn," the "great staff" of backcountry life, was also new. Guidebooks touted the Indians' grain as the ultimate "lazy man's crop," almost a spontaneous production of nature, but the mysteries of corn culture from clearing, to planting, to hoeing, to shocking, to shucking, to shelling were hardly self-evident.[48]

Nor was tradition entirely transferred in stock raising. Emigrants, particularly those hailing from northern parts of the British Isles, had considerable background grazing livestock on common range, a practice which relocated readily to the backcountry. Indeed, some foraging livestock multiplied rapidly in the mid-Atlantic backcountry. But not all stock transferred so well. Experience proved pigs best suited to the woodland range, and hogs assumed a far more prominent place in the backcountry than they had in the old country.

The independence of swine introduced novel problems. As pigs were left to forage in the woods, they lost their domestic attachments and became "so wild that even the wolves dared not attack them." Endangering persons and property, the unmarked offspring of wandering stock also presented questions of ownership. These were settled by the evolution of what backcountry inhabitants called a "right in the woods," which entitled "each person in possession of a plantation . . . to a certain proportion of the live stock that runs wild."[49]

In crop and stock raising, backcountry settlers underwent a seasoning process; in hunting, they started almost from scratch. Those with soldiering experience in Europe presumably had some familiarity with guns. In British America, militia exercises and frequent target shooting contests improved the marksmanship of adult white males. The handiwork of Pennsylvania-German gunsmiths, whose rifles became the preferred weapon of backcountry men, augmented accuracy and range. These rifles were prized and personalized possessions, which explains Daniel Boone's reluctance to exchange his for the inferior French musket offered by Will Emery.[50]

Technology obviously mattered to hunters, but technique counted more. The sharpest shooters were not always the surest hunters. Michael Stoner, for example, was "an indifferent hand to shoot at mark. I co[ul]d beat him," boasted his brother-in-law. "But at game, he was the best man" in southwestern Virginia, for he "seemed to understand the motions of living animals." Knowing the habits of animals was a prerequisite for successful tracking. "A succession of intrigues" was how one backcountry man described the movements of hunter and game. Even where game was unusually abundant, a solid education in animal habits and habitats meant the difference between success and very serious failure. In Kentucky in the 1760s and 1770s, the size of buffalo herds made it seem that anyone could kill a buffalo. The best hunters, though, knew to "kill the leader if you could find it out, and you might kill three or four of them." Once the leader of a herd fell, the rest often hovered. "Had we been disposed," remembered Abraham Thomas, we "might have shot the whole gang." Less experienced hands, however, did not get that opportunity. They gave their position away by getting on a herd's windward side or shot the wrong buffalo first. Either miscalculation risked setting off a stampede in the direction of the hapless hunter.[51]

It took a long time to acquire this intimate acquaintance with animals. Good tutoring helped, but instructors were hard to find in the early eighteenth century when few backcountry men had mastered the art of hunting. Scandinavian Pennsylvanians, the descendants of the colonists of New Sweden, had the most experience and provided some guidance in hunting to their neighbors. For the most part, however, European colonists learned the essentials of hunting—how to dress, how to track, how to decoy, how to wait patiently and silently, how to live off the land—by watching and listening to Pennsylvania Indians.[52]

The borrowing of techniques enabled backcountry men to add wild meat to their subsistence repertoire and heightened the resemblance between Indian and white hunters; yet even as hunters mingled, crucial differences persisted. While Ohio Indians had no tradition of stock raising and assigned women primary responsibility for cultivation, the backcountry subsistence system placed men in charge of all three legs. Thanks to the remarkable adaptability of hogs, hunting remained less important to the diets of backcountry settlers than to Ohio Indians. It was no less anticipated, however. Backcountry men yearned for the slack times when the agricultural schedule permitted a hunting break. If things went well, after the ground was ploughed and the corn was planted, "came a sort of leisure time" when fathers and sons would steal some late spring and summer days in their preferred diversion. As among Ohio Indians, longer hunts awaited the completion of the harvest. Then, hunting fever raged. Once the crops were in and the leaves were down, backcountry farmers "became uneasy at home. Everything about them became disagreeable," remembered a resident of western Virginia, "even the good wife was not thought for the time being a proper companion." To restore domestic tranquillity, able-bodied men took to the woods. But unlike Ohio Indians, backcountry men left women behind.[53]

In extending the scope and span of their excursions, long hunting parties entered a unique single-sexed world. Military service also took men away from women, but the conventions of warfare in both backcountry and Indian country favored short campaigns that did not interfere with other commitments. Agricultural responsibilities and localist predilections discouraged militiamen from participating in extended operations that left farms untended and homes undefended. Kentucky-bound hunters, by contrast, strayed farther and stayed away longer.[54]

Long hunting companies also deviated from the well-ordered hierarchies idealized by colonial gentry. Instead of leaders appointed on the basis of wealth and rank, long hunting parties chose guides on the basis of their woodsmanship and made—or tried to make—decisions by the consent of the company. Station camps, an outlet for rambunctious sociability, served more importantly as a central depository for skins and a place to reallocate hunting supplies. When enough skins were accumulated to fill the capacity of the pack horses, the hunters divvied up the proceeds. Risks, resources, and material rewards were shared in a way that paralleled the mutuality among Ohio Indian hunters.[55]

Trans-Appalachian hunts amplified the toughness that backcountry (and Ohio Indian) men revered. Near home, shooting games, wrestling brawls, and drinking bouts afforded convivial all-male settings in which backcountry men practiced their toughness and measured one another. As if the stakes of manhood won and lost were not already high enough, the most accurate marksmen raised the risks. The boldest supposedly outdid William Tell by aiming at targets placed between legs instead of atop heads: probably a tall tale, but graphically illustrative of the connection between marksmanship and manhood. Yet trans-Appalachian hunts intensified the test of toughness. The trip itself, over the steepest mountains and through some of the densest, wettest forests in eastern North America, was arduous. Once on the western slopes, long hunters separated into groups of two or three to pursue game stealthily. For months they hazarded Indians, animals, and the elements.[56]

While commitments to mutuality and constructions of manhood were common traits among white and Indian hunters, the absence of women from backcountry hunting parties differentiated the cultures. Long hunting groups usually included a number of men brought along to tend the station camp, dress the skins, and prepare food: in other words, to do what women did for Ohio Indian hunters. Little is known of these camp keepers, whose exploits were deemed unworthy of recording. They seem to have been hired hands rather than equal partners. Indeed, camp keeping often fell to slaves, who bore their share of risks and displayed their toughness, but remained the property of other men.[57]

The most profound distinction between hunting cultures was not in the relations between men but in those between men and animals. To be sure, the contrast was not a stark and simple one between Christians and animists. Backcountry and Indian hunters each ascribed magical powers to the animate world. Like Indians, backcountry hunters firmly believed that dreams foretold the future. Whether hunters were asleep or awake, croaking ravens, howling dogs, and screeching owls portended ill. Drawing on a trove of folk knowledge, hunters wore charms, uttered incantations, and performed rites to ward off evil spells, reverse bad omens, and cure cursed rifles. But backcountry men recognized no kinship with animals. While Ohio Indians credited animal partners for surrendering themselves, backcountry men saw the hunt as an act of mastery, and by extension, an affirmation of manhood. In exercising their biblical dominion over lesser beasts, hunters owed no obligation to their prey, no duty to kill only what they needed.[58]

Wherever backcountry hunters trod, depletion of game soon followed. One year, the long hunter Isaac Bledsoe discovered a salt lick so crowded with bison that he was afraid to dismount. When he returned the next year, he found thick cane growing about the lick. The growth of vegetation and the absence of buffalo briefly convinced Bledsoe that he was in a different spot—until he approached the lick and looked out on an expanse of bleached bones. Backcountry hunters accused Frenchmen from the Illinois country of having perpetrated this offense, of having wasted thousands of buffaloes merely for their tongues and tallow. But the record of backcountry hunters was no better. Large herds of buffaloes had once roamed east of the Appalachians. But they had been killed, observed Thomas Walker, for "diversion." That continuing wasteful slaughter of animals, especially buffaloes, incensed Indian hunters, making long hunts even more dangerous.[59]

Under these perilous and demanding conditions, it was not surprising that long hunting was primarily a young man's game. Physically, young men were best suited to the rigors of trans-Appalachian hunting, and psychically, they were most in need of the affirmation of manhood that long hunts brought. Exploits in hunting, like those in warfare, compensated for what young men typically lacked—ownership of land and dependents over whom to exercise patriarchal authority. On long hunts, then, youthful backcountry bachelors found a respite from farm work and from emasculating dependence.[60]

There were conspicuous exceptions to the prevalence of unmarried youths and to the seasonal character of hunting. To cite the most renowned, Daniel Boone turned thirty-five shortly before his meeting with Will Emery. When he departed from his Yadkin home, he left behind a wife of thirteen years and six children with a seventh on the way. His departure on May 1, 1769, upended the normal calendar in which the beginning of long hunts was postponed until after the conclusion of the harvest. That year and the next, Boone did no farming. Nor did Elisha Walden, a long hunter of long standing, who boasted of having "never cultivated the soil." Henry Skaggs was another in the select group of life-long hunters who avoided farming and stock raising. "So ignorant was Henry Skaggs of the modes of civilized life," reported a neighbor, that when the aging hunter finally retired to a farm in southern Kentucky "he did not know how bacon was made."[61]

Thanks to the labors of other family members, especially that of almost abandoned wives, the dependents of Boone, Walden, Skaggs, and other "full-time" hunters did not live without bread and bacon. In 1769 and 1770, Daniel's dereliction meant more work and less companionship for his wife, the former Rebecca Bryan, and their older children. The eldest two, boys then twelve and ten, had just graduated to field work and were still not capable of a full day's labor. If James and Israel Boone were like other sons of the backcountry, they already dreamed of their own escape from field work, of accompanying their father or making bold hunts of their own into Indian country.[62]

Neighbors, especially relations, helped out Rebecca. Boones and Bryans proliferated in the Yadkin country, having moved their extended families together from Pennsylvania to Virginia to North Carolina. Like other migrants to successive backcountries, the Boones and the Bryans cemented their neighborliness by intermarriage. In 1755, a year before sixteen-year-old Rebecca wed twenty-one-year-old Daniel, her uncle had married Daniel's younger sister. Even the welcome aid of nearby relations, however, did not offset the prolonged absences of her husband. Relations unfortunately were not nearby enough. Compared to the clustered homes and outlying fields that characterized Ohio Indian settlements, the dispersed pattern of backcountry farmsteads isolated Rebecca from kith and kin and limited the assistance that "neighboring" households lent her.

No wonder protective patriarchs steered daughters clear of young men still addicted to the hunting life. Having decided to make hunting his lifelong occupation, James Finley sensibly resolved "to get me a wife suited to this mode of living." That did not sit well with the father of Finley's chosen bride, who did his utmost to discourage the marriage. When his daughter eloped, the enraged father refused to let her fetch her clothes.[63]

While long hunters rated poorly as spouses and sons-in-law, their demonstrated manliness and mutuality earned the respect and even adulation of neighboring men. Henry Skaggs' ignorance of bacon making and rumors about the illegitimate paternity of one of his offspring did not diminish his standing as a man with a "high sense of honor." Nor did Daniel Boone's inadequacies in husbandry and as a husband diminish him in the eyes of his neighbors. In the fall of 1774, when Dunmore's War broke out, Boone and his family had taken temporary shelter in a cabin in southwestern Virginia. Yet he was so esteemed by men in the Clinch River Valley that they petitioned William Preston, the local gentry leader, to have Boone appointed commander of the forts in that part of the backcountry. Though a newcomer to the region, Boone's reputation preceded him. His popularity confirmed the analysis of another son of the backcountry: for gaining the respect of peers, "a good hunter was the greatest honor to which any man could attain."[64]

IN CROSSING THE APPALACHIANS, Daniel Boone and other great hunters breached the geographic and cultural boundaries between backcountry and Indian country. Mostly young and single men, but also older husbands and fathers, long hunters rejected the restraints that Indians, elites, and their own female relations sought to impose upon them. In Kentucky, they met Indian hunters with whom they had much in common, if too much in conflict.

Strife between backcountry and Indian men was something the British crown wished to avoid. Keeping peace with Ohio Indians was in the empire's interest. War interrupted the fur trade and reopened the continent to French influence. But individual interests often conflicted with imperial purposes. On both sides of the Atlantic, gentlemen thirsted for Ohio Valley lands to be open to private empire builders. Divided internally, British and British American gentry realized their worst fears. They lost control of the frontier between Indian country and backcountry to "hunters," to peoples whom gentlemen considered near equals in their savagery.

Seeking to avoid a destructive war, some Ohio Indians bid for a peaceful resolution that would protect their hunting range in Kentucky.

The alternative, as Will Emery appreciated, escalated into bloody wars of retribution. Unfortunately backcountry poachers did not get the message, and colonial officials responded inadequately to appeals from Indians for protection from interlopers. And so came Dunmore's War, resulting in the Shawnees' coerced concession of hunting rights in Kentucky. Anglo-American colonization of Kentucky followed in the spring of 1775. With the settlement of trans-Appalachia, the worlds of Indian and backcountry hunters came together and fell apart.

TWO *The Parting of Hunters*

A LITTLE MORE THAN EIGHT YEARS after their introduction, Daniel Boone and Will Emery met again. On the morning of February 7, 1778, Boone was hunting near the Lower Blue Licks in northern Kentucky when he was surprised and eventually overtaken by four Shawnee men. Boone surrendered and was escorted to the Indians' main camp. Amidst the scores of warriors assembled there, Boone spotted Will Emery. It took Emery a moment to recall when and where the two had previously met, but with some prompting from Boone, Captain Will remembered and exchanged hearty "howdydos" with his once and present captive.[1]

The events of 1778 figure prominently in any recounting of the life of Daniel Boone and the history of the Kentucky frontier. In 1778, Boone was in his early forties, at the midpoint of a long life. It was also a turning point, for Boone, for fellow Kentucky pioneers, and for nearby Indian peoples. Prior to falling into Indian hands, Boone commanded the highest respect of his comrades, for the early years of Kentucky's colonization accented the gallantry of hunters. In the wake of his capture, Boone's world and that of Ohio Indians converged as never before. It seemed that Boone would be incorporated into Indian society, one of several strategies tried by Ohio Indians. But Boone's integration was not completed, and the men captured along with him aborted the birth of a new common world. While the ways of hunters continued to cross after 1778, the coexistence of Indians and pioneers became impossible along the Ohio River. In central Kentucky, what came to be called the Bluegrass country, the freelance existence of hunters—of men like Daniel Boone and Will Emery—also became a thing of the past.

I

Significant as hunting was to the mix of backcountry subsistence and the making of backcountry men, its prominence increased during the initial Anglo-American settlement of Kentucky. Deprived of alternative fare and tormented by Indians, pioneers lived "on their guns" and turned to men like Boone to feed them and lead them. A hero in hunting and warfare, Boone epitomized the ideal of pioneer manhood, though he was older than most pioneer men. The hunters' Kentucky was very much a young man's country.

From the outset of colonization in 1775, the presence of Indians and the prodigious consumption of pioneers complicated the task of hunters. On March 10, 1775, a party of thirty colonizers led by Boone set out from southwestern Virginia to blaze a trail from the Cumberland Gap to the Kentucky River. There they intended to establish a "station." Cutting a road through thick woods was hard work, but for two weeks the men worked enthusiastically and feasted on fresh meat supplied by Boone and other hunters. Before daybreak on March 25, however, Indians attacked the company. Two men were killed, another wounded, and the rest dispersed. Some turned back. More might have done so had Boone and a few others not conveyed "firmness and fortitude." As much as Boone's power of example and persuasion, the sight of two to three hundred buffaloes pounding along the Kentucky River plain lifted the company's spirits and kept the fledgling colony intact. During the tense days of fort building and corn planting, buffalo meat supported pioneers at the station that they named Boonesborough in honor of Boone's leadership under fire. But hunters decimated the local herd in a few weeks' time. Thereafter, hunting became more dangerous and less certain. By mid-May, the men at the half-finished fort were "almost starved" as they waited for hunters to return from expeditions that took them up to thirty miles from the relative safety of Boonesborough.[2]

Over the next few years, thousands of pioneers repeated the experience of Boonesborough's original settlers. Hunting fed migrants on the overland route. Those who made it safely to Kentucky continued to rely on their guns to survive the initial season of settlement. In the absence of alternative foods, hungry pioneers devoured enormous quantities of wild flesh. Even when their deprivation was short-lived, they treated the return of fresh meat as a feasting time. Their inability to preserve the spoils of the hunt no doubt elevated their consumption to gluttonous proportions. The country was "plentifully furnished . . . with salt springs," explained Boone and seventy-five other Boonesborough settlers in a 1777 petition to the Virginia legislature. Distilling sufficient quantities of salt from brine required several weeks' work in the open. "The incursions of the different Nations of Indians" made this too risky. Settlers might have cured meat by "jerking" it, as Ohio Indians did, that is, by cutting it in strips and letting the sun dry the flesh. But here pioneers did not follow Indian ways.

Fort Boonesborough in about 1778. From George W. Ranck, *Boonesborough: Its Founding, Pioneer Struggles, Indian Experiences, Transylvania Days, and Revolutionary Annals,* Filson Club Publications, no. 10 (Louisville, 1901).

The pioneers' preference for salty foods and extravagant feasts resulted in the squandering of tens of thousands of pounds of flesh. If a buffalo was not "young and fat," hunters took only the hump and tongue and left the rest to rot.[3]

As they did at Boonesborough, pioneers paid for their wastefulness. Newcomers assumed that dependence on hunting would be limited to their first months in the "wilderness," but Indian raids and geographic isolation compounded the normal problems of frontier farm making and prolonged the hunting season well beyond initial expectations. The forts in which settlers defended themselves from Indian raiders left outlying fields and wandering stock untended. Pioneers were helpless to prevent the burning of their crops, the killing of their stock, and the stealing of their horses. With these settlements too distant and too exposed to be resupplied from the other side of the Appalachians, wild meat became the staff of life. But reckless hunting meant men had to travel longer distances with less assurance of finding sufficient meat.[4]

The dangers of hunting and frontier life unsettled many settlers. During their journey to Kentucky in the spring of 1775, a party of forty men counted almost one hundred people "turning Back for fear of the indians." Only three of the men who had planted corn near Boonesborough that spring remained at the fort four years later. Some had moved on to other stations, but already forty-seven people had died in defense of the fort or while hunting. Others, finding prospects dim and perils daunting, fled back across the Appalachians.[5]

Most likely to come and most likely to stay were young bachelors. According to Richard Henderson, the mastermind behind the founding of Boonesborough, the majority of persons there in the spring of 1775 were "single, worthless fellows," an intractable band in search of adventure, not settlement. Their defiance of authority began at home; many Kentucky pioneers, like the eighteen-year-old Abraham Thomas, ventured out "against the positive injunctions" of their fathers. As often, however, young men acted as scouts for their fathers and their extended families, smoothing the way for future migrants. For some time after 1775, Kentucky attracted relatively few family men and many fewer female settlers. A census taken at Harrodsburg in May 1777 tabulated only twenty-four adult white women as against eighty-five men. One husband who went for a look but did not linger decided it was no country for a "growing family." [6]

It was, however, a good young man's country, for there were plenty of opportunities in hunting and warfare to separate men from boys. When Indians chased pioneers behind station walls and destroyed their crops and stock, hunting became "an unwelcome business for all but the most intrepid." Facing starvation, the boldest men slipped out under cover of darkness. In squads of four or five, they rendezvoused at secluded places. Gone from these hideaways was the boisterous conviviality that had prevailed when long hunters converged at their station camps. Sleep was light, guns kept at arm's length, and moccasins tied about the knees to have shoes ready for a hasty exit. To avoid giving away their position, hunters did without fires, exposing themselves to winter cold, summer mosquitoes, and year-round wolves. Without light, they could not engage in fire hunting, the customary means of spotting deer and other game at night; during the day, they also had to restrict their shooting. When Indians were known to be about, hunters dared not shoot at even the easiest prey. Keeping the fast became another test of manliness. To a hunting party out of Boonesborough, "a fine young buffalo" appeared a perfect breakfast, until one member "reproached them for their *boyish* conduct" and exhorted his fellows "to exhibit more self denial and fortitude and act like men." Chastened, the rest of the hunters agreed to maintain their silent fast and "see who the *boys* are and who evince[s] the most fortitude." [7]

In this milieu, cowardice carried an awful stigma. To admit to faintheartedness was to fail as a man. To reveal terror in a more physical form condemned one to a lifetime of ridicule. Pity men like poor Joe Smith, who during an encounter with Indians "fouled his pantaloons as a consequence of his extreme fear." His companions never let Smith forget his stain. But demonstrations of manliness won fearless hunters the admiration of neighbors and strangers; so even more did expressions of mutuality. Under normal circumstances, backcountry custom granted an animal to the hunter who drew first blood. But at those times when the subsistence system stood on a fragile single leg, the spoils were equally divided—and not just among those with a role in the killing. Adept hunters were quick to offer rations to any pioneer in need. John Taylor gratefully discovered this after he removed to central Kentucky and found himself ill-equipped to supply his own meat from the woods. Taylor survived, thanks to the "common generosity of hunters," who "admit[ted] me to share in the profits, so far as meat went."[8]

That altruism did not come wholly free of reciprocal obligations. Sometimes hunters accepted a gift in kind or a promise of one in the future. Often neighbors agreed on a mutually beneficial division of labor. While some men supplied meat to the ad hoc collective, others took responsibility for cornfields that in the present situation were held in common. These compacts assigned no exact value to the contributions of hunters and farmers. They promised only an equal share to all participants.[9]

For their fortitude and their "gifts" of food, the foremost hunters earned more than their share of respect and authority, though they led more by example than by edict. Pioneer men preferred it that way. As among long hunters, colonists promoted temporary "captains" to supervise hunting parties and direct the defense of settlements. It was, for example, "by general consent" that the founders of Boonesborough put themselves "under the management and control" of Daniel Boone. In practice, the need to maintain consensus limited the exercise of authority. "I was captain, but we were all heads," remembered the elected leader of one pioneer troop. To aristocratic observers, however, this system of rule by ruffians seemed no system at all. Where were the permanent ranks based on hereditary privileges? Where were the coercive mechanisms that kept order among the "lower sort"? The fact that "no person did actually command entirely," struck a gentry visitor to Boonesborough in 1775 as "all anarchy and confusion."[10]

Whereas the pioneers' system of leadership by example and persuasion diverged sharply from gentry notions of immutable hierarchies, it more closely paralleled that of Indian adversaries. Ohio Indians typically divided leadership between war chiefs and peace (or village) chiefs. The former won their authority for their heroism in combat, their talents in arranging attacks, and their success in exhorting warriors. By Shawnee tradition, would-be war chiefs had to lead at least four parties into the enemy's country. On each occasion, they had to return with at least one scalp, while suffering no casualties of their own. By contrast, the position of village chief generally passed from father to son, though succession was not always hereditary. Nor was authority unchallenged. Peace chiefs usually spoke first in village councils, but they did not monopolize the floor. Amidst many voices, leaders were only as powerful as they were oratorically persuasive, as they were through vivid metaphors and dramatic gestures able to build consensus for their views on making and breaking peace.[11]

Silent in formal councils, Shawnee women nonetheless participated in decisions about village affairs, most directly through the interventions of female war and peace chiefs. These posts customarily were occupied by the mother, sister, or another close relative of the male chief. The female village chief's principal duty was to oversee the activities of women. She scheduled planting and arranged feasts. She was also responsible for conveying the consensus of village women to a male war chief. According to an early-nineteenth-century ethnographer, when the wishes of women opposed those of a male war chief, the female village chief "seldom fail[ed] to dissuade him."[12]

Pioneer women had no equivalent official stature or influence. Numbers accounted for part of the difference. During the 1770s, few white women moved to Kentucky. Of course, in backcountry neighborhoods where women and men were roughly equal in number, women enjoyed no formal authority either, though they surely shared the hardships of frontier life. In Kentucky, when times were toughest, women followed livestock into the open woods to see what might be foraged. Their collection of wild greens often complemented the meat brought in by hunters. Yet even when gathering substituted entirely for meat, gatherers did not become chiefs of any kind.[13]

Nor did the assumption of male roles promote pioneer women. Disguising women as men to make the defenders of a fort appear more abundant was a favorite trick of pioneers. These women did not just dress the part. Some were crack shots and expert hunters. Indeed, at a marksmanship match in 1777 at St. Asaph's Station, Esther Whitley's first shot topped all participants. Neighboring men continued until dark, unable to beat her. Sharpshooting won Whitley a place in local lore. It did not vault her into local leadership. Among Kentucky pioneers, the best men were men, even when bested by a woman.[14]

II

Across the frontier, Ohio Indian leaders struggled to confine the influx of young backcountry men to Kentucky and to contain the insurgence of their own young men. From 1775 to 1777, older leaders sought an accommodation with American pioneers that would make the Ohio River a permanent frontier between Indian and backcountry. Their youngers, however, rallied to the banner of confederation, hoping that together, and in alliance with the British, Indians might regain Kentucky.

The "greatest difference" between whites and Indians, suggested Thomas Alford, a Shawnee memorialist born in 1860, "is the deference paid to age, and in the association of the sexes." Certainly Shawnee women of the late eighteenth century enjoyed more freedom of association than their backcountry counterparts. The clustering of homes, the pooling of field and domestic work, and the permissive customs concerning premarital sexual relations and divorce gave Shawnee women an advantage on the women of dispersed backcountry neighborhoods. As for the elderly, Alford insisted they were beloved and respected. "In all our gatherings, older people had the floor." Eighteenth-century sources confirm the consideration extended to the opinions of the elderly. But the years after 1775 were turbulent times in which young men also made themselves heard.[15]

The tumult raged across the Ohio Valley, and nowhere more immediately than in Cherokee country. In the winter of 1775, more than a thousand Cherokees assembled at Sycamore Shoals to negotiate with Richard Henderson, a former justice of the North Carolina superior court. In a daring enterprise to be considered in the next chapter, Henderson sought to buy much of Kentucky from the Cherokees. In March, the influential headman Attakullaculla, as well as the revered warriors Oconostota and the Raven, agreed to terms with Henderson. Reconciled to some backcountry expansion, they endorsed a bargain that provided their people with several wagonloads of goods and for the moment directed colonists away from Cherokee country. While Cherokees hunted the lands they ceded, their towns were at some distance from Henderson's proposed colony and ideally would remain so. That logic, together with the prestige of Attakullaculla, Oconostota, and the Raven, swung many Cherokees behind the deal. But there was no consensus. Throughout the public negotiations and after the purchase was concluded, Attakullaculla's

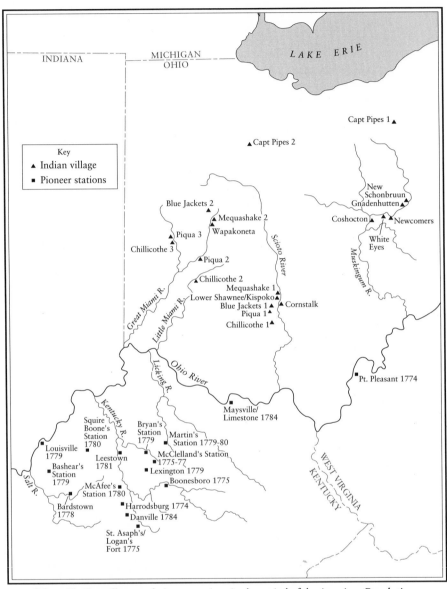

Selected Indian villages and pioneer stations in the period of the American Revolution.

son Dragging Canoe denounced accommodation. Hundreds joined him, principally young men, who feared that appeasement would cost them their role as hunters and would lead eventually to the occupation of their entire country.[16]

To break the deal, unreconciled Cherokees ambushed Boone's party on its way to the Kentucky River. Though Boone led this company by "general consent," Cherokees knew from his attendance at earlier negotiations that he was Henderson's man and that Boonesborough was the beachhead of Henderson's colony. Hoping to scare off pioneers before they became entrenched, opponents of appeasement attacked on the morning of March 25. Thanks to the inspiring example of Daniel Boone, the assault failed to turn pioneers back. But the killing of two of Boone's men aggravated divisions among the Cherokees. Blaming the "accident" on "Two Ill disposed Malicous of our men," Oconostota apologized and asked whites to resist thought of revenge. The attack, of course, was no accident. Nor was it likely that only two men were involved in an attack against thirty pioneers. No matter how many were actually present, they had hundreds of supporters.[17]

As Anglo-American colonization pushed closer to the Cherokee heartland, the number of militants swelled. In the summer of 1776, 150 warriors led by Dragging Canoe turned their fury on settlers in the Watauga Valley. They were defeated, but a force four times as large planned a new campaign to drive settlers out of eastern Tennessee. Instead, the war came to Cherokee country, with disastrous results for Cherokee subsistence and Cherokee unity. In the summer and fall, back-country militiamen burned Cherokee towns and fields. With ammunition and food in short supply, older leaders again asserted the need for accommodation. In May and July 1777, Attakullaculla, Oconostota, and the Raven agreed to cede lands to the revolutionary governments of Georgia, South Carolina, North Carolina, and Virginia. Dragging Canoe and his followers were adamantly opposed. So irreconcilable were the differences within Cherokee councils that militants seceded. Known to Anglo-Americans as the Chickamaugas and to themselves as *Ani-Yuniwa* or "the Real People," the militants moved west, establishing towns in the Tennessee River Valley. The new location, affording better access to British supplies, enabled the secessionists to continue the battle against pioneer expansion.

At the same time, militants awakened to the idea of pan-Indian resistance. Just a few years earlier, calls for a united front against Anglo-American expansion won little backing in Cherokee councils. Only a handful of Cherokees joined the Shawnees during Dunmore's War. Most rejected the pan-Indian message declaimed by emissaries of their long-standing enemy. Yet in the spring of 1776, Dragging Canoe clasped the war belt proffered by Shawnee envoys, and the majority of young men agreed with the Shawnee orator that "it was better to die like men than to dwindle away by inches." A confederation of Shawnees and Chero-kees had once seemed as unlikely as a union of American colonists; in the spring of 1776, it appeared more revolutionary than the American Revolution, which seemed to Ohio Indians nothing more than an Anglo-American civil war.[18]

Ever since the Fort Stanwix Treaty, Shawnees had roused other Indian peoples to make war together to halt the inland spread of pioneers; not all Shawnees, however, advocated militancy or confederacy. Like other Ohio Indians, Shawnees lacked a single center of authority; all politics were truly local. Even more than other Ohio Indians, they lacked an abiding tribal identity. Shawnees had historically been grouped into five "bands," each with its own specific responsibilities and often split about the course of tribal affairs. By the eighteenth century the ethnic bonds that tied the bands together had also weakened. One hundred years on the move ex-posed the Shawnees to many peoples and bloodlines. Back in the Ohio Country, Shawnee villages became more heterogeneous, ethnically and politically. But opposition to the Fort Stanwix Treaty cut across village, band, and ethnic identities. From 1768 to 1774, Shawnees achieved greater internal unity, though they failed to gain much external support. De-feated in Dunmore's War, they divided once more.[19]

Convinced that encroaching "long knives" meant to occupy the en-tire Ohio Valley and that expansion could not be stopped, hundreds of Shawnees adopted a familiar strategy. Just as Pennsylvania Shawnees had earlier migrated to the Scioto Valley, so scores of Ohio Shawnee families gradually left for new homes west of the Mississippi. Unlike Cherokee militants, these migrants opted to leave rather than to die or dwindle away by inches.[20]

The leaders who remained retained a more accommodating, as well as a more localistic, outlook. Cornstalk returned to his pursuit of peaceful coexistence. Having marked a treaty ceding Shawnee hunting rights south of the Ohio River, Cornstalk, along with like-minded headmen among the Shawnees and neighboring Delawares, implored Anglo-Americans to reciprocate by staying away from the game and lands north of the river. Violence, these spokesmen attributed to "your young men . . . destroy-ing our Deer," which inspired our "foolish Young People" to strike back "without the Knowledge of the Chief[s] of their Nation." Keeping hunters apart by confining them to one or the other side of the Ohio River was the road to coexistence. To maintain peace, village leaders also disavowed pan-Indian sentiments. When youthful culprits came from outside their village or region, accommodationists deflected blame where it belonged, lest misunderstanding lead to misdirected retaliations.[21]

The problem of irascible young men prompted White Eyes, a Delaware chief, to move beyond the standard formula for coexistence. At a treaty conference in Pittsburgh in October 1775, he promised to "be Strong and Prevent my young Men from hunting" on the south side of the Ohio River. That pledge was expected, but he coupled it with an extraordinary proposal to makeover young Indian men. He preferred they not hunt at all, that "rather they wou'd employ themselves in planting Corn in their own fields."[22]

White Eyes' exhortation went beyond what other accommodationist leaders imagined in 1775. His recommendation to give up hunting jeopardized the mixed subsistence of Ohio Indians. His endorsement of corn planting as a proper activity for men imperiled their definition of masculinity. What White Eyes seemed to envision was not accommodation but abdication. To Ohio Indians, it sounded like the cultural reformation pushed by missionaries, especially the Moravians with whom White Eyes mingled. To young men, it looked like surrender.

Through 1775 and into 1776, Indian men expressed their disaffection with acculturation and accommodation by menacing Moravian missionaries and ambushing Kentucky-bound travelers and trans-Appalachian pioneers. The alienated represented the vanguard of pan-Indianism. In July 1776, thirteen Cherokees united with four Shawnees to kill two Kentucky men. A smaller party of two Cherokees and three Shawnees splintered off and captured Daniel Boone's teenage daughter Jemima, as well as two of her Boonesborough peers, Elizabeth and Frances Callaway.[23]

The symbolism of age-old enemies fighting side by side as yet outweighed the military significance of this and other raids. Within days, a rescue party led by Boone caught up with the Indians, freed the girls, killed two of their captors, and sent the survivors fleeing. The rescue was exceptional, but the raid was not. Typically, this "mischief," as White Eyes called the unauthorized forays, yielded some horses, produced a few casualties, and persuaded numbers of migrants and settlers to leave Kentucky. Raids on this scale and of brief duration, however, could not dislodge pioneers once they took shelter inside their stations. The Indians "do not adopt the same ideas of bravery," observed a British official. Certainly this was true if bravery entailed a frontal assault on a fortified position; no war chief or would-be war chief risked his men in such a lethal action. Laying siege to the station was the next available option, but raiders lacked the manpower and the supplies to carry out a long operation. Young men also lacked the will; what glory was there in starving out an enemy? Instead they gathered their plunder and withdrew, perhaps adding the scalps of a stray hunter or two on their return home.[24]

Absent the outbreak of the American Revolution, the disaffection of young men would not have so decisively derailed the pursuit of peaceful coexistence. Once the British began to arm and encourage western Indians, it tipped the balance of power away from pioneers and away from accommodationist leaders. With British supplies, Ohio Valley Indians more effectively harassed the backcountry. In 1777, Indian raiders conducted their most sustained attacks to date on Kentucky settlements. In March, two hundred Ohio Indians led by the Shawnee war chief Blackfish began hit and run strikes that harassed pioneers and kept them in their stations through July. By fall, when that year's "Indian summer" finally ended, seven stations had been abandoned; just four remained. These were in disarray, their inhabitants nearly destitute of corn and livestock.[25]

Despite these conflicts, American officials and accommodationist leaders repressed hostilities as best they could. Promising presents, American negotiators endeavored to win Indians to the patriot cause. Failing that, they strove to keep Ohio Indians out of the war with assurances that Kentuckians would "forbear hunting on the Other side of the River Ohio." To varying extents, accommodationists obliged. White Eyes agreed to let the Americans establish garrisons in Delaware country and to act as a guide and courier for them. Cornstalk steered a more neutral course, successfully defying pressure from militant Indians and the British to take a firm anti-American stand. To preserve the neutrality of his people, he apprised Americans of the activities of militants, even urging Kentuckians in the summer of 1776 "to waylay and kill" a party of fifteen Shawnees that had gone to the Cherokees "on some bad design."[26]

Unfortunately for Cornstalk and for accommodationists, pioneers waylaid and killed Indians indiscriminately. Into 1777, in spite of the failure of Americans to deliver promised supplies, Shawnees remained approximately evenly divided between militants and neutrals. But the "retaliatory" campaigns carried out by backcountry militias paid no heed to Indian factions, murdering whatever Indians were available. Among the Shawnees, accommodationist sentiment disappeared with the cowardly assassination and gruesome mutilation of Cornstalk in November 1777.

Cornstalk had gone to Fort Randolph, near the site of the 1774 Battle of Point Pleasant, to broker a new peace between Americans and his people. Instead of negotiating, the American commander, Matthew Arbuckle, took Cornstalk and his party hostage. A few days later, revenge-minded backcountry men broke into the prisoners' cell and commenced firing. "If we had anything to expect from" the Shawnees, wrote the American general Edward Hand when he learned of the incident, "it is now vanished."[27]

The death of Cornstalk enraged all of Shawnee country and united Ohio Indians against Americans. Erstwhile accommodationists demanded immediate reprisals, if not against the well-fortified perpetrators, then against whatever Americans were most vulnerable. On that score, Kentuckians were obvious targets. While Ohio Indians did not usually make war during the winter hunting season, Blackfish led more than one hundred men across the Ohio River during the first week of February 1778. Their destination was Boonesborough, their mission to revenge Cornstalk's death and rout Kentucky pioneers.[28]

III

Daniel Boone's capture at the Lower Blue Licks abbreviated the Shawnees' expedition against Boonesborough and caused a change in plans. Instead of killing Boone, Blackfish adopted him. Instead of wiping out Boonesborough, the Shawnees determined to assimilate the pioneers of Kentucky. The strategy of incorporating enemies, including backcountry captives, had a long history among Ohio Indians. Indeed, Ohio Indians so effectively assimilated their adopted captives that returning them became a persistent sticking point in negotiations with British authorities in the decade before the American Revolution. At the end of the Seven Years' War, the Shawnees were obligated to release all Anglo-American prisoners. But to fulfill their obligation, the Shawnees were compelled to bind hundreds of adoptees, lest they run away before being "freed." According to a witness, the white prisoners, mostly women and children, greeted their liberation with "the utmost reluctance." Several quickly "found means to escape," while others "continued many days in bitter lamentations, even refusing sustenance." Given their success in incorporating backcountry captives, the Shawnees' change in plans was sensible. But what the Shawnees contemplated in 1778—absorbing an entire pioneer community, children, women, *and* men—was unprecedented.[29]

Blackfish's men would not have chosen to incorporate Boone's men but for Boone's cooperation after his capture. In early January, Boone had left Boonesborough, captaining (pioneer-style) a group of more than two dozen men on a saltmaking expedition at the Lower Blue Licks. The leader, not coincidentally, was also the company's hunter, performing his task with the usual bravery and skill. Boone's courage and his credentials as a leader, however, became the subject of controversy after his bloodless surrender. Without consulting his company, he arranged their peaceful capitulation. To convince saltmakers to disarm without displaying any "manly" defiance, he assured them they would be well treated by the Indians and released to the British at Detroit. Imagine their surprise, then, when a few hours later they heard Boone promise to conduct his captors to Boonesborough in the spring "when the weather will be warm, and the women and children can travel . . . to the Indian towns." Then, we will "all live with you as one people," and "the young men," referring to the saltmakers who expected to be ransomed to the British, "will make you fine warriors, and excellent hunters to kill game for your squaws and children."[30]

Boone's declamation followed several hours of animated speeches by Shawnee warriors. The debate, remembered saltmakers, was vigorous, though, with the talks carried out in Algonquian, our witnesses recalled the particulars of only Boone's address. Had the proceedings been in English, the saltmakers, like other backcountry captives, would still not have truly understood. Ohio Indians packed their speeches with metaphors whose meanings were not easily discerned by those unfamiliar with the idiom. From the gestures of Indian orators, pioneer auditors could tell that the Shawnees were divided. From Boone's speech, they learned the alternatives were their execution or their amalgamation. Not thrilled by Boone's bombshell proposal, the saltmakers naturally preferred it to the alternative. By a two-vote margin, sixty-one to fifty-nine, the Shawnees elected to spare the saltmakers and return in warmer weather to complete the adoption of the people of Boonesborough. In fact, the final decision on the fate of the captives awaited the return to Chillicothe, where Shawnee women would blacken them for execution or accept them for adoption.[31]

While Boone presented assimilation matter-of-factly, as a question simply of logistics, his men resisted the idea of living as one people with the Indians. On their march north to the Shawnee towns, saltmakers displayed their defiance. Several refused to carry the baggage that their captors had confiscated from them. Even Boone, perhaps to regain the stature that his surrender cost him, scuffled with a warrior who wanted him to tote a kettle filled with salt.[32]

To a point, Indian warriors understood and respected the obstinacy of pioneer men. When James Callaway, a typically headstrong seventeen year old, balked at carrying some of the salt he had made, one of the Indians raised his tomahawk. In a dash of youthful bluster, Callaway pulled off his hat and dared his antagonist to strike. Smiling at this show of courage, the warrior lowered his weapon. Boone's behavior when he was forced to run the gauntlet also gained him stature, among both saltmakers and Shawnees. The blows of more than one hundred men staggered Boone, but he won cheers from captives and backslaps from captors after he ran over and laid flat his last assailant.[33]

Beyond a certain point, the unruliness of saltmakers became too much trouble. It was, after all, a lack of battlefield manliness that saved these captives from execution. To Shawnee warriors, the saltmakers' submission manifested a deficiency of physical and spiritual power; nothing would be gained by their execution. By contrast, the British offered bounties for American prisoners. After marching the saltmakers to Chillicothe, forcing them to run the gauntlet, and allowing village women to inspect the "live flesh," the Shawnees decided to adopt only about half of their captives. They deemed the remaining prisoners too rough or not rough enough for the life of an Indian hunter. Those unfit for adoption were sent to Detroit and consigned to the British.[34]

The arrival of Shawnees and their rejects frustrated the British commander at Detroit, Lieutenant Governor Henry Hamilton. In Kentucky, it was widely rumored that Hamilton paid Indian allies for pioneer scalps, but in this case, as was his policy, he ransomed and then imprisoned the captives. Hamilton's disappointment was not with the Indians' "humanity," though at least one of the saltmakers recollected that they were "much better treated by the Indians than by the British." What bedeviled Hamilton was that "the Savages could not be prevailed on to attempt the Fort [Boonesborough], which by means of their prisoners might have been easily done with success." What Hamilton only slowly grasped was that while his Ohio Indian allies fought with British supplies against a mutual foe, they conducted their campaigns on their own schedule, by their own tactics, and for their own purposes.[35]

Hamilton was, however, pleased by the information he received from Boone. The situation in Kentucky, Boone told Hamilton, was desperate. Faced with starvation, expecting no hope from Congress, and impressed by the benevolence of the Indians, the settlers at Boonesborough would gladly surrender, said Boone, when he returned with the Shawnees. For telling Hamilton what he wanted to hear, Boone was promised a horse, a saddle, and some silver trinkets.[36]

But Hamilton could not ransom Boone. Despite a reported offer of £100, five times the bounty paid for the other saltmakers, Blackfish would not sell. He had already adopted Boone. One of Blackfish's sons had been killed during the rescue of the daughters of Boone and Richard Callaway in 1776. The custom of Indian country encouraged Blackfish to "cover the dead" by adopting a substitute for his slain child. Fittingly, the war chief chose Boone, the leader and hunter of the pioneer company, as a surrogate son. The rites of adoption that turned foe into family member had already been completed before the trip to Detroit. Earlier Boone had run the gauntlet, a ceremony intended to let grieving Indians vent their anger over the loss of loved ones. While at Chillicothe, Boone's hair had been plucked in the Shawnee style and his skin scrubbed. "I never was washed so clean before or since," remembered one captive of his scouring by Shawnee women. Symbolically purged of his whiteness, Boone was re-named Sheltowee, meaning Big Turtle. Finally, a grand feast was held to welcome Boone and other adoptees.[37]

Upon his return from Detroit, Sheltowee settled into his place in Blackfish's household and among Ohio Indians. Although Blackfish was only a few years older than Boone, Sheltowee got along easily with his father and with the rest of his new kin. As with his backcountry neighbors, Boone earned the "applause" of his Indian peers "for my activity at our shooting matches." In a matter of weeks, he gained the affection of his relatives, the friendship of his neighbors, and the trust of his father, who soon allowed Boone to hunt at his liberty. Boone, no doubt, was delighted when his father told him not to worry about planting and tending corn, for "your mother can easily raise enough for us all." That had always been Boone's view, though in the backcountry, it was not entirely respectable to leave farming to women. So pleased did Boone appear that suspicions arose among less adaptable adoptees. Typical was William Hancock, who had been adopted by Boone's old acquaintance Will Emery. Showing none of Sheltowee's flexibility, Hancock despised his adopted kin and wondered how Boone could be content among "a parcel of dirty Indians."[38]

Boone's unexpected appearance on June 20, 1778, at the gates of Boonesborough raised the suspicions of pioneers. Earlier the people at Boonesborough had heard that Boone and the saltmakers had been killed by the Indians. Then escaped captives had returned with the even more disturbing news that Boone had consorted with the British and joined the Indians. Now Boone was back, exhausted and hungry after a four-day journey from Chillicothe to Boonesborough. Regaining his strength, he vigorously denied the accusations against him. His surrender, he insisted, had saved lives and delayed the assault on Boonesborough; his dealings with Hamilton and his apparent serenity among the Shawnees was all deception.[39]

Maybe so, but Boone's subsequent actions reinforced doubts about his leadership and his loyalties. To restore his reputation, Boone proposed and led a preemptive strike against Ohio Indian towns. The foray failed in all its objectives and deprived the fort of its most able defenders. This, at a time when the largest Ohio Indian force yet assembled, a mixed group including Shawnees, Wyandots, Miamis, Delawares, Mingoes, and even a contingent of British militia, was on the march. Having killed few Indians and secured no plunder, Boone's company of about twenty men beat a hasty retreat, arriving at Boonesborough on September 6, one day ahead of Blackfish's 350-man army.[40]

What happened next intensified the controversy regarding Boone's allegiances. Before launching any assault against outnumbered pioneers, Blackfish and other war chiefs negotiated, first with Boone and later with other representatives from Boonesborough, outside the station's walls. Blackfish reiterated his offer of good treatment if the men submitted peaceably and death if they did not (the women would still be adopted). By good treatment, he meant a trip to Detroit or adoption by Indians. To ease the journey of women and children, he brought forty horses; to entice men, he conjured a country teeming with game. The offer appealed to Boone, who restated to Blackfish his preference to surrender the fort. Boone lied to Blackfish when he claimed he had run away merely to see his wife and children and when he denied participation in the previous days' raid. But his desire to surrender was sincere. In discussions inside Boonesborough, he urged men to trust the Indians' word. As Boone had already discovered, Ohio Indians preferred to incorporate, not eradicate, their backcountry counterparts. Boone, however, was outvoted. Still, he pressed for more talks, hopeful that "they could make a good peace." [41]

Among those suspicious of Boone's intentions, Richard Callaway was the most vocal. Callaway had opposed the raid across the Ohio, and he distrusted the faith that Boone placed in "savages." Callaway's hatred prevailed. The defenders, including Boone, resolved to die to the last man. To put up a more imposing front, Callaway resorted to a familiar trick, instructing "the Women to put on hats and hunting shirts and . . . git up on the top of the wall . . . as they might appear as a great many men." For Callaway, it was better for women to die like men than to live as one people with the Indians.[42]

The September 1778 parley between Ohio Indians and Boonesborough settlers, depicting whites escaping from the clasp of Indian warriors and running to the fort. The original caption read, "Treachery of the British and Indians." From George W. Ranck, *Boonesborough: Its Founding, Pioneer Struggles, Indian Experiences, Transylvania Days, and Revolutionary Annals*, Filson Club Publications, no. 10 (Louisville, 1901).

Because Ohio Indians declined to storm the fort, no pioneer women and only two white men died during the ten-day siege of Boonesborough. The campaign turned into a sniping contest, as Indians and pioneers exchanged verbal insults and long-distance shots. Owing to their exposed positions, the Indians lost thirty-seven men, but heavier casualties did not cause them to leave. However, like frontal attacks, long sieges were not congruent with the Indians' way of war. Since the pioneers were well-provisioned, having already harvested their corn, Indians began to tunnel under the walls to increase the pressure on the population of the fort. When the shaft collapsed prematurely, the attackers lost heart. With the hunting season approaching, most of the warriors withdrew to attend to their other duties.[43]

The departure from Boonesborough signaled the failure of the Shawnees' strategy of mass incorporation. Blackfish had embraced Boone as a son, had treated the saltmakers with humanity, had shown good faith throughout the negotiations, and had nothing to show for it. The people at Boonesborough had renounced Boone's pledge and refused to come away. Earlier Boone had run away, and in the months before and after his desertion, at least seven other adopted saltmakers had attempted to flee.[44]

Not all saltmakers were eager to escape. Joseph Jackson stayed among the Indians until 1799 and fought with them against his former comrades. Micajiah Callaway also remained for five years among the Indians and served as an interpreter during negotiations with the Americans. Even after Callaway returned to Kentucky in 1783, he remained a man of two worlds, continuing in his role as a translator and cultural mediator.[45]

But the rest of the adopted saltmakers fled when they could, and most of these got away. While Boone and other adoptees reported they were closely watched, Indian wardens were in general rather inattentive. After all, returning, not retaining, captives had previously been the problem. The episodes from the 1760s, however, predated the most recent hostilities that accompanied the colonization of Kentucky and intensified frontier animosities. In the past, women, children, or men who had grown up after being captured at an impressionable age composed the ranks of the acculturated. These were easier to guard and easier to indoctrinate.

From February to September 1778, the Shawnees attempted a bolder absorption, beginning with the hardest to absorb. They failed. The flight of the saltmakers indicated that misunderstanding and hatred now overwhelmed any affinities between Kentucky pioneers and Shawnees.

IV

Along with the previous collapse of accommodation, the unwillingness of pioneers to assimilate darkened and bloodied the Kentucky frontier. Through the end of the American Revolution and for another decade, Ohio Indians threatened Kentucky colonists. But the battleground was shifting. Boone's raid across the Ohio was untimely. In the years after 1778, however, offensives into Indian country proved decisive in the conquest of the Ohio Valley. American invasions repeatedly destroyed Indian towns and fields, forcing Ohio Indians to survive by hunting alone. But the supply of game could not withstand the enlarged demand, which arose in part from the Indians' expanded subsistence needs, but mostly from their deepening dependence on the fur and liquor trade.

When the Indians lifted their siege of Boonesborough, about one hundred warriors, mostly Shawnees, remained behind. Breaking into smaller groups, lingering warriors reverted to an older and less ambitious strategy of hit and run strikes. But these lacked the potential to reclaim Kentucky for Indian hunters or remake Kentuckians into Indian hunters. Regrouping a month later in their towns, Shawnees weighed their options anew.[46]

Once again, Shawnees divided. In the spring of 1779, upwards of four hundred warriors and their families uprooted from Chillicothe, joining an earlier wave of westering migrants in Missouri. The following year, another group of Shawnees resettled on the Tennessee River between Cherokee and Chickasaw settlements. Outmigrations left only about one hundred warriors at Chillicothe, but these and other Shawnees, reported Henry Hamilton, were "inveterate against the Virginians." In April and May 1779, the Shawnees sharply rebuffed an American overture delivered by accommodationist Delaware chiefs. By the spring of 1780, American military leaders in the west characterized Shawnees as "the most hostile of any Savage Tribe" and resolved to make them "pay for all the mischief they have done" in Kentucky and across the backcountry.[47]

Yet Indian raids across the Ohio continued and grew bloodier. In the first nine months of 1781, Indians killed or captured 131 people in the vicinity of the Falls of the Ohio, about one-eighth of the population of Jefferson County. The next year came a fresh wave of small incursions and one large invasion that culminated in a decisive Indian victory at a battle at Blue Licks. There, Indians killed sixty-one Kentuckians, a third of the enemy force. Afterwards the commander of the Fayette County militia revised upwards to 860 the number of settlers in the central Bluegrass region killed by Indians since Daniel Boone led the party of trailblazers to the Kentucky River in 1775. Though Shawnees took much of the blame and incurred much of the wrath of Kentucky militiamen, they did not act alone. True, Shawnee leaders sometimes criticized other Indian peoples for not lending adequate assistance. But at Blue Licks, as in earlier engagements, the Indian force comprised warriors from across the Ohio Country and Great Lakes Region.[48]

Shawnees and other Ohio Indians aimed their loudest complaints at their British partners. The coalition of British and Ohio Indians, in fact, was not what either side desired. While English officers castigated the Indians' tactics and treatment of prisoners, Ohio peoples complained that their ally was slow to supply them with promised gifts. Trust disintegrated as American offensives ravaged Shawnee country. In a May 1779 raid against Chillicothe, the Shawnees lost their cabins, their household items, their horses, and their principal chief, Blackfish, as well as an unknown number of men, women, and children. The long, bitterly cold winter of 1779–80 was hard on the Shawnees, but the summer of 1780 was even harder. In August, an army commanded by George Rogers Clark laid waste four Indian villages and burned hundreds of acres of not yet harvested corn. Destitute of corn, warriors talked openly of a break with the British, who had failed to supply them with sufficient ammunition to defend their women and children. A Delaware chief wished for the return of the French, advising his English "brother" that Ohio Indians had "never known of any other Father." Relations with the British disintegrated to the point that some Ohio Indians, including some Shawnees, threatened again to make peace with the Americans.[49]

Unfortunately for reawakened accommodationists, Kentucky pioneers continued to kill their Indian friends as readily as they did their enemies. In November 1778, American militiamen ambushed White Eyes while he was acting as a courier for the Americans. Moluntha, a Mequashake Shawnee, who emerged from Cornstalk's band as the chief proponent of coexistence with the Americans, met an end as tragic as his predecessor's. In 1786, an enraged (and depraved) Kentuckian bludgeoned Moluntha, while the Shawnee chief clutched a recently signed treaty with the Americans in one hand and a flag with thirteen stripes in the other. The murderer, Hugh McGary, was subsequently court-martialed, but the sentence was only a one-year suspension from command. While the murderer acted alone, the burning of Moluntha's village, which had been occupied by neutrals, was the work of an entire company. Still, Kentuckians offered no apologies for their generic Indian hating. "The Indians have always been the aggressors," explained Federal District Court Justice Harry Innes, and "the savage mode of war" made it "impossible to discriminate" between hostiles and neutrals.[50]

American arrogance quashed any lingering chance for peaceful coexistence. Benjamin Logan, the commander of the expedition against Moluntha's town, disdained the protocol of Indian diplomacy. Like Lord Jeffrey Amherst after the Seven Years' War, Logan and other Kentuckians treated negotiations with the Indians as an opportunity to dictate terms to a vanquished people.[51]

But Shawnees and other Ohio Indians no more considered themselves conquered by the Americans than by the British. The end of the Revolution diminished but by no means eliminated the Ohio Indians' ability to menace Kentuckians. Between September 1783 and December 1787, Innes guessed that three hundred Kentuckians were killed and twenty thousand of their horses were stolen. Over the next two and a half years, he reported almost three hundred more deaths. Although the death rate tailed off at the end of the decade, especially in the interior counties, settlers were still not safe from small bands of raiders. Nor was their property. In just three months of 1789, a Kentuckian counted twenty dead, five captured, and upwards of a hundred horses stolen. Appeals to the national government for assistance failed to stem Indian depredations. These continued in the 1790s, prompting influential Kentuckians to contemplate secession from the new American republic to seek the protection of a foreign empire.[52]

Indeed, in the early 1790s, a confederation of Ohio Indian warriors twice routed the armies of the barely united states. In the second and more decisive defeat in November 1791, the American force of fourteen hundred lost more than six hundred men. Afterwards, leaders of the national government briefly assumed a humbler pose in negotiations with Ohio Indians. Instead of condescending to "children," American officials referred to Indians as "brothers" and matched conciliatory language with conciliatory terms. Leaders of the Indian confederacy, however, rejected all proposals that did not guarantee the Ohio River boundary between the United States and Indian country. While older chiefs and younger warriors omitted calls for the return of former hunting territory, they insisted on compensation for lands south of the Ohio River and vowed to overrun Kentucky if their demands were not met.[53]

Despite the confidence-building triumphs over invading American soldiers and the terror-inspiring raids against American settlements, Ohio villagers lacked the manpower to overrun Kentucky and the reserves to maintain their hold on Indian country. Nearly forty years of war, along with waves of outmigration and recurrent epidemic diseases, had reduced Indian populations, even as their enemies' numbers expanded exponentially. By 1790, the combined population of Ohio Indian villages was probably one-tenth that of Kentucky, and the disparity was growing. While Indian warriors inflicted greater casualties than they suffered, invasions from across the Ohio wrecked the subsistence system of Ohio peoples. Once Kentuckians discovered the vulnerability of Indian villages and cornfields, they burned and plundered with devastating effect. Just as Kentucky pioneers in the late 1770s were forced to live on their guns, so Ohio Indians in the 1780s often found themselves with no alternative but to hunt. The security of their mixed subsistence system in ruins, Ohio Indians grew more dependent on the British for weapons and sometimes for rations.[54]

The subsistence crises of the 1780s accelerated a dependence on foreign supplies that had bit by bit been transforming the material and economic cultures of Ohio Indians. For more than a century, Ohio Indians had exchanged furs for European products. Initially, most imported metal items paralleled the function of neolithic crafts, and the trade goods circulated within existing networks of reciprocity and redistribution. The impact of the fur trade, while substantial, did not immediately disturb

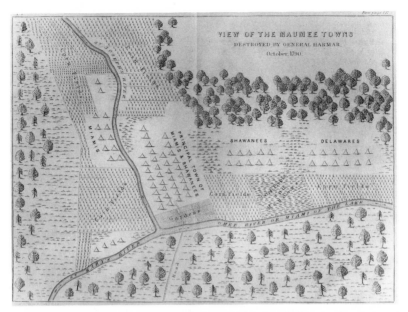

A multiethnic Ohio Indian village in about 1790, showing the layout of gardens and cornfields. From *The Record of the Court at Upland, in Pennsylvania, 1676–1681, and a Military Journal, Kept by Major E[benezer] Denny, 1781 to 1795*, Memoirs of the Historical Society of Pennsylvania, no. 7 (Philadelphia, 1860).

conventions of village exchange. As late as the early 1770s, a Presbyterian minister witnessed the custom among Delawares of ceremonially "present[ing] the skins of the animals and a considerable part of the meat to the widows and the aged." But as European tools and weapons supplanted native technologies, the hunting economy of Ohio Indians acquired a two-tiered structure. By the early 1790s when the adopted captive Jonathan Alder went hunting with his Shawnee kin, separate rules governed the disposition of meat and skins. As in earlier times, Alder provided venison and bear meat to his parents and to fellow villagers. Yet Alder no longer shared his pelts with widows and elders, for "all the profits accruing from the sales of skins and furs" were his alone.[55]

It was no accident that Alder, a "white Indian," announced the partial conversion to more egoistic, commercial practices. Like the saltmakers who stayed, Alder lived among Indians, but between worlds. That intermediary position enabled Alder and Micajiah Callaway to act as cultural brokers. It also made them witting and unwitting cultural breakers, the transmitters of European values and procedures.

Heading the list of cultural breakers were the purveyors of alcohol. In

A Shawnee Indian, wearing the blue cloth shirt and breechclout, red cloth leggings, and silver ear and septum ornaments that demonstrated the incorporation of European styles into Ohio-Indian material culture. Original drawing in the Bibliothèque Nationale, Paris.

addition to metal goods, ammunition, blankets, cloth, and other foreign items, the skin trade brought unscrupulous traders and a ruinous credit system. However, except for alcohol, the demand for European commodities was limited, and so was the Indian hunters' pursuit of peltry. By contrast, the demand for alcohol was elastic. Again and again, village headmen and visionary prophets denounced liquor traders and called for the prohibition of alcohol. Elders expressed special concern that traders not give "our young Men . . . a drop of strong Liquor," lest they behave foolishly or violently. But demand could not be contained, and suppliers exploited the one commodity that allowed them to circumvent the traditional protocol of exchange. For their part, drinkers guarded against the imprudence that drunkenness occasioned by disarming themselves and appointing a few men "to keep sober to prevent mischief." These "designated drivers" did not restrain the flow of liquor, however. After a few days of trading skins for liquor, drinkers had only the memories of "unbounded riot and intoxication" to show for a winter's hunt.[56]

The fur-liquor trade gradually altered the ways of Ohio Indians. For women, who were responsible for dressing skins, the expansion of commercial hunting meant more work. For men, it meant more hunting. In the wake of a drunken spree, hunters had no choice but to resume their pursuit of deerskins. The deer population, already under pressure from increased need for meat, neared exhaustion. Owing in large part to the influence of alcohol, taboos against overhunting fell away. In distancing themselves from their animal kin, Indian hunters drew closer to the ways of pioneer hunters.

The closing of ways only hastened the closing of the Ohio River frontier. As Ohio Indians became more dependent on traders, their independence eroded. The failure of the British to provide essential protection and trade goods eventually enabled American invaders to wrest control of the southern half of Ohio. Pushed north and west, Ohio Indians lost contact with their former hunting ground of Kentucky.

V

By the time the Indians were gone, Kentucky was not the hunters' country it had been. For some years after 1778, wild meat nourished pioneers, and hunters profited (in enhanced local status) by their manliness and mutuality. But the commercial inducements of the fur trade together with the mandates of manhood rapidly depleted the biggest game. As Indian attacks relented and the hunting environment deteriorated, the subsistence system reverted to the ordinary backcountry mixture. Hunting gradually lost its prominence, and hunters their eminence.

For Daniel Boone, diminished status came more quickly. Suspected of selling out to the British and hanging out too happily with the Shawnees, Boone came under scrutiny upon his return to Boonesborough in June 1778. His raid across the Ohio won majority support, but its failure further eroded confidence in his leadership. When Blackfish arrived at Boonesborough and instructed Boone to fulfill his promise to surrender the fort, Boone replied truthfully that he no longer commanded. When he subsequently spoke in favor of the Indians' terms to the men of Boonesborough, Richard Callaway "swore he would kill the first man who proposed surrender." After the Indians lifted their siege, Callaway's accusations against Boone's treasonous, cowardly, and foolish leadership led to the convening of a court-martial at nearby Logan's Station.[57]

Boone was exonerated, and his superiors in the Virginia militia affirmed the correctness of the verdict by promoting him from captain to major. Still, the experience was humiliating. In some respects, too, the higher rank conferred less authority, for his commission to lead derived from the governor of Virginia and not from the respect of his comrades. At Boonesborough, the passions excited by Callaway did not subside. To avoid lingering opprobrium, Boone removed in December 1779 from the station that bore his name.[58]

At that point, the "hard winter" of 1779–1780 was well under way. Coming on the heels of a fourth consecutive "Indian summer," deadly cold weather brought the threat of mass starvation to Kentucky. Already in the fall of 1779, the settlers at Boonesborough complained that the "Barberous ravages of inhuman savage[s]" had "reduced many of us so low that we have scarce cattle amongst us to supply our small Family's." Across Kentucky, Indian attacks curtailed the harvest. The scarcity of corn became a major concern as the deep freeze stretched from the beginning of November through the end of February, killing much of the remaining livestock. And so men lived again on their guns. But the prolonged cold also froze game in great numbers and what survived was often reckoned too poor to ingest. Some wondered what had ever possessed them to remove to a "Dreary Wilderness" where "we Don't know when we shall if ever get anything to eat." Once more the manliness and mutuality of hunters rescued the three thousand or so colonists in Kentucky.[59]

As always, mutuality had distinct limits. Local demand dictated the worth of perishable meat, and in making gifts, hunters conformed to the customs of good neighborship. There was little or no market for wild meat, which ordinarily only supplemented backcountry diets. In Kentucky during the Revolution, with no alternatives available, the market for meat was potentially much greater. But with survival at stake, hunters gave it away. They declined to profit from neighbors in need. The value of skins, however, was not a neighborhood matter, and with this commodity, hunters sought out the highest bidder. European demand pushed the price of peltry to levels that surpassed the cost of transportation to the coast and across the Atlantic. The sale of deerskins furnished hunters from the southern backcountry with money to buy land, pay taxes, and procure imported supplies that were unobtainable through local networks of exchange. In pursuit of increased revenues, long hunters expanded the scope and span of their excursions. Dissatisfaction with the prices offered by backcountry merchants led some long hunters to carry their skins to Natchez or New Orleans in hopes of striking a better deal with Spanish traders. Later hunters looked to take advantage of similar commercial opportunities. Whereas hunters invited John Taylor to "share in the profits so far as meat went," they offered no portion of the profits derived from skins.[60]

The omission underlined the boundaries between mutuality and profit-mindedness. As in Ohio Indian country, one set of rules governed the sale of skins and another the disposition of meat. So long as precepts of exchange fell into neat compartments, commercial dealings and good neighborship coexisted easily. But, as in Indian country, the pursuit of skins did interfere with good hunting. Year after year, long hunters collected large numbers of buffalo, deer, and bear skins. A good hunter easily amassed sixty to eighty in a single season; an exceptional one gathered four or five hundred skins. That limit held only because few men had the horses to pack more out. Already in 1767, George Morgan, the Illinois-based agent of the Philadelphia mercantile firm of Baynton, Wharton, and Morgan, accused skin hunters of having "so thinn'd the Buffaloe & other Game" in Kentucky "that you will not now see the $\frac{1}{20}$ Part of the Q[uantity] as formerly." An exaggeration no doubt, but after another decade of unrestricted skin hunting, buffalo and other big game was much harder to find, even as the need for wild meat was greater than ever.[61]

Commercial incentives do not alone account for the depletion of game in the 1760s and 1770s. Like Indians, backcountry hunters had limited wants when it came to most commodities offered in exchange for skins and furs. Implements of farming and items of fashion were not high priorities for many long hunters. As one backcountry boy observed of the hunting men he wished to emulate, "the stimulus of success never animated them," for "they have no artificial wants which wealth can gratify."[62]

Nor do subsistence imperatives explain the orgy of buffalo killing that occurred during the 1770s and 1780s. At Boonesborough before the local herd was extinguished, "some would kill three, four, five, or $\frac{1}{2}$ a dozen buffaloes and not take half a horse load from the all." It was not hunger, but the exhibition of manhood that motivated this and hundreds of other sprees. "Many a man killed a buffalo just for the sake of saying so," admitted one pioneer. Deerskins were more profitable, but it was tales of buffalo hunting that boys and men recounted.[63]

The rapid depletion of buffalo inspired a number of unsuccessful proposals to better manage hunting. In the spring of 1775, at the first and only convention of the House of Delegates of the Transylvania Colony, Boone had forwarded a bill for preserving game. This idea was quickly buried, as were other schemes to restrain hunters. At Blue Licks in the early 1780s, the increasing scarcity of game prompted an agreement between the settlers to allow only the neighborhood's best hunter to kill buffaloes. But this effort was designed more to lessen the stench of rotting buffaloes and reduce the magnet for wolves than to save a dwindling resource. About the only ceiling that pioneer hunters observed was that set by the supply of powder and bullets. And so by the middle of the 1780s, buffaloes disappeared from central Kentucky.[64]

"Cane and game," it was often said, sustained Anglo-American colonists, yet pioneers maintained neither flora nor fauna. Growing up to twenty feet high, with quills several inches thick, "canebrakes" covered much of central Kentucky. While pioneers struggled through dense clusters, cane's value as a provender for domestic stock and a hideout from Indians made its presence and preservation essential. Cane also nourished wild herbivores, especially buffaloes, whose presence and preservation determined the pioneers' survival. But whereas wild meat saved the first settlers from prolonged starvation, few pioneers considered it an ideal diet. Complaints about the monotony of their fare or the hardships of doing without bread figure prominently in the reminiscences of pioneers. A diet that mixed bread and meat was deemed essential to the good life, especially if Kentucky was to become more than a young man's country. "If we have a plenty of Turkeys we will never die," summarized a Kentucky-bound slave in the fall of 1785. "But if we have bread and bacon too, we would live a heap longer."[65]

To secure bread and bacon and make Kentucky a fit country for families, pioneers busily transformed the landscape of central Kentucky. With the end of the Revolution, great numbers of families embarked for Kentucky, changing forever the composition of the population and the face of the countryside. Thousands and then tens of thousands of men, women, and children poured in during the 1780s, slashing and burning away the towering cane to make way for pastures and cornfields. As bluegrass succeeded the indigenous range, the women who handled dairying responsibilities discovered that cane-fed cows actually provided more and better milk. Nonetheless, the "improvements" satisfied most men. While the "Bluegrass region" of Kentucky lost its biggest game and its trademark cane, the new look established the pioneers' occupation and improvement. It affirmed that their collective claim to the land was superior to that of Indian hunters. Evidence of occupancy and improvement also buttressed the claims of individual pioneers to a piece of the land. On the basis of land ownership, as the next chapter relates, men graduated to a more mature manhood reserved for those who had achieved "independence."[66]

EVEN AFTER THE CONQUEST and colonization of the Bluegrass, the trip to Kentucky from the southern backcountry still involved a journey across a hunter's frontier. Migrating from Virginia to Kentucky in 1785,

Harry Innes discovered that the approach to the Cumberland Gap was inhabited by "all sorts of indolent, ignorant people, who raise a little corn, but depend chiefly on hunting for their support." Living in "little log huts, destitute of every convenience of life," these hunters wanted "only salt and whiskey." Further into the "wilderness," the signs of settlement thinned; Innes found only "a few scattering huts, which are possessed alternately by [white] hunters and Indians." Here was a country in which hunters still existed and coexisted.[67]

That was no longer true at the end of Innes's journey. The "maturation" of the Bluegrass displaced hunters. For Indian hunters, the occupancy of Anglo-American colonists ruined an already improved land. Through intimidation and in combination, Ohio Indians, especially young warriors, fought to preserve a way of life based on seasonal hunting in Kentucky. At the same time, some of their elders endeavored by cooperation to coexist with pioneers, conceding hunting rights south of the Ohio River to protect what was left of Indian country. Boldest of all strategies undertaken by Ohio Indians was incorporation, the attempt to turn captives into kin so that Indian men and women might continue to live as they pleased. Pioneer men, however, were unshakable, uncooperative, and unassimilable, and Indians were compelled to retreat from Kentucky and its borders. Thanks to the valor and generosity of pioneer hunters, colonists persevered and the central Kentucky landscape acquired a new face.

Yet the hunters who made that possible did not persist. In the Bluegrass region, the eradication of wildlife and the improvements to land very quickly doomed the hunting way of life cherished by Daniel Boone and by many young backcountry men. Not that hunters were innocent victims of progress. Like Indians, pioneer hunters contained profit-minded behavior by limiting consumer demand and by refusing to take advantage of neighbors in making gifts of meat. The compartmental hunting economy, however, did not curb the depletion of game. Years later, Boone and other pioneer hunters expressed regret about the unchecked pursuit of game and the destruction of the best hunter's country they had ever seen; at the time, though, the pursuit of land diverted their attention.

THREE *Land Hunting*

THE PURSUIT OF LAND and the "mature" manhood that came with its ownership inspired the colonization of Kentucky. The hunt for modest homesteads, which were the basis for patriarchal independence, drove Daniel Boone—and nearly all white men who crossed the Appalachians in the latter part of the eighteenth century—westward. Land hunting also fired grander visions among many of the colonizers of Kentucky.[1]

Pioneers divided land seekers into two categories. On one side stood actual settlers who braved wilderness and Indians in hopes of acquiring fee-simple titles to frontier land. Blocking their objective were the claims of the second brand of land prospectors: nonresident speculators. Across the continent, pioneers condemned engrossing speculators, but their animus peaked on the Appalachian frontier in the years before and after the Revolution. From Maine to Georgia and into the Ohio Valley, backcountry residents accused gentlemen of using unfair influence to acquire immense and illegitimate grants. Invoking what historian Richard Maxwell Brown has defined as the "homestead ethic," backcountry settlers challenged the legitimacy of speculator holdings. They insisted that by virtue of their occupancy and *agricultural* improvements their own claims to a "family-sized farm" superseded those of absentee engrossers. In the latter part of the eighteenth century and extending into the nineteenth, clashing claims and rising antispeculator sentiments boiled over in a series of bloody confrontations.[2]

In Kentucky, as in other eighteenth-century backcountries, the hopes of homesteaders collided with the plans of great speculators. On both sides of the Atlantic, ambitious gentlemen vied to grab Kentucky. Initially great speculators paid little attention to the demands of homesteaders. Seeking to rule as well as own Kentucky, the most ambitious paid lip service to the welfare of occupants, but in general aspirants to land empires regarded other gentlemen, not ragged pioneers, as their rivals. By petition and extralegal protest, Kentucky pioneers got the attention of magnates, but the system, with its favors for speculators, survived. Unrest never reached as fevered a pitch as on the other side of the mountains. Among the reasons why rebellion did *not* break out was the behavior of trans-Appalachian pioneers, which too often blunted the radicalism of their antispeculator rhetoric.

No individual better illustrated the violation of homesteader principles than Daniel Boone. A longtime companion confirmed that, as a hunter of game, Boone "never made an effort to accumulate" the consumer goods that the fur trade made available. Yet the scale of his and other pioneers' real estate accumulations made apparent that backcountry men were as susceptible to a speculative spirit as gentlemen. In Kentucky, pioneers acted too much like profiteers; in doing so, Boone and other Revolutionary-era settlers undermined the independence for which they fought and the good poor man's country that they sought.[3]

I

In Kentucky, the acquisitiveness of great speculators achieved a new scale, and their clashing ambitions made for a particularly intriguing, if often secretive, drama. Beginning in the 1740s, excitement about the lands beyond the Appalachians, especially those west of Virginia and south of the Ohio River, spread among potential speculators. The Ohio and Loyal Land Companies, each composed of prominent Virginia gentlemen, obtained grants from King George II to 1,300,000 acres of unspecified lands in the Ohio Valley. The outbreak of hostilities interrupted their plans to locate the lands and bring colonists to it, and George III's Proclamation of 1763 also discouraged the schemes of the two speculating concerns. But rival companies and individuals were entering the field, seeking grants of their own from the crown. Speculators who missed the "present opportunity of hunting out good lands," warned George Washington, "will never regain it."[4]

Against considerable odds and opposition, a group of North Carolina lawyers and merchants under the leadership of Judge Richard Henderson seized the opportunity most decisively. Henderson was a man of enormous ambition. On the recently settled Carolina piedmont, he served as a deputy to his father, the sheriff of Granville County, and spent a year reading law under the tutelage of John Williams. Henderson married Williams' stepdaughter, Elizabeth Keeling, who was herself the daughter of an English peer. As a well-connected attorney in the 1750s and 1760s, Henderson earned a substantial income plying his craft in the North Carolina upcountry. Handling mostly debt collection suits for gentry clients, Henderson also reaped the wrath of many dispossessed occupants.

Seeking the surest way to enhance his status and advance to the heights of economic and political power, Henderson chose land speculation, a business which further alienated him from the common folk of the back-country.[5]

In North Carolina great speculators conducted their affairs in a particularly predatory manner. Unscrupulous land agents and corrupt colonial officials defrauded hundreds of would-be buyers. Instead of acquiring clear titles, many settlers paid exorbitant fees only to discover that their payments had been mislaid or that others had previously patented their claims. When the fleeced looked to the law for redress, they found officers of the court to be more interested in adding to their own fortunes than in protecting poor men. In matters of land, observed a North Carolina merchant-planter, the practice among speculators and fee collectors was to "screw as much as they can from a stranger for it."[6]

"Screw unto others," the golden rule of land dealers and colonial officials, antagonized residents of the North Carolina backcountry. Styling themselves "Regulators," the disaffected demanded that priority be given to those who occupied and cultivated the land. "The peaceable Possession, especially of back waste vacant Lands," declared Regulator leader Hermon Husband, "is a Kind of Right." By engrossing land and evicting squatters, land speculators interfered with the customary right of the poor from "time out of mind" to "move out, from the interior Parts to the back Lands, with their Families and find a Spot, whereon they built a Hut and made some improvements." Speculators' false promises of North Carolina as a new Eden "encouraged so many Thousands of poor Families to bestow their All, and the Labour of many Years" only to have title to the land pass to a "few roguish Individuals," who by their legal chicanery might dupe another generation of would-be homesteaders.[7]

In hopes of silencing discontent, Governor William Tryon appointed Richard Henderson an associate judge of the North Carolina Superior Court in 1768. With the elevation of Henderson, whom he considered a man of "candor and ability," Governor Tryon believed he had answered the grievances of western settlers. In Henderson, Tryon thought he had a judge for whom the estranged "entertain an esteem."[8]

Tryon was mistaken. Regulators damned all lawyers, but they especially despised Richard Henderson. The "Lawyer's Art," according to Husband, made a "Libel of the Lord's Prayer." Lawyers, and "others in Connection with them," by which Husband generally meant the county courthouse ring, were the "greatest Burden and Bane of Society." When Husband and his followers moved from general condemnation to specific targets, they singled out Judge Henderson and his connections. In October 1770, a crowd of Regulators invaded Henderson's courthouse at Hillsborough. There they "severely whipped" a number of local luminaries, including Henderson's mentor and legal partner, John Williams. Also flogged were John Luttrell, the clerk of Henderson's court, and Thomas Hart, the sheriff of Orange County and Hillsborough's leading merchant. Ignoring the Regulators' demands for justice, Henderson dismissed the crowd as "abandoned to every principle of virtue." A few weeks later, Regulators set fire to Henderson's barn and stables. Two nights after that arson, they burned down his house.[9]

All this preceded disclosure of Richard Henderson's most daring speculation. In the 1760s, together with John Williams and Thomas Hart, Henderson quietly formed a company to acquire a vast domain on the other side of the Appalachians. During the years of planning, Henderson and his partners likely turned to long hunters, possibly including Boone, to scout land. No documents confirm Boone's employment by Henderson prior to 1774. Indeed, the surviving evidence from the late 1760s points to an adversarial relationship between the two men, with Henderson filing a suit against Boone for an unpaid debt of £20 in 1768. Henderson continued to press his case until he won a judgment in the spring of 1770. Afterwards, he secured a warrant for Boone's arrest, which awaited the long hunter's return from Kentucky.[10]

Still, while Boone was probably not yet Henderson's man, the strategy of using long hunters as covert land hunters made sense. "The Success of the Scheme," speculators understood, "depend[ed] upon the Secrecy with which the Business is conducted." Not only did Henderson fear the wrath of Regulators should his plans become public, but he also did not want to tip off rivals, who could use their influence with colonial officials to sabotage the venture. Similarly concerned with confidentiality, George Washington instructed his land agent in the Ohio Valley to proceed with "the operation carried on by you under the guize of hunting game."[11]

The ruse worked. By the time Henderson's scheme and Boone's role came into the open, Regulators had been defeated and land-grabbing rivals outmaneuvered. After playing a prominent role in crushing the Regulator insurrection, Henderson enlisted new partners for the speculative enterprise, which was rechristened first the Louisa Company and later the Transylvania Company. The Transylvania partnership eventually boasted nine of the wealthiest and most politically influential men in the North Carolina upcountry. These piedmont luminaries, however, lacked the high profile and imperial connections of rival speculators. Making a

virtue of necessity, the North Carolina partners bypassed customary chan-
nels. Instead of seeking a grant from London as other land adventurers
did, the Transylvania Company adopted Henderson's controversial plan to
bargain directly with the Cherokees. With Boone in attendance, Henderson commenced negotiations in the fall of 1774. Even before concluding
the deal, the partners advertised terms for settlers in a Williamsburg newspaper. And on March 10, 1775, with no treaty yet signed, Henderson
dispatched Boone at the head of a party of thirty axmen to cut a road and
establish a station as headquarters of the new Transylvania Colony.[12]

Henderson nearly unveiled his plans too early. In March 1775, the approximately one thousand Cherokees who assembled at Sycamore Shoals
to dicker with Henderson remained deeply divided about the wisdom of
ceding land. Most of the younger men, fearful of losing their hunting
grounds, opposed any sale. Even those who supported a deal were not
prepared to give the Transylvania Company what it wanted. At first, the
Cherokees proposed to part with only small tracts. When Henderson rejected this approach, the Cherokees responded by offering to sell the land
between the Kentucky and New Rivers. But Henderson refused this deal
as well, believing that by earlier treaties the Cherokees had ceded those
lands to Virginia. Finally, on March 17, with Boone's axmen halfway to
their destination, the Cherokees struck a deal with the proprietors of
the Transylvania Company. For £10,000 worth of goods, the Cherokees
deeded to Henderson and partners the lands between the Kentucky and
Cumberland Rivers, as well as a 200,000-acre parcel east of the Cumberland Gap to serve as a pathway to the new colony.[13]

Predictably, Henderson's bold coup alarmed government officials and
their allied speculators. "There is something in that affair which I neither
understand, nor like, and wish I may not have cause to dislike it worse
as the mystery unfolds," wrote George Washington of the Transylvania
Company's no longer secret negotiations. With their own plans for engrossing Kentucky threatened, colonial governors in Virginia and North
Carolina issued proclamations denouncing Henderson's stroke. In his decree, Governor Josiah Martin of North Carolina warned that "Henderson
and his confederates" aimed to create "an Asylum to the most abandoned
fugitives from the several colonies." Privately, Martin feared that the success of the company was inspiring comparable conspiracies. "If some
effectual stop is not put to these daring usurpations," argued Martin,
"such Adventurers will possess themselves soon of all the Indian country."
Governor Dunmore of Virginia also censured the piracy of "Henderson

and his abettors." But unlike his North Carolina colleague, who saw the Transylvania Colony as a refuge for "freebooters," Dunmore fretted that the generous terms advertised by Henderson would drain from Virginia "Numbers of Industrious People."[14]

Through their accomplices in the Virginia Assembly, jealous rivals challenged the validity of the Transylvania Company's land claims. Hostile Virginia legislators appointed a commission to investigate the purchase, ostensibly to ascertain whether Henderson had tricked the Cherokees. The appointment of the committee, oddly enough on July 4, 1776, presaged the end of independence for the Transylvania Colony. Though the committee failed to turn up evidence that Henderson had swindled the Cherokees, the legislature moved ahead with the destruction of the colony.[15]

Henderson pressed on, but he had already muffed the company's best chance to win influence in Virginia's ruling circles. Back in early 1775, Patrick Henry intimated that he wanted in on the company's deal. Henry admitted that in 1774 he and several prominent Virginia gentlemen, including William Byrd, John Page, Ralph Wormeley, Samuel Overton, and William Christian, contemplated a similar purchase from the Cherokees. In March 1775, Christian told an associate that in "Mr. Henry's opinion" the Transylvania claim was valid, and the colony "would stand." In April, the proprietors wrote Henry to thank him for his "noble and patriotick exertions," adding the hope "to have it in our power to give you a more substantial evidence of our gratitude." But Henry received no presents from the company. Nor was he allowed to buy into the partnership, because, remembered the grandson of one proprietor, Henderson feared the loss of his status as "guiding spirit" to the dynamic Virginia orator. Once snubbed, Henry became a determined opponent, as did his many powerful relations. As governor of Virginia, he prodded the legislature to invalidate the Transylvania claim. Similarly jilted legislators were pleased to do so.[16]

Henderson and his fellow partners alienated potential allies by trying to shut them out of the speculating game. In September 1775, the partners voted to sell tracts larger than 5,000 acres only to those who immediately settled on the land, precluding absentee speculators from gaining a foothold. The proprietors also charged more for all quantities of land above 640 acres, diminishing the resale profits of large purchasers. And the partners resolved not to sell more than 100,000 acres to any purchaser on any terms. In addition to these discriminations against "secondary" speculation, they reserved all of the choice tracts adjacent to the Falls of the Ohio, widely viewed as the site likely to become "the most considerable mart in this part of the world," entirely for themselves. The last action especially "roused the attention of a number of people of note." [17]

The opposition of noteworthies doomed the Transylvania Colony. An attempt to sidestep the objections of Virginia leaders by appealing to the Continental Congress failed, because congressmen did not want to offend powerful Virginians. The fate of the colony returned to the unfriendly Virginia Assembly. On December 7, 1776, the legislature made official Virginia's jurisdiction over all of Kentucky. Turning a deaf ear to Henderson's strenuous protests, the assembly created the County of Kentucky, which essentially ended the life of the Transylvania Colony.

Rivals also frustrated Henderson's efforts to obtain "fair" compensation for the exertions and expenditures run up by the partners. After a series of postponements, the Virginia House and Senate finally closed the Transylvania business in November 1778. As the last debate proceeded, a dejected Henderson conceded that he "believe[d] the Virginians do not mean to be very liberal or generous." A few weeks later, the House and Senate voided the Transylvania purchase. As compensation, the Virginia assembly initially granted 800,000 acres, but amended it down to 200,000 acres to be located at the mouth of the Green River. Embittered and financially embarrassed, Henderson and his partners expressed no thanks for the inadequate restitution offered by Virginia.[18]

II

The intrigues of competing speculators in Virginia resulted in the demise of the Transylvania scheme, but the challenge to the legitimacy of the proprietors' claim also emerged from within the colony. In rising numbers, Kentucky pioneers repudiated the authority of the Transylvania partners. Rebellious settlers revived the rallying cries of Regulators. Pioneers—men far more enthusiastically than women— insisted that title to parcels adequate to insure "independence" properly belonged to those who risked their lives to occupy and improve the land. More than the self-promoted contributions of absentee investors, what borderers called "getting land for taking it up" pushed the boundaries of white settlement across the Appalachians. Soldiers, who glimpsed the Ohio Valley during the wars of the late colonial period and received land bonuses for their services, spread the word about the expanse of good land in Kentucky. Even without military bounties, reported William Christian, the troops fully expected that migrants to Kentucky "would be deemed proprietors by occupancy of at least some valuable tracts." Hunters, who explored the game-rich district after the war, disseminated more news of fertile lands, "unoccupied" by Indians, waiting to be claimed by possession and cultivation.[19]

At least three parties—from Pennsylvania (led by James Harrod), Virginia (led by James and Robert McAfee), and North Carolina (led by William Russell and Daniel Boone)—initiated settlement plans in central Kentucky in 1773. While Boone abandoned his squatting ambitions and became a faithful employee of Henderson and partners, the Harrods and McAfees, together with new land prospectors, returned in 1774 and 1775 to build cabins and plant corn, thus fulfilling what they deemed the customary prerequisites of occupancy and improvement.[20]

These pioneers, and those who followed them, downgraded the rights of Indian peoples who had long claimed Kentucky and improved it as a hunting ground. The Indians' claim, summarized one pioneer, "is like the claim of the children: it is mine, for I first saw it—or what that of the Buffaloe might be—it is mine, for I have first run over it." Because agriculture "is most favorable to the support of the greatest numbers, and consequently productive of the greatest happiness, . . . any right . . . not founded in *agricultural occupancy*" was worthless. Here, of course, pioneers conveniently overlooked the agricultural improvements that Indian peoples had made across the Ohio. Ohio Indians, no less than pioneers, occupied and improved land. Like pioneer squatters, they claimed the right to possess what they cultivated. But unlike pioneer men, Indian women did not claim permanent, individual ownership of the fields they farmed. Theirs was a group right and a use right, not an individuated and perpetual tenure.[21]

Quick as squatters were to fault the Indians' tenure, pioneers initially abided the new claim of Henderson and his partners. In fact, through most of 1775, Henderson skillfully reconciled occupants to the rule of the Transylvania Company. When Henderson first reached Boonesborough, he found all in disorder. In public, Henderson maintained a commanding front in the face of widespread demoralization. Privately, he damned his recruits as "a set of scoundrels who scarcely believe in God or fear a devil." Henderson wisely sweetened his dictates with promises of land, and his inducements won over the majority of Boonesborough settlers. Within a month of his arrival, he enthusiastically noted that at least around the company's headquarters "everybody seemed well satisfied."[22]

Once the situation at Boonesborough stabilized, Henderson turned to a more daunting task. While the Transylvania Company had recruited many of the settlers at Boonesborough, pioneers in other parts of Ken-

The first and only meeting of the Transylvania House of Delegates, near Boones-borough, in May 1775. From George W. Ranck, *Boonesborough: Its Founding, Pioneer Struggles, Indian Experiences, Transylvania Days, and Revolutionary Annals*, Filson Club Publications, no. 10 (Louisville, 1901).

tucky owed no allegiance to the partners. According to John Floyd, an agent of would-be land magnate William Preston, the majority of border-ers who relocated to Kentucky in the spring of 1775 preferred squatting to other methods of obtaining ownership. "The people in general seem not to approve of the governor's instruction with regard to settling the land; nor will any that I have seen purchase from Henderson, they rather choose to settle, as they have done on Holston," by cabin and cultivation rights. These squatters worried Henderson, especially those affiliated with James Harrod, whom he dismissed as "a body of lawless people."[23]

Bidding for recognition of Transylvania authority, Henderson invited emissaries from each of the four stations then established in central Ken-tucky to an assembly at Boonesborough. At the convention in May 1775, Henderson assumed a commanding stance. He insisted on holding a feu-dal ceremony to mark the transfer of suzerainty from the Cherokees to the Transylvania proprietors. In his address to the delegates, the former magistrate spoke in a style designed to awe his audience. With a bow to the "perfect balance" of the English constitution, Henderson outlined a government for the Transylvania Colony consisting of three branches: a lower house with representatives chosen by the people, a council of up to twelve men possessed of landed estates, and the proprietors. As to land, he reaffirmed the proprietors' power to sell it on their own terms and to collect quit-rents not exceeding two shillings per hundred acres.[24]

Henderson emerged from the four-day conference bounding with confidence. While the assembly did not assent to the proprietors' division of powers and land distribution system, the delegates did not reject the plan either. The results, wrote Henderson, left "everybody pleas'd," including even James Harrod, now favorably described as "a very good man for our purpose." John Floyd concurred with Henderson's prognosis. "All the settlers have received Col. Henderson as proprietor of that side of the Kentucky [River] which is called Transylvania Colony," Floyd informed William Preston.[25]

What Floyd did not say publicly was that he had also been brought into the Transylvania fold. When Floyd first visited Boonesborough in early May, Henderson had expected difficulties, since "he was Surveyor of Fincastle under Col Preston[,] who had exerted himself against us." But Floyd had startled Henderson by inquiring on what terms his men at St. Asaph's Station might settle Transylvania lands. Realizing that it was "most advisable to secure" Floyd "to our interest," Henderson promised him land and gave him a lucrative job as a surveyor for the Transylvania Colony. Through the rest of 1775, Floyd, and by extension Preston, did not meddle with the Transylvania claims, confining Fincastle surveys to the north side of the Kentucky River.[26]

With Floyd in his pocket and the squatters affiliated with Harrod seemingly compliant, Henderson gloated over the remarkable progress of the Transylvania Company. In a letter to the proprietors remaining in North Carolina, he summarized the course of events, emphasizing the dark days of March and April when Indians, hunger, squatters, and speculators challenged. But now, in early June, Henderson assuredly looked ahead. The Indians had not menaced for two months, the corn was doing well, and "everything has succeeded to my wish with respect to title."[27]

And then Henderson and his partners miscalculated. Believing their rule secure, the Transylvania proprietors set new terms for Kentucky land. At a meeting in September 1775, the partners voted to reserve 200,000 acres for themselves, including all lands adjoining salt springs, as well as all gold, silver, copper, and lead mines. They also reaffirmed their intention to collect quit-rents on all lands beginning in 1780. Finally, they doubled the price of land to all buyers who had not planted corn the previous spring.[28]

This last action enraged many recent emigrants to Kentucky and swelled the ranks of the disaffected. George Rogers Clark, who in July 1775 had reconciled himself to the rule of the Transylvania Company as "Reasonable Enough," now began to agitate against the excesses of the proprietors. Settlers at other stations joined in protesting the abuse of authority. In the fall of 1775, a number of settlers departed Boonesborough and aligned with the antiproprietary camp. In his year-end account of the state of the Transylvania Colony, partner John Williams reported that a conspiracy, led by Abraham Hite, had started around Harrodsburg, made up of settlers refusing to "hold lands on any other terms than those of the first year."[29]

In passing the obnoxious land rules, the proprietors crossed a line between acceptable and illegitimate exercise of authority. As in North Carolina, popular dissatisfaction in Kentucky began as an outcry against the excesses of rulers. Apparently, the Transylvania partners did not learn any lessons from their brush with the Regulators. By what was generally perceived as brazen profiteering, the proprietors provoked a revolt. By their disdain for the limits of authority, the partners turned fence-sitters into foes. As George Rogers Clark put it, Henderson and his associates "work[ed] their own Ruin."[30]

What began in the fall of 1775 as agitation against the arrogance of proprietors rapidly matured into an appeal for independence from Transylvania rule and a clamor for homestead rights. In March 1776, eighty-eight "aggrieved Transylvania settlers" petitioned the Virginia Convention to condemn the "insatiable avarice" of the proprietors, question the validity of the purchase from the Cherokees, and "implore to be taken under the protection of . . . the Colony of Virginia, of which we cannot help thinking ourselves still a part." Three months later, settlers around Harrodsburg gathered again to denounce the "pretended proprietors" for their "usurped authority" and their "exorbitant price" on land. So as "not [to] entail *Slavery* upon our posterity," the settlers repeated their request that the Virginia government "claim this country." But the petitioners sought more from Virginia than jurisdiction. Invoking the "ancient cultivation law," they asserted the rights of those who "by Preoccupancy" had inhabited the frontier. Recalling Hermon Husband's demands, Harrodsburg squatters claimed that improvers of vacant lands deserved title to sufficient acreage "to provide a subsistence for themselves and their Posterity."[31]

The petitioners' expression of the homestead ethic articulated the aspirations of a generation of pioneer men. Concern for land and lineage was uppermost on the minds of male migrants to Kentucky. When pressed to explain the decision to pack up belongings and remove families to dangerous, distant Kentucky, westering men referred to the same hopes as the Harrodsburg petitioners. Kentucky-bound fathers with growing families dreamed of being able to give "each of [their] children a sufficient portion." "The prospect of seeing all his Children settled Comfortably in one Neighborhood[,] their Arms open at any time to receive and assist," afforded a pioneer father "a greater degree of Happiness than any other situation."[32]

For pioneer mothers, moving afforded much less happiness. Susannah Johnson recalled that her father, like so many other men, decided to up-root from South Carolina and settle in Kentucky because "his family was now large, and he wished to locate where his children could find homes around him when they chose." Johnson's mother was not consulted, but recognizing that "her children, when arrived at maturity, might seek homes in new countries, and for the sake of keeping the family together, she consented to remove." As the departure day approached, however, "she wept incessantly" and when the family set off, "she sobbed convul-sively." Beyond her husband's earshot, she told Susannah that she "would willingly see every thing we possess on earth in flames, if that would take us back to our old home!"[33]

Backcountry-bred women resigned themselves to a peripatetic life, but past experiences did not prepare them for the journey to Kentucky. While most pioneer women had uprooted several times before, the dis-tance and the danger was never as daunting as the transmontane trip to Kentucky. The migrations that took thousands of families from Pennsyl-vania to the Virginia and Carolina backcountries were typically spaced out over several decades. But Kentucky was hundreds of miles away and had to be reached in one extremely perilous move. Once there, at least during the Revolution and through the 1780s, the situation of pioneer families remained precarious. No wonder many wives begged their rest-less husbands to stay put.

Unlike men whose pursuit of independence overwhelmed former at-tachments, women's fantasies incorporated a wider circle of friends and relations. Mother "would rather live in a little smoky cabben in Kentucky then in a good house in Carolina," Mary Adair wrote her sister, but only "if she could . . . have you and Betsey and your families near hir and with-out that she never will be happy any where." Adair's mother, like other pioneer women, put greater value on the proximity of extended families than men. That reflected the essential support backcountry women gave and received from female neighbors and relations. The company of kin folk, especially kinswomen, reconciled mothers and wives to moving to Kentucky. Their absence made the prospect truly dreadful.[34]

Differences between men and women mattered, but not to the fate of the Transylvania Colony. The remonstrances that emanated from Kentucky spoke in a masculine idiom. Homesteader protests against the Transylvania proprietors focused on the denial of independence to white male settlers, not the lack of support networks for female colonists.

III

The overthrow of the Transylvania Colony was a victory for rebellious male colonists; however, substituting the rule of Virginia gentlemen was no triumph for the cause of homesteading. Under the jurisdiction of Virginia, the land situation in Kentucky grew more chaotic and the distribution more concentrated. Disputes resulting from conflicts over landownership multiplied. Instead of one company monopolizing speculation, scores of monied men engrossed land. The majority of actual settlers did not realize their dreams of land sufficient to insure independence for their families and their descendants. Bitterness prevailed. Adherents of the homestead ethic again were forced into resistance.

The results confounded the intentions of Thomas Jefferson, who as governor of Virginia had overseen passage of the law to distribute lands in Kentucky. As a Whig pamphleteer, Jefferson had affirmed the homestead ethic, granting that a settler "may appropriate to himself such lands as he finds vacant, and occupancy will give him title." In the Virginia Constitutional Convention of 1776, he proposed giving fifty acres of frontier land to landless whites. Later that year the now Governor Jefferson disclaimed his untempered defense of squatting rights, calling it "a very hasty production." The land act of 1779, drafted by George Mason, with Jefferson's assistance, did *not* grant free lands to actual settlers. Yet the law retained elements of Jefferson's earlier endorsement of the rights of occupants.[35]

The law provided, as Jefferson desired, a process by which squatters could turn their "right" of occupancy into legal titles to fair-sized tracts. The act offered "actual settlers" the right to purchase 400 acres at a price below that available to nonresidents, with the lowest charge to the earliest occupants. Those who had made improvements, which entailed the building of a regulation-size cabin, were entitled to "preempt" an additional 1,000 acres at a slightly higher rate than settlement rights. Four commissioners were appointed to travel to Kentucky, hear the claims of occupants and improvers, and award certificates for 400, 1,000, and 1,400 acres. All lands not claimed and purchased by occupants and improvers or reserved for soldiers were put on sale through treasury warrants for forty shillings Virginia currency per hundred acres. No limits on amounts were set.[36]

The sale of treasury warrants invited speculation and concentration. Since the price of these warrants remained stable while the value of

Virginia's paper currency depreciated rapidly, the purchase of Kentucky lands became an increasingly attractive investment for grand speculators. Within a year of the law's taking effect, Virginia had sold treasury warrants redeemable for 1,925,796 acres of Kentucky land. Over the next decade, millions of additional acres passed into the hands of nonresident purchasers. Under Virginia's parceling of Kentucky, twenty-one individuals or partnerships acquired grants in excess of one hundred thousand acres.[37]

Rather than being a boon to actual settlers, the introduction of improvement rights spurred speculation. In determining the priority of claims, the 1779 act assigned preference of location to the earliest occupant. In defining the maximum size of settlement and preemption rights, however, the law reversed itself, providing 400 acres for occupancy and 1,000 acres for improvement. The discrepancy, as an October 1779 petition from the inhabitants around Boonesborough bitterly complained, allowed men who "only raised a small cabbin [and] perhaps never stayed three weeks in the country" to claim 1,000 acres. Meanwhile, those coming to Kentucky after the deadline for preemption rights, "who have suffered equally as much as the first setled," were restricted to 400 acres, and that at a higher price. "It had been well for us," lamented the Boonesborough petitioners, "if we had all been such cultivators and never come to settle in the country untill there had been a peace."[38]

Indeed, some cabin builders never intended to occupy their improvements on a permanent or even temporary basis. Many of the earliest "cabins" consisted only of stacks of three or four logs arranged in a square. "Improvements" often amounted to little more than a few square yards of cleared ground. Already in the summer of 1775, John Floyd reported that the best Kentucky lands were being preempted by "land jobbers," who "go about in companies and build 40 or 50 cabins" on vacant tracts. Floyd later warned his Virginia connections against compensating these invisible improvers, lest they expect "bloodshead soon." Yet Virginia lawmakers rewarded land jobbers. Although the land bill theoretically restricted individuals to a single preemption warrant, land jobbers easily evaded that limitation. To escape notice, crafty cabin builders disguised their handiwork by blazing the initials of friends on their improvements. In time, they assigned the improvements to these fronts and sold their preemption certificates to migrating settlers or absentee speculators.[39]

Procedural defects compounded the woes of actual settlers. Delays in the voiding of the Transylvania claim and in the formulation of a new system for parceling land allowed overlapping claims to proliferate. In June 1776, shortly after receiving the original protest of the Harrodsburg squatters, the Virginia Convention resolved that persons making settlements and improvements to vacant Kentucky lands should have preference in gaining title to those lands. Nearly three years passed, however, before the Virginia assembly made official the rights of occupants and set up a schedule of payments and fees leading to the establishment of legal titles.

When the commission finally arrived in October 1779 to issue certificates, disorder reigned—an unfortunate reality that the four commissioners tried their best to ignore. Over the next seven months, the commission conducted 79 sessions, heard from over 1,400 claimants, and dispensed 1,328 certificates encompassing 1,334,050 vaguely located acres. At that pace—an average of sixteen certificates issued per day—the commissioners had no time to inquire into potentially conflicting property lines. The certificate for 1,400 acres issued on December 24, 1779, to Daniel Boone, for example, specified that the tract lay "on the Waters of licking [River] including a small spring on the North East side of a small branch[,] a Camp & some Bushes Cut down at the same about 20 Miles East from Boonesborough." More precise than most settlement and preemption warrants as to location, Boone's certificate nonetheless lacked any detail about the configuration of the tract in question. The actual boundaries of Boone's property awaited the official survey, which he and other certificate holders had three years to accomplish. Rather than quieting controversies, the snap decisions of the commissioners bedeviled the courts of Kentucky well into the nineteenth century.[40]

Though lawsuits entangled almost all claims, few who crossed the mountains anticipated difficulties in securing clear titles. Guidebooks touted Kentucky as a haven for homesteaders, "the best place in the world for people to remove with large families . . . if the view of the Emigrant should be to render himself and his posterity independent." Edenic visions of an easy life lured tens of thousands of emigrants to Kentucky in the 1770s and 1780s. "What a Buzzel is amongst People about Kentuck?" wondered a Virginia gentlemen in May 1775. "To hear people speak of it[,] one Would think it was a new found Paradise." A decade later, Judge Harry Innes was struck by how the Kentucky-bound "seem absolutely infatuated by something like the old crusading spirit to the holy land." To migrants, Kentucky was "the Canaan of the West." Or, as one western preacher reversed the metaphor, heaven was a "Kaintuck of a place."[41]

The promised land inevitably disappointed. Not only were titles constantly contested, but the land itself failed to live up to its Edenic reputation. Migrants like William Nichols who imagined a "delightful Country where the Spontaneous productions of the soil alone must ever prevent the most Indolent from wanting the necessaries of life" found that procuring a subsistence was not so simple. Pioneers like Sarah Graham who came to Kentucky envisioning harvests of 190 bushels of corn per acre quickly learned how unrealistic were their projections. Much of the testimony about crop yields mistakenly generalized on the basis of the best lands, which actually covered only a fraction of Kentucky. Other exaggerations were pure fabrications concocted by speculators and their literary mouthpieces.[42]

Betrayed expectations stiffened opposition to Virginia's jurisdiction among actual settlers. In 1779, the Virginia land commissioners "received several letters intimating that a Combination of People were forming at the Falls to seize the Commissioners['] books and burn them." That extralegal conspiracy did not materialize, but the concentration and litigation inspired by Virginia's land system continued to incite protests and threats. At Harrodsburg in 1781, an assembly of fifty to sixty men had to be "dispersed in a forseable manner" after declaring their plan to petition Congress "to set aside . . . the land laws of Virginia."[43]

As tempers rose, the specter of rebellion menaced. Some of those disappointed with the land policies of Virginia's patriots turned into Tories. In Kentucky, loyalism gained strength during the Revolution. According to one observer in 1780, Kentuckians were so infuriated by the "Nabobs in Virginia taking all the lands" that, were the English to offer Kentuckians uncontested title to adequate parcels, "the greatest part will join" the loyalist cause. After the Revolution, foes of Virginia looked to Congress to right wrongs and reward occupants with fair and free headright grants. Agitators pronounced Virginia's claims "no better than an oak leaf" and spread rumors about congressional invalidation of the 1779 act. Partisans of redistribution argued that "to grant any Person a larger quantity of Land" than he needed for himself and his family was "subversive of the fundamental Principles of free republican government." Thus, the homestead ethic became a measure of true republicanism, and Virginia's aggrandizement of speculators became a justification for revolution. All seemed set for a new backcountry uprising.[44]

IV

In spite of all the dissatisfaction, in Kentucky, unlike on the other side of the Appalachians, there was no bloody insurrection. The threat of violent confrontation loomed during and after the Revolution, but extralegal intimidation remained on a relatively small scale. The insurgency of disappointed homesteaders never coalesced, in part because interference with the homestead ethic came from inside as well as outside Kentucky. The rhetoric of squatting rights did not reflect the reality of pioneer behavior. Many early pioneers, most notably Daniel Boone, were themselves caught up in the ethic of speculation.

When and where settlers breached the homestead ethic cannot be pinpointed, given their imprecise notions of the meaning of independence and the size of an appropriate family farm. Neither the 1776 petition from Harrodsburg squatters nor later entreaties praying revival of the "ancient cultivation law" specified how much land pioneers deemed sufficient to "provide a subsistence for themselves and their posterity." At the very least, independence implied possession of enough land to produce a "competence" for the present and an equal status and standard of living for posterity.[45]

By the latter part of the eighteenth century, the tradition accepted by many western Virginians set the proper size of a homestead at 400 acres. When his family moved with other squatters to the Monongahela Valley in 1772, Joseph Doddridge recalled that people considered private holdings above that size to be a wrongful expropriation of land. "My father, like many others, believed that having secured his legal allotment, the rest of the country belonged of right to those who chose to settle in it," remembered Doddridge. Presented the opportunity to add two hundred adjoining acres to his farmstead, Doddridge's father secured a patent. "But his conscience would not permit him to retain it in his family; he therefore gave it to an apprentice lad whom he had raised in his house."[46]

To judge by the praise lavished on Kentucky, independence required less land than ever before. While Kentucky was not the paradise real estate promoters extolled, the soil, especially in the central Bluegrass plain where pioneers clustered, was genuinely special. Reliable observers verified corn yields double and triple that of the most productive lands in Pennsylvania, Virginia, and North Carolina. Half as much land might furnish as ample a subsistence. "I thought if I could get but ten acres" for "my children in this rich new land," determined pioneer William Hickman, "it might be to their advantage."[47]

No Kentucky pioneer, though, expected to settle for ten acres. Nor did the majority of land seekers risk their lives and meager fortunes to obtain only a few hundred acres. It did not matter that a hundred-acre farmstead, with 20 percent under cultivation, could with supplements from the woods provide a subsistence for a small family. Nor did it matter that a slightly larger estate with more cleared and planted acreage could produce a surplus for which there was no market. Regardless of how many acres they needed, pioneers wanted more land. The self-restraint on land accumulation shown by Doddridge's father in western Virginia was rare in Kentucky. The October 1779 petitioners from Boonesborough complained that the 400-acre settlement right, approved on the Monongahela, was too "small a compensation" for the "loss[,] trouble[,] and risk" of moving to Kentucky.[48]

Of the forty-six Boonesborough petitioners, who included Boone, twelve men and two women received a settlement warrant for 400 acres. Only three carried their warrants through to grant. The rest sold out or acquired more land than the 400-acre standard. Overall, as Table A.1 details, twenty-nine of the petitioners received a certificate for 400 (S), 1,000 (P), or 1,400 (S+P) acres. Just five kept possession of their warrant through the next stages—survey and grant. Fourteen sold all or part of the lands to which they were entitled, while nine purchased additional holdings.

The buying and selling of claims began immediately. Hardly had John Floyd procured a certificate from the commission for a 1,400-acre tract before he "was immediately offered six fine young Virginia born negroes for it." Given the "keenness" of the market in settlement and preemption warrants, Floyd expected to obtain plenty of warrants for William Preston and other Virginia gentlemen who employed his land-locating services.[49]

The money of nonresident speculators backed Floyd and accounted for much of the buying and selling of settlement and preemption warrants. The land commissioners were themselves quite active, despite obvious conflicts of interest. According to John May, who witnessed the proceedings of the tribunal, the commissioners repeatedly passed judgment on claims in which they had purchased an interest and granted certificates in their own names. No one, however, was as active a purchaser of settlement and preemption warrants as May, a Petersburg merchant who, with the financial backing of Samuel Beall, attempted to corner the market. Because so "many of the Claimants have not Money to clear out their Lands," May believed warrants could be had very cheaply. And by purchasing choice land now at prices well below market value, a "very great Profit" was anticipated. Seeking money in the spring of 1780 to buy up an additional 100,000 acres of warrants, May predicted that within a year he could resell the lands at a profit of £200,000. "If I had 100,000 at this Time[,] I could, in six weeks Time, locate them on Land that would be worth half a Million."[50]

Though lacking the vaulting ambition of John May, homesteaders of smaller means and dreams also drove the booming market in settlement and preemption certificates. As with the Boonesborough petitioners, a substantial minority of those pioneers who received warrants on the basis of having actually settled or improved Kentucky lands purchased additional claims. Of the 138 pioneers issued preemption warrants for having raised a cabin in Kentucky between 1773 and 1775, 43 (31.2 percent) eventually acquired grants for more than 1,000 acres. Recipients of certificates for improvements without actual settlement were widely accused of land jobbing, so it was not surprising that only about one in six qualifying cabin builders maintained their land claims at 1,000 acres. Yet the percentage of preemption warrant holders who bought additional tracts was essentially the same as the proportion of actual, corn-raising occupants falling into that category. As Table A.2 shows, 56 of the 176 pioneers (31.8 percent) receiving settlement and preemption warrants engaged in land acquisitions that ran counter to the restraints of Monongahela homesteaders.

Table A.3, which summarizes the land transactions and holdings of the thirty-six men who built cabins at Harrodsburg in 1774, further illustrates the departure of Kentucky pioneers from the self-imposed lids of the homestead ethic. This first squatting company included at least three men who acted as land jobbers, erecting cabins and choosing lots on behalf of absent persons. Fourteen of the cabin builders eventually received settlement and preemption warrants. Among this group of actual settlers, nine obtained grants for more than 1,400 acres.

The acquisitiveness of Harrodsburg squatters exhibited considerable range. For three of the settlement and preemption warrant holders, the increase in landholdings amounted to only a few hundred acres apiece, within the limits of the homestead ethic. The other six settlement and preemption warrant holders who enlarged their holdings did so more significantly. Their grants at least tripled the original 1,400-acre certificate. While these half dozen occupants did not approach the 100,000-plus-acre holdings of the twenty-one biggest nonresident speculators, their grants, ranging between 4,200 and 12,200 acres, far exceeded the immediate requirements of independence.

To be fair to the Harrodsburg squatters and other land-grabbing pioneers, their engrossments were not simply evidence of a profiteering spirit. Part of their acquisitiveness, at least, was a reasonable response to the chaotic situation in Kentucky. Overlapping claims created endless and expensive litigation. It also made likely the loss of some or all of one's land grants. So acquiring "surplus" lands was a smart way to guard against legal reversals. In addition, independence was conceived in multigenerational terms. Providing land for posterity certainly raised requirements, especially since pioneer families were typically quite large. Neither the uncertainties of law nor the independence of dozens of grandchildren, however, warranted homestead rights of several thousand acres.

Daniel Boone's land hunting demonstrated the corruption of the homestead ethic. Boone first attempted to obtain land in Kentucky apart from any speculating company. In 1773, he persuaded a number of neighbors and relatives to join him in a bold occupation of Kentucky. Rather than purchase from Indians, speculators, or colonial governments, Boone appealed to the homestead ethic to legitimize the planned claims in Kentucky. In September, some forty individuals had assembled in Powell's Valley in southwestern Virginia ready to claim lands in Kentucky on the basis of possession and cultivation. Concerned that other squatters might preempt the best land, Boone exhorted the party to move forward quickly. The Kentucky-bound travelers had not yet reached the Cumberland Gap when an ambush by Cherokee warriors dashed their homesteading quest. Boone's eldest son, James, was killed in the attack. While Daniel urged the expedition to push on, the rest of the would-be homesteaders refused. Reluctantly, Daniel, Rebecca, and their surviving children turned back.[51]

Boone then fell in with Richard Henderson and company. With the voiding of the Transylvania purchase, Boone lost a 2,000-acre grant promised him by the proprietors in 1775. Yet unlike other employees who sued the partners, Boone remained loyal. Even after the properties he had counted on to secure independence for himself and his posterity were revoked, Boone continued to hunt land for some of the partners. And on at least one occasion in 1785, he donated his locating services for free, for "Reasons of past favors and good friendship."[52]

After Virginia took over the allocation of Kentucky, Boone made hunting land for absent treasury warrant purchasers his primary means of support. For old friends, he occasionally located vacant tracts and marked boundaries for no charge. From most clients, however, Boone exacted a hefty fee, for which he promised "to locate the land on as good as the Country will admit." He also contracted to "forever Defend the land and premises hereby bargained" if any problems arose about the clarity of title. For their services and their pledges, especially in the dangerous years of the Revolution, he and other land hunters received "the customary price," half the land clear of all expenses. In 1782, Boone was appointed a deputy surveyor of Fayette County, enabling him to perform the official survey at the same time as he made the initial location. The following year, he received a similar commission to make surveys in Lincoln County.[53]

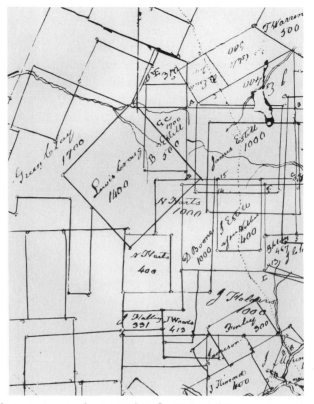

Plat displaying various overlapping and conflicting land claims near Boonesborough in the 1780s. Daniel Boone himself laid claim to a tract of some 1,000 acres. Courtesy of Special Collections and Archives, Eastern Kentucky Libraries.

During his term as an surveyor, Boone began to speculate more extensively. In his four years as a deputized official, he executed close to one hundred fifty surveys. Surveying warrants varying from 15,000 to 50 acres, Boone struck side deals entitling him to thousands of acres. He made surveys in his own name for 20,279 acres. Between 1783 and 1786, he sold his rights to 11,900 of these acres. He carried more than 8,000 acres through to grant.[54]

Because so many early settlers acquired at least a paper right to lands beyond a "family-sized farm," redistributionist energies dissipated. As one's claims multiplied and the size of one's potential estate expanded, so did one's stake in salvaging at least a *part* (one's own) of the existing system of land distribution. Already in 1781, John May, who had the most to lose should the Virginia system be overturned, recognized that the opening of speculative opportunity "disposed" Kentucky men "to submit to the Laws of Virginia." Then the most daring speculator in Kentucky lands, May assured his nervous partner Samuel Beall that there was no reason to rush into a hasty sale. "That Clamor which was at first raised against Monopolies [has] entirely died away, and every body seem[s] determined to monopolize as much as they can." Four years later, May was still busy calming Beall, still expressing certainty that as long as "nine out of ten of the Inhabitants are large speculators," no popular movement was going to wipe out Virginia warrants or otherwise reduce the "value of lands."[55]

MAY'S CONFIDENCE IN THE SECURITY of the system flew in the face of some important facts. As the distribution of land evolved through the 1780s, it did not provide family-sized farms for most men. Instead, the parceling maintained the stranglehold of landlords, primarily absentee, over Kentucky. The fall of the Transylvania Company rid Kentucky of the intolerable governance of Richard Henderson and partners, but it did not clear the field of land engrossers. How could it have when rival speculators largely engineered the fall of the Transylvania Colony? While the rule of Virginia opened the way for fee-simple titles, it also promoted confusion, litigiousness, and enormous landholdings by nonresidents. In 1792 when Kentucky achieved independence from Virginia, two-thirds of adult white male residents owned no land. The majority, in the words of Moses Austin, were "at last Oblig'd to become hewers of wood and drawers of water," to live as dependents, as tenants. Many others, remembered pioneer John Hedge, "squatted down on lands, not knowing or caring whose they were."[56]

Frustrated in their efforts to have and hold the basis of independent manhood, Kentuckians identified speculators and allied land jobbers as the cause of their distress. Pioneer men lashed out at engrossments that blocked access to land for occupancy and improvement. Squatters, tenants, and small landowners with uncertain holds on independence screamed loudest about vast uncultivated tracts in the hands of nonresidents. Though habits of deference died hard, backcountry folk had shown their intolerance of too abusive authority. The North Carolina Regulation in the 1760s and the popular rejection of the Transylvania proprietors in the 1770s broadcast the mutinous potential of backcountry settlers. Given the history of these and other backcountry disturbances, Kentucky seemed ripe for a rebellion in the 1780s.

There were many reasons why no additional insurrection disrupted the colonization of Kentucky. Most obvious was the persistence of an external threat. Colonization and conquest occurred simultaneously, which delayed any day of reckoning for Virginia's land system. During the Revolution, when the first colonists arrived, no place in Kentucky was safe from Indian attackers. Until the mid-1790s, lands away from the center of the Bluegrass plain could be occupied and improved only at great risk. Thousands of would-be homesteaders concluded that in the short term it was better to rent than to squat. Better to follow the "prevalent custom for persons to take a lease on lands in the more central parts, free from probable incursions of the Indians," reasoned John Hedge, than to get killed challenging absentee ownership of outlying tracts. Generous terms made tenancy easier to take. Anxious to get tracts cleared and homes, outbuildings, barns, and fences constructed, landlords designated yearly improvements in lieu of rental payments. Leases generally ran for several years, during which tenants kept their harvest and stock, while landlords were spared portions that did them little good in the absence of a market.[57]

By the time Indian dangers diminished and tenants moved off in search of estates of their own, the colonization of lands north of the Ohio reduced pressures on the Virginia land system operating south of the river. Beginning in the late 1780s, Kentuckians began to cross the Ohio to occupy and improve lands. Much has been said about how the United States government learned from the chaos of Kentucky and arranged for a more orderly distribution of public lands in the Northwest Territory. Less has been made of the safety valve that Ohio lands provided for Kentucky frontiersmen. The effects of outmigration were invisible; they were apparent only in what did not happen. Yet if thousands of pioneers had not moved on, Kentucky's colonization would have been even more chaotic and probably less peaceful.[58]

Finally the spread of speculative behavior undermined the solidarity of homesteaders and erased the chance for a general redistribution. The land claims of Daniel Boone and other pioneers, though hardly on the scale of a Richard Henderson or a John May, also impeded the rights of later migrants to acquire title by virtue of occupancy and improvement. The cause of homesteading suffered not only from the engrossment of speculators, but also from the acquisitiveness of early homesteaders.

"The spirit of speculation was flowing in such a torrent that it would bear down every weak obstacle that stood in its way," wrote the Reverend David Rice of his first visit to Kentucky in the early 1780s. "I looked forward to fifty or sixty years," he observed, "and saw the inhabitants engaged in very expensive and demoralizing litigations about their landed property." Rice, the father of Kentucky Presbyterianism and the new state's foremost opponent of slavery, displayed remarkable prescience about the consequences of undammed—though oft damned—speculation.[59]

FOUR *The Rules of Law*

AS DAVID RICE PROPHESIED, for a half century and more after their American colonization, Kentucky lands were the objects of speculation and litigation. As absentee and settler speculators enlarged their claims, lawsuits entangled almost every tract in central Kentucky. Already in 1786, a French traveler sadly determined that Kentuckians "would hardly know how to buy a piece of land without involving themselves in a lawsuit, often ruinous, always long and wearing."[1]

After Kentucky gained statehood in 1792, the disastrous legacy of the Virginia land system confronted the new state's governing officials. As lawsuits proliferated, judges tried to sort conflicting claims and invent some rules to reduce the chaos. Legislators wrestled with the problems of widespread landlessness and universal uncertainty about titles. Upon these rulings, judicial and legislative, rested the property of residents and nonresidents.

The rules of law cost Daniel Boone all the lands he *thought* he owned. From the time he signed on with the Transylvania partners, Boone traveled with speculators. But while he served great speculators and tried to emulate their acquisitiveness, he never mastered the imitation. In the world of hunters from which Boone hailed, good neighborship meant giving meat away to folks in need; courage and generosity were the measures of manhood and the basis of local authority. In the world of great speculators, however, accumulation of land established noteworthiness. To maximize self-advantage, the "worthiest" land brokers bent rules. In Kentucky, concluded a transplanted Pennsylvanian, speculators must "much deceive others or lose very considerably." Boone was ill-equipped for the cut-throat practices of notable speculators. He was out of place in the courthouses and legislative halls where successful engrossers won their most important victories.[2]

For Boone and other Kentuckians who lost their lands or never obtained any, the rule of law was synonymous with the misrule of lawyers. Pioneers and their descendants yearned for a less complicated and more

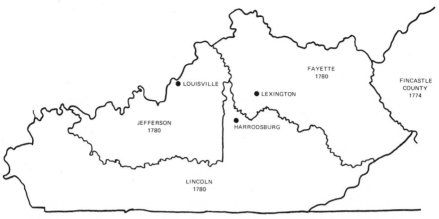

County jurisdictions in Kentucky (1780–84). Courtesy of the Kentucky Historical Society.

democratic legal system, which they hoped would diminish the role of lawyers and assign a family-sized farm to all adult white men. To the dismay of those who hoped it would become the best poor man's country, the new state of Kentucky became a paradise for lawyers. It was this reputation that brought Henry Clay to Kentucky. First as a litigator and then as a legislator, Clay became prominent in the resolution of land matters. His developed into an effective voice for the preservation of an independent judiciary and the protection of gentry property.

Yet despite evidence to the contrary, the rule of law was more than the self-interested jurisdiction of wealthy lawyers and their monied clientele. In Kentucky and across the early republic, democratic influences curbed the power of bar and bench. Responding to popular pressures, decisions of courthouse and statehouse ameliorated dissatisfaction with the distribution of land. That popular pressures did not bring a more radical redistribution exhibits the remarkable capacity of republican government to preserve comity while conserving property. Similarly, the quieting of conflicts over slavery depended on this kind of settlement. During the first decade of Kentucky's statehood, as exasperation with the maldistribution of land peaked, agitation about slavery also crested. But opposition to slavery, like that to land distribution, did not in the end upend the rules of law or the security of private property.

I

On January 31, 1803, a fire consumed the office of the Fayette County clerk. As an early resident of the area admitted, " 'twas believed the office was set on fire to destroy land claims." Yet no one in the vicinity of the clerk's office fingered the arsonist. The flames, it seemed, served the interests of neighbors who hoped the destruction of old records would result in a straightforward and fair redistribution of land among occupants.[3]

Arson was an extreme remedy, but the uncertainty of land possession summoned drastic measures. Virginia's allocation of warrants prior to verifying location created chaos aplenty. Claims, observed Kentucky's first historian, were scattered "as autumn distributes falling leaves." In one case cited by Henry Clay, "the same identical tract" was "shingled over by a dozen claims." Kentucky legislators exacerbated the confusion by continuing to grant lands haphazardly. In 1797, the surveyor general of Kentucky reported to the legislature that while grants for approximately twenty-four million acres had been issued, the state contained only half that much acreage.[4]

Inequality of holdings compounded the problem. In 1800, the richest tenth of taxpayers owned nearly a third of the Kentucky lands in private hands. At the same time, a third of adult white males held less than two hundred acres and more than half possessed no land at all. No owners, smallholders especially, felt their titles safe.[5]

In the late 1790s Boone joined the ranks of the dispossessed. From the state of Kentucky, he procured grants to thousands of acres in addition to those he had secured from Virginia. But he never managed to finish the acquisition process by gaining clear titles. Again and again, overlapping claimants contested Boone's claims, and ignorance of the intricate provisions of laws inevitably deprived him of ownership.[6]

Boone's deficiencies as a locator and surveyor cost him dearly. As more and more of his locations were discovered to conflict with other claims, Boone became enmeshed in numerous lawsuits. At one session of the Bourbon County Court in May 1788, three different men sued Boone "for breach of his promise and assumption." All of the plaintiffs won judgments against him. Through the 1790s, Boone listened to litigants impugn his honesty and accuse him of performing "chimney corner" surveys, making up instead of measuring boundaries. Outside of court, he received assassination threats.[7]

Boone blamed his misfortune on complicated laws and insidious lawyers. As damage awards piled up against him, he became acidic about the injustices done him by judges and lawyers. Eventually he stopped appealing adverse judgments. Frequently he did not appear in court to defend himself. His surrender resembled the abdication of his brother and longtime hunting partner, Squire, who grew so tired of giving depositions and answering suits that he became "principaled against going into town . . . on any business whatsoever." In the fall of 1798, when Daniel failed to respond to a plaintiff's complaint over six thousand acres of lost land, the judge ordered the sheriff of Mason County, where Boone resided, to take the absent defendant into custody. But the sheriff could not find Boone, who had decided to leave Kentucky forever.[8]

Tens of thousands of Kentuckians shared Boone's sense of futility. As the volume of litigation multiplied, despair of gaining justice within the legal system deepened. Exasperation with the slow, expensive, and complicated workings of the courts made litigation a Hobson's choice for many claimants. As one set of pioneer petitioners recounted, "Ignorance of the Law" threatened to "complete our Ruin." Yet to "prosecute our Claim[,] the last Cow and Horse must be sold to maintain the Suit"; to "decline the contest, the Land upon which we had Hopes of supporting ourselves and Families in peace during the Remainder of our Lives will be wrested from us."[9]

Venting frustrations, folk wisdom ridiculed lawyers—and those who resorted to them. One joke told of a sick lawyer, who made out a will in which he left everything to the people. Asked why, the lawyer replied "from such I had it, and to such I give it again." "Before you go to law, the *controversy* is whether the money is your's or another's," advised a Lexington almanac; "once the suit is begun, the *contrivance* is, that it be neither your's nor the other's, but their's who pretend to defend you both."[10]

Punchlines packed a walloping message: in lawsuits only lawyers won, for their livelihoods "depend[ed] upon the contentions, broils, and vices of our citizens." Thus, lawyers deliberately complicated proceedings to justify excessive fees. The "custom of the country in giving one half [in payment to lawyers] to save the other is too large" resolved a meeting of Fayette County farmers in 1798. That meeting, along with many similar gatherings, called for a new constitution and a rewriting of the laws to make them understandable to "simple" farmers. Most in need of simplification were the land laws, "a chaos of Gothic ignorance," designed to slow the course of justice, while enriching lawyers.[11]

As a group, the lawyers of Kentucky did not earn much respect for their educational accomplishments. Defenders of legal intricacy argued that the land laws required "half a life well spent to master," but few lawyers studied so diligently. In the last years of the eighteenth century and the first decade of the nineteenth, admission to the Kentucky bar required no formal training. The schooling of most lawyers consisted of a year as a clerk in the office of a prominent attorney. Anything more, claimed one member of the Kentucky bar, made the fledgling lawyer "an overmatch for half who practice." Micah Taul, who built a substantial practice, boasted that when he received his license he "had *looked* into" but had never actually "*read a Law Book*." That hardly crippled Taul, since most of his fellow attorneys "studied Hoyle more than they did Blackstone." [12]

That lawyers liked to drink and gamble did not injure their reputations, for these pastimes were endemic among free white males. The aggressive culture of backcountry men celebrated the conviviality and competition of all kinds of gamesmanship. Boasting was an integral part of betting. "The way to be popular in Kentucky," discerned the transplanted New Englander Amos Kendall, was to "drink whiskey and talk loud, with the fullest confidence." [13]

Lawyers preferred poker, however, where the emphasis on bluffing countered the spirit of self-assertive gamesmanship. Unlike shooting or brawling, where contestants demonstrated their superiority directly and openly, where participants talked and hopefully shot straight, the greatest satisfaction in poker accrued to players who did not have to reveal their hands. Horse races, cock fights, wrestling matches, and shooting tournaments were not immune from devious manipulation, but only in cards was deception part of the game.

To lay people, law resembled poker. At law, as in poker, the best claim did not necessarily win. A large bankroll, though no guarantee of success, helped at cards and in courts. Those who could call a bluff and raise the stakes possessed a significant advantage, as did those who could raise the cost of litigation through procedural delays and appeals. Those with the most resources could also retain the most capable lawyers, who, like the best poker players, knew how to manipulate circumstances to favor their clients.

The dispossessed dreamed of a simpler, swifter, surer system of justice. After Boone left Kentucky, he briefly realized his juridical fantasy in Missouri. Appointed syndic by the Spanish governor in June 1800, Boone dispensed his brand of quick, but popular, justice. In criminal matters, he ordered violators whipped, with the lashes "well laid on." In land disputes, Boone frequently faulted both parties and dictated his own compromise.[14]

Boone's system of justice appealed to Kentuckians tired of lawyers and courts. For claimants with sufficient financial resources, the easiest way to avoid lengthy legal entanglements was to buy out the owners of overlapping tracts. Those of limited resources often compromised with their neighbors. "For friendship" Benjamin Swope and George Smith "agreed to give up to each other the part of interference." Other disputants escaped the time and expense of law and lawyers via arbitration. Baptists, and to a lesser extent members of other evangelical churches, relied on lay referees to mediate between complainants and insure that squabbles did not cause a "breach of fellowship."[15]

These alternatives hardly solved all conflicts. Neighbors often refused to be neighborly, and so, as François André Michaux found out on his tour of Kentucky in 1802, litigators had no trouble finding litigants. At every house Michaux stopped, the inhabitant "was persuaded of the validity of his own right" and "dubious of his neighbor's," an attitude that mustered lawyers and deflected arbitrators. "The temper of the day is too much opposed to accommodation of disputes," confessed an advocate of arbitration. As long as "claimants too passionately enslave themselves with the shackles of the law," lawyers were free to carry out their "artful" orchestrations.[16]

The search for a panacea to the problems of maldistribution politicized the citizenry of Kentucky. "The people of Kentucky are all turned Politicians," Federal Court Judge Harry Innes wrote Thomas Jefferson in 1791. "The Peasantry are perfectly mad . . . They say *plain honest Farmers* are the only men who ought to be elected." Particularly unsettling to Innes and other gentry leaders were the calls by plain farmers for a redistribution of land.[17]

Through the 1790s, redistributionist sentiment focused on the concentrations of land in nonresident hands. However, plans to impose confiscatory taxes on the lands of nonresidents ran afoul of the 1792 separation compact with Virginia. The separation agreement stipulated that lands belonging to nonresidents "shall not be in any case taxed higher than the lands of residents . . . nor shall a neglect of cultivation or improvement of any land . . . subject such non-residents to forfeiture or other penalty" for at least six years. Barely a year had elapsed, however, before redistribution-minded legislators, eyeing the uncultivated, undivided lands of nonresidents, began to push owners to make improvements or sell off tracts. At their 1793 session, lawmakers passed a revenue act that classified land as first, second, or third rate according to the quality of the soil. By assessing land on the basis of potential, resident politicians pressured owners to make their lands productive.[18]

Not surprisingly, nonresident speculators objected to the new code. The partners of the Transylvania Company, trying to uphold the value of their 200,000-acre "consolation" grant, denounced the progressive tax as a land grab by resident politicians "calculated for the purpose of speculating on the lands of Absentees." Resentful that their rights as "the principal promoters of the settling" of Kentucky were being trampled, the partners saw no way to pay the tax on lands "in their present unproductive State." Because of the tax bill, the Transylvania partners were forced to sell off their grant in a manner they deemed hasty and premature.[19]

Land reform at the expense of nonresidents came also with the enactment by Kentucky's lawmakers of "occupying claimant" statutes. At its 1794 session, the lower house, whose members faced annual election by voters angry with the current land situation, approved a bill freeing ejected occupants from back rents and forcing their ejectors to compensate them for improvements made by those with "color of title." The Senate, whose members did not have to answer to voters every year, rejected the bill on the grounds that it violated the terms of the separation compact. Three years later, however, a similar bill made it through both houses. The occupying claimants act of 1797 provided residents, who, "deducing a fair title from the record," had settled and improved land from which they were "afterwards evicted," with compensation for their investment of labor.[20]

Since legislative remedies still faced court tests, reformers concentrated on democratizing the state's judiciary. That meant dismantling constitutional guarantees insulating judges from majority sentiments. The issue of judicial independence moved front and center in the fall of 1794 in the case of *Kenton v. McConnell*. By a two-to-one vote the magistrates of Kentucky's highest court handed down a decision jeopardizing thousands of titles encompassing hundreds of thousands of acres. The ruling precipitated a loud and immediate uproar. Editorialists blasted "the opinion of two fallible men" and questioned the vesting of so much power in so few hands. Petitioners barraged the legislature with remonstrances, seeking new judges who would render opinions "with as little formality and legal criticisms as possible."[21]

Although one of the judges switched his vote the following term and thereby reversed the decision, the debate over the independence of the judiciary stayed atop the legislative agenda. Members of the lower house responded to public pressure by initiating an inquiry into the conduct of the judges. The two-thirds majority required for impeachment was not attained, but the legislature censured the judges for a decision "contrary to the plain meaning and intent of the law." The assembly also moved to restructure the court system. A 1795 act rescinded the Court of Appeals' original jurisdiction over land cases and vested it in six district courts. The same year saw passage of a law authorizing arbitration as an alternative to litigation.[22]

Radicals agitated for more far-reaching reforms. This resulted in 1802 in the replacement of district courts with a system of circuit courts. Opponents branded the reform a "legislative absurdit[y]." Proponents hailed it as a means of making justice more accessible and less expensive for common folk. To make the circuit courts more friendly, the act mandated that two of the three judges riding each circuit be unschooled in the law. Thus, the majority would depend on common sense instead of legal trickery in reaching their decisions. But the circuit court plan backfired; the role of lawyers increased. Fanciful arguments readily swayed untutored justices. "Our lawyers, and not our judges, too often decide causes," conceded one writer, admitting the failure of the simplifying scheme.[23]

The pace and scope of legislative reform during Kentucky's first decade of statehood raised hopes without rectifying the problems of insecurity and inequality. Legislators, summarized Henry Clay, had "attempted much and done little." At the beginning of 1803, the situation regarding the land and the law was still a mess. No wonder, then, that the perpetrator(s) who torched the office of the Fayette County clerk were not identified.[24]

II

Next to the maldistribution of land, the future of slavery was the most contentious problem facing Kentucky lawmakers in the first decade of statehood. Kentucky's 1792 constitution protected slavery, but emancipationists pressed their cause through the 1790s. Along with frustration over land matters and resentment of too independent justices, antislavery fervor of one strain or another galvanized a solid majority of Kentucky voters behind a new constitutional convention. Yet instead of democratizing the judiciary or ending slavery, the 1799 constitution left most checks on popular governance in place and secured slave property from legislative meddling.

No one was more disappointed by this result than the Reverend David Rice, who had championed emancipation from his first days in Kentucky. After graduating from the College of New Jersey in 1761, Rice commenced his ministerial career in his native Virginia. Like other Virginia men with growing families, Rice ventured west in 1783 to secure independence for himself and his sons. But the disarray of the land situation in Kentucky persuaded Rice to return to Virginia, which he would have done permanently had not a petition signed by three hundred Presbyterian pioneers beseeched him to come back. Responding to the petitioners, Rice organized the first three Presbyterian congregations in Kentucky in 1784. Though Rice brought slaves with him, he was a devout opponent of slavery. As Kentucky moved toward statehood, he emerged as the most forceful exponent of the antislavery position. At the 1792 constitutional convention, he led the fight for emancipation of slaves and for prohibition of slavery.[25]

Rice's antislavery combined scriptural and secular objections. Slavery, he insisted, violated God's law. It was also "inconsistent with good policy," for slavery bred idleness, stimulated vice, and sapped political virtue. Immediate abolition, so that the new state would not "be born in this sin," was the only salvation for Kentucky's republican government.[26]

At the 1792 constitutional convention, Rice's crusade came up short. By a vote of twenty-six to sixteen, delegates defeated an antislavery plank. Though Rice had resigned before the decisive poll was taken, ministers still accounted for six of the sixteen antislavery votes. Five of the other ten delegates who made up the minority were active laymen in Presbyterian and Baptist congregations. But the majority, all of whom were slaveowners (as were twelve of the minority), were not swayed by Rice's arguments. Determined to protect their property and preserve order, most delegates rejected emancipation as economically disadvantageous and socially dangerous. Kentucky's first constitution did grant the legislature "full power to prevent slaves being brought into this State as merchandise" and "to prevent any slave from being brought into this State from a foreign county." Article IX, however, deprived the legislature of its "power to pass laws for the emancipation of slaves without the consent of their owners, or without paying their owners, previous to such emancipation, a full equivalent in money for the slaves so emancipated."[27]

Kentucky's first constitution was largely the handiwork of George Nicholas, a Virginia-born lawyer of great distinction and a Kentucky land speculator of grand designs. Nicholas wished to remake Kentucky in Virginia's image, to replicate the well-ordered, gentry-dominated government and society of the Old Dominion in the new state of Kentucky. While Nicholas stepped away from Virginia precedent by eliminating ownership of land as a qualification for voters, he deliberately checked the property-threatening tendencies introduced by adult white male suffrage. In addition to the shield it afforded slavery, the 1792 constitution affirmed the validity of all lands granted by Virginia and provided lifetime appointments for justices of the state's highest court—to block any radical confiscation and redistribution schemes that might arise in the future.[28]

A campaign for a more democratic constitution began almost at once. While the 1792 charter was never ratified by a popular vote, Article XI promised "citizens . . . an opportunity to amend or change this Constitution in a peaceable manner." If a majority of voters supported a new convention in 1797 and again in 1798, then a third election was to be held to choose delegates "for the purpose of readopting, amending or changing this Constitution." Because these ballots enfranchised all adult white males, the electorate was sure to be very different from the framers of the constitution. At the 1792 convention more than 90 percent of the delegates owned slaves; that year only 23 percent of the electorate were slaveholders.[29]

A substantial proportion of this nonslaveholding majority disliked slavery, albeit for different reasons than Rice. Indeed, the influence of clergy men at the 1792 convention exaggerated their leverage over the general population. Instead of biblical exegesis or republican ideology, practical concerns about competition drove popular antislavery. White tenants naturally resented their displacement by black slaves. Antislavery also appealed to propertyless men who anticipated that elimination of unfree competitors would encourage the breakup of large plantations and improve tenants' chances to acquire lands of their own.

Unfriendly competition between slave and free labor dated back to the prestatehood era when gentry landowners sent dependents to take possession of tracts, clear fields, build homes, and make other necessary improvements. Often this entailed leasing lands to tenants. The precarious situation and the difficulties of opening a frontier farmstead, however, necessitated that generous terms be offered; typically, tenants negotiated agreements that deferred payments for the first year or two of a four- or five-year lease and kept subsequent rents relatively light. Where possible, landowners employed slaves, who lacked the bargaining power of free tenants.[30]

The shift from tenants to slaves troubled some slaveholders. In the late eighteenth century, misgivings about slavery haunted the Virginia gentry. Many gentlemen assuaged their consciences by touting the fatherly attentions they expended on their "people." But this rationale did not comfort slaveholders who exposed their slaves to the hardships and dangers of the trans-Appalachian frontier. In 1780, when Kentucky was truly a dark and bloody ground, Thomas Hart, one of the Transylvania partners who employed Boone, agonized about the morality of "send[ing] a parcel of poor slaves where I dare not go myself." But Hart, who would become the father-in-law of Henry Clay, like other slaveowners, reconciled himself to having slaves smooth the way for his family.[31]

Ultimately, most masters worried less about the safety of their slaves than about the security of their property. "Not being able to hire a Man on any Terms," John May opted to bring his "most valuable Slave" on a land-hunting venture in 1780. But May's bondsmen quickly "fell in with some worthless Negroes who persuaded him to run away & attempt to get with the Indians." While this slave returned after a ten-day absence, May concluded that the frontier was "a bad place to bring Slaves to, being so near Indians that they will frequently find their way to them." But as Indians retreated from the borders of Kentucky, slaveowners became more concerned with internal threats to their chattel. Before heading west in the early 1790s, John Breckinridge dispatched twenty slaves to Kentucky. With antislavery feelings running high and the possibility of a new constitutional convention looming, Breckinridge confessed to being "somewhat afraid of the Kentucky politicians with respect to negroes." [32]

It fell to Breckinridge to defend slavery and gentry rule against pressures from Kentucky politicians and people. After his slaves prepared the way, Breckinridge relocated to a plantation near Lexington in 1793 and entered into the practice of law. In December of that year, Governor Isaac Shelby appointed him as the state's attorney general. Four years later he was elected to the Kentucky House of Representatives. Fearing that a new constitution would excessively democratize government and disturb property rights, Breckinridge became the chief spokesmen for the "friends of order." Assuming the mantle of gentry leadership from George Nicholas, Breckinridge charged that proponents of constitutional revision were radical emancipationists, motivated by envy not principle. These "political upstarts" hoped only to "come in for a better share of the *loaves* and *fishes* than they now enjoy." Their goal was theft, for "where is the difference whether I am robbed of my horse by a highwayman, or of my slave by a set of people called a Convention?" Both were "species of Property," insisted Breckinridge," and both were "equally sacred." Extending this line of attack, Breckinridge submitted that emancipation endangered the landholdings of all Kentuckians. "If they can by one experiment emancipate our slaves; the same principle pursued, will enable them at a second experiment to extinguish our land titles; both are held by rights equally sound." [33]

Advocates of constitutional change denied Breckinridge's charge and hammered the undemocratic checks enshrined in Kentucky's 1792 charter. Particularly galling was the indirect election of members of Kentucky's upper house. Proconvention writers also engaged in fear-mongering of their own. One broadside warned that the same principles that justified slavery sanctioned the disenfranchisement of poor white men. [34]

Henry Clay, a twenty-one-year-old newcomer to Kentucky, penned the most comprehensive refutations of Breckinridge and the most thorough expositions of the need for a new constitution. Born in Hanover County, Virginia, on April 13, 1777, Clay often spoke of his humble beginnings. Yet while Clay was not to the manor born, neither were his origins so modest. Growing up in middling circumstances, Clay's ascent began with a clerkship in the office of George Wythe, the eminent jurist who had trained Thomas Jefferson, George Nicholas, and many other prominent lawyers in Virginia and Kentucky. After leaving Wythe, Clay moved west in 1797, where he quickly built a solid practice. But the young attorney, technically underage when he obtained his license to practice law in Kentucky, initially distanced himself from the conservatism of Nicholas and his coterie. In April 1798, writing as "Scaevola," Clay authored a blistering indictment of the 1792 constitution's unrepublican principles. Rejecting judicial and upper house curbs on popular sovereignty, Clay contended that "the will of the enlightened representatives of a free people should not be checked by any power upon earth, except it be the people themselves."[35]

The following February "Scaevola" published another tract, which accused Breckinridge and the anticonvention forces of perpetrating "a contemptible subterfuge" by suggesting that redistribution of land was the hidden agenda of emancipationists. Echoing Rice, he insisted that "justice and policy both recommend" the end of slavery. "Neither justice nor policy," however, "recommend[s] a [re]division of all the property in this state." As for ending slavery, Clay, true to his later reputation, advanced a compromise. Departing from Rice's contention in 1792 that the sin of slavery must be eradicated without delay, Clay proposed that emancipation be implemented gradually. This moderate course would allow the commonwealth time to adjust to a free-labor economy and to educate freedmen for the responsibilities of citizenship.[36]

Although George Nicholas belittled the newcomer as a "beardless boy," Clay's political talents were undeniable. He was already an accomplished orator. One listener credited the youthful Clay as "the best three-year old he had ever seen on the turf." The "depth and sweetness of his voice" and "the gracefulness of his enunciation and manner" reminded others in the audience of another famous Hanover County orator — Patrick Henry.[37]

The results of the preliminary elections of 1797 and 1798 cheered Clay and other supporters of fundamental change. The first referendum on whether to call a new convention brought 5,001 votes in favor to just 425 opposed. Anticonvention spokesmen claimed that the low turnout invalidated the election, but in the following year's contest a substantial majority (and a much larger number of voters) again backed a new convention. Opponents then tried to overturn the results by having nonvoters counted as negative voters, but this blatantly undemocratic maneuver collapsed. While Breckinridge persisted in his obstructionism, cooler gentlemen reconciled themselves to a new convention and made plans to control it. As George Nicholas counseled Breckinridge, "a convention I do not wish to see, but opposition to it, will only increase the fever, and render the opposers personally obnoxious." [38]

Having kept a public silence during the elections of 1797 and 1798, Nicholas returned to the fray in the spring of 1799. Despite his prominence as an attorney and as the chief framer of Kentucky's first constitution, Nicholas preferred to stay out of electoral politics. "I never intend to have any hand in the game of government," he informed a friend, "but wish to know how the hands are managed." The successes of proconvention forces, and the threat of unchecked democracy and emancipation, however, obliged Nicholas to exercise his managerial skills anew. In the months before the May 1799 election of convention delegates, Nicholas, with Breckinridge's assistance, organized a slate of candidates to run against the radicals and drafted a five-point platform. [39]

Nicholas's platform again demonstrated his willingness to concede battles in order to win wars. In 1792, he had acquiesced to the enfranchisement of propertyless men. As Fredrika Teute has argued, this incorporation of "the unpropertied into the body politic" contravened classical republican wisdom, which held that only independent men with a propertied stake in the system could be trusted with the vote. Nicholas, however, understood what other gentlemen were slow to realize: by giving the unpropertied a stake in the political system, the extension of suffrage might "divert conflict away from radical action over economic inequalities." In 1799 Nicholas repeated the formula. Sacrificing one check on popular governance, Nicholas's platform called for direct election of members of the upper house. But it also reaffirmed the essential principles of "safe government": preservation of an independent judiciary, prohibition of legislative emancipation without consent or compensation, and protection of the separation compact with Virginia (and thus protection of the landholdings assigned by Virginia). [40]

Nicholas died suddenly on July 25, 1799, just three days after the constitutional convention got under way, but the shape of the final document was clear. At the May ballot to choose delegates, the Nicholas-Breckinridge slate reversed the results of the two previous elections and routed proreform candidates. Only four emancipationists were elected, and these delegates were of different minds about the means and timing of the process. The religious contingent, so prominent in the antislavery faction of 1792, was reduced to just three ministers, one of whom quoted scripture to defend slavery. Lawyers, by contrast, were more numerous at the second constitutional convention. This group too divided on many questions, but to a man they opposed radical schemes to confiscate property or democratize government to the detriment of the rule of law.[41]

The new constitution of 1799 satisfied Breckinridge, who as a member of the convention played an important role in its drafting. It would also have pleased Nicholas, as the final product bore the imprint of his platform for safe government. In a bow to democratic sentiments, the new constitution mandated direct election of upper house legislators. On the crucial issues, however, the 1799 charter restored the status quo. The independence of the judiciary remained intact, the Virginia land grants remained inviolable. The 1799 constitution also reaffirmed Article IX of the 1792 constitution, and then amplified its defense of slavery. To remove potential impediments to the growth of unfree labor, delegates denied legislators the authority even to prohibit the future importation of slaves into Kentucky. As for Kentucky's free blacks, the 1799 convention overrode the precedent of the 1792 constitution and deprived them of their right to vote.[42]

III

A decade of legislative reform and constitutional revision, then, had seemingly not relieved the sources of popular dissatisfaction. At the beginning of the nineteenth century, landlessness was still the unfortunate lot of half of Kentucky householders, and overlapping claims still impeached the titles of the luckier half. Yet, as in the prestatehood era, no bloody uprising upset the distribution of land. Rancor remained, but the rule of law successfully contained discontent and protected property. Indeed, slavery not only endured, it expanded.

If one man deserved credit for saving the system, it was Henry Clay. In the 1790s, George Nicholas and John Breckinridge were the preeminent guardians of gentry property and authority; in the first decade of the nineteenth century, Clay emerged as their successor. That role hardly befit the young firebrand who had launched his political career championing emancipation of slaves and democratization of the state constitution. Fortunately for the gentry cause, Clay shed his youthful radicalism rather swiftly.

Rarely can one date ideological conversions as exactly as in the case of Clay, where a shift in political views corresponded with a change in personal status. In April 1799, after a brief courtship, Clay married Lucretia Hart. Daughter of Thomas Hart, a partner in the Transylvania Company who had subsequently established himself as one of the leading merchants in Lexington, Lucretia brought her husband a handsome dowry and entry into the Bluegrass's most elite circles. Clay's roster of clients expanded dramatically, and it soon included many of Lexington's wealthiest businessmen–land speculators. Through his father-in-law, whose mercantile connections extended widely, Clay gained a number of nonresident clients as well. Firms in Baltimore, Philadelphia, and New York signed on with Clay. The heirs of Thomas Hart's brother, Nathaniel, also retained Clay in a suit against Daniel Boone, whose faithfulness to the Transylvania partners was forgotten. Clay, though, lost this case for lack of evidence "to convict Boone of fraud."[43]

Marriage agreed with Clay, as measured in his net worth. In 1799, he listed taxable property of only one horse. Just five years later, Clay's stable of horses numbered five. More important, his landholdings topped 2,500 acres. Included in that total was a tract of 125 acres acquired that year on which Clay began to build a home and plantation. While Clay continued to express opposition to the peculiar institution, he owned six slaves in 1804. Over the next few years, he added to his lands and improved his plantation, a mile outside of Lexington, which he named Ashland. A decade after his arrival in Kentucky, Clay possessed more than ten thousand acres and held fourteen slaves. By then, he lived in a fine brick mansion, from which he oversaw a thriving plantation. In the fashion of Bluegrass planters, Clay raised hemp and fine-blooded horses, of which he then owned forty.[44]

Clay's radicalism ebbed as his clientele changed and as he transformed himself into a hemp-raising, horse-breeding, slaveowning planter. In 1801, when John Breckinridge went to Washington to take a seat in the United States Senate, he entrusted Clay with his legal practice. Two years later, Clay followed Breckinridge's footsteps into political office. In August 1803, six months after fire consumed the county clerk's office, Fayette County voters elected Henry Clay to his first term in the Kentucky House of Representatives. As a legislator, Clay spoke up as ably for gentry interests as he had earlier promoted those of plain farmers. He promised to rejuvenate the independence of the judiciary. To bring stability and safeguard property, he espoused higher salaries for judges. At the same time, he attacked the circuit court's unlearned judges for rendering incorrect and unpredictable verdicts.[45]

Yet Clay simultaneously supported occupying-claimant laws. "A farm, with all its fields, houses, orchards, gardens, lawns, and shrubberies no more resembles the same land in its native state than a piece of Brussels lace does the flax out of which it is wrought," reasoned Clay. Compensating improvers and shortening their uncertainty about title was the right thing to do. It was good politics, too. Every legislator understood that occupying-claimant statutes disadvantaged nonresidents. Absentees correctly complained that entrusting the valuation of improvements to a jury composed of the occupying claimant's neighbors led to inflated assessments. Stories of "apple trees not bigger than a man's arm" valued at ten dollars, of half-rotten fences at the full price of new rails, and of decrepit log houses judged equal to stone or brick mansions substantiated the fears of nonresidents. Absentee land claimants, however, could not vote. In the courts, Henry Clay represented nonresidents; in the legislature, he did not.[46]

In Clay, the gentry acquired an able defender of their real estate; however, quieting simplifiers and redistributionists was not the work of a single individual. The system, in large measure, saved itself. Had the higher courts of Kentucky not cooperated, the legislative consensus behind occupying-claimant laws would have foundered. The refusal of the Kentucky Court of Appeals to extend the privileges of the statutes to occupants without color of title dismayed some squatters. In general, however, the decisions of Kentucky's highest court caused more dissatisfaction among out-of-state claimants. The justices repeatedly upheld the constitutionality of the statutes, finding no violation of the compact between Virginia and Kentucky. Nor was Kentucky's highest court willing to quash the assessments of local juries except where "the most convincing and satisfactory evidence of the incorrectness of their estimate" existed.[47]

Aware of the anguish and anxiety produced by tangled land titles, the justices of the court of appeals stretched their interpretations to help unshingle claims. Judges devised precepts to standardize the shapes of tracts. They also bent rules of identity to allow honest, if faulty, entries to pass muster. Rejecting "uncertain, repugnant or impossible calls in an entry," the justices set "notoriety" as the critical test. By notoriety was meant that the entry contained expressions and allusions to objects as would "communicate to *others* a competent idea of the intended appropriation." Further defining notoriety as the "knowledge of the objects by the generality of persons conversant in the neighborhood" provided an advantage in court to residents over nonresidents.[48]

By the early nineteenth century, the justices of the court of appeals had improvised a property code unique to Kentucky. According to John Marshall, Chief Justice of the United States Supreme Court, the invented principles contradicted his own views. Yet Marshall was reluctant to overturn them. "The very extraordinary state of land titles in that country has compelled its judges in a series of decisions to rear up an artificial pile, from which no piece can be taken by hands not intimately acquainted with the building without endangering the structure and producing a mischief to those holding under it," wrote Marshall for a unanimous court in *Bodley and Hughes v. Taylor* (1809).[49]

Marshall's recognition that the Kentucky courts lived by different rules explained why nonresidents usually pressed their claims in federal court. Citing how "tardily" the state courts handled land cases, attorneys advised their nonresident clients to sue in the Federal Court of Kentucky presided over by Judge Harry Innes. Crowded dockets provided a convenient excuse, but the choice of courts ultimately hinged on the desire to escape the local favoritism of Kentucky's state courts.[50]

The specter of federal judges tampering with the state's makeshift land rules terrified Kentuckians, and also worried Innes. A year before Innes was appointed to the bench, he worried about the disastrous implications of concurrent jurisdiction. In disputes between the residents of Kentucky and other states, Innes forecast that outsiders would sue in federal court and "the citizens of Kentucky . . . will nine times out ten lose." [51]

At least in the period from 1789 to 1816 when Innes sat on the bench, the Federal Court of Kentucky showed remarkable sensitivity to resident interests and local anxieties. By his diligent respect for the unusual precedents of Kentucky state courts, Innes undercut apprehensions about the federal courts. By his preference for juries and by his adherence to their findings, Innes checked his own powers. He also removed the taint of nonresident favoritism from the Federal Court of Kentucky, since juries were composed of residents only.[52]

Juries played a crucial part in legitimizing the judicial system. Because they were not paid for their duty, jurors handled business rapidly. They did not spend much time reflecting on their contributions to the legal system. As Innes understood, however, juries provided a local stamp of approval on the controversial rulings of courts in land cases. If juries sometimes contradicted Innes's own understandings, that was a price he was willing to pay to maintain the public's esteem for the judicial branch. The independence of juries helped preserve the independence of the judiciary.

These three factors—regard for the jury system, state and federal court rulings sympathetic to occupants, and legislation privileging residents over nonresidents—enabled the legal system to survive Kentucky's tumultuous early years of statehood. To be sure, distribution of land remained grossly unequal, and nasty comments about lawyers remained commonplace, especially among those unable to obtain clear titles. Tens of thousands of Kentuckians continued to vote with their feet, relocating across the Ohio River or joining Boone in Missouri. Within Kentucky, however, the rule of law retarded the spread of insurrectionary resentment. The mysterious blaze at the Fayette County clerk's office did not become a wildfire.

Nor did the proslavery provisions of the 1799 constitution immediately sound any fire bells in the night. The citizens of Kentucky never formally approved the 1799 constitution. Still, the election of convention delegates was as democratic a canvass as late-eighteenth-century American political culture permitted, and the results spoke loud and clear: the majority of voters rejected emancipation, with or without delay. Defeated at the polls, the antislavery crusade staggered into the nineteenth century. David Rice and a few clergymen continued to assault slavery as inimical to the word of God and contrary to republican principles. The strength of their convictions, however, were muffled by divisions within the churches between opponents and defenders of slavery.[53]

As a political force, antislavery declined after the constitutional question was resolved. A few slaveholders continued to voice their doubts. Even after he softened his antislavery radicalism and accumulated dozens of slaves, Clay remained an outspoken critic of the Peculiar Institution. In 1816, he accepted the chairmanship of the newly organized American Colonization Society. For more than a decade, he spearheaded the society's drive for gradual emancipation and deportation of all free blacks to Africa. But without a realistic plan to compensate slaveowners, the society's goals could not pass constitutional muster. In the absence of a firestorm of antislavery protest among the citizenry of Kentucky, emancipation moved to the political margins.[54]

In the opening years of the nineteenth century, no conflagration returned antislavery to the fore. Among the citizenry of Kentucky, still largely composed of nonslaveholders, the 1799 election of delegates confirmed that popular antislavery was waning. In part, this reflected the diminishing proportion of tenants in the adult white male population. While not all that radical redistributionists desired, legislative and judicial remedies had reduced the rate of landlessness from two-thirds of heads of households in 1792 to slightly more than half in 1802. American colonization of Ohio also weakened antislavery feeling within Kentucky. Because the Northwest Ordinance had banned slavery in the territory north of the Ohio, those lands lured fervent antislavery people out of Kentucky. In some cases, entire congregations resettled north of the Ohio River. Ohio lands also attracted tenants who tired of competing with slaves for unskilled agricultural labor.[55]

More and more, those who stayed developed a stake in the system. During the 1790s, the number of slaves in Kentucky nearly quadrupled, outpacing the growth of the white population (which had only tripled). The percentage of slaveowners also rose slightly, so that by 1800 more than one in four households owned at least one slave. This statistic underestimates the pervasiveness of slavery, however. Because many farmers could not afford to purchase, they chose instead to "hire out" slaves on a seasonal or annual basis. These short-term arrangements permitted small farmers and tenants to take advantage of otherwise unaffordable slave labor.[56]

By turning unfree labor from competitor to contributor, hiring out won slavery support from nonslaveholding farmers and tenants and gained slave property a more secure base. As Daniel Drake remembered, his father "never purchased a slave for two substantial reasons: *first*, he had not the means; & *second*, [he] was so opposed to slavery that he would not have accepted the best negro in Kentucky." But "now & then," when family labor was insufficient, "he hired one" from a neighboring slaveholder. Renting slaves, it seemed, was amenable to antislavery men of pliant principles.[57]

DURING THE 1790S, the maldistribution of land and the protection of "aristocratic" property, particularly slaves, put the rule of law under fire. Because the allocation of Kentucky lands left so many landless or insecure about their titles, the laws and the lawyers who made them heated popular passions. Resentment of unfree labor and of constitutional curbs on majority governance further inflamed radical demands for the redistribution of lands, the emancipation of slaves, the simplification of laws, and the establishment of a truly democratic charter. While radicals succeeded in dismantling Kentucky's first constitution, the compact that replaced it safeguarded land and slaveholdings and left the judiciary independent. Nor did legislative reformers accomplish much in the way of making courts more friendly to plain farmers. These failures fueled the sense of betrayal felt by men for whom independence remained elusive. In the colonial backcountry, such betrayals of homesteader hopes had periodically exploded into incendiary violence; yet in republican Kentucky, the situation turned out to be less combustible.

The gentry stewards of republican Kentucky deserve credit for smothering fires before they blazed out of control. At the 1792 constitutional convention and again in the months before the 1799 convention, gentry concerns were well served by the leadership of George Nicholas. The openness of Kentucky's ruling elite to men of exceptional talents and rising fortunes contributed as well to political stability. Thus did the gentry admit Henry Clay to their ranks and enlist the onetime radical in the cause of safe government and secure property.

Credit for the maintenance of stability also belongs to the rule of law. For all its flaws, for all the disadvantages at which it put common folk, the rule of law cooled rebellious impulses. What E. P. Thompson has said of the rule of law in Hanoverian England applied to Kentucky in the early days of the "Age of Clay." To rule by law necessitated that gentry rulers appear fair, and to appear fair, they often had to be fair. In fact, Thompson's conclusions were more true of republican Kentucky than of monarchical Britain. In eighteenth-century England, as Thompson has shown, the threat or instigation of crowd action pressured rulers to be just. Kentuckians also resorted to extralegal avenues, but unlike their English counterparts, they exercised additional control over the rule of law through the arsenal of republican government. With ballots and verdicts, Kentuckians—that is, the adult white male minority who voted and sat on juries—alleviated the sources of their frustration. Not all, to be sure, but enough to save the system.[58]

FIVE *Rights in the Woods*

NEARLY ALL WHITE MEN from Boone to Clay pursued private ownership of land, but considerable variation existed over the scope of rights
conferred by private titles. Boone and his cultural compatriots, though
devoted to homestead privileges for occupants, also emphasized the
"right[s] in the woods" that belonged to all (white) backcountry people.
Hunting and open-range herding, activities central to the subsistence of
backcountry families, depended on unrestricted access to "waste" lands.
In the southern backcountry before the Revolution and in Kentucky after
the war, good fences did not make good neighbors. By contrast, Tidewater gentlemen zealously policed the exclusivity of their property rights.
As far as slaveowning tobacco planters were concerned, order and prosperity depended on an owner's unrestricted dominion over his property.[1]

Once the retreat of Indians diminished the urgency of common
rights, Kentucky planters and their legislative accomplices criminalized
customary prerogatives in the woods and codified the privatization of
natural resources. Unlike the distribution of land, which mobilized protest
against the rules of law, the new property regime provoked no sustained,
collective resistance from the citizens of Kentucky. Yet these rulings foreclosed the world of Daniel Boone and enclosed the landscape of Henry
Clay's Kentucky. To its champions, privatized property enhanced the
profitability of agriculture, which benefited farmers at every level; to its
foes, the new regime primarily enriched slaveowning planters at the expense of those who still claimed rights in the woods.

Its most resolute foes were found not in Kentucky settlements but
across the Ohio River in Indian villages that had been relocated away from
Kentucky's northern border. Yet even after surrendering their rights in the
Kentucky woods, Ohio Indians witnessed the spread of new property relations into their villages. For many Ohio Indians, both semiprivate and
fully privatized property threatened sacred values. Indian seers preached
a return to an old world order. Animated by prophetic visions of a land-

scape restored to its game-filled past, Indian hunters warred against alien ideas and American domination.

On the south side of the Ohio, the hunters of Kentucky did not mobilize in defense of their customary rights. Only isolated incidents disrupted newly privatized relations. Although hunting remained a distinctive element in the culture of Kentucky men, a defining rite of manhood, it was by the 1790s a secondary economic pursuit. Distancing themselves from pioneer economic culture, tenants and family farmers subordinated public rights to personal interests. Their ferocious pursuit of private lands weakened commitments to rights in the woods and eased accommodation to a more fully privatized regime.[2]

When conflict about property rights did occur in the early statehood era, divisions between gentry and backcountry gave way to more confusing and transitional alignments. Disputes over rights in the waters, for example, created shifting alliances that cut across ranks of rich and poor. In contentions over the improvement of waterways, proponents and opponents shared a commitment to commercial development; the question was the form that development would take.

I

The world of Daniel Boone restricted the rights of private land use, though never to the same degree as neighboring Indian peoples. The temporary usufruct privileges that Indian horticulturists respected were not for pioneers, who considered ownership of land the cornerstone of patriarchal independence and regarded property rights as perpetual. Still, an informal consensus among occupants limited private enjoyment of individuated property. Pioneers presumed that unimproved land, whatever its legal status, was semipublic property. They cultivated and enclosed only a small fraction of their fields; the rest, at least temporarily, remained like the unclaimed woods, a common on which all white inhabitants had certain rights—to cross at will, to range stock, to collect dead timber, and most important in Revolutionary Kentucky, to hunt game. With survival at stake, pioneers insisted that public needs eclipsed private rights.[3]

A 1777 petition to the Virginia General Assembly regarding the disposition of Kentucky's salt springs expressed the narrow conception of private property rights held by pioneers from the southern backcountry. Signed by Boone and seventy-five other settlers around Boonesborough, the appeal complained that while "bountiful Nature hath plentifully furnished this Country with Salt Springs," the inhabitants "have for some time past been almost destitute of the necessary Article Salt." Indians hindered production, but so, said petitioners, did absentee owners who failed to improve their properties. The petitioners requested that, "if the Claimants do not immediately erect Salt Manufactories at the different Springs claimed by them," the Virginia Assembly declare the springs "publick Property."[4]

The entreaty received a cool response from the Virginia Assembly. Even though the government of Virginia passed occasional acts "encouraging the making of salt," legislators were in 1777 and afterwards unprepared to make improvement a condition of ownership. To have done so would have threatened the property of all of the Virginia speculators who had not found buyers or tenants for their Kentucky tracts. Through the 1780s, a number of salt springs remained in the hands of absentee proprietors and production lagged far behind capacity.[5]

Pioneers did not wait for legislative blessing; they took what they needed, though a loose moral economy structured their confiscations. In western Virginia during Dunmore's War, Daniel Trabue remembered that when merchants "hid their salt, . . . People gethered in companys and went and hunted up the salt . . . and Divided it," paying the nominal owners "a reasonble prise." Less than three months after petitioning the Virginia Assembly, and without waiting for an answer, Boone led a party of saltmakers to Blue Licks. No one at Boonesborough contemplated compensating owners, who had not fulfilled their obligations. Nor, for that matter, did the saltmakers expect to profit—had their operation not been interrupted by Blackfish's war party. At odds with the statutes of Virginia, neighborhood convention legitimized access to precious resources. Where lawmakers were distant, saltmakers determined that rights in the woods ruled.[6]

Once survival became a less urgent concern and Virginia gentlemen began to occupy their Kentucky lands, local solidarity eroded. The consensus that had formerly guaranteed public access to game and timber deteriorated. Backcountry assumptions about the "rights in the woods" of all (white) inhabitants came under attack. Broadcasting the breakdown of the pioneers' consensus, "no trespassing" notices in Kentucky's early newspapers announced an end to the era of untrammeled access. These published bans jeopardized a variety of backcountry practices. Warnings were given not to hunt, fish, or fowl on privately held land, nor to remove timber from these properties. Interlopers were also advised not to let stock roam across exclusive domains, nor even to cross the grounds themselves without permission of the owner. One advertisement listed all of these activities and cautioned trespassers to refrain as well from "stripping them-selves and washing in my pond." Another privatizing notice ominously promised "to make an example of" any "such strolling transgressors."[7]

For the most part, privatizers relied on the law to intimidate un-reconstructed woodsmen. By statutes and contracts, the rules of prop-erty were gradually rewritten. To conserve game and exclude unwanted hunters, some gentlemen turned a portion of their estates into private hunting parks and asked the courts to enforce Virginia game laws that had been transferred to Kentucky. Virginia's hunting statutes stipulated fines and whippings for convicted poachers, though legislation had always exempted meat hunting by residents of frontier counties. Those laws re-mained technically in force after Kentucky became a separate state. As settlement thickened in central Kentucky, privatizers claimed the immu-nity of meat hunters no longer applied.[8]

New statutes, particularly a 1798 act "for preventing trespasses," fur-ther diminished customary common rights. In itself the 1798 fence law appeared an innocuous piece of legislation. It did not close the open range. Landowners were still expected to fence in crops, not animals. The act merely clarified what constituted a "lawful fence" and spelled out a schedule of reparations. But privatizers seized on the letter of the law and lengthened fences. Some owners encircled their entire property with law-ful fences, so that unbroken barricades ran for miles through the Bluegrass country.[9]

Because fence building contributed to deforestations, landlords at-tached great importance to the preservation of their private woodlands. To avert the depletion of timber, they pressed leases on tenants that restricted wood rights. When Clay rented a part of his Ashland estate in 1815, he for-bade lessees from axing any living trees. Later, he rescinded "any privilege of fire wood, the preservation of my wood being an object to which I at-tach great value." An 1818 act subjecting convicted timber thieves to stiff fines afforded Clay and other privatizers still more protection.[10]

Lawmakers were not completely blind to the nuisances that endless enclosures created. Responding to the inconveniences caused by extended fences, the legislature eventually ratified a law insuring public passage through private lands. The passway act, approved in December 1820, offered some relief from three decades of privatization. It hardly reversed the trend. The statute suspended trespassing laws only in places where a jury of "four housekeepers" deemed public crossing "indispensable." The jurors then designated a route, measuring no more than fifteen feet wide, across the enclosed lands. Owners retained the right to present a "suitable alternative." Once laid out, the public way was opened only to "those who may be legally and necessarily required to attend courts, elections, &c."[11]

The passway act, then, did not restore the pioneers' balance between private property and public necessity. The activation of old Virginia hunting laws and the enactment of new enclosure and trespass measures put the power of the state behind the destruction of backcountry customs. The enlargement of individual property rights imperiled the future of hunting and open-range herding. To the chagrin of pioneers and their descendants, who cherished a way of life founded on rights in the woods, the laws of property sculpted a landscape more congenial to gentry tastes.

II

It was certainly not a landscape suited to a hunter's lifestyle, as the resistance of Ohio Indians demonstrated. Concurrent with the privatization of the Kentucky landscape, Indian peoples in the upper Ohio Valley also saw customary notions challenged. The resulting reformation did not extend to the commodification of land; the idea that a piece of land could be owned exclusively by an individual and that it could be bought and sold like any other product or service remained as outlandish to Ohio Indians as it was common to white Kentuckians. But the expansion of commercial relations, the disintegration of traditional means of subsistence, and the influence of foreigners induced Ohio Indians to adopt innovative strategies for preserving their independence. These included experimentation with previously alien forms of property and of property holding. Though the resulting privatization was far more limited than in Kentucky, Indian defenders of custom launched a fierce counterattack against the "Europeanization" of the landscape.[12]

The inroads of Europeanized property relations followed the fur trade into the Ohio Valley. As European tools and weapons replaced native technologies and alcohol became a cultural staple, Ohio Indians drew stiffer distinctions between the territorial rights of meat and skin hunters. While hungry men without a local right in the woods were permitted to take meat for personal consumption, long hunters and other skin seekers were deprived of their pelts and ejected, or worse.

In the last years of the eighteenth century, with hunting grounds constricting and game supplies dwindling, outsiders became less welcome in the woods surrounding one of the Ohio country's villages. It no longer mattered whether the foreign hunters were after meat or skins. This assertion of exclusivity referred to villages, not individuals, but it marked a step in the direction of a privatized landscape. With individual hunters forsaking redistributive rituals to take charge of the disposition of their skins, Indian rights in the woods increasingly imitated backcountry conventions.

The addition of livestock broadened the correspondence between Ohio Indian and backcountry cultures. Prior to the advent of Europeans, woodland Indians had little experience with domesticated animals. Ohio Indians kept dogs for hunting and for food and eagerly adopted horses for packing loads of fur and transporting warriors, but they domesticated no cattle, sheep, or hogs. Well into the eighteenth century, the absence of such stock on one side of the frontier and the abundance of domesticated animals on the other disclosed a cultural fault line between Ohio Indian and backcountry worlds. Minimizing the distinction, they occasionally likened wildlife to livestock. The analogy served a purpose. By maintaining that "the Elks are our horses, the Buffaloes are our cows, [and] the deer are our sheep," Ohio Indians justified their "ownership" of game and their right to punish foreign poachers. But the reasoning was flawed, for Shawnees, Delawares, and their Indian neighbors more typically condemned the idea of owning game *and* domesticating stock. Both actions, it was believed, desecrated the spirituality of animals.[13]

These denunciations, however, lost some potency once Ohio Indians began to kill deer exclusively for their skins and raise livestock. Already in the 1760s, European visitors to the Ohio Country remarked on the Indians' cattle and on their skill in making butter and cheese. After the Revolution, livestock herds increased in size and importance. As overhunting reduced the supply of game, Ohio Indians compensated by raising more cattle and hogs.[14]

With livestock came fences. In the backcountry manner, Indians left their stock to graze on the open range, but roving cows, pigs, and horses still had to be kept out of cornfields. At the Shawnee town along the Au Glaize River in northwest Ohio, geography solved the problem. In one direction from the river, pasture lands stretched behind the village's thirty or forty cabins. Across the Au Glaize, safe from marauding livestock, extended acres of unfenced cornfields. Other towns, however, lacked adequate natural barricades, which necessitated the construction of man-made fences. Advised by officials of the United States government, Christian missionaries, and assorted white intermediaries, Ohio Indians, to varying extents, chopped trees, split rails, and enclosed fields.[15]

Fence building and other signs of a Europeanized landscape reached their greatest extent in the communities of Christian Indians founded by Moravian missionaries. Having initiated missions among the Delaware in eastern Pennsylvania, Moravian evangelists followed Indian refugees into the Ohio Country. There Christian emissaries faced opposition from nativist prophets, who saw to it that indifference and hostility greeted haughty proselytizers. Nevertheless, the Moravians, under the steward-ship of David Zeisberger, persevered where other missionaries failed. At a series of sites in the Ohio Country, Zeisberger supervised the construc-tion of Christian towns by Indian converts. Boasting well-tended gardens, fine orchards, neatly fenced cornfields, and sprawling pastures supporting large herds of cattle, hogs, and horses, the landscape surrounding these Moravian Indian villages took on a decidedly European character.[16]

For Zeisberger and his brethren, no less than for missionaries of other sects, saving "savages" required that they be "civilized," that their world be remade along European lines. Although Moravians displayed more sensitivity than rival missionaries, they too proposed a thorough refor-mation of Ohio Indian life. To facilitate the civilizing process, Moravian missionaries closely regulated the lives of Indian neophytes. Immediately targeted for extinction were beliefs and rituals that competed with Chris-tianity. The banning of dances, sacrifices, and other "heathenish festivals" manifested this intolerance of syncretism. Because hunting was deemed incompatible with civilized life, it was discouraged and restricted. Mis-sionaries prohibited residents from soliciting supernatural aid in hunting. Men were told not to go on any long hunts without informing the village minister. To give women "more time to attend to their domestic con-cerns," females were prevented from going at all. By this separation, it was hoped, "the men will be induced to return home sooner." Thus did Moravian missionaries shrink hunting time, while encouraging men to industry in civilized pursuits: raising livestock and cultivating crops.[17]

And putting up fences. These were intended not only to block wan-dering stock, but also increasingly to demarcate property boundaries. At New Gnadenhutten mission in the 1780s, for example, fences encircled the town's orchard, which was tended by all inhabitants. A decade later, at the Moravian village of Goshen, the orchard remained a community con-cern, but adult male converts owned their own homes, raised their own livestock, and fenced and cultivated their own "plantations."[18]

To Zeisberger's delight, these revolutionary arrangements made each Moravian community a "city on a hill." Indians from near and far visited the Moravian settlements to inspect the buildings and grounds and assess the prospects of Christian Indians. Zeisberger understood that the ap-pearance of prosperity attracted new converts. "Many for this reason like to live here, being weary of wandering about," Zeisberger explained, "for they see that our Indians in their manner of life fare better."[19]

To Zeisberger's dismay, Ohio Indians were neither so readily impressed nor so easily converted. They liked to visit and trade more than they wanted to stay and live as Christians. "For the word of God," confided a missionary at the Moravian's White River settlement, "they have no ears, and in no wise show any desire whatever to hear it." After growing rapidly in the late 1780s, the population of Christian Indians dipped sharply in the early 1790s. Although the numbers rebounded a bit later in the decade, the census showed only slight increases. At the turn of the century, conversions slowed and backsliding plagued Moravian communities.[20]

Missionaries tried to shield fickle converts from "the pleasures of the heathen," but neophytes did "not seem able to resist the temptations with which they are surrounded." At White River, converts John and Catherine Thomas exemplified the problem. In 1803, the mission's scribe noted the departure of John and Catherine for an Indian town thirty miles away. The Thomases claimed their trip was timed to harvest corn before other Indians stole it. Suspicious of this rationale, the Moravian diarist surmised that the Thomases "wanted an excuse to go among them and join in their heathenish practices." A few months later, a repentant John and Catherine reappeared at White River. To escape future enticement, the Thomases agreed to move to another mission, away from the baneful influence of their infidel kith and kin. En route, however, they changed their minds and went hunting with their former friends and relations. Following the winter's hunt, Catherine returned again to the Moravian town, blaming her husband's devotion to alcohol for her backsliding. But Catherine held to her declaration of renewed faith for less than a year. In the spring of 1805, she left once more to participate in a festival at the nearby Indian town of Woapicamikunk.[21]

By adhering to their own creeds or syncretizing Christian and native rituals, Ohio Indians resisted the agenda of missionaries. Into the early nineteenth century, Ohio Indians accepted new beliefs and economic practices selectively, rejecting those recommendations at odds with their ideas of the good and virtuous life. Men refused to give up hunting, disdained instruction in how to labor as white people, and declined to venerate industry. "We do not need anyone to teach us how to work," a Quaker missionary was lectured. "If we want to work, we know how to do it according to our own way and as it pleases us." After more than a century of trading skins, Ohio Indians remained cold to the untamed pursuit of advantage. "They still think that those who have something are in duty bound to share with them," recorded a frustrated missionary at White River.[22]

Domesticated animals and fenced fields gave the landscape a more European look, but appearances deceived. Indian women remained in charge of the fields and took on responsibility for livestock. Missionary efforts to revamp Indian gender relations made little headway. To the contrary, in the last years of the eighteenth century and the opening years of the nineteenth, the arrogance of culture-breaking missionaries, together with the unceasing demands of American officials for additional land cessions and further trade concessions, stimulated an extreme reaction.[23]

Deaf to Christian evangelists, Ohio Indians flocked once more to hear of the dreams of nativist prophets. The Shawnee prophet Tenskwatawa, the brother of Tecumseh, was the most famous visionary, but he was not alone in urging Indians to cleanse their world of European artifacts and influence. Nativist rejection of things European had a long history in the Ohio Country, although, according to the White River missionary in 1805, "never . . . have the Indians been in such a state of revolution as they are at present." From in and around White River, Indians traveled to Woapicamikunk to listen to an old woman recount how her grandfather had appeared and told her: "You are to live again as you lived before the white people came into this land. You are to dress in skins and everything that you have from the white people you must put away, and the cattle must be killed. In that event, you will have wild game enough, and the deer will come in front of your huts. At present the deer are under the earth. If you do what I have told you, they will once more come out."[24]

Hundreds of Ohio Indians turned prophecy into practice. Seeking salvation from a gloomy present and a darker future, the disciples of visionaries renounced the imitation of white ways. Responding to the exhortation of prophets, they gave up alcohol and shed European garb. Readying for the return of departed game, they slaughtered cattle and tore down fences. Inspired by Tenskwatawa and united by Tecumseh, militant Indians from the Ohio Valley and the Great Lakes determined to restore the world they had lost. The militants' crusade did not aim for a completely revitalized landscape, however. While Tenskwatawa commanded his followers to de-Europeanize their world by killing cattle and hogs, he accommodated to the presence of horses. Neither the Shawnee prophet nor his pupils desired a return to an equine-less way of living.[25]

Militants succeeded in driving Moravian missionaries from the White

River, but their ends again stopped short of full restoration. In 1805, a band of Indians invaded the Moravian town and shot the mission's best hog. For the Moravian brethren, "the most painful part . . . was the fact that we had to see that our worst enemies lived here in our village." Threatened by militants and backsliders, the Moravians abandoned the mission in 1806. Before they left, though, the Delaware chief Hacking-pomsga warned them not to clear out their livestock or sell off their improvements. Rather than exterminating the Moravians' stock in a nativist rite, Hackingpomsga insisted that since the cattle grazed on Indian land, Indians deserved half of the animals. Because the village's "houses and everything made of wood" were also built with Indian timber, the chief demanded half for his people.[26]

The irony of Hackingpomsga's claims escaped the Moravians' notice. While Hackingpomsga believed his was a sacred mission to purge Indian country of foreign influences, his demands reflected a deep-seated attachment to European things and European thinking. In effect, his expropriation of Moravian holdings evidenced a landlord's logic. Indeed, by Kentucky standards, Hackingpomsga cheated his tenants, who as occupying claimants could have kept all of their livestock and more than half the value of their improvements! Nonetheless, neither the contradictions nor the collapse of the Ohio Indians' uprising detract from its impact. Even as they sometimes employed European thinking to take possession of European things, Indian rebels managed to delay the thorough Europeanization of their country. Ohio Indian hunters lost, but they did not lose quietly.

III

Across the Ohio River, pioneers relinquished their rights in the woods without much resistance, revealing their complicity in the process of privatization. In Kentucky as elsewhere, the retreat of Indians had inflated land values and inspired a speculative frenzy. The proliferation of conflicting claims, together with the possibility of great profits, encouraged pioneer "right in the woodsmen" to guard their landholdings more jealously — though this necessarily interfered with the rights in the woods of others. Anxious to defend shaky claims, they asserted their exclusive possession and enjoyment more forcefully, especially to woodlands that displayed little if any sign of occupancy and improvement. As the informal ceiling that the homestead ethic set on landholdings gave way to unrestrained acquisition, pioneer-speculators moved toward a more privatized vision.

Unable to reconcile his open country ways with the new regime,

Daniel Boone chose to flee instead of fight. Faced with mounting debts and endless legal difficulties, he and Rebecca slipped out of Kentucky in 1799. Heading for more sparsely settled country west of the Mississippi, Boone put a positive spin on his removal from Kentucky. He left, he reportedly said, because he "want[ed] more elbow room." Even before Boone exited, hunters of his ilk were being displaced from Kentucky. Formerly the primary means of survival, hunting declined in importance once the eviction of Indians made it less necessary, the depletion of game made it less dependable, and the migration of families made it less respectable. To be sure, hunting continued to contribute to the subsistence of Kentucky households and it retained enormous symbolic significance as well, but try as they did to emulate Daniel Boone, the hunters of post-frontier Kentucky were not the men they wished they were.[27]

During the 1780s and 1790s, the resettlement of thousands of men, women, and children changed the character of Kentucky's population and altered pioneer standards. To live nearly exclusively by hunting was still acceptable for young men, but it was not considered a respectable pursuit for husbands with wives and children. Like many other boys raised in the backcountry, James Wade dreamed of devoting himself to the chase. When he first arrived in Kentucky, he made a happy go of the hunter's life. For Wade and many other young migrants to Kentucky, hunting was not so much a stage of society as it was a stage of life. "When I got me a family," concluded Wade, "I found hunting was no way to make a living." The chase was too uncertain.[28]

Hunting, Wade knew, was not conducive to settling down. Following the game meant an especially peripatetic existence. Among westering Americans, whose "restlessness" astounded European visitors, the itinerancy of those who continued to live by hunting stood out. To keep up with the game, Abraham Snethen's father moved his family, which eventually numbered eleven children, thirty-four times in thirty-two years. For Wade settling down required selling his rifle. "I knew as long as I had a gun, I codn't farm with success," he explained. For three years, he diligently confined himself to working the land. And then he had second thoughts. Squirrels were taking a large portion of his corn. Game, though not as abundant as formerly, was still sufficient to make hunting a rewarding diversion from the labors of his fields. So Wade again obtained a gun—to protect his farm from pests, to augment the fare of his family, and to enjoy anew the stimulation and the test of the chase.[29]

The progression of James Wade from bachelor hunter to family farmer (and recreational hunter) personified the larger evolution of Kentucky. The "Age of Boone"—when the survival of Kentuckians had depended on their hunting—had passed. Yet just as Wade ultimately refused to live without his gun, hunting did not disappear with the closing of the frontier. Long into the nineteenth century, the rifle occupied a central place over the mantle or the door of most Kentucky farmsteads. Indeed, a European visitor remarked, in choosing a rifle, the Kentuckian was "even more particular than in selecting a wife."[30]

The placement and choice of the rifle expressed some practical meaning. Hunting and the complementary rewards of fishing filled an essential prescription for the economic well-being of nonslaveholding households. In an age when agriculture remained vulnerable and variable, the availability of fish and game provided an insurance policy against starvation. As long as wild meat could be procured, farmers relieved their families from an endless diet of "hog and hominy." David Meriwether, who grew up on a sizable farm near Louisville, recalled that his family subsisted in the spring on fresh fish. Spending his Saturdays on the banks of the Ohio, Meriwether boasted that he often caught enough to supply his family with enough food for the whole week. In the fall he and his father went hunting. Each year's hunt yielded several dozen wild turkeys, as well as numerous coons, possum, and deer. When smoked, the meat generally lasted through the next summer.[31]

Fish and game provided a significant protein supplement, but the spot reserved for the rifle was as much symbolic as it was pragmatic. With Indians no longer lurking and livestock and corn typically more than satisfying subsistence requirements, rifles really did not have to be kept so prominently at hand. For a good part of the year, their usage was limited to purging squirrels and other pests from cornfields. Many counties offered bounties for the scalps of female wolves, though an act of the Kentucky legislature amended the terms of payment to discourage scalpers believed to be secretly breeding the predators. In 1795, the Kentucky legislature passed an act requiring every white male over sixteen to kill a certain number of squirrels and crows annually. To fulfill their obligations, neighbors periodically came together for daylong contests in which rival companies vied to top their opponents' squirrel count. Usually conducted in April or May after planting, the largest of these hunting competitions netted over five thousand squirrels in a single day. Afterwards the furry prey became the featured course in a festive barbecue and burgoo. On an everyday basis, however, the incessant chore of shooing away pests was left for young boys. This they accomplished with the aid of dogs and the shotgun, a weapon conceived "entirely beneath the *dignity* of genuine" Kentucky hunters.[32]

For men confined much of the year to the civilized pursuits of farming and stock raising, shooting matches provided intermittent opportunities to pull down their beloved rifles. "Driving nails," "snuffing candles," and "barking squirrels"—that is, shooting just beneath the bushy-tailed rodents so that they were sent flying from their perch—remained popular contests in nineteenth-century Kentucky. These tournaments, often held with other aggressive and bloody contests on court and militia training days, established the pecking order among neighborhood shooters. The continuing equation of marksmanship with manhood heightened the stakes of shooting matches and squirrel hunts. To shoot a squirrel anywhere but in the head was "reckoned very unsportsmanlike." Such poor sportsmanship diminished a man's standing in the local community. By contrast, the best squirrel hunters were the object of much adulation, especially since squirrel hunting and target shooting contests often involved high-stake betting.[33]

Momentous as these and other rough games were in establishing a man's credentials among his neighbors, the real thrill and the supreme test of male prowess still lay in the pursuit of big game. Nails, candles, and squirrels were poor substitutes for multipointed bucks or "master" bears. Like the long hunters of the 1760s and 1770s, nineteenth-century Kentucky hunters talked a great deal of luck and paid careful attention to local superstitions. But like the desperate hunters of the Revolutionary years, they knew that success ultimately depended on possession of a range of talents and calculations. The chase still demanded ample patience, sharp senses, and an education in animal habits and habitats. In fact, the exhaustion of big game stocks made bagging a deer or a bear a greater challenge than ever.[34]

In the 1790s and the early nineteenth century, men looked forward to passing days and weeks in the woods, testing themselves against their prey and their companions. Times spent hunting or to a lesser extent fishing held a special niche in the memories of Boone's contemporaries and of Kentuckians of the next generation. Farm boys in nineteenth-century Kentucky treasured days when they could slip off to local fishing holes. They still dreamed of killing more beasts than even Daniel Boone. Memoirists wrote reverently of the thrill of their first big kill.[35]

As adults, they retained this childhood enthusiasm for the pleasures of hunting and fishing, often mixing those amusements with steady drinking. An ample supply of bourbon was thought an "indispensable article" for trips into the woods. On cold mornings, nothing revitalized hunters like "a good toddy." Among fishermen, remembered one avid sportsman, the "Custom whenever they Caught a fish" was to take "a Nip." The system generally worked well. Occasionally, however, "the Best of old Bourbon" got the best of a successful fisherman, who was "too Drunk to fish Before his Companions Had Caught anny." [36]

As had been the case among farmers in the colonial backcountry, the year's biggest, longest, and best hunting awaited the completion of the harvest. These fall and winter excursions often brought together a dozen or more hunters. Packing their horses heavy with guns, tents, blankets, cooking utensils, sugar, coffee, cornmeal, salt, and, of course, bourbon, the hunting party frequently traveled thirty or forty miles to woods where "the country was not fenced up." The combination of trusted rifles, faithful dogs, friendly competitors, and resourceful quarry made hunting the fulfillment of male fantasies. In hunting, as in the other all-male gatherings, the participants vied not only with each other but also against a standard of rough and readiness set by an earlier generation of pioneers. Spending days tracking red deer and black bears with the aid of canine companions, passing the night swapping stories, comparing trophies, drinking corn liquor, wrestling, whittling, and drinking some more, many imagined themselves latter-day long hunters.[37]

The imitators did not impress Daniel Boone. Returning to Kentucky after an absence of some years, the aging long hunter was saddened by the dwindling game. Once "thousands of Buffaloes" inhabited Kentucky "and to hunt in those days was a pleasure indeed." Now, Boone supposedly informed John J. Audubon, he found none, "and a few signs only of a deer were to be seen." But "as to deer itself, I saw none." [38]

In the thinly settled regions of the state where bear and deer remained plentiful, a few men still lived mainly "on their guns." For these last backwoodsmen, the chase was neither a leisure-time departure, nor a way to measure their manhood against the valor of an earlier generation. In the mountains of eastern Kentucky, hunting remained a primary activity of men, as well as a major contributor to the family table. Living in what better-heeled outsiders considered the rudest poverty, these hunters jealously guarded their way of life. As in the early years of colonization, Appalachian hunters cooperated to insure the subsistence of all neighboring families. These hunters also happily shared their homes and their meals with strangers who passed through their country. Their generous hospitality did not extend to sharing hunting grounds, however. Those who came to kill game were made most unwelcome, for rights in the woods belonged exclusively to residents.[39]

Elsewhere in Kentucky, as hunting became less important, residential rights in the woods yielded to privatized property. This new regime did not gain absolute dominion nor go entirely uncontested. Hogs continued to range in the woods and occasionally trespassed into fields where they did not belong. Timber continued to be taken without the consent of landowners. To a limited extent, the independence of jurors, who refused to convict trespassers or who rewarded insufficient damages to plaintiffs, inhibited the enforcement of privatizing statutes. But defiance of new property codes was disorganized. The individuals who committed transgressions had no designs on civil disobedience. Through the passage from the world of Boone to that of Clay, open-range herders, timber thieves, poachers, and assorted trespassers never seriously disturbed the peace, nor halted the reorganization of law and landscape.[40]

IV

While the disparity between backcountry and Indian responses reinforces an earlier conclusion about the gap between backcountry and Indian worlds, the relative peacefulness with which Kentucky's privatization progressed reminds us again that the rule of law was not simply the rule of lawyers. Far from merely ratifying gentry interests, the consequences of law often escaped easy classification. In conflicts over rights in the woods, the law elevated conceptions of property that were hostile to backcountry expectations. In controversies over rights in the waters, however, the cultural origins of antagonists muddied. Instead of public-minded pioneers versus privatizing gentlemen, riparian disputes roused changing coalitions behind competing approaches to commercial development.

Not all waterways caused splits, nor did commerce per se divide Kentuckians. Indeed, the demand for free commercial navigation of the Mississippi united Kentucky's citizenry. Factions arose, however, about what kind of commercial society Kentucky would become: one designed to make Kentucky a better poor man's country by catering to households that generated modest marketable surpluses or one favoring men of more substantial means, whose lands and "hands" (tenants and slaves) produced commodities on a far larger scale. The difference, it must be emphasized, was not always clear.

Through the 1780s and 1790s, merchants, planters, and lawyers took the lead in petitioning and negotiating for the opening of the Mississippi

River to Kentucky traffic. Gentry leadership was to be expected, given that post-Revolutionary political culture retained a still significant reverence for traditional hierarchies and that the economically advantaged had the most to gain from the broadening of commercial opportunities. The more Kentucky land one owned, the more important the Mississippi became. "The Value of Land here will much depend on the Convenience of Navigation," recognized John May at the outset of his speculations. Complaining that foreign control over the "natural" outlet to the sea kept Kentucky in an undeveloped state, gentry spokesmen railed against the federal government's failure to settle the issue. The most influential leaders covertly conferred with Spanish officials to see if a separate arrangement between Kentucky and Spain could be worked out. These dealings became and remain the source of much controversy, though at the time plans to detach Kentucky from the United States in exchange for navigation rights on the Mississippi were a well-kept secret.[41]

For their more patriotic public positions, gentry leaders encountered no opposition from within Kentucky. Smallholders, squatters, and tenants voiced no objection to opening the Mississippi to American commerce, since gaining access to the market world via the Mississippi was to their benefit as well. It promised to decrease the price of imported necessities, and by simultaneously increasing the volume of agricultural exports, it offered profits which could be used to buy land. Nor did the Mississippi River trade "cost" backcountry settlers their traditional exchange relations. Marketing produce to outsiders for as high a price as possible did not disrupt mutuality among neighbors any more than selling deer skins at a premium interfered with gifts of meat by hunters. In an economic culture that compartmentalized rules of neighborhood and long-distance exchange, translocal commerce presented no ethical dilemmas.

When the scene shifted to waterways within Kentucky, divisions emerged, but these did not pit backcountry and gentry factions. The struggle over the development of Stoner's Fork of the Licking River, which began with the 1789 motion of Laban Shipp to build a grist mill, was a case in point. Shipp's proposal ignited a deep split among the residents of Bourbon County. Supporters and opponents of the mill tended to cast the controversy in terms of public versus private or rich versus poor. In fact, the sides were never so clearly defined.

When Shipp applied in December 1789 to the Bourbon County Court for permission to erect a milldam near the confluence of Stoner's and Hinkston's Forks, he anticipated no resistance. Bourbon County magistrates approved about half a dozen construction permits each year in the late 1780s. Following Virginia law, the magistrates appointed a jury to view the site, examine potential threats to the "health of [the] Neighborhood," and assess possible damages to surrounding houses, orchards, and fields. Once the jury of twelve men reported its findings, the justices entertained objections from neighbors. If no one protested, the magistrates accepted the jury's report, ordered appropriate reimbursement, and granted the mill builder's application. That many of the mill applications originated from one or another of the justices undoubtedly sped along the process, but a widespread agreement on the benefits of water-powered grist mills is confirmed by the low compensation to landowners offered by juries.[42]

Shipp's request initially proceeded according to form. In January 1790, the site-inspection jury found no injury to person or property likely. The magistrates then licensed Shipp, who immediately set to work. However, in an unprecedented move in March 1790, foes of the project appealed to the Virginia General Assembly to prevent erection of Shipp's mill. Shipp countered with a memorial of his own. Through the rest of the year, supporters and opponents traded charges and petitions.[43]

Both sides insisted that concern for the commonweal motivated their positions. In his petition, Shipp cited the "Great inconvenience" suffered by resident families on Stoner's Fork "for want of water Grist mills." Inhabitants were forced to travel up to thirty miles to the nearest mill. Once there, the backlog of orders necessitated long waits, often stretching overnight. Worse still, customers could arrive after a long journey only to find the mill closed for insufficient water flow. The time, expense, and uncertainty of transporting corn to distant mills meant that the inhabitants of Stoner's Fork had to grind their grain by mortar and pestle or by horse-powered mill. Shipp promised to relieve the residents of this arduous and inefficient labor. By freeing manpower, his mill would stimulate a substantial increase in the size of corn harvests, protecting the well-being of farmers for many miles around and providing a tenfold increase in property values. So although he had "nearly spent his fortune in erecting this usefull Building," Shipp "felt himself happy in a prospect of being Usefull to his country and his family."[44]

Opponents of the mill countered with their own version of localism and public-mindedness. If built without restrictions, as originally approved by the Bourbon County Court, Shipp's mill would impede the passage of fish, threatening the subsistence of poorer inhabitants. More important, though, was the mill's potential to obstruct navigation by boats, condemning "the Greater part of the Inhabitants" to an onerous

"Land Carriage of Many Miles." Above all, Shipp's adversaries sought to preserve, if not improve, water access to a tobacco inspection station recently established at the confluence of Hinkston's and Stoner's Forks. Brought to Kentucky by the post-Revolutionary emigration of Virginia gentlemen, tobacco enlisted in its cause those who wished to replicate the culture of the Tidewater in the fresh lands of the Bluegrass. For transplanted slaveowners, the duplication of a gentry-dominated society based on landownership and slave labor was unthinkable without tobacco. Not surprisingly, Bourbon County's slaveholders tended to attach their names to petitions opposing Shipp's bid.[45]

But Shipp's was not a poor man's cause. Nearly every taxpayer in the county went on record on the issue, and more than twice as many signed on with the tobacco lobby as endorsed Shipp's proposal. As Ellen Eslinger has shown, the majority included a sizable component whose taxable property fell below the county's average assessment. Most residents of Bourbon County planted corn, but the majority of small farmers and tenants remained skeptical about the commercial value of a mill. While hundreds of families would have welcomed a respite from hand grinding, water mills were too expensive to relieve their subsistence-oriented labors. Miller's fees devoured up to half of the customer's grain, so patrons brought only their excess corn to water-powered mills.[46]

In 1790, corn cultivators in Bourbon and neighboring counties had little stimulus to increase their use of grist mills. As long as Spain closed navigation of the Mississippi, the market for even finely ground corn was severely restricted. The high cost of transporting surpluses overland precluded selling corn in Atlantic ports. Over the Wilderness Road, a horse could barely pack its own feed, much less carry a load of surplus corn. Tobacco also suffered from constraints on Mississippi navigation, but statutory incentives improved its commercial prospects. After a 1787 Virginia law made tobacco the closest thing to legal tender in Kentucky, it supplanted skins as the preferred currency. As in Virginia, tobacco was acceptable in payment of taxes. Even tenants and small landowners, who had no wish to transplant Tidewater hierarchies, found tobacco the best way to raise money for land and taxes.[47]

The strong backing given warehouse and inspection facilities in Bourbon County and elsewhere in central Kentucky showed the broad support for tobacco culture. In the late 1780s, residents in all of the newly created Bluegrass counties agitated for the establishment of official tobacco stations. From Nelson County, at least five separate requests originated between 1787 and 1789. Over four hundred inhabitants signed one or more of these petitions. As Table A.4 details, Nelson County's advocates of tobacco culture tended to own more land than those whose names did not appear on the petitions. Petitioners against the mill were also three times more likely to own slaves than nonsigners. As in Bourbon County, however, support for tobacco culture reached across land and slaveowning classifications. Nearly one-fourth of the Nelson County signatories owned no land. Another third possessed holdings of less than 200 acres. More than 60 percent of petitioners owned no slaves.

Eventually, Bourbon County justices of the peace acceded to the demands of the pronavigation contingent. The magistrates ordered that Shipp and other mill owners on Stoner's Fork build their dams so as not to obstruct the "ordinary navigation" of tobacco-filled boats. "Ordinary navigation," the court determined, meant the erection of locks and slopes allowing the safe passage of boats up to "twelve feet wide and forty feet long."[48]

Initially, the Kentucky legislature also favored tobacco boats over grist mills. At its first session in 1792, an act "to prevent obstructions in water courses" was passed, which levied fines against the builder of any obstruction which interfered with navigability. Turning to the lingering controversy over Stoner's Fork at their second session, lawmakers went beyond the County Court's decree. Legislators prohibited new dams on Stoner's and appointed a commission to raise money to improve the navigability of the Fork. The commissioners did not, however, receive enough subscriptions to effect the desired results. A decade later, the legislature named a second commission, including Henry Clay, to ascertain natural obstructions, estimate expense of removal, and collect funds to clear the stream. The law of 1804 aided the commissioners by appropriating all fines against mill owners to the improvement campaign.[49]

The statutory tilt toward navigability was gradually balanced by a series of acts granting extensions and exemptions to mill builders. The 1793 law allowed the owners of existing milldams eight years to comply with lock building provisions. Yet eight years later, the legislature condoned another delay for completing locks on Stoner's Fork. Lawmakers approved additional postponements in 1806 and 1811. At the 1812 session, the legislators reversed their earlier pronavigation stance entirely. They repealed the 1811 deadline for erecting proper locks and opened the way for new mills by extending lengthy indulgences "to those who may hereafter build mill-dams" on Stoner's Fork.[50]

The legislative reversal was an acknowledgment of growing popular demand for water-powered mills, even when their siting interfered with public navigation. The shift in sentiment registered loudest in Nelson County. Where a substantial cross section of pioneering householders signed petitions in favor of tobacco warehouses and unimpeded navigation, nineteenth-century residents of Nelson raised a "considerable riot" when the county court—composed of the local gentry—ordered the removal of a milldam in the summer of 1825. When workers arrived to carry out the order, a visitor reported that "the country people in the neighborhood twice made a slight resistance and threatened vengeance." In Nelson, at least, magistrates could no longer count on popular acquiescence to the primacy of tobacco culture.[51]

The rising tide of support for mills, in fact, had its origins in the eighteenth century. In 1789, about twenty miles east of Laban Shipp's proposed site, the fortuitous concoction of limestone-impregnated water and sour mash in charred kegs provided a new raison d'être for water-powered mills. Bourbon whiskey, named for the county where it was invented, invigorated the commercial possibilities of corn. In the early 1790s with the Mississippi closed, bourbon carried a sufficiently high price in Atlantic ports to justify overland transportation. Corn still did not enjoy the special legal privileges accorded to tobacco, but in distilled form it emerged as the informal currency of Kentucky. Income from the sale of bourbon in distant markets allowed tenants to purchase land and claimants to buy out disputed tracts. As sale of skins and furs had done for backcountry hunters, the sale of bourbon afforded Kentucky farmers a means of purchasing otherwise unobtainable items from import merchants.[52]

During the 1790s, defiance of Alexander Hamilton's excise tax disclosed the centrality of whiskey to the competences of Kentucky farmers. In the late 1790s an exasperated revenue officer estimated that in Kentucky and what would become Ohio between 250,000 and 500,000 gallons of locally distilled whiskey annually escaped taxation. Enforcing the tax was a dangerous job. Threats and violence discouraged collectors. In 1793 in Nelson County, two collectors were assaulted by enemies of the tax, who "rescued" confiscated whiskey from the revenue officers. In Fayette County, a third collector was pulled from his horse, tarred, rolled in leaves, and warned of worse to come.[53]

What frustrated revenue officials was not extralegal intimidation but legal obstructionism. Federalist leaders had trouble finding an attorney in Kentucky willing to prosecute cases against delinquent distillers. George Nicholas, the most powerful lawyer in Kentucky, rejected George Washington's offer. As long as the national government failed to guarantee passage down the Mississippi for Ohio Valley produce, Nicholas pledged his opposition to the "oppressive and unjust" excise law. Even the appointment of a federal attorney did not bring a rush of convictions. Although their membership was limited to wealthier property owners, grand juries refused to indict tax evaders. When for the first time two indictments were presented—against a distiller for an unregistered still and another man for assaulting a revenue collector—the trial juries acquitted both defendants. Through the four-year tenure of prosecutor William Clarke, not one of fifty defendants was convicted. With Federal Court Judge Harry Innes impeding prosecutions by strict adherence to all legal technicalities, with prominent Kentucky lawyers refusing to serve as federal attorney, and with grand and petit jurors acquitting in spite of the facts, evasion of the whiskey tax continued through the administration of John Adams.[54]

The whiskey rebellion, like other movements against outside foes, united white Kentuckians. Putting aside divisions about rights in the woods and the waters, Kentucky men joined together in defiance of Indians, nonresident speculators, and federal excise taxes. Divergent interests reemerged when "foreign" threats abated, but because of the complicity of lawyers, judges, and juries, the rule of law endured to structure the economic future of Kentuckians.

IN THE OHIO VALLEY before the completion of American conquest, frontier property regimes detached from any fixed or absolute system of land tenure; across the Anglo-Indian frontier, the intersection of cultures changed the landscape and transformed the social constructions of property. In the mutual process of "frontiering," both Indians and pioneers adopted novel arrangements that balanced private and public rights. "Rights in the woods" meant different things on opposite sides of the shifting border between backcountry and Indian country. But frontier property regimes shared a commitment to the commons.

Under pressure from within and without, however, frontier regimes crumbled in the middle Ohio Valley. Conquest deprived Indians of their rights in the woods and hastened the commodification of their Ohio Valley lands. Already committed to land as commodity, Anglo-American colonizers were prepared to sacrifice their rights in the woods to save their private holdings. That renunciation opened the door to a privatized regime. Yet it was law that oversaw the transformation of Kentucky from the world of Daniel Boone to that of Henry Clay. From the statehouse in Frankfort and courthouses across the Commonwealth issued ordinances and decrees that determined the distribution of land and, less noticeably, the rights of property owners.

The law was obviously essential in solidifying the gentry's privatized regime, but its makers and interpreters did not usually choose between diametrically opposing economic cultures. In contrast to the uprising in Indian country, the assault on backcountry customs elicited no re-vitalization crusade in Kentucky, an absence that attested to the shared values of white male inhabitants. Widespread beliefs—in independence premised on private ownership of land, in preferences for residents over outsiders, in the liberty to distill and drink whiskey without interference from federal tax collectors, and in the promise of some form of com-mercial development—bridged cultural cleavages between lay people and lawyers, between plain farmers and gentlemen planters, between right-in-the-woodsmen and privatizers. Nevertheless, beyond these confluences, conflicts about political economy, especially about the character of labor, remained to be settled before consolidation of the world of Henry Clay was complete.

SIX *The Bluegrass System*

THE TRANSFORMATION FROM THE WORLD of Daniel Boone was most complete at the center of the Bluegrass region. On one level, life in the early-nineteenth-century Bluegrass resembled that in the eighteenth-century Virginia Tidewater. The fertility of fresh soils, the relative health-fulness of the climate, and the privatization of property made the lands around Lexington, the Inner Bluegrass, a magnet for migrating gentry. For gentlemen of Tidewater and Piedmont, burdened down by worn-out lands, excess sons, and unprofitable slaves, the Inner Bluegrass proved a hospitable environment in which to replicate and regenerate the planter culture of eighteenth-century Virginia.

But the world of Henry Clay was not simply a duplication of the world of George Washington and Thomas Jefferson. Migration to the Bluegrass revived the declining fortunes of planters and their offspring. Fresh, fertile soils altered the way landowners in possession of large num-bers of slaves viewed the world. This divergence of gentry cultures in Vir-ginia and Kentucky was manifested in the emergence of Lexington as the hub of the Bluegrass. From Lexington radiated a vibrant commercialism quite unlike the economic apprehension pervasive among the planters of Revolutionary Virginia. From the beginning of the nineteenth century to the War of 1812, Lexington reigned as "the greatest inland city of the west-ern world," the grandest emporium west of the Appalachians. The lawyers, merchants, and planters who believed themselves responsible for Lexing-ton's preeminence were determined not to let the Bluegrass slip into the stagnation afflicting the Tidewater. These elites, who received the great-est benefits from the prominence of Lexington, resolved to maintain the prosperity of the Bluegrass by improving their own economic well-being.[1]

The dynamic vision of economic development found its visionary in Henry Clay. In his private life, Clay exemplified the essence of Bluegrass entrepreneurialism; in his public life, he served as a spokesman for this spirit of gain; as a legislator, he masterminded a program to throw the endorsement of the state behind the system of commercial and industrial

progress unfolding in Lexington and its environs. Along with his wealthiest constituents, Clay considered the favors of government indispensable
to the development of the Bluegrass. Even after he moved his statesman-
ship to the federal stage, when he explicated his vision of an "American
System" for a national audience, his eyes remained locked on the fortunes
of the "Bluegrass System."

Clay saw the embryonic Bluegrass System and the mature American
System as a political economy for all the people, but his line of sight was
limited. He mistook the interests of the elite portion of his constituency
for the interests of the whole community. Clay always felt that the Bluegrass System bettered the lives of white and black laborers in and around
Lexington. He did not see that it in any way betrayed the dreams of poor
men, free and unfree.

I

The half century after Daniel Boone first scanned "the beautiful level
of Kentucke" brought dramatic changes to the landscape of central Kentucky, but the Bluegrass region retained its power to inspire. "Here is the
best land that mine eyes have yet seen," enthused the Methodist circuit
rider Joseph Thomas about the undulating plain north of the Kentucky
River. The Bluegrass was "not surpassed in riches in any other country,"
according to the guidebook author D. B. Warden. It was "the Garden . . .
of the world," echoed the gazetteer Samuel Brown. From the immensely
fertile soil, unprecedented yields of fifty, seventy-five, even one hundred
or more bushels of Indian corn per acre were reported. Similar successes
were recited for other crops.[2]

The extravagance of the tributes to the Kentucky Bluegrass smacked
of land speculator propaganda, and opponents of emigration readily deflated exaggerated claims. Both Warden and Brown maintained that the
entire region bounded by the Ohio, the Kentucky, and the Big Sandy
Rivers consisted of first-rate land. In fact, as the English traveler Thomas
Ashe pointed out, the lands within this area—one hundred fifty miles
long and fifty to one hundred miles wide—varied widely. Near Lexington lay "a small portion of highly beautiful land," encompassing about
eighteen hundred square miles. The rest of the treasured Bluegrass region,
insisted Ashe, was composed of indifferent, broken tracts. Other touring
writers concurred, discriminating between the gently rolling lands surrounding Lexington and the more rugged terrain that dominated as one
moved away from the center of the Bluegrass.[3]

Even the most critical visitors to the Inner Bluegrass came away impressed by the magnificence of the terrain. Though one Pennsylvanian found the region "badly watered," he raved that "the country around Lexington, for many miles in every direction, is equal in beauty and fertility to anything the imagination can paint." In a similar vein, New England-born Amos Kendall gushed that "poetry cannot paint groves more beautiful or fields more luxuriant" than those around Lexington. Kendall was especially taken by the "exuberance of verdure, [the] many orchards in bloom, and [the] many gardens laid out with taste." Touring the parklike setting, another newcomer wondered if "they sweep the woods here?" [4]

The impressions of observers suggested that the Inner Bluegrass had become a new Tidewater, dominated by estates befitting English lords. Stately brick mansions, elegant formal gardens, and luxuriant bluegrass pastures gave the landscape around Lexington a genteel ambience. "Everything announced the opulence" of the owner, remarked François André Michaux. That a number of the largest landowners turned a portion of their estates into private hunting preserves heightened the likeness to English country seats. [5]

The barons of the Bluegrass lived like Tidewater grandees, and they thought like them also, styling their behavior and appearance to impress equals and awe inferiors. In attire and address, the patriarchs of Bluegrass estates imitated the fashions and customs of Virginia, and by extension English, gentlemen. Their dress and comportment, their houses and grounds displayed the same fondness for ostentation. On both sides of the Appalachians, aggressive sociability was an integral component of the gentry code. "The profusion and display at our entertainments has ever been a matter of astonishment to strangers," observed Margaretta Brown, who recognized that competition drove this extravagant hospitality. "For fear of being thought mean, . . . we could not invite a friend to dinner, but the table must groan with costly piles of food." [6]

Like Anglo-Virginians, Bluegrass planters lived for times spent convening and competing in the "agreeable company" of other gentlemen. While entire neighborhoods engaged in squirrel hunting tournaments, gentlemen preferred fox hunting, which carried a more aristocratic ancestry. The cultural lineage from Tidewater to Bluegrass gentry was perhaps most conspicuous in the blend of conviviality and contest which characterized dancing in both regions. "We all danced as soon as our legs and arms were manageable," remembered one boy who grew up on a Kentucky plantation. Already in the late 1780s, a number of dance instructors had opened schools in Lexington to teach students the essentials of cotillions, hornpipes, allemandes, waltzes, gavottes, and reels. Such instruction was indispensable to those aspiring to gentility, for when Bluegrass planters danced they "made use of every exertion in trying who could dance the best."[7]

In some respects, most notably their devotion to improving the breed of horses, Bluegrass gentry outshone their Tidewater mentors. At court days, Francois André Michaux noticed that among Kentuckians "horses and law-suits comprise the usual topic of their conversation." By 1800, Kentucky was home to ninety thousand horses, the highest per capita in any state of the Union. For the most part, these were draft horses with undistinguished pedigrees, cheap animals good for carrying loads and working fields. But gentlemen imported top stallions from Virginia and Great Britain to produce sleeker, faster animals. With stud fees ranging up to twenty dollars per cover and forty dollars for a live foal, the owners of successful stallions made a great deal of money from the breeding business. Profits, though, were just part of the reward that accrued to the owner of the fastest horse. As in colonial Virginia, owning an exceptionally swift horse and staking large sums of money on its racing ability boosted a Bluegrass planter's status as a gentleman.[8]

Whether in dancing, horse racing, or any other competition, Bluegrass planters were quick to answer all insults to their dignity as gentlemen. To lose face was to risk one's status as a gentleman, which in Kentucky, as in colonial Virginia, depended on the vigilant defense of personal honor. According to one British traveler, the importance Bluegrass planters attached to matters of honor went beyond the attentive standard set by English noblemen. "A Kentuckian," observed Elias Fordham, "is an Englishman with a little more pride." In keeping with the unwritten code of gentry behavior, Bluegrass gentlemen satisfied their wounded pride in the ultimate contest: pistols at ten paces.[9]

Of course, a gentleman did not live (and die) by honor alone. More than fancy attire, polite manners, fast horses, and inflated sense of self, the ownership of vast lands and numerous hands ultimately determined who was a gentleman. The pyramid of land and slaveownership in the Bluegrass region eliminated all but a handful of aspirants, and the top was becoming more exclusive. In Woodford County, as Table A.5 makes clear, only one in twelve householders owned more than one thousand acres in the mid-1790s, a proportion that declined to one in twenty-two in 1810, and to just one in forty-two in 1825. In Woodford, slaveowners

Kentucky county map, 1820. Reprinted with permission of Charles Scribner's Sons, an imprint of Simon & Schuster Macmillan, from *Kentucky: Atlas of Historical County Boundaries*, ed. John H. Long; compiled by Gordon Denboer. Copyright © 1995 The Newberry Library.

actually composed a majority of householders by 1825. Yet, as Table A.6 lays out, only a small fraction ever attained planter status, which by common understanding required the possession of twenty or more slaves.[10]

Although the Bluegrass elite modeled themselves on the Tidewater gentry, the economic culture of early-nineteenth-century Kentucky planters diverged from that of eighteenth-century Virginians. Where tobacco infused the worldview of colonial Tidewater gentlemen, the well-being of Bluegrass planters depended more on hemp, supplemented by stock raising. These activities, together with the distance of the Bluegrass from Atlantic outlets, turned western planters away from eastern outlooks. Gone, too, was the sense of doubt and decline that weighed heavily on the tobacco growers of Virginia. Rising prices—for stock, for hemp, and for land—generated a vigorous and optimistic spirit among Bluegrass gentry.[11]

Discouraged by the uncertainty of marketing tobacco, the instability of its price, and the knowledge of what the weed had done to Virginia soils, Bluegrass planters successfully diversified their land use strategies. Livestock offered the great advantage of being able to walk itself to cis-Appalachian markets. While most Kentuckians who engaged in animal husbandry followed backcountry practices, allowing their cattle, hogs, and horses to forage in the "common" woods, a few of the largest landowners enclosed their fields and concentrated on raising more expensive stock.[12]

The lands of Bluegrass planters were also perfectly suited for the cultivation of hemp. The interior location of Kentucky dictated that any staple grown there command a high price per pound in distant markets, but, as Henry Clay complained, there was "too much bulk and too little value in Tobacco and Flour." Experiments with cotton fizzled because of early frosts. But the cotton boom that spread across the Deep South did provide Bluegrass planters with a highly valued staple. Bales of cotton needed to be roped and bagged, and slaves who worked in cotton fields needed to be clothed. Hemp, grown in the Bluegrass region, fit those demands. The highest price was fetched for the long, fine fibers produced from the deep, loamy soils of the Inner Bluegrass. By the beginning of the nineteenth century, over forty thousand pounds of raw hemp fiber were annually exported from Kentucky to the lower South. On the eve of the War of 1812, Kentucky monopolized the supply of hemp to the whole cotton kingdom. With yields ranging up to one thousand or more pounds of fiber per acre and hemp prices rising through the early years of the nineteenth century, the owners of Inner Bluegrass plantations looked ahead to the future in a way that gentlemen in Virginia no longer did.[13]

Inner Bluegrass planters possessed the lands and the hands necessary to exploit the opportunities presented by hemp cultivation. While hemp culture was less meticulous than tobacco, the production of first-rate fibers also required intensive, year-round labor. Accordingly, Kentucky planters referred to hemp as a "nigger" crop, because, they said, blacks understood the eccentricities of breaking and hackling hemp stalks to free the fiber from the wood; more to the point, slaves could be compelled to perform the back-breaking tasks associated with raising hemp from seed to stalk. From the beneficence of their lands and the efforts of their slaves, Bluegrass hemp planters built a style and a standard of living that reproduced and then surpassed that of the world they left behind.[14]

II

The booming agricultural economy of the Inner Bluegrass made the city of Lexington the commercial and industrial capital of western America. Already in the 1790s, the level of commercial activity in Lexington amazed visitors. By then, the town boasted more than a dozen general stores, stocked with an array of briskly selling commodities. "I never saw a town the size of Lexington, where there is more the appearance of Traffic & Business carrying on," reported an English traveler. The hustle and bustle of daily life in fin-de-siècle Lexington reminded commentators more of Philadelphia than of the tranquil Virginia countryside. With the explosion of the hemp trade in the first decade of the nineteenth century,

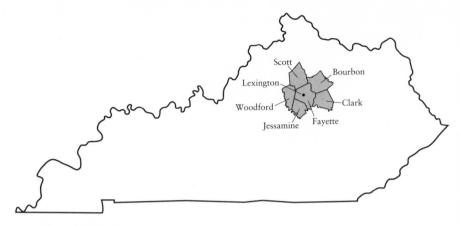

The Inner Bluegrass.

Lexington prospered. Its population jumped from eighteen hundred in 1800 to over four thousand three hundred in 1810.[15]

In developing so spectacularly, Lexington overcame the drawbacks of its location. True, the city was situated at the center of the Inner Bluegrass, surrounded by lands of extraordinary fertility, but exporting the products of the area was a complicated and perilous proposition. Unlike Philadelphia, or any of the other leading Atlantic cities, Lexington was not a seaport. Nor was it adjacent to a major waterway. The Kentucky River, whose course at one point took it within fifteen miles of Lexington, was the nearest outlet to the Ohio River. Steep gorges limited access, however, and even when goods reached the river, navigability remained unpredictable. Too little or too much water resulted in frustrating and costly delays of several months. Instead of by river, most goods went overland to the Ohio. The sixty-four-mile road connecting Lexington and Limestone (later Maysville) on the Ohio River was the main artery in and out of the Inner Bluegrass, yet it, too, was in dreadful shape. "Full of holes" and covered with large stones, "which seemed as if put there on purpose to annoy equestrians," the road was pronounced "beyond all comparison the worst I had ever seen" by one critic in the early 1820s. Loaded wagons made no more than fifteen miles a day on dry days, less in winter or the frequent wet days when the road turned to knee-deep mud.[16]

The condition of the Limestone Road and other avenues to Lexington added to the perils of doing business in the Inner Bluegrass. In the 1780s, wagoning from Philadelphia to Pittsburgh and from Limestone to Lexington inflated the Kentucky price of imported European and West

Indies goods as much as 500 percent above their seaport tab. In the 1790s and 1800s, transportation costs subsided, but the price of European goods in Lexington was still 50 to 100 percent above the Philadelphia price. The trip between Philadelphia and Lexington took two months, time in which drayage charges mounted and market conditions fluctuated. Passage from New Orleans by river and road also extended over several months.[17]

A number of economic factors compounded the geographic disadvantages under which Lexington merchants carried on their affairs. Goods bought from coastal merchants were generally purchased on six to twelve months' credit, forcing Lexington traders to watch inventories carefully, lest interest penalties accumulate. Seaport merchants also wanted payments made in specie, which, as central Kentuckians constantly lamented, was very scarce in their part of the world. Except for sales to the army, Lexington businessmen conducted few transactions on a hard-money basis.[18]

Lexington merchants had to find alternatives to cash that were acceptable to both local patrons and distant creditors. As in other specie-poor inland settlements, the balancing of accounts was a complex procedure. "The smallest transaction between two individuals can be carried out only by inconceivably roundabout and circuitous means," complained one would-be central Kentucky merchant. The account book of J. C. Owings, who owned stores in Lexington and nearby Paris, illustrates the intricacies of exchange. Only about one in twenty customers who appeared in Owings' book for 1790–1791 settled up in cash. Slightly more than a tenth of the accounts included some hard money, but also entailed some form of barter. Better than 80 percent of Owings' customers balanced their accounts through promises and payments in kind, by an exchange of goods and/or services. That one in four settlements involved a third person underscored the flexibility that was essential for completing transactions in Lexington.[19]

To satisfy out-of-state creditors, Lexington merchants needed a commodity that was literally as good as gold. Only a few Kentucky products held a high enough value to meet that test. As in the presettlement era, skins and furs continued to function as an acceptable substitute for gold and silver (or notes backed up by gold and silver reserves). Into the nineteenth century Lexington merchants like Samuel and George Trotter advertised their willingness to take pelts— especially beaver and otter skins —in exchange for wares brought from Philadelphia and other seaports. Trotter and Company annually sent between thirty and forty thousand dollars of deerskins to the coast as a way of balancing its accounts with

Philadelphia merchants. In postfrontier Kentucky, however, fur-bearing wildlife was increasingly sparse, threatening the viability of this form of barter. Whiskey served as a better specie substitute; only the ineffectual intrusions of federal revenue officers endangered its production.[20]

To discourage complicated barter and risky credit arrangements, Lexington merchants increasingly discriminated in favor of cash customers. "Every thing has two prices, the *trade* and *cash* price," observed one consumer. Customers paying in kind and seeking to postpone the settlement of their bills paid a stiff interest penalty for these indulgences. During the 1790s, some commodities began to be available "for ready money only." At the beginning of the nineteenth century, a number of prominent Lexington merchants renounced barter and credit altogether. Traditionalists denounced the discontinuation of customary forms of exchange. Invoking the rhetoric of classical republicanism, protesters accused merchants of putting private interests above public and patriotic obligations and urged customers to shun cash retailers who were "the enemy of the community."[21]

Merchants dismissed these criticisms; theirs was a hazardous business, in which failures outnumbered successes and risk-takers deserved rewards. As for critics who questioned his practices and prices, merchant John Wesley Hunt received an appropriate rejoinder from his brother: "I do not [at] all doubt that taking goods to Kentucky is occasioned with a great deal of hard labour[,] Trouble & Anxiety & a Person ought to get well paid for it," rationalized Abraham Hunt. John Wesley Hunt was indeed well paid. He parlayed his shrewd judgment of market conditions and 40 percent profit margins into a fortune that made him the first millionaire west of the Appalachians.[22]

With the sales of some mercantile establishments surpassing one million dollars per year and annual incomes reportedly reaching sixty thousand dollars in the first decade of the nineteenth century, the most successful Lexington merchants enjoyed a standing in the community and a standard of living superior to that of the wealthiest planters. By 1808, at the height of the boom, the real and personal property of the sixteen wealthiest merchants accounted for over one-third of the total valuation of taxable property in Lexington. Thanks to increasing hemp prices, the wealth of these merchants continued to grow through the end of the decade. Between 1808 and 1809, the value of William Leavy's holdings nearly doubled, from $25,817 to $46,710. The property of George Trotter increased from $61,564 to $100,300. Like the lawyers, who made fortunes in land litigation, the merchants of Lexington allocated a portion of their profits to planter-style extravagances. "What a pleasure we have in raking up money and spending it with our friends," declared Thomas Hart, echoing the sentiments of countless gentlemen. The "politeness and liberality" exhibited by Hart and other traders and the opulence displayed in their mansions, their carriages, and their clothing indicated the correspondence between the culture of planters and merchants.[23]

The ventures of Lexington merchants, on the other hand, parted from the customs of Virginia planters, with significant results for the economy of Kentucky. In addition to traditional investments in conspicuous display and land speculation, merchants branched out into manufacturing. A variety of enterprises attracted the attention of Lexington merchants, though, not surprisingly, they invested heavily in hemp-related manufactories. Despite his fondness for the good life, Thomas Hart saw clearly the opportunities awaiting merchant-manufacturers. In the mid-1790s, he opened a rope-walk, as well as a number of other industrial concerns. By 1800, five rope-making enterprises operated in Lexington. Early in the nineteenth century, John Wesley Hunt established himself as the most prominent hemp manufacturer, capitalizing an immense bagging manufactory in 1803. By 1810, Fayette County was home to five manufactories devoted to the production of bagging for cotton. The number of rope walks had risen to thirteen, eight of which were located in Lexington. The annual value of rope manufactured in Fayette County approached $200,000, while the value of cotton bagging neared $400,000. In little more than a decade, the value of these hemp manufactures had multiplied fortyfold.[24]

That hemp and hemp manufacturing escaped the depressing consequences of Jefferson's embargo heralded a brilliant future for Inner Bluegrass planters, dealers, and manufacturers. Prices for hemp fibers, as well as for Kentucky-made ropes and bags, inflated even as other commodities slumped. As Philadelphia and other seaports experienced severe recessions, Lexington continued on its flourishing course. Given the progress of the "Philadelphia of the West," merchant-manufacturers and hemp planters entertained hopes that the City of Brotherly Love would eventually be known as the "Lexington of the East." One writer even anticipated that the "seat of [the] general government will probably be removed" to Lexington.[25]

III

The merchants, lawyers, and planters who piloted the economic advancement of the Inner Bluegrass were ambitious men. They recognized that keeping Lexington as the greatest inland city, not to mention turning it into the greatest city in all of the United States, required an alliance of private enterprise and public finance. Even though the Bluegrass elite was dominated by men who considered themselves good Republicans, they embraced a political economy that swerved away from the localism and agrarianism associated with one strain of the Jeffersonian movement. Out front of this nationalist and developmental persuasion was Henry Clay.

Clay was an ideal spokesman for the "Bluegrass System," the political economy backed by the elites of Lexington and vicinity. In appearance and manner, he was the epitome of a Bluegrass gentleman. Among the slaveowning planters, risk-taking merchants, and enterprising lawyers with whom he socialized, Clay swaggered with the best of them. True to the self-assertive values of his class, Clay cherished his honor, and when his character was attacked, he saw "no alternative than that of demanding personal satisfaction." His personal economy combined the money-making activities associated with Bluegrass elites. Although he initially made his living as a lawyer, Clay married into the merchandising and manufacturing family of Thomas Hart, and he sank large amounts of capital into a number of commercial and industrial enterprises. He devoted his most careful attentions to Ashland, his showplace plantation on the outskirts of Lexington. There Clay raised, or rather his slaves raised, hemp. At Ashland, he attended as well to the business of breeding blooded stock, spending vast sums importing Hereford cattle and thoroughbred stallion prospects from England. Toward the end of his life, Clay made explicit the connection between the personal and the political: "I am executing here [at Ashland], in epitome, all my principles of Internal improvements, the American System &c."[26]

The "American System" that Clay pieced together for a national constituency in the second and third decades of the nineteenth century was in essential respects an enlarged version of the program he had previously espoused in the Kentucky General Assembly. As the representative from Fayette County in the Kentucky Lower House, Clay forwarded the interests of Bluegrass planters and Lexington merchants; as a national legislator, he continued to champion their cause. Though cloaked in nationalistic rhetoric, the protective tariffs, internal improvements, and banking policies that Clay advocated in Washington retained their Bluegrass flavoring.[27]

Denying class or local preferences, Clay deemed the encouragement of domestic manufactures vital to the preservation of the fledgling Republic. As a member of the Kentucky House in 1809, he sponsored a resolution calling for members to "clothe themselves in productions of American manufacture" as a symbolic protest against European disregard for the independence of the United States. In the United States Senate the following year, Clay sought to give substance to the symbolism through tariff protections for crucial industries, arguing that "the nation that imports its clothing from abroad is but little less dependent than if it imported its bread." Taking as his example "the well regulated family of a farmer," Clay credited "the harmony" of the contributions made by the different members with securing the independence of the household. Just as members of the family performed different roles, so "some of us must cultivate; some fabricate." Thus, his American System promised a balanced economy, harmonizing sectional and occupational divisions and resulting in a republic greater than the sum of its parts.[28]

Still, it was hardly a coincidence that Clay's first speech in favor of domestic manufactures targeted the hemp industry for special protection. His protectionist declaration was delivered in 1810, the year in which Kentucky hemp, after a decade of rising prices and expanding production, had suddenly fallen sharply in value. Although Clay did not single out Bluegrass hemp, he obviously understood that preferential treatment would profit central Kentucky planters and Lexington manufacturers. Privately, he admitted a degree of local and self-interest in his campaign "to rig the Navy with cordage made of American Hemp–Kentucky Hemp–Ashland Hemp."[29]

Clay's allegiance to federally financed internal improvements was also rooted in the Bluegrass. Nothing dampened the trade of central Kentucky more than inferior roads and inaccessible rivers, and Clay's experience in the Kentucky House taught him that state governments were unable to tackle grand projects. In early Kentucky, the condition of roads and streams was basically the concern of the county courts. The archaic system of maintenance and construction proved plainly inadequate in dealing with a problem that crossed county lines. Efforts by the state government to coordinate local projects and fund general improvements came up short as well. In its first decade, the Kentucky legislature passed a series of laws intended to ameliorate the state's deficiencies in river and road transport, but rather than appropriate money from the state treasury, lawmakers empowered private companies to sell stock subscriptions or conduct lotteries to pay for transportation projects. Inability to raise the authorized capital doomed most of these private ventures.[30]

Lexington merchants and manufacturers organized a number of turnpike and canal companies. For several years, a proposal to cut a canal through the Inner Bluegrass from the Kentucky River to the Elkhorn River inspired a great deal of conversation, though as usual funding problems halted actual construction. Cheaper costs made turnpikes more feasible, and early in the nineteenth century, Lexington leaders began to talk of building turnpikes from Lexington to Louisville and Limestone utilizing the latest macadamizing technology. In 1811, the legislature authorized a lottery to raise $5,000 to improve a portion of the Limestone Road. After this approach failed, the legislature passed a new act in 1817 incorporating the Lexington and Maysville Turnpike Road Company, as well as a Lexington-Louisville corporation. The Maysville Road, which attracted the most enthusiasm, was granted the right to raise $400,000 through the sale of stock, with the state agreeing to purchase $50,000.[31]

The boosterism of corporate officers outran their ability to underwrite turnpike projects. Maysville Turnpike directors predicted confidently that the "enhance[d] value" of adjoining lands "will alone be sufficient to defray the whole cost of the undertaking." Yet within a few years, confidence in private financing waned. "Everyday we become more wedded to the opinion that this Road should be a *state concern*," explained one officer. Increasingly, the directors thought it "even more desirable" that the Maysville Turnpike "belong to the United States." And so the American System became their best hope of winning a "liberal appropriation . . . from the General Government."[32]

As the congressional representative of the Inner Bluegrass, Henry Clay made public funding of internal improvements a major element in the American System. While this component presumed unparalleled expenditures by the federal government, he maintained that he "had imbibed his political principles" from Jefferson's most trusted friend and successor, James Madison. In 1817, after Madison vetoed the Bonus Bill, which earmarked the federal surplus for internal improvements, Clay claimed that the action was "irreconcilable with Mr. Madison's own principles," in that Madison, like Jefferson before him, understood that bettering the transportation infrastructure was critical to promoting commerce and preserving the republic.[33]

Clay held an elastic view of Jeffersonian principles. On one decisive ingredient of the American System—a national bank—his position underwent a startling reversal, yet he denied "the slightest contradiction" in his flip-flop. In his speech on rechartering the Bank of the United States in 1811, Clay sounded Jeffersonian alarms against paper aristocracies and foreign control of the institution's stock, and as Speaker of the House, he blocked the rechartering of the First Bank of the United States. Five

Henry Clay as a young man, at about the time of his departure for the peace negotiations at Ghent in 1814. Courtesy of the Kentucky Historical Society.

years later, however, Clay acted as legislative midwife in the birth of the Second Bank of the United States.[34]

In fact, Clay's stand in 1816 appalled Thomas Jefferson, and for some time Clay's view of banks had run counter to Jefferson's. Clay spent a good portion of his first several years in the Kentucky House fighting off attempts to repeal the charter of the Kentucky Insurance Company, a Lexington-based corporation granted the right to circulate notes and lend money at interest. In debate, Clay rejected Jefferson's fear that banks concentrated wealth in the hands of a venal paper aristocracy. Like the merchants of Lexington, who invested in the insurance company and de-

Lithograph of Ashland, Henry Clay's estate outside Lexington, by Bascom Cooper (1852). Courtesy of the Filson Club Historical Society.

pended on its notes and loans to expedite trade, Clay dwelled on the benefits derived by the entire community when commerce flourished.[35]

As a state legislator, Clay did not favor all banks. He defended unsuccessfully the inviolability of the corporate charter of the Kentucky Insurance Company mostly to preserve the Lexington concern's statewide monopoly on banking privileges. Clay never welcomed outside competitors calmly, especially ones in far-away Philadelphia that were controlled by foreigners and Federalists. In 1811, Clay's localist attachment to the Lexington commercial elite overrode his nationalist vision. What changed, then, between 1811 and 1816? The financial crisis of the United States during the War of 1812 undoubtedly broadened Clay's nationalism and made him more disposed to the necessity of a national bank. Also in its favor, the Second Bank of the United States contemplated a branch office in Lexington. Indeed, Clay's influence over the Second Bank allowed him to recommend ten of the first thirteen directors of the newly established Lexington branch. Clay subsequently handled a large volume of the Second Bank of the United States' legal business in the West.[36]

The man who voted for the National Bank and espoused the American System clothed a Hamiltonian political economy in Jeffersonian garb. Contravening his fidelity to the aims of Jefferson and Madison, Clay's vision of economic development clearly deviated from principles of agrarianism and limited government. Nonetheless, ample as his nationalism

became, Clay never lost sight of local interests. Through his long government service, Clay operated from the proposition that what was good for
Lexington merchants was good for the Bluegrass, and what was good for
the Bluegrass was good for the United States.

IV

Henry Clay's experiences in turn-of-the-century Lexington provided
the foundation for his faith in the universal benefits of economic development and for his certainty that the Bluegrass System improved the lot
of rich and poor alike. When Clay arrived in Lexington in 1797, the town
already boasted a reputation as the West's best city for men on the make.
In the boomtime that coincided with Clay's rise to political prominence,
Lexington retained its status as a favored destination for migrating artisans and laborers, as well as lawyers and merchants. But while the political
economy pressed by Clay blurred the distinctions, the advantages that
made Lexington a good poor man's city did not coincide with the interests
of enterprisers. The onset of harder times after the War of 1812 exposed
the dissonance.

Lexington's standing as a good place for artisans rested on the dearth
of trained craftsmen, which allowed skilled craftsmen an unparalleled
chance to get ahead. After visiting Lexington in 1806, John Melish related
that "industrious journeymen very soon become masters." Though opportunity and wages varied considerably between crafts, a correspondent
to *Niles' Weekly Register* reported in 1815 that "mechanics of all descriptions receive nearly double the price for their labor that they get to the
eastward." The comparatively low cost of living in Lexington helped as
well. François André Michaux pointed out that artisans in New York and
Philadelphia toiled four days to pay their boarding charges and meet other
most basic needs. In Lexington, where boarders paid only one to two dollars per week for room and board, single journeymen "can subsist a week
with the produce of one day's labour." And for those with rifles, the woods
around Lexington, though no longer a game-filled paradise, still might
supplement a journeyman's subsistence.[37]

In his memoirs, the papermaker Ebenezer Stedman recalled the turn
of the century as a golden age for Bluegrass artisans and laborers. In
those years, claimed Stedman, workingmen were respected, and so was
their "Good[,] Substantial work." Stedman remembered that his father,
a skilled mechanic, was "looked upon as a man of more than ordinary
Importance. Men of the Highest Standing Sought his acquaintance," including Henry Clay. Stedman waxed nostalgic for his father's day when

there were "no overgrown wealthy Capitalist[s] to Screw down the wages of honest workmen & cause them to Slight their work." [38]

The age was less golden than Stedman recollected. If skilled workers enjoyed the benefits of relatively high wages, elevated social status, and frequent holidays, few turn-of-the-century artisans managed to savor the independence that came only with the ownership of land. Inequality in the distribution of land emerged early in Lexington, and it was more pronounced than anywhere else in Kentucky. When Clay arrived in Lexington in 1797, more than three-quarters of the town's taxpayers owned no real estate. By 1805, the proportion of landowners dropped below one in five. For all but the most successful masters in the most profitable crafts, the dream of holding fee-simple title to Inner Bluegrass land proved elusive. Less than one in ten craftsmen listed in the 1806 Lexington directory owned any real estate. Only one artisan, a silversmith, possessed more than the median. Those denied land often took up a new occupation or drifted out of town, having failed to secure independence. Just 51 of the 138 craftsmen enumerated in the 1806 directory were still carrying on the same business twelve years later when an updated volume was published. And these were master craftsmen, who had already graduated to the top of the artisanal hierarchy. [39]

Landless dependence and rootlessness were facts of life for ordinary mechanics and unskilled day laborers. Leisure time was not always a matter of choice, since Lexington workingmen often found only seasonal or sporadic employment. Periodic water shortages forced many Inner Bluegrass journeymen into an itinerant lifestyle. When the paper mill in which Ebenezer Stedman and his father worked shut for want of water, the two, along with other papermakers, traveled on foot from mill to mill all the way to Ohio, hoping to find enough work to avoid starvation. Back in Lexington, Stedman found temporary residence in a boarding house. Though rates were affordable, the nickname of the house, "Cold Comfort," suggested the meager accommodations and monotonous fare that transients endured. No wonder, then, many boarders turned to the bottle for warmth and solace. [40]

"Bottle fever," as the well-digger John Robert Shaw termed it, ruined the careers of countless workers. Shaw's life and misfortunes illustrated the colorful, but destructive, consequences of an alcohol-saturated existence in boomtime Lexington. After settling in central Kentucky in the mid-1790s, Shaw initially wandered about working for food "and whatever other compensation my employer thought proper." Entering into the well digging business, Shaw developed a solid reputation for divining water. His talents in locating water and his poetic advertisements brought him dozens of clients and a growing personal estate. Blown up four times while blasting wells, Shaw lost one eye, four fingers, and seven toes. He eased his pains, as other workers drowned their uncertainties, with alcohol. Unfortunately, drunkenness caused him to be defrauded by several customers. Intemperance and related extravagances eventually plunged him into debt, forcing him to forfeit much of the property for which he had sacrificed various body parts.[41]

Ultimately, the well-being of the free labor force hinged on factors beyond any single individual's control. Master craftsmen understood the need for collective action to implement uniform prices. Ordinary mechanics were slower to this realization, though in 1811, twenty-one journeymen cordwainers banded together to protest unfair wages. At a meeting in February of that year, the assembled shoemakers resolved not to work for any master paying substandard wages nor to associate with any journeyman violating the accord. But low persistence rates made enforcement of a compact among Bluegrass journeymen difficult in the best of times, and maintaining those standards became impossible when the economy of Lexington slid after the War of 1812. The economic plunge hit both rich and poor, but working people, who lived near the margins of subsistence, faced the more desperate situation.[42]

Cracks in the boom surfaced before the war, though the full impact of the slump remained concealed for several years. The decline in hemp prices, which began in 1809, signaled trouble ahead and started calls for protection. The war, which temporarily removed British competition, suspended Clay's tariff campaign and restored the appearance of prosperity. By 1814, however, Lexington merchants complained of "gloomy" times. Peace brought a flood of cheap British goods, creating a crisis for Lexington manufacturers. The hemp industry suffered a terrible blow from which it never fully recovered. By the middle of 1815, all fourteen rope walks in Lexington had shut down. Most did not reopen or they resumed operation on a much smaller scale. In other industries, a similar contraction occurred. By 1819, factories in the vicinity of Lexington representing $500,000 in capital investment were idled. The manufacturing census of 1820 revealed the magnitude of the depression in Lexington. Discontinued or drastically diminished operations characterized virtually every Inner Bluegrass industry.[43]

The simultaneous collapse in commercial volume intensified the severity of Lexington's postwar plummet. The proliferation of steamboats on western waters after the War of 1812 doomed inland Lexington's reign as the entrepot of the Ohio Valley. Regional trade that had formerly been handled by Lexington merchants shifted to the river cities of Cincinnati and Louisville. To stem the decline, Lexington merchants launched canal proposals and lobbied anew for government encouragement of domestic manufactures. Henry Clay heard the call of his most influential constituents and stepped up his campaign to obtain federal funding of internal improvements. Even had these efforts succeeded, Lexington's pre-steamboat preeminence was gone forever.[44]

Investments in lands in and around Lexington partially insulated merchants and manufacturers from the shock of failing industries and languishing commerce. Fueled by the liberal loan policies of western banks, speculation in trans-Appalachian lands reached a frenzy in the years after the War of 1812. Across the Ohio Valley, land values skyrocketed, with the most exorbitant bids recorded for urban real estate. In Lexington, land prices climbed as high as $400 per acre. For wealthy investors, who reaped a bonanza from the sale of Lexington lots, the tremendous increase in property values blunted the impact of the economic downturn. Working-men, though, had no cushion against the postwar crash. The closing of manufactories and the decrease in trade threw hundreds of mechanics out of work. Land speculation permitted merchant-manufacturers to maintain a genteel standard of living, while "poor people" had "great difficulties in making a living for their families."[45]

The reopening of manufacturing companies did not restore prewar conditions for Lexington's free workers. Snapping up bankrupt enterprises at reduced prices made good sense to merchant-manufacturers with bank notes to spare. After the cotton and woolen factory built by Lewis Sanders at a reported cost of $150,000 defaulted on bank loans in 1816, a group of merchant-manufacturers purchased the property at the bargain price of $21,000. But the new board of directors understood that returning the Sanders property to profitability required changes in management, changes that would alter the circumstances and composition of the labor force. Before resuming operation, the directors hired George Lockebie to restructure the organization of the factory.[46]

Lockebie forwarded a remarkably prescient proposal in February of 1818. In his report, Lockebie invoked time-honored clichés, urging the directors to operate the plant with the "utmost economy," reminding them that the "loss of time is loss of profit." This was standard advice, repeated endlessly in every country almanac. What was new in Lockebie's exposition were the details of his plan to minimize waste and maximize economy. Likening a factory to "a busy hive," he maintained that it was crucial to arrange operations so "that no part may be standing still on account of another part having fallen behind." His vision of an integrated operation, in which each operative performed a specific task, went far beyond the decidedly unscientific management that had been the rule in Lexington craft shops and manufactories. To make the operation function "with as much precision as a military corps," Lockebie advocated closer supervision of all hands. Denying the humanity of the labor force, the new-style manager argued that a tardy or absent worker "ought to be dismissed as [a] piece of machinery that does not answer the ends proposed." Lockebie also advised the directors to open a store convenient to the manufactory to "obviate the necessity of paying all the wages in ready cash" and to augment the control that employers exerted over their employees.[47]

V

Oddly, Lockebie's prescription for industrial recovery made no mention of one ingredient of growing importance to the Bluegrass labor system: slaves. With slavery secured by Kentucky's second constitution, the transition in the composition of the Bluegrass labor force accelerated. In the Inner Bluegrass, slaves accounted for a quarter of the population in 1800. With the expansion of hemp cultivation, their number multiplied as Bluegrass landowners replaced tenants with slaves. By 1820, slaves constituted more than a third of the Inner Bluegrass census.[48]

From farm to factory, the cultivation of hemp and its conversion into rope and bagging material was almost entirely in black hands. After the War of 1812, Lexington industrialists increasingly relied on unfree hands to resuscitate their enterprises. In spite of generally depressed conditions, the 1820 Manufacturing Census reported that 424 people, including 168 children and 10 women, were employed in Fayette County hemp works. The digest did not break down employment by race, but judging by the testimony of witnesses, black workers dominated and did well by their employers. At one cotton bagging factory, employing between sixty and one hundred "negroes of all ages," a skeptical observer came away impressed with the performance of the laborers, who showed "more skill in the management of their machinery than I had supposed the slaves possessed."[49]

Like Lockebie, Henry Clay avoided the subject of slaves in industry. Preaching the harmony of interests, Clay contended that the American System provided "adequate security . . . against oppression on the part of capitalists towards the laboring portions of the community." Here and elsewhere, Clay restricted his remarks to free white males, pretending that the laboring portions included no slaves. Though the history of the Bluegrass illustrated how profitably slaves could substitute for white workers in agriculture and manufacturing, Clay remained mute about the effects of the competition on free labor. The unspoken importance of slaves to the Bluegrass System accented the contradictions between Clay's political and personal economy. "No man," asserted Clay, "is more sensible of the evils of slavery than I am, nor regrets them more." Yet his antislavery principles did not stand in the way of his ownership of slaves. Clay acquired his first slaves after his marriage to Lucretia Hart, and over the next half century, he added to his contingent of human property, which eventually numbered forty. In dollar value, his investments in slaves ranked behind only his stake in real estate.[50]

Denying the permanence and emphasizing the benevolence of their mastery soothed the consciences of Clay and other Bluegrass slaveholders. Seldom referring to slaves as property, Bluegrass masters favored kinder, gentler euphemisms. Older bondsmen and women became "uncles" and "aunts," though all slaves remained "children" in the eyes of their masters. "It is our duty to do all we can to render them happy in their life of bondage," avowed one self-sacrificing owner. Kentucky planters almost convinced themselves that bondage was in the best interests of their slaves. Had not the Englishman John Melish deemed the slaves of Kentucky "better fed, better lodged, and better clothed than many of the peasantry in Britain"? Had not virtually every observer commented on how much more benign slavery was in the Bluegrass than elsewhere? Clay clearly believed that his slaves lived comfortably and he deeply resented it when they disturbed his illusions. He complained that one runaway fled "for no other reason than because we have spoiled him by good treatment."[51]

Clay and fellow planters blamed "indifferent overseers" for whatever abuses occurred on Bluegrass plantations and in Lexington manufactories. Their response to risks that slaves faced from persons other than their owners was an 1816 statute protecting blacks "from the violence of the wanton and unfeeling." Keeping with paternalistic understandings, the act was written "to enable the owners of slaves to protect" their bondspeople from extralegal corporal punishment. Masters submitted the 1816 law, and the relatively mild slave code of which it was a part, as proof of the exceptional humanity of the Bluegrass System.[52]

Lexington manufacturers offered their own evidence of the compassion of the Bluegrass System. Instead of purchasing slaves outright, industrialists typically rented unfree workers from their owners, usually for one-year terms. "Hiring out," as the contracting of slaves was called, allowed manufacturers flexibility to expand and contract their labor force in response to changing demand. But the practice also had advantages for hired slaves, for whom the experience brought "a taste of freedom." Factory supervisors downplayed traditional coercive methods for extracting slave labor in favor of a task system with daily quotas. To motivate hands to meet and exceed their minimums, managers paid generous bonuses for any "over-work." According to a New England visitor to a Lexington hemp manufactory, the incentive plan stimulated the ambition of slaves and left them "happier" than any "set of workmen" he had ever seen. Without hesitation, the New Englander affirmed that "there is more health, wealth, strength and happiness, more real freedom of body, and quite as much independence of mind among the slaves of Kentucky, as there is in Blackburn, Sheffield, Birmingham or Paisley." Moreover, for slaves who turned their taste of freedom into something permanent, the Bluegrass System fulfilled its benevolent promises. Hiring out furnished a number of Kentucky slaves with the means to purchase their freedom. In a few cases, "over-work" bonuses saved over many years permitted hired bondsmen to emancipate their entire families.[53]

Still, the freedom of freed blacks was severely limited. While Henry Clay supported gradual emancipation, he considered free blacks "corrupt, depraved, and abandoned." Manumitted slaves were supposed to leave the continent. At the very least, they were encouraged to leave Kentucky. The laws of the Commonwealth discriminated against free blacks across the board. The 1799 Constitution excluded blacks from bearing arms, serving in the militia, and voting in elections. An 1808 act prohibited the "future migration of free Negroes and Mulattoes" to Kentucky. Other statutes required free blacks already in the state to carry certificates attesting to their status, be gainfully employed or face imprisonment for vagrancy, and observe curfews that made no distinction between free and enslaved. Suspicion fell on free blacks whenever there was an unsolved crime.[54]

For most African Americans, the benevolence of the Bluegrass System proved a heartbreaking fraud. Under the best of circumstances, buying freedom was an expensive proposition. Before manumitting slaves, owners received all of the annual hiring out fees. Masters also exacted up to a thousand dollars in over-work earnings, though the market value of adult bondsmen did not approach that level. Accumulating the necessary bounty took slaves years of overtime toil. After decades of saving, some slaves discovered that verbal agreements carried no force if owners chose to forget old pledges. In other unfortunate cases, new owners disclaimed knowledge of manumission promises made by former masters. As a slave song warned, "My ole Missis promised me/Dat, when she die, she'd set me free/She lib so long; her head got ball/She swore she's *nebber* die-at all/But, now ole Missis—dead en-gone/She's lef *me* here—a hoein de cawn."[55]

Dishonorable deeds stripped the paternalistic veneer from the Bluegrass System. Slavery in the Bluegrass ultimately rested on the same power of the law and the lash as it did further to the south. Boasting only good intentions, masters cheated slaves of their freedom and whipped them for insubordination. The kindest masters sometimes displayed the cruelest streaks. At least one of Clay's bondsmen accused him of brutality. In nine years at Ashland, Lewis Richardson complained he received no "hat[,] nor cap to wear, nor a stitch of bed clothes, except one small coarse blanket," with "nothing but coarse bread and meat to eat and not enough of that." After Lewis returned late from a visit to his wife, he recounted, Clay ordered "me stripped and tied up, and one hundred and fifty lashes given me on my naked back." Richardson exaggerated, Clay's overseer insisted, and he was a drunken incorrigible, neighboring planters testified. But his allegations of mistreatment were partially corroborated by other fugitives whom Clay professed to coddle. And when Clay was not around, his sons terrorized the slaves at Ashland. No wonder slaves in the Bluegrass were heard singing: "Heave away! Heave away!/I'd radder co't a yaller gal/Dan work for Henry Clay."[56]

In fairness to Bluegrass slaveholders, theirs was undoubtedly a better country for blacks than the Lower South. But Clay and his slaveowning peers inhabited a world where hardheaded economics overruled softhearted paternalism. Thus one slaveowner wondered "if it is right to call human beings property," and in the same breath advised his son that "there is no species of property . . . that improves an estate as fast as a healthy breeding negro woman whose children do well." The sale of slaves, especially the breaking up of families, exposed the triumph of profit-mindedness over paternalism. Around the Bluegrass, blacks learned to fear New Year's Day, for that was a day when debts were settled and slaves sold to meet obligations. "Justice forbids . . . traffic in human flesh," wrote an overextended William Little Brown in 1812. Alas, concluded Brown, "necessity compels me to sell Abram," a trusted servant, for $450. Esteeming the money "so much borrowed from Abram," Brown promised "at some future date to redeem him and give him his liberty." The anguish of slaveowners did not impress sold-off slaves. As one bondsmen acidly summarized, Bluegrass paternalists "mind no more selling children away from slaves, than they do calves from a cow." Indeed, sellers often exchanged slaves for livestock.[57]

The protestations of slaveholders became more hollow as the volume of sales increased after the War of 1812. The growth of the cotton kingdom, together with the postwar slump in Lexington industries, combined to make slaves more valuable in the Lower South than in the Bluegrass. As Lexington faded as the headquarters of trans-Appalachian commerce, it became a center for the transfer of human property from the Bluegrass to the Deep South.[58]

Slaves registered their discontent with the Bluegrass System in a variety of ways, with flight being the most obvious means of resistance. Through the 1790s, a few slaves ran off to live among Ohio Valley Indians. But the fears of masters about massive defections of slaves to Indian country were exaggerated. Just as Anglo-Kentuckians were not easily converted into white Indians, so Afro-Kentuckians did not become black Indians in large numbers. For many slaves, as for many white women, the worst aspect of moving to Kentucky was the separation from family and friends who stayed behind. Escaping to Indian country made reunions even less likely. As the slave trade with the cotton kingdom expanded, however, running north became the best available option for slaves facing sale to the South. Before being sold down the river, hundreds of Kentucky slaves fled or tried to flee across the Ohio.[59]

Slaves remaining in the Bluegrass generally settled for more discreet forms of rebellion. On farms, pigs, chickens, and eggs frequently "disappeared." According to slave Lewis Clarke, it was "a kind of first principle" that those who "worked had a right to eat." Elaborating on the slaves' labor theory of value, Henry Bibb declared his "moral right" to take "a little from the abundance" which his exertions produced. In manufactories, hired slaves resisted efforts to speed their work. Complaints by factory managers of slaves "falling behind" indicated that enslaved black laborers, like their free white counterparts, slowed the pace of work to a schedule of their own and not their employers' choosing.[60]

A rash of suspicious fires struck a more damaging blow against the Bluegrass System. Blazes consumed at least nine manufactories in Lexington in the half dozen years before the War of 1812. The hemp works owned by John Wesley Hunt was victimized by incendiaries twice in less than five years. On the first occasion in November 1807, a hired slave boy was convicted of arson. In January 1812, a second fire caused $20,000 worth of damage to the rebuilt factory. The same week three other blazes damaged Lexington manufacturing establishments. Within two weeks of the conflagrations, two male slaves under fifteen were sentenced to be hanged for torching Hunt's establishment. Citing the age of the convicts, the governor commuted the sentences. The reprieve outraged manufacturers, who saw it sending the message that "boys may burn houses with impunity."[61]

The anger with the governor's decision disclosed more deep-seated fears within the master class. Even before the latest arson wave, slaveholders and slave hirers were on edge. On several occasions, rumors of slave insurrections spread around Lexington and the Bluegrass countryside. In December 1810, the discovery of a supposed conspiracy involving free and enslaved blacks in Lexington sent propertied residents into "an uproar," renewing demands for better policing and regulations on hiring out.[62]

The insurrections never materialized, and some doubt exists whether the convicted arsonists were guilty. Although the blazes may have been protests by disgruntled blacks, they may also have been set by displaced white workers. Arsonists targeted factories such as Hunt's, which hired large numbers of slaves and few free laborers. Nothing, it was said, stirred up the animosity of white mechanics as much as the sight of slaves "clad in better attire than honest white persons who labour for their living." A verse in one of John Robert Shaw's advertisements put the resentment of white workers almost in rhyme: "The great men are determin'd/All the negroes to have/To work in their factories/The poor men to starve."[63]

IN THE BLUEGRASS REGION of early-nineteenth-century Kentucky, Henry Clay gave full play to the spirit of gain. Born in modest circumstances, Clay achieved his dream of getting forward. Together with other successful Bluegrass lawyers, merchants, and planters, he realized a style and a standard of living that was the envy of Virginia gentlemen. In the "Philadelphia of the West," he and fellow Lexington elites flourished. Even the end of the economic boom did not diminish their optimism.

Clay and his principal backers believed that the Bluegrass System, wedding public and private interests, offered men of enterprise their best opportunity to exploit fully the resources of the trans-Appalachian West. In his legislative career in Frankfort and Washington, Clay articulated a political economy that promised to reconsolidate the capitalist world order. In the new world order imagined by Clay, the Bluegrass (and the United States) would escape its colonial dependence on the English metropole and reap the benefits of being its own integrated center of agriculture, commerce, and manufacturing.

The rumblings of the discontented showed that not everyone shared in the blessings of the Bluegrass. Enslaved blacks and poor whites did not rejoice for Clay's political economy. Yet because they competed as laborers, white and black workers posed as much of a threat to one another as they did to the Bluegrass System.

But the masters of the Bluegrass did not feel entirely safe either. The burning of factories kindled doubts. Amidst the swirl of rumors of slave conspiracies, Margaretta Brown confessed her "apprehensions" that "if the *Monster* Slavery does not destroy the people of Ken[tuck]y before long, it will only grant them the same sad favor that Polyphemus granted to Ulysses—to be the *last which it will devour.*" Also to be resolved was a confrontation with homesteaders from Kentucky's Green River Country. At stake for Henry Clay and fellow Lexington elites was the future of the Bluegrass System; at stake for Green River homesteaders was the future of their good poor man's country.[64]

SEVEN *The Blueing*

of the Green River Country

THE ENGROSSMENT OF LAND, the rule of lawyers, the privatization of property rights, the power of merchant-manufacturers, and the entrenchment of slavery transformed the Bluegrass from the world of Daniel Boone to that of Henry Clay. Away from Lexington, however, backcountry ways persisted; outside the Inner Bluegrass, the ascendancy of lawyers, planters, and merchants remained unrealized to the end of the eighteenth century. From these hinterlands arose a challenge to the Bluegrass System.

During the 1790s, the Green River Country, south and west of the Bluegrass, emerged as Kentucky's best poor man's country. Unlike the Bluegrass, which had fallen under the sway of speculators from the opening of the Kentucky frontier, the Green River Country was initially a refuge for squatters. The settlement of this area, also called the "Southside," promoted by generous homesteading terms, produced a broader and more equitable distribution of land than in the Bluegrass. Here at last was a country in which nonslaveholding family farms predominated.

In the statehouse, the representatives of the Southside, proclaiming themselves defenders of these yeoman farmers, initially assailed the "aristocratic" political economy of Henry Clay; yet the "Green River Band" ultimately voted to enlarge the Bluegrass System. Their endorsement transformed the Green River Country. During the first two decades of the nineteenth century, the economic culture of the Southside grew increasingly like that of the Bluegrass and the country became less accommodating to poor men.

I

The Green River Country never captivated travelers as did the Bluegrass. Whereas visitors rhapsodized about the splendors of the Bluegrass, the few brave souls who ventured south of the Green River expressed no enthusiasm for the prairies that greeted them. Raised to assess the quality of "virgin" land based on the number and types of trees it supported, early comers to the "Barrens," as the grasslands of the Southside came to be known, disparaged the fertility of the whole country and denigrated the landscape. Less than a third of the land in the Green River district was actually prairie, but the sight of treeless meadows so shocked eighteenth- and nineteenth-century travelers, accustomed to dense American forests, that the Barrens inevitably dominated their blighted vision of Southside scenery. Typical was the view of Thomas Ashe, who declared the Barrens "so sterile and inhospitable that neither man nor beast can reside there."[1]

The Barrens enjoyed a better reputation among hunters. Through the use of fire, Ohio Valley Indians extended the range of the prairies to attract more game and facilitate hunting. So successful were they in luring buffalo to the newly cleared pastures that the first French hunters named the Green River after the animal. But bad reports about agricultural potential dampened the enthusiasm of land speculators and discouraged any rush of settlers to the Green River Country. Because Tidewater and Piedmont gentry directed their acquisitive energies to the Bluegrass, Virginia was free to offer the territory south of the Green River as an inducement to her Revolutionary soldiers. The Virginia legislature set aside the largest grants for colonels, however, and consoled the proprietors of the Transylvania Company with a 200,000-acre parcel at the mouth of the Green River. During the 1780s, over 1,500,000 acres were located on military warrants in the Green River district, but few grantees moved there.[2]

In the early 1790s, the population of the Green River Country consisted of a handful of squatters, who hunted game, ranged livestock, grew a little corn, and, judging by contemporary accounts, raised a lot of hell. Indeed, when Peter Cartwright arrived in 1793, he claimed that criminals constituted a majority of the inhabitants in Logan County, which was thus nicknamed "Rogues Harbour." According to a Bluegrass planter, the Southside was "filled with nothing but hunters, horse thieves and savages . . . where wretchedness, poverty and sickness will always reign."[3]

Yet the reputation of the Green River Country underwent a startling reformation in the years after Kentucky attained statehood. Avoiding the prairies, the first squatters had built their cabins in what they assumed to be the more fertile, wooded lands that bordered the Green River and its tributaries. But the soil's fertility pleasantly surprised farmers who defied conventional wisdom and planted a small patch of prairie. Once they became aware of the productivity of the grasslands, Southside settlers forgot their time-honored landscape prejudices. "You can form no idea of the Beauty of the Barrens . . . from anything you have seen in Virginia," wrote W. L. Underwood of Warren County to his sisters back in the Old Dominion. "The Barrens in the Spring," exulted Underwood, "afford the most beautiful and variegated prospect in the world, the whole face of the earth is thickly matted with a beautiful green grass, and the flowers of all colors putting forth thick gives the whole a fragrancy of appearance not describable." As word seeped out of yields of forty to fifty bushels of Indian corn per acre, only about 20 percent below that of the finest Bluegrass soil, excitement spread about the previously shunned district. An increasing number of squatters took up residence in the early 1790s; in Logan County, which then encompassed most of the Barrens, the number of tithables nearly tripled between September 1792 and October 1795.[4]

Still, the inability of squatters or would-be settlers to gain title to lands south of the river discouraged emigration to the district and left the vast majority of those already there legally landless. In 1795, more than eight out of ten Logan County families owned no acreage. Raising anew the banner of occupancy and improvement, landless Southsiders petitioned the Kentucky legislature to offer the same bargain-priced settlement and preemption rights that Virginia had earlier extended to settlers north of the river.[5]

The pleas of would-be homesteaders were as usual countered by those of land speculators, whose interest had been piqued by news of the Barrens' beneficence. In 1794, Harry Toulmin and Thomas Hart Jr., son of the Transylvania Company proprietor, proposed to buy 250,000 acres for $25,000. A joint committee of the Kentucky House and Senate favored acceptance of the offer, but the bill was referred to the next session, where it was not reintroduced. That same session the attempt by Lexington merchant Andrew Holmes to take over ownership of a sizable portion of the district was defeated in the Senate. In 1795, a company composed equally of Philadelphia speculators and prominent Bluegrass political leaders, under the direction of Elisha J. Hall, audaciously bid for all the remaining unappropriated land south of the Green River. The Hall Company pledged to settle 500 families within five years and offered liberal terms on modest-sized tracts to current squatting occupants. As with the Toulmin and Hart proposal, the joint committee, operating on traditional notions about the quality of the Barrens and no doubt powerfully influenced by the eminence of the Hall Company's Kentucky investors, endorsed the immense sell-off. In mid-December of 1795 the Kentucky Senate voted accordingly. However, the House, whose members were annually answerable to both landed and landless voters, deemed it "impolitic for the waste and unappropriated lands south of Green River in this state to be disposed of to any company of individuals" and defeated the sell-out proposal.[6]

The legislature then turned around and enacted a settlement and preemption bill. Signed into law just a few days after the Hall Company's land grab had been foiled, the 1795 act "for the relief of settlers on the South side of Green River" confirmed the rights of squatters to the tracts they had illegally occupied. The law allowed actual settlers, who had cleared two acres and planted a crop of corn before January 1, 1796, to purchase up to 200 acres at the comparatively low price of thirty cents per acre. Following the not terribly successful model of the Virginia land law of 1779, the Green River homestead act provided for the appointment of three commissioners to adjudicate conflicting claims.[7]

Although the 1795 law explicitly warned that future squatting on vacant lands "with an expectation of being granted the preference of settlement" would not be tolerated, the Kentucky legislature soon reversed itself. In March 1797 an act "for encouraging and granting relief to settlers" extended the eligibility for claiming settlement rights to those occupying vacant lands south of the Green River on or before July 1, 1798. The statute also entitled occupants who had missed the first deadline to gain legal possession of between 100 and 200 acres at prices of sixty cents per acre for first-rate land to forty cents per acre for second-rate soil.[8]

In the wake of the homestead acts, emigration to the Southside surged. By 1800 the population of the Green River Country had passed 30,000. Nearly one of six white Kentuckians lived in what a few years before had been a largely uninhabited territory. At the same time, the settlement and preemption laws led to a dramatic rise in the number and proportion of landholders. Before the 1795 act, less than one in five heads of households in the Green River Country owned any land; by 1800, a majority, about five out of nine, heads of households had gained legal possession of real estate. In those counties south of the Green River that contained the now attractive Barrens, landowners accounted for an even higher proportion. In Logan, where two out of three householders owned land, the proportion of resident landowners topped all other Kentucky counties. Four of the top five counties on that list lay all or in part in the former Green River Country.[9]

What really distinguished the structure of landholding in the Green River Country was not so much the higher percentage of owners as the startlingly equal apportionment among them, especially in comparison with the Bluegrass. The homestead act of 1795 allowed actual settlers to preempt up to 200 acres, and most did precisely that. At the end of the eighteenth century, more than half, and in some counties close to three-quarters, of the landowners held exactly 200 acres. Just one in seven residents possessed more than that amount (see Table A.7).[10]

The vast plantations that lent the Bluegrass its grand and opulent character remained as yet foreign to the Green River Country. Only about one of five households south of the Green River owned slaves. And the minority who were slaveholders generally owned fewer blacks than their Bluegrass counterparts. Only one-quarter of slaveowners possessed as many as five slaves. Wholly dependent on family labor, the majority of Southside farmers lacked the manpower to clear and plant more than a fraction of their 200 acres and left their stock to forage across unfenced pastures. With timber so scarce in the Barrens, fencing was considered a waste of time and wood, as well as an unneighborly act. Horses and cattle raised on the open range compared unfavorably with stock nurtured on enclosed bluegrass pastures; for generations, a skinny Kentucky woman was described as being "as bony as the hips of a Green River cow." But pigs, which were the principal stock of Southsiders, were appraised by one Lexington merchant as "equal to any in the world." [11]

As in the Appalachian backcountry, fish and game supplemented corn and hogs in the diet of Green River homesteaders. "Full-time" hunters disappeared with the extinction of the buffalo in the 1790s, but bear, deer, and smaller game still abounded, and Southsiders continued to enjoy wild meat. Fishing also provided an important element in the subsistence of Green River folk and a pleasant escape for Southside men and boys. The Green, recalled one fisherman, "abounded more than any river I have ever known." [12]

Backcountry traditions also survived in the rough play and hard drinking of Green River men. "Squirrel barking" and "gander pulling," in which riders at full gallop attempted to yank the head off a live goose tied to a tree, remained favored sports. Southside men also enjoyed letting human blood run, judging from the eye-gouging, hair-pulling, nose-biting brawls in which they occasionally engaged. Alcohol, of course, animated such games. At harvest time, "the rule of this country," explained one Southsider, is "to turn into drinking and stay till late if not all night" at it. When the flow of alcohol temporarily ceased at this harvest, fighting erupted, and "blood soon began to run." But peace was restored when "there was more whiskey to be Drunk." [13]

Life, like play, was rough in the turn-of-the-century Green River Country. Material conditions progressed only slowly beyond the ascetic styles of frontier days. "The improvements are all in a slovenly manner having no appearance of neatness or taste," complained one resident. "In their manners and ways of living," concluded Thomas Joynes, the inhabitants of the Southside "approximate nearer to the aborigines of the country than any I have ever seen." The crowded, unfinished, "miserable log huts" that Green River folk called home shocked Joynes. "When bed-time came," wrote Joynes disgustedly, "men, women, children and dogs had to sleep in a filthy little room," crammed together on a bug-infested, "stinking, straw bed."[14]

This life especially tried Green River Country women, who, according to Joynes, were "*continually* employed" in cooking, dairying, and "*manufacturing all clothing*." Recalling the daily routines of a Green River woman, Susannah Johnson's partial catalog included "milking and making butter and cheese, washing, ironing, and bleaching." At the top of the list was making all of her family's clothing, for this "required incessant exertion." Susannah Johnson and other farm women did not buy their clothing in stores, but their labors were often sold. To supplement the meager income of her husband, an itinerant Methodist preacher and part-time farmer, Johnson took up sewing for neighbors and shopkeepers. Other Southside women marketed poultry, eggs, and vegetables, though the earnings from the sale of women's produce were frequently recorded in the names of their husbands and fathers.[15]

While men conducted their families' business, women stayed at home. With neighboring farmsteads often at a distance, women and men endured periods where contact was limited to immediate family members. As late as 1810, Joseph Thomas passed only two houses in a thirty-five mile stretch of Barrens along the road from the Cumberland Country of middle Tennessee. But as in other recently colonized rural areas, the gendered division of labor within Green River households intensified the seclusion of women. Although wives and daughters typically helped husbands and fathers in field work and stock raising, much of "women's work" sequestered them within the home and its immediate environs. On his 1802 tour of the Southside, François André Michaux visited a woman who had seen no one but her husband and children for eighteen months. During the time that Susannah Johnson's husband rode his preaching circuit, gathering news from across the country, she confessed she "saw or heard but little of the world."[16]

A good poor man's woman, Susannah Johnson endured the privations of Green River Country life. What else could she have done? Where else could she have gone? A poor man's wife had few options. After her first husband died, Mary Adair returned to her parents' household. But when her father's health declined, Adair knew his death would leave her "destitute of any other home." Because it was unthinkable for a woman to live alone and because she did not want to move in with a sibling, Adair "conclude[d] it best to alter my way of life" by accepting a marriage proposal. Once married, or in the case of widows remarried, women had even fewer choices. A few Southside women left their husbands and took up with another man in a different locale. But divorce records show the reverse was much more likely. Almost always it was women who filed for divorce after their husbands had abused and abandoned them. In any case, divorce was very rare, and though the courts sometimes granted women control of the family property, the circumstances of a divorced woman were unenviable. A pragmatic woman made the best of her situation.[17]

Without good women, there were no good poor men's countries. Like backcountry hunters, Green River men benefited from the gendered division of labor. Because "the labour of the woman . . . is much the hardest labour done," Charles Lewis of Livingston County allowed that Green River men "don[']t work more than one fourth of their time" and still had "more corn than they know what to do with as well as meat." Thomas Joynes concurred. The Green River Country, averred Joynes, was "well suited for lazy men," for they "are not generally employed in labor more than one-fourth of their time." Even quarter-time taxed the work limits of Southsiders, who, Joynes joked, dreamed of an Edenic "land that will produce loaves of bread already baked, and hams of bacon already boiled."[18]

It was no paradise for men (and much less for women), but thanks to charitable homesteading acts, the colonization of the Green River Country spread 200-acre farms across the landscape. Although the land was not the best, it yielded families a ready competence. As one resident summarized, the Southside "is not a country that a man can ever calculate on getting rich from farming," but, he added, "this country is well calculated for a man who has but a small property and a large family who he wishes to procure lands for and to have it in his power to procure with a tolerable degree of ease bread & meat for them."[19]

II

Green River homesteaders knew that countries such as theirs had an inauspicious history. Many Southsiders had fled in debt and disappointment from lands east of the Appalachians after speculators gained control over land, expelled squatters, and raised the price beyond poor men's means. Some had suffered several years of tenancy in the Bluegrass, frustrated by the stranglehold that great landlords and absentee speculators held over that rich man's region. When the Kentucky legislature opened the Green River Country to actual settlers, homesteaders won an important victory, but the contest over land and political economy was by no means settled.

The passage of the Green River settlement act of 1795 had certainly not squelched the desire of engrossers to extend their land empires in the region. The encouragement the law gave to homesteaders abetted speculators as well. Indeed, Samuel Hopkins, the agent for the Transylvania Company, boasted that he had played a crucial behind-the-scenes role in the enactment of the 1795 statute. After all, nothing inflated the value of the company's consolation grant more than increasing settlement around it. Immediately following the enactment of the homestead law, the company, which had done little to promote the peopling of its 200,000 acres for the previous fifteen years, appointed a surveyor "to enable us to divide Green River lands speedily."[20]

The price of Green River lands tempted monied men. At a time when the United States charged two dollars per acre for considerably less safe lands north of the Ohio River, the Kentucky legislature's homestead price seemed a superior bargain to speculators. Engrossers evaded the 200-acre-per-homesteader limit, as an earlier generation had exceeded the 1,400-acre ceiling set by Virginia in 1779. To profit from Southside acreage, speculators still had to clear their lands of competing claimants and parcel their tracts for resale. Once seated, occupants were not easily removed. Employed by a wealthy easterner to eject squatters, Robert Triplett found "the occupants refused to surrender the land." Nor, wrote a frustrated Triplett, would they acknowledge any tenancy. Hamstrung by occupying-claimant statutes that made ejection costly, Triplett sought to convince occupants to purchase lands for a reasonable price. Unfortunately, prospective buyers almost always required credit and defaulted enough to make credit risky. In case conciliation failed, Triplett carried a dirk for protection from menacing occupants.[21]

In their confrontations with speculators, Southside homesteaders discovered the strength in unanimity. No man, it was said, could be elected to the legislature from the Green River Country who did not vow to save the homesteaders' "little all" from falling "prey to . . . mercenary speculators." Voting as a bloc and log rolling for additional support, the "Green River Band," as antagonists tagged Southside representatives, secured passage of a 1798 act which allowed homesteaders to pay for their land in four equal, annual installments. Two years later, the legislature extended the time of payments to twelve years. Periodically, the Kentucky House and Senate passed absolutely, final deadlines, but each time the "Green River

Band" united to prolong the extensions. Year after year, the state restructured the debt of its Southside citizenry. In 1823, a quarter century after the debts were supposed to have been retired, the amount due the state for head-right claims to Green River lands had instead ballooned to $33,000.[22]

For the Green River Band, debt relief skirmishes galvanized a multifront challenge to the domination that Bluegrass elites exercised over the government of Kentucky. Led by Felix Grundy, Green River legislators fought for judicial reform, a campaign which culminated in the establishment of circuit courts in 1802. Invigorated by their success in postponing land debts and decentralizing the court system, Grundy and his followers broadened their attack against Bluegrass hegemony. In 1804 Grundy rallied his supporters to oppose the reelection of John Brown, one of the wealthiest Bluegrass lawyer-planters, to the United States Senate. Although Henry Clay's skilled management of Bluegrass forces denied victory to Grundy's candidate, the Green River Band served notice of their growing strength by unseating Brown.[23]

Simultaneous with the battle over the senatorial election, Grundy and his backers declared war on a centerpiece of the Bluegrass System. During the 1802 session, while Grundy and his followers had diverted their attention to the circuit court bill, a petition from Lexington's leading merchants, seeking a corporate charter for an insurance business, had slipped through the legislature and into law. Tucked away in the bill were two little-noticed, but carefully styled, clauses permitting the corporation to tender paper and charge interest on loans. When Grundy learned of the "secret" privileges conferred upon the Kentucky Insurance Company, he made revocation of the charter the focus of his 1803 reelection campaign. Through the summer, Grundy, now a resident of Washington County, well north of the Green River, toured the Southside thundering against the latest aristocratic trickery. Returned to the Kentucky General Assembly, Grundy moved from a defense of homesteaders to an offensive against the Lexington corporation. Over the next three sessions, he worked to repeal the loopholes that permitted the insurance concern to loan money at interest—to wipe out what for Grundy signified Bluegrass privilege.[24]

Privately, Clay, a stockholder in the company, lambasted the "truly astonishing" ignorance of those who opposed the legitimate profits of the Bluegrass's bank; on the assembly floor, Clay was more statesmanlike, patiently outlining the ways in which the bank facilitated commerce in Lexington and across Kentucky. In defending the insurance company, he developed his vision of government "encouragement" of private enterprise to promote commercial prosperity. Anticipating also the Marshall court's rulings on the inviolability of corporate charters, Clay argued that any amendment prohibiting or restricting the insurance company's banking privileges contradicted the contract clause in the state and federal constitutions.[25]

Grundy countered with a different view of constitutionality and political economy. He contended that because the insurance corporation's charter was obtained fraudulently it was unconstitutional. Where Clay proclaimed the universal benefits of the bank's services, Grundy contended that the ninety-day loans extended by the Kentucky Insurance Company hardly satisfied the longer terms required by ordinary farmers. Instead of prizing the work of honest yeoman, the issuing of paper money rewarded speculation, enabling a privileged few "to become affluent without *labour*." Grundy blasted the "exclusive privilege" granted to the Lexington bank for "creat[ing] a distinction among our citizens and . . . promot[ing] the spirit of aristocracy, which is already too prevalent." Left unchecked, the bank threatened to "prostrate" the people to the speculations of Bluegrass gentry.[26]

The survival of the Kentucky Insurance Company depended not so much on floor debate as on back-room deals, however. Tactically, Clay outmaneuvered Grundy again and again. Each time Grundy seemed on the verge of victory, Clay persuaded enough antibank men to switch sides to save the fledgling institution. Hoping to demonstrate the universal benefits of the bank to wavering representatives, Clay pushed the Kentucky Insurance Company's promise to rescue farmers facing dispossession for failure to pay federal land taxes. In 1804, after much behind-the-scenes bargaining, Clay split the Green River Band by gaining the votes of the representatives from Henderson and Muhlenberg counties and staved off repeal by one vote. Recovering from this narrow setback, Grundy introduced a bill to discourage speculative lending practices by holding all stockholders liable for notes issued by the insurance company. Recognition of the overwhelming sentiment for some regulation convinced the friends of the bank to drop constitutional objections and accept a compromise reform bill that made the bank's officers personally accountable for any overissue of paper. But this regulation, signed into law in December 1804, lacked provisions for enforcement, minimizing its consequences.[27]

The possibility for more effective reforms, if not outright repeal, grew dramatically the following year. In the August 1805 election, the opponents of the bank won an apparently decisive victory, registering a net gain of fourteen seats in the Kentucky House. The opponents of the bank even made inroads in the Inner Bluegrass, with Jessamine now in the repeal column and Woodford and Scott Counties' representatives divided. To the dismay of Clay and other insurance company stockholders, one of Fayette County's three legislators defected to the opposition. The election of a Green River man, John Adair, to the United States Senate over the Bluegrass candidate seemingly foreshadowed the results of the bank battle. The repeal bill passed both houses by substantial margins. Vetoed by Governor Christopher Greenup, who cited Clay's constitutional reservations, the objection was easily overridden in the Grundy-led assembly.

With the Kentucky Senate poised to do the same, the bank's defenders desperately sought to avoid abolition. Bluegrass merchants shrewdly petitioned for the establishment of a branch of the Bank of the United States in Lexington, thinking that given a choice the opponents would prefer the locally controlled Kentucky Insurance Company. As it happened, what derailed the opponents was less the threat of the Bank of the United States than the introduction by Clay of a bill to force payment of the Green River land debt. Clay's resolution split the Southside faction from its coalition partners. Forced to choose between bank or land, the Green River Band reluctantly abandoned its long-time allies at the moment when the hegemony of the Bluegrass barons was most precarious. Once more, the Kentucky Insurance Company escaped with its banking privileges intact.[28]

But the Lexington firm's exclusive possession of that right, like the Bluegrass elite's control of the state's government, neared its end. Paradoxically the 1806 elections returned even stronger antibank majorities in both houses; yet the subsequent legislative session witnessed a consensus between Bluegrass and Green River representatives to expand, not erase, the banking system. The legislative voices that had railed against the antirepublican principles of banking were soon silenced and forgotten, at least for a time. After years of resisting schemes to entice him out of the statehouse, if not out of the state altogether, Felix Grundy accepted an appointment to the circuit court of appeals in December of 1806. Although he was promoted to chief justice just four months later, the low salary, which he had been so instrumental in maintaining, did not support Grundy and his growing family in the style to which he aspired. In 1807, he resigned from the Kentucky bench and moved to Tennessee.[29]

Even before he had left the Kentucky assembly, the tide of legislative sentiment had turned against Grundy's rejection of loaning institutions and paper money. At the 1806 session, the opposition shifted away from mistrust of banks in general to a more easily resolved jealousy of the Kentucky Insurance Company's monopoly. When Henry Clay's kinsman,

Green Clay, one of the largest landowners in the Bluegrass, introduced a bill to erect at Frankfort a new bank, whose capital was to be equally divided between the state and private investors, a resolution of the long conflict between Bluegrass and Southside appeared in reach. Grundy himself supported the measure. In the vote on Green Clay's proposal, tied in classic log-rolling practice to a plan to appropriate the Green River debt to fund the state's portion of the stock offering, Southside legislators overwhelmingly approved the chartering of the Bank of Kentucky. A little more than a year later, the legislature established a branch of the Bank of Kentucky in Russellville, the county seat of Logan County, cementing the foundations of banking in the Barrens. And so after years of thundering against paper aristocrats, Grundy and his followers accommodated to the spread of banks.[30]

The reversal of the Green River Band invited skepticism about their commitment to the hard money principles they had so fervently championed. As far as Henry Clay and his Bluegrass cohorts were concerned, the turnaround on banks and the unseemly bartering of votes showed their opponents lacked republican principles, lacked virtue. Their attacks on the Kentucky Insurance Company, like previous challenges to the constitution, the court system, slavery, and land distribution, were the products of envy. And for playing to the people's prejudices against the Bluegrass System, Grundy's opponents deemed him an "unprincipled demagogue."[31]

Grundy and his band were certainly not the small farmers with whom they identified themselves politically. Grundy's origins were humble, but his ambitions were not. Educated in the Lexington office of George Nicholas, the chief architect of Kentucky's first constitution, Grundy carried an impressive legal pedigree. Like so many other enterprising young lawyers who found breaking into the overcrowded Lexington legal market nearly impossible, he set off in 1795 to make his fame and fortune in the Outer Bluegrass, where he had grown up, and in the Southside, where the demand for attorneys to handle conflicting land claims was expanding fastest. Though his income never approached the level of Henry Clay and other top-echelon Lexington lawyers, Grundy accumulated sizable holdings of land and slaves, the possession of which distinguished him from the 200-acre Southside homesteader. Other men elected to the state legislature from the counties south of the Green River, like those who represented the Bluegrass districts, also tended to own more land and more slaves than their constituents.[32]

At the turn of the century, Southsiders still imbibed much of their political culture from the Bluegrass and from its colonial antecedents. That political culture assumed proper deference to "the better sort." The people were expected to "freely vote for him who merits most." Those who voted in national elections, and few did, voted for congressional candidates who swore themselves faithful Republicans. That oath entailed less a positive affirmation than a categorical denial of hated Federalists. By virtue of his persecution by despised Federalists, Matthew Lyon, an émigré from Vermont, entered Livingston County a Republican hero. That Lyon's devotion to political principle ran shallow mattered little to his southwestern Kentucky constituents. That Lyon could, in the words of Micah Taul, a contemporary Green River political aspirant, "drink Grog all the day long without getting drunk" and "tell pretty good rough anecdotes" qualified him as "altogether . . . a good Electioneer." On the state level, the old campaign rules also held sway. "It would have been an *Insuperable Objection* to a candidate for office," commented Taul, "if he did not drink" and distribute alcohol and other treats liberally.[33]

To be sure, the political culture was evolving. Across the United States, the colonial ideal in which gentry candidates styled themselves as wise fathers was giving way to a new persona in which office seekers ran as "friends of the people." In the Southside of Kentucky, where few candidates had the bearing and the wealth to inspire awe and deference, the shift was especially pronounced. Political aspirants ritually professed their friendship with plain farmers. Even so, few members of the Green River Band were plain farmers. The governing oligarchy opened to allow in rising talents like Felix Grundy, but government in the Green River Country retained its gentry slant.[34]

The possession of extra land and added hands distanced the elected from their electors. When the Bank of Kentucky promised to extend its services to the Southside, the members of the Green River Band found the temptation to get in on the banking bonanza irresistible. Fear of the corruptions of banks yielded to the desire to share fully in the commercial boom that loans and notes helped to perpetuate. After the War of 1812, the Southside delegation campaigned for a banking proliferation. To break the domination of the Bank of Kentucky by Bluegrass interests and spread the benefits of banking throughout the state, the Green River Band combined in 1818 with other aspiring outsiders to charter forty-six independent banks. The counties south of the Green River received eleven of the shakily capitalized financial institutions, significantly one more than was chartered in the Bluegrass.[35]

Green River representatives recognized that banks alone could not make the Southside the commercial equal of the Bluegrass; the Green River Country needed an improved transportation infrastructure. Instead of interfering with the Bluegrass System's program of internal improvements, Southside legislators sought to equalize the government's entitlements. When the state legislature debated making internal improvements on the Kentucky River, which flowed through the Bluegrass, the Green River Band held up approval until an equal amount was appropriated for improving the navigability of the Green. In pressing the case for a fair share of budgetary allocations and banking privileges, the Green River faction reaffirmed its conversion to Henry Clay's political economy.[36]

III

The rapprochement between Bluegrass and Green River Country, however, had its limits outside the statehouse. Clay recognized that his personal popularity was "confined to the region of Lexington, or at the farthest to the North Side of the Kentucky River." The extension of Clay's Bluegrass System disturbed the Southside's plain folk, in that privatization of property endangered their rights in the woods and publicly funded internal improvements necessitated higher taxes, which cash-poor homesteaders did not favor. Banks enriched speculators and corrupted society, or so plain folk assumed.[37]

By their cold response to the Russellville branch of the Bank of Kentucky, Green River farmers demonstrated their misgivings about the expansion of the Bluegrass System. Efforts to educate the public to the riches that the bank would bring to the region had "little effect on my fellow citizens," conceded a propagandist for the Russellville branch. To ease the misgivings of homesteaders and stimulate flagging business, the directors of the Russellville branch pledged to give "preference in discounts" to borrowers who intended to apply the loan to land payments. But against the bank's advertising campaign stood folk knowledge censuring usury and enjoining debt. "The man whom necessity urges to borrow," went the popular couplet, "is drag'd to a business which dips him in sorrow." Worried about finding money to pay off taxes and land debts, Southside farmers looked upon the new bank as yet another threat to their simple agrarianism. Except for a disappointing number of loans used by settlers to pay the installments on land debts, the Russellville branch generated little business in its early years.[38]

Yet the reticence of plain folk did not stem the transformation of the Green River Country. As Table A.8 details, an increasing number and proportion of landowners reached the higher brackets of real estate holdings. In December 1800, a new act for further "settling and improving the vacant lands of this Commonwealth" permitted free persons above eighteen years of age to preempt up to 400 acres. Green River homesteaders who had claimed under the old limits were allowed to appropriate an additional 200 acres. Old and new settlers jumped at the chance to add to their domains.[39]

The raising of preemption limits presaged the emergence of Bluegrass-like patterns of landownership in the Green River Country. To be sure, the proportion of landowners remained above the levels characteristic of the Bluegrass. In the Barrens, the percentage of landowners declined only slightly from turn-of-the-century heights. Despite massive migration and seemingly endless conflicts over land titles, about three in five households in Logan and Barren Counties were still headed by landowners in 1825. Yet while the overall percentage of landowners in the Green River Country remained steady, the distribution of land among those owners veered away from the egalitarian pattern that had stamped the young Southside a good poor man's country. At the time of its creation in 1792, Logan County boasted only two residents owning more than 1,000 acres, and they just barely topped that amount. Eight years later, only thirteen householders had surpassed the thousand-acre threshold. By 1810, seventy-seven residents of Logan, better than one in ten landowners, held over 1,000 acres; six of these had acquired estates of over 10,000 acres.

During the first decades of the nineteenth century, engrossers profited handsomely from their speculations. Those who bought up tracts at the state's price sold them at a hefty markup. In 1807, Ninian Edwards, for many years Logan County's representative, asked between two and three dollars per acre for unimproved prairie that carried a homestead price less than a tenth that amount. Speculators who held onto their lands scored even bigger coups, particularly in the Barrens where land prices soared. In 1817, Logan and Christian County sellers sought up to eight to ten dollars per acre for barely improved tracts.[40]

In Kentucky, where speculators went, slaveholders and slaves followed. In Logan County, the percentage of slaveowners doubled during the first quarter of the nineteenth century. By 1825, better than two out of five householders had acquired at least one slave, a proportion as high as in some Inner Bluegrass counties. Logan's neighboring counties did not match its percentages, but they experienced substantial broadening of the slaveholding population as well (see Table A.9). During the same years, the number of slaves in the Green River Country was increasing much

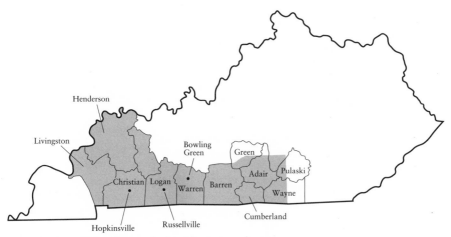

The Green River Country in the early nineteenth century.

faster than the region's white population. After an eightfold increase in the first twenty years of the nineteenth century, slaves accounted for more than one in five inhabitants of the Green River Country.[41]

Like their Bluegrass brethren, Green River slaveholders denied avaricious motives. Theirs, they reassured themselves, was a benevolent mastery. In his diary, Warner L. Underwood, one of the largest of Southside slaveholders, denied ever having made money from his slaves. All profits, he assured himself, had been expended on keeping up those too old or too young to labor. "I have supported my negroes and not they me," he concluded his private defense. Writing his brother in slaveless Ohio, Charles W. Short, a doctor and land speculator in Christian County, repeated the familiar justifications of Bluegrass paternalists. "As far as the use of negroes," Short explained, "a person who feeds, clothes, and treats them well should, surely, require their labour from them without having himself much disturbed on the score of feeling." In a twist on that standard rationale, one of Short's Christian County neighbors, Robert Henry, blamed his wife for making slaveownership necessary. Slaves, observed Henry, eased the labors of women and "exempt[ed] the lady of the House from that wretched system of suspicion & *espionage* which are the greatest curses of housekeeping." For his wife, then, he gave up the dream of moving to Illinois. "The prospect of living in a free state, however fascinating it may look upon paper," he judged, "too utopian . . . for my notions & for those of my family." Dropping paternalistic pretense, Short acknowledged that slavery had its rewards for masters as well as mistresses. If one were determined to cultivate the soil, "you might as well make money by it as not." As speculation drove up the price of land, making money became a greater imperative, and slaves, well-managed, made owners money.[42]

Some Green River slaveholders attempted to duplicate the profitable strategies of Bluegrass planters by investing heavily in pedigreed livestock. Early in the nineteenth century, Southside breeders began to import Bluegrass-raised stallions to stand in the Green River Country. The merino sheep craze also spread to the Barrens.[43]

For most Southside slaveholders, not stock but tobacco made their investment in human property pay off. The Green River Country generally lacked the first-rate land required to raise hemp as successfully as in the Bluegrass, but the Southside's soil and climate were ideally suited for the cultivation of tobacco. Especially in the Barrens did tobacco and its planters fare well. With the Mississippi opened, Southside planters exploited their financial opportunity. Green River growers pioneered the development of new strains of Burley leaf, which met an enthusiastic response in foreign markets. After the War of 1812, superior quality Burley from the Southside sold for three times the price of Bluegrass-grown leaf. Near Hopkinsville, the seat of Christian County and the center of the tobacco region, Charles Short reported with a mixture of awe and disdain that some planters cleared five to ten thousand dollars per year from the sale of the "dirty article." High tobacco prices also inflated the worth of Green River land, providing an added bonanza for planter-speculators. In December 1818, Short bragged that his acreage had doubled in value in just two years.[44]

The tobacco boom spurred the progress of a diversified economy in the Green River Country, including the growth of commercial centers. In the 1790s, the villages of the Green River Country had been towns in name only, generally little more than places in which the county court assembled a couple of days each month. Permanent population and establishments were rare, and with the volume of market exchange so low, few merchants were inclined to set up fixed stores. Instead they packed up a wagon of goods or several horses and peddled their way across the sparsely peopled countryside, stopping in town to trade wares on county court days. In 1800 the town of Henderson, situated at the mouth of the Green River, claimed just 205 inhabitants. Nonetheless, the Transylvania Company's last best hope for speculative consolation dwarfed the tiny villages upriver. And because of Henderson's advantageous location, the proprietors' agent, Samuel Hopkins, confidently forecast that the town would soon achieve its "commercial Manhood" as the entrepot of all trade entering and exiting the region's principal artery.[45]

Hopkins accurately predicted the region's economic "masculinization," but his optimism about Henderson's advance was misplaced. Despite the rising importance of the Mississippi trade, the progress of the town of Henderson disappointed its proprietors. By 1810 the town's population had slipped to 159. At the same time, upriver communities in the heart of the tobacco-growing Barrens enlarged substantially. Glasgow, Bowling Green, Hopkinsville, and, most of all, Russellville emerged as handsome villages, boasting sizable mercantile concerns and a wide range of mechanics. So great was Russellville's economic growth that its mercantile community fancied the town "the Lexington of the Green River."[46]

Boosterism aside, neither Russellville nor any of the other Green River villages posed a threat to Lexington's position as the "Philadelphia of the West." Despite the rapid increase in town dwellers, the population of the Green River Country remained overwhelmingly rural through the nineteenth (and much of the twentieth) century. In 1820 less than 5 percent of the Southside population resided in towns. More than 90 percent still reported agriculture as their primary vocation. Less than 1 percent reported commerce as their principal occupation.[47]

The numbers do not tell the impact of the mercantile one percent, however. In the Southside, merchants initially adapted their trade to the rules of the countryside, to the barter arrangements that characterized exchange among neighboring households. Rule number one, explained Charles Short of Hopkinsville, was that "nothing is done in this country without credit." Short might have added that almost nothing was done in cash. Accordingly, merchants who hoped to do any business, with flourishing tobacco planters or with poorer corn and hog raisers, sold their commodities on loose terms—loose, not only in the time stipulated for making payment but also, as in neighborhood exchange, vague as to the type of payment.[48]

The loose terms appeared in many respects to conform with the principles of rough reciprocity governing neighborhood exchange, but the resemblance was deceptive. Country merchants did what was necessary to facilitate trade with cash-poor farmers, but that did not keep them from finally imposing the rules of the market on all manner of exchanges. In the early years of the nineteenth century, the Southside merchants and other tradesmen advertised their willingness to exchange their inventory for cash, skins, or farm produce. As in the Bluegrass, nearly every adver-

tisement specified that preference in price would be given to those purchasing with specie or bank notes. Such favoritism was natural, given that
the creditors of country merchants preferred specie and that Green River
farmers otherwise had no incentive to settle their accounts promptly.[49]

What was unnatural, or at least antithetical to the principles of reciprocity, was the extent to which merchants pressed their preferences on
their customers. At a time when neighborhood convention proscribed the
calculation of any interest and law forbade rates above 6 percent, Green
River traders extracted usurious premiums for credit and barter purchases.
Newspapers, the herald of the outside world, led the way in making
exorbitant demands on debtors. In 1809, subscribers to the Russellville
Farmer's Friend paid two dollars in advance or two dollars and fifty cents
at the end of the year, a 25 percent interest rate that made the paper no
friend to poor farmers. Ten years later, the Russellville *Weekly Messenger*
charged the same two dollar basic subscription, but upped the payment to
three dollars for those waiting just three months to settle their accounts.[50]

The steep difference between the cash price and the trade price and
exorbitant rates of interest handicapped those Southside farmers who
preferred to conduct their commercial business according to the customs
of neighborhood exchange. More and more, those farmers found their
credit and barter options foreclosed. Already before the War of 1812, several merchants advertised that their commodities were available for "cash
and notes in hand only" (see Table A.10). While some merchants continued to accommodate themselves to the older realities of Southside life,
an increasing number of Green River Country tradesmen insisted that
their customers adjust to the hard rules of commercial exchange. Life in
the Green River Country was indeed becoming more like life in the Bluegrass.[51]

THE "BLUEING" OF THE GREEN RIVER COUNTRY altered the character of the Southside. What had been one of Kentucky's best hunting
grounds was fast becoming a facsimile of the Bluegrass. What had once
been Kentucky's best poor man's country was by the second decade of
the nineteenth century a good land for those with slaves and capital to
grow rich marketing tobacco. Prosperous plantations and bustling villages
made the Barrens a region where Henry Clay would have felt at home.

The transformation of the Green River Country required the enlargement of the Bluegrass System. The challenge mounted by the Green River
Band to that system withered after 1806. The establishment of the Bank
of Kentucky marked a new era in the geographic alignment of the state's

political factions. Save the issue of retiring the Green River land debt, the legislative spokesmen of the Green River Country typically voted with the representatives of the Bluegrass counties in passing laws and appropriating funds to improve the commercial infrastructure of Kentucky. The ideological protest raised by Felix Grundy to the antirepublican and aristocratic tendencies of the Bluegrass System was temporarily silenced. In the decade after 1806, Green River legislators banded not to overthrow the Bluegrass System but to secure a fair share of its spoils for themselves and their constituents.

Not all Southsiders, or Kentuckians in general, converted as easily as Green River politicians to the platform of more banks and improved transportation. For many, the spread of the Bluegrass System appeared more daunting. Speculation and slavery, after all, undermined the foundations of a good poor man's country. Seeking a better way, some men and even more women invested their hopes in the next world.

EIGHT *Worlds Away*

"HOW WE LIVE IN THIS WORLD and what Chance we have in the next we know Not," wrote Daniel Boone to his sister-in-law in 1816. As he was then in his eighties, a widower of three years, Boone's thoughts naturally drifted from this world to the next. Though born a Quaker, as an adult Boone had occasionally identified himself as a Presbyterian. Yet he never joined any church, and he espoused a simple, ecumenical creed: "All the relegan I have [is] to Love and fear god, beleve in Jeses Christ, Do all the good to my Nighbour and my Self that I Can, and Do as Little harm as I Can help, and trust on god[']s marcy for the Rest." The rest—his chances in the next world—did not trouble Boone, for "god never made a man of my prisipel to be Lost."[1]

Three decades later, an aging Henry Clay also contemplated his after-life, along with his political future. Though he was raised by Baptists, Clay, like Boone, belonged to no church for most of his adult life. Indeed, his well-chronicled fondness for ostentatious display and bluffsmanship hardly conformed with the Baptist ideals of simplicity and humility. In 1844, as a Whig presidential candidate, Clay found himself under attack for his lack of church membership and his love of gaming. Endeavoring to quiet the concerns of an increasingly evangelical electorate, he expressed hope that he might "yet be inspired with that confidence in the enjoyment of the blessings, in another state of existence, which [Christianity] promises." His prayers were not answered in the election of 1844: his highest worldly aspiration remained out of reach. In 1847, though, the man who would not be president found the faith that "disarms death of all its terrors." In his seventieth year, he became a member of the Episcopal church in Lexington.[2]

To biographers, the religious views of Boone and Clay usually merit only a few pages. While millions of their contemporaries came to focus on the next world, Boone and Clay kept their attentions very much on this one. Neither man subscribed to the evangelical enthusiasm that transformed the western country at the beginning of the nineteenth century. Indeed, evangelicalism constructed a world apart from those of Boone and Clay. For as long as he could, Clay tried to ignore evangelicals. In 1801 what came to be called the Great Revival was in full swing. At Cane Ridge, just fifteen miles northeast of Clay's Lexington home, the volcanic eruption of enthusiasm created a spectacle that was impossible to overlook. Yet Clay said nothing—or at least never mentioned Cane Ridge or the Great Revival in any of his public writings or extant private correspondence.

In this case, it did not matter what Clay said or did not say. News of the "miraculous" happenings at Cane Ridge spread rapidly and sparked a religious revival across the Ohio Valley and the southeastern United States. Cane Ridge quickly became synonymous with the evangelical persuasion that dominated American Protestantism in the nineteenth century. "Both for what it symbolized and for the effects that flowed from it," historian Paul Conkin nominated the Cane Ridge meeting as "the most important religious gathering in all of American history."[3]

The exuberant piety displayed at Cane Ridge reshaped the history of the United States, but within Kentucky, the meeting was as much a culmination as a beginning. The meeting on the grounds of the Cane Ridge Presbyterian Church, near the small Bluegrass town of Paris, capped several years of mounting religious enthusiasm, the origins of which were in the Green River Country. The diffusion of revivalism from the Southside to the center of Kentucky thus countered the expansion of the Bluegrass System: Cane Ridge, from this perspective, marked the "greening" of the Bluegrass.

Evangelical ways defied the cultural hegemony, if not the political economy, of the Bluegrass System. The selfless spirit of evangelicalism starkly contrasted with the gentry's self-assertive spirit of gain. The warm embrace of evangelical communities offered an alternative to the legal injustices, the impersonal exchanges, and the unequal relations of the Bluegrass System. For the least powerful in general and for slaves in particular, evangelicalism provided a refuge from the world of Henry Clay.

It was a world away from Daniel Boone's as well. Evangelicalism rebuked rough manhood, substituting a transcendent sentimentality for backcountry sensuality. A sanctuary from patriarchal domination, the company of evangelicals exhilarated rural women.

Evangelical excitement transformed Kentucky, but it vanquished neither backcountry toughness nor the Bluegrass System. While evangelicals easily overcame the opposition of staid Presbyterians, the confrontation with rougher men ended in a draw. And the challenge to the Bluegrass System largely dissolved once evangelicals, like others before them, compromised on the question of slavery.

I

The Green River Country in the 1790s was an unlikely birthplace for the Great Revival. The rush of homesteaders into the region in the middle of the decade made the Southside less a haven for "hunters and horse thieves," but the roughness of pioneer settlement remained a fact of everyday life. Economically and culturally, the Green River Country was still backcountry: in the 1790s, it was certainly not God's country. "A stupid & ignorant people" greeted Presbyterian minister John Rankin when he arrived in southwestern Kentucky in 1796. Not "a single individual" around the Gasper River Church in Logan County "seemed to have any light or knowledge of living religion, or any desire for it." Instead, remembered Logan County's Peter Cartwright, "Sunday was a day set apart for hunting, fishing, horse-racing, card-playing, balls, dances, and all kinds of jollity and mirth."[4]

Across the Kentucky countryside, clergymen bemoaned the sunken state of religious affairs. Protestant ministers, who disagreed vigorously with one another's theological constructions and ecclesiastical credentials, agreed that indifference, infidelity, and anticlericalism prevailed among Kentuckians. "Of all the denominations," summarized Baptist preacher David Barrow in 1795, "the Deists, Nothingarians and anythingarians are the most numerous."[5]

Clergymen fixed on Barrow's first and second category. Their epistles assailed the rampant rationalism and materialism of the 1790s. Such jeremiads were by no means limited to the western country. In New England, both Calvinist clergy and Federalist elites recoiled from the infectious spread of anti-Christian Jeffersonian-Jacobinism. In Kentucky, though, an embattled clergy stood alone against the "deism" and "nothingarianism" of the state's Jeffersonian gentry. Kentucky's 1792 constitution had excluded practicing ministers from serving as legislators, and the following year the legislature had dispensed with the services of a chaplain. According to ministers, these moves left the state government in the hands of infidels. The ruling Bluegrass gentry in particular had succumbed to Paineite "universalism."[6]

Beyond affluent Bluegrass circles, "anythingarians" far outnumbered universalists and atheists. The majority of Kentuckians were hardly "rationalists" or unbelievers. To the contrary, most accepted that invisible forces immediately shaped human destiny. This was especially true for people who lived in or near the woods, for the "wilderness" was still considered a dark and mysterious place. To master the mysteries of the forest, hunters subscribed to an array of superstitions. Some of this magic lore derived from neighboring Indians, but the mysticism of backcountry people was not born on the American frontier. Animistic beliefs, as students of popular religiosity have detailed, had deep roots in the European past. On both sides of the Atlantic and the Appalachians, animism and Christianity blended into an "anythingarianism" that incorporated Christian doctrines and rituals with alternative forms of supernaturalism. "The belief in ghosts, wizards, and witches prevailed to a considerable extent," recalled James Ireland of the early decades of settlement. He also remembered that when anything went wrong—when "any of the stock died or was afflicted in a peculiar manner, . . . or if a child came into the world deformed, hair-lipped[,] or any peculiarities about it," it was assumed to be the result of bewitchment. In Ireland's neighborhood, as was often true elsewhere, blame fell on "an old decrepit woman."[7]

If not strictly unchristian, anythingarians were nonetheless unchurched. There was no established church in the post-Revolutionary West, and no denominations could keep pace with Kentucky's rapidly growing population. Many of the first pioneers had Presbyterian connections, and a Presbyterian minister, David Rice, organized the first church in Kentucky. But a disillusioned Rice "found scarcely one man and but few women who supported a credible profession of religion." Rice's efforts and that of other pioneering Presbyterian ministers made a very limited impact. Methodist circuit riders and Baptist pastors also failed to bring many Kentuckians into their churches. As the state's population nearly tripled between 1790 and 1800, the proportion of Baptists declined from about one in twenty to one in forty. By the late 1790s, only about 5 to 10 percent of Kentuckians belonged to a Christian church.[8]

But the situation was changing south of the Green River, and the chief catalyst was James McGready, a Presbyterian minister recently relocated from Orange County, North Carolina. In 1796 Rev. McGready took over the Gasper River, Muddy River, and Red River Presbyterian churches in Logan County, Kentucky. McGready was an experienced revivalist, having sparked a religious awakening in North Carolina. His fiery sermons, evoking the terrors of hell awaiting unregenerate sinners, stirred the Piedmont's plain folk from their Sunday slumber. At the same time, McGready's pointed comments about the fate of immoral gentlemen in the next world generated a backlash. After his church was vandalized and his life threatened, McGready accepted a call from former parishioners who had relocated in the western country.[9]

Migration to Logan County in the Barrens of Kentucky did not diminish McGready's determination to shake up the "universal deadness and stupidity" of his parishioners, no matter whom he offended. In the Green River Country, he once more worked his homiletic magic. In May 1797, "a very considerable number" of congregants at Gasper River "awakened to a deep and solemn sense of their sin and danger." That summer, the Muddy River and Red River churches also witnessed a rousing of religious sentiments. Things quieted again during the fall and winter, but enthusiasm reappeared at Gasper River in the summer of 1798, then spread to the other Presbyterian congregations in Logan County. The ebb and flow of excitement alternated over the next two years, until fervor erupted in June 1800.[10]

That month between four and five hundred people gathered at Red River for three days and nights of exhortation. This was a stunningly large assembly; the population of nearby Russellville, the so-called "Lexington of the Green River," was only 117. The meeting was remarkable too for its interdenominational character; in the spirit of unity, McGready invited Baptist farmer-preachers and Methodist itinerant circuit riders to join in what was essentially a Presbyterian communion service. Together the clergymen focused the attention of the crowd on their fate in the next world. And then, with collective anxieties at a fevered pitch, an amazing catharsis swept across the multitude. It began, remembered the Reverend John Rankin, when "an alarming cry burst from the midst of the deepest silence." What happened next amazed Rankin, who had taken over from McGready as pastor at Gasper River: "some were thrown into wonderful & strange contortions of features, body & limbs frightful to the beholder[;] others had singular gestures with words and actions quite inconsistent with presbyterial order."[11]

A few weeks later, a second, even larger, gathering convened at Rankin's Gasper River Church. Authorities from the Synod of Kentucky rushed to Logan County to ascertain the true nature of the "strange operations which had transpired at the previous meeting." So also came hundreds of excited curiosity seekers, many from as far away as a hundred miles. For three days, wagons filled the rising ground to the west and south of the Gaspar River log church. By Sunday, the third day of the gathering, the anticipation of the crowd peaked. That evening, large numbers of repentant sinners began to tremble and shake, to shout and groan, and then to fall prostrate on the earth.[12]

News of the Green River Country meetings ignited an unprecedented upsurge in religious feeling. Beginning in the summer of 1800 and continuing the next year, the revival spread across the Green River Country and into the Bluegrass, as well as into neighboring Tennessee. One observer likened the movement to a "fire that has been long confined—bursting all its barriers and spreading with a rapidity that is indescribable." The blaze raged especially among Baptists. In the Green River Country, Baptist churches doubled their membership. In the twelve months *preceding* the Cane Ridge camp meeting, Baptist churches in the Bluegrass also multiplied their membership. At the Great Crossings Church in Scott County, a few miles east of Cane Ridge, newly baptized members numbered 142 in 1800. The following year, 117 more converts joined the church, 110 of whom entered before the Cane Ridge meeting commenced. The Elkhorn Baptist Association, with which the Great Crossings Church was affiliated, showed similar increases across the Bluegrass region. In August 1800, the association counted 1,642 members in 27 reporting churches; a year later, their census of 36 congregations tallied 4,853, including 3,011 newly baptized brothers and sisters.[13]

Growth in church membership crossed racial lines. During the winter of 1800–1801, hundreds of slaves and free blacks were baptized and welcomed into Baptist churches. Slaves accounted for nearly a third of the new members at Great Crossings, a percentage that slightly exceeded the proportion of African Americans in the population of Scott County.[14]

The revival, then, was in full swing in August of 1801. From across the Bluegrass region, pilgrims made their way to Cane Ridge. Along with the already converted, the Cane Ridge meeting drew thousands of people who desired, but had not yet experienced, a spiritual rebirth. Beginning on the sixth of August, they converged on the Bourbon County site in numbers never seen before in one place in Kentucky. By Saturday the tenth, the fields surrounding the meetinghouse overflowed with between ten and twenty thousand people. The multitude within this instant city reminded one observer of the scene in downtown Philadelphia; indeed, the population at the meeting dwarfed that of Lexington.[15]

Cane Ridge restaged the Green River camp meetings on a larger scale, for a longer duration, and with a greater intensity. As at the gatherings south of the Green River, a Presbyterian church hosted the sacramental communion at Cane Ridge, but the affair was ecumenical. Barton Stone, the minister at the Cane Ridge church, took over McGready's organizing role, but he was joined by seventeen Presbyterian ministers, including some who had witnessed McGready's work in North Carolina or the

The scene outside Cane Ridge Church, August 1801. Courtesy of the Kentucky Historical Society.

Green River Country. Also on the grounds were a number of Baptist and Methodist preachers, and sectarian rivalry was set aside, to the common goal of saving souls. Moreover, Cane Ridge, like previous camp meetings, was an interracial, if not an entirely integrated, gathering. Because the crowd at Cane Ridge was so large, several preachers exhorted simultaneously from different parts of the field. Blacks tended to congregate on one side of the field where African American preachers entreated them to pray, sing, cry, and rejoice for God's mercy.[16]

Hour after hour, day after hot summer day and long into the nights, the preaching continued and the excitement of the assembly built. The pandemonium sounded to one witness like the "roar of Niagara." Hundreds danced spasmodically, shouted wildly, wept hysterically, and fell "as if a battery of a thousand guns had been opened upon them." Descriptions of these convulsive physical and emotional outbursts dominated eyewitness accounts of Cane Ridge and the Kentucky Revival. It "appear'd like dancing at a distance," but closer up, Reverend John Lyle found the motions and emotions more frantic and more ecstatic. "She felt through her flesh like the prickling of pins and a dead heaviness[,] as though the blood had stopped or was about to cease from circulation," reported one "fallen" woman to Lyle. Before swooning, others also remembered "deadness . . . as when your leg is asleep," only in this instance, their whole body seemed paralyzed. According to numerous testimonies, the collapse that followed was like being shot.[17]

How many were actually "gunned down" was unclear. Richard McNemar, who was among the revival's greatest champions, put the number seized at Cane Ridge at three thousand. Skeptics deflated his claims about the extent of the exercises. More conservative assessments reduced the number stricken to less than a thousand and as low as three hundred. Of course, even the lower figures were high enough to make quite an impression on the most cynical spectator.[18]

Both believers and cynics agreed that the ranks of the afflicted included previously heathenish men. On the edges of the Cane Ridge congregation, ruffians mocked and taunted worshippers. About a hundred of these men adjourned to a nearby tavern, where, twenty-year-old James Finley remembered, they "engaged in drunken revelry, playing cards, trading horses, quarreling, and fighting." For several years, Finley had lived as a hunter and had enjoyed the typical amusements favored by backcountry men. Like other young men, he especially loved when other men "listened to" his hunting stories "with the greatest excitement." Entering the tavern, Finley defiantly swore he "would not have fallen to the ground for the whole state of Kentucky," for "such an event would have been an everlasting disgrace" to his "boasted manhood and courage." But in the tavern, amidst men who shared his taste for rough living, Finley felt "as near hell as" he "wished to be." That night he prayed, "cried aloud for mercy and salvation, and fell prostrate." Like Finley, many "rough" men were unexpectedly affected by their attendance at revival gatherings. "He would not fall for a thousand dollars," and "he did not believe in heaven[,] hell[,] or devil," boasted one of these men just before he fell. After "he lay speechless for an hour or two," he arose with new convictions to "seek Christ" and live righteously.[19]

Such dramatic personal transformations were not limited to men. At Cane Ridge, according to the Englishman Henry Alderson, women constituted the majority of those "struck down." A year later at a camp meeting outside of Lexington, Frenchman F. A. Michaux observed the same pattern. But other anecdotal evidence contradicted the impressions of Alderson and Michaux. The Reverend John Lyle, for example, contended that during the last day of the Cane Ridge meeting the "exercised . . . were almost all men." Church records suggest a balance between the sexes. At the height of the revival in 1800 and 1801, the Mount Tabor Baptist Church in Barren County welcomed 41 newly baptized men and

48 women into the congregation. At the Great Crossings Baptist Church near Cane Ridge, the division between newly baptized men and women was closer still: 130 men versus 129 women.[20]

Although men and women seemed equally susceptible to convulsions, the experience especially challenged backcountry-bred males. As James Finley acknowledged, falling "disgrace[d]" his "boasted manhood and courage." The code of self-assertive manhood to which the hunter Finley adhered proscribed confessions of fears and displays of weakness. Yet Finley and other felled men succumbed to the terrors of eternal damnation. A tormented Jacob Young "wept bitterly," while other men, like the women about them, "melted into tears." Crying and swooning stripped Finley and Young of their aggressiveness, and prepared them for rebirth, a metaphor which reinforced the "female" character of religious conversions. Of one newly reborn man, James McGready wrote, "he is all tenderness," choosing a word that was the antonym of toughness, the antithesis of backcountry manhood.[21]

More significant to McGready than the gender of converts was their age. At the Green River meetings, "little children, young men and women, and old grey headed people, persons of every description . . . were to be found in every part of the multitude." But it was "the life, zeal, and visible evidences of the power of God, operating through young converts" that McGready deemed especially "worthy of observation." Again and again, he returned to the youth of converts, citing numerous tales of young boys and girls, "who on the first days of the solemnity, could not behave with common decency, now lying prostrate on the ground, weeping, praying, and crying out for mercy."[22]

At Cane Ridge, according to one witness, "particularly Boys and Girls about 8 or 10 years old" fell. From a purely demographic standpoint, the preponderance of younger people among the fallen was no surprise, for at the turn of the century younger people predominated in Kentucky. During the precarious times of the 1770s and 1780s, Kentucky was a young man's country, but the population actually grew slightly younger as Anglo-American settlement "matured." The migration of thousands of older men and women was more than balanced by the migration and birth of tens of thousands of children. James Finley was only twenty when he was converted, yet he was already five years past middle age, that is, past the median age of white Kentuckians.[23]

From the Green River Country to the Bluegrass, the contagion of enthusiasm inspired thousands of women and men, black and white, old and especially young to forsake secular concerns and cease sinful practices.

After Cane Ridge, according to the Presbyterian minister George Baxter, "a religious awe seemed to pervade the country." Taking note of the absence of profane swearing, once the lingua franca of rough manhood, Baxter designated Kentucky "the most moral place I had ever been in." In the winter of 1802, the reformation of manners was striking, but there was talk and hope of an even greater revival the coming summer.[24]

II

For Presbyterian authorities, promise quickly yielded to despair. The ministrations of James McGready kindled the revival and Presbyterian churches hosted the greatest camp meetings, but the months and years after Cane Ridge were not kind to western Presbyterianism. The attempts by synod authorities to dampen enthusiasm and impose order from above split the church. At Gasper River, where McGready first stirred enthusiasm, and at Cane Ridge, where excitement peaked, clergymen, along with much of their congregations, rejected Presbyterial authority and orthodox theology. These ex-Presbyterians, together with tens of thousands of Kentuckians, turned to evangelical sects that better satisfied their emotional needs and their populist sensibilities.

For Presbyterianism, the crest of the revival crashed quickly. Already in April of 1802, John Lyle noted that while religion continued "lively" at Cane Ridge and two neighboring Presbyterian congregations, few new conversions had occurred since the previous November. More disturbing was the reversion of recent converts to worldly ways. Such relapses sometimes occurred even before the close of a camp meeting. That was the case with "one Dougless," who, Lyle recorded, "fell as if shot but was drunk a day or two after at meeting." In November 1802, Lyle's review of the previous year's additions to the Sugar Ridge church turned up only two or three people who were still "professors of good report." The rest had in various ways "turn'd back like a dog to his vomit": Harper "drinks too much at times"; Becca Bell "is with child to one Brown"; Kate Cummins also "got careless" and "had a bastard"; Patty McGuire "has been whoring," while her husband John has been "drinking & fighting"; Haris Jones "curses & swears rapidly"; Polly Hardistan was "at times serious[,] at others vain and foolish."[25]

The apostasy of the recently reborn convinced Lyle that enthusiasm did not endure. When he had first witnessed people "falling down in distress," he had hoped the displays might "arouse the attention of a sleeping world & convince deists and gainsayers." At the Cane Ridge meeting, Lyle was genuinely impressed by how the fallen "arise & speak to their friends" in "orations [that] consist of the plain & essential truths of the Gospel . . . with all the feeling & pathos that human nature . . . is capable of." But Lyle warned parishioners to guard against excessive emotionalism and he preached the need for good order in worship, for proper gesture, voice, and "humility in prayer." Once the extent of backsliding became evident, Lyle decried false enthusiasm. He then joined David Rice and other Presbyterian clergymen who opposed the unruly emotionalism of camp meetings. Recognizing that hours of hortatory preaching generated "religious insanity," Rice recommended, and Lyle endorsed, an evening curfew on camp meeting services. To prevent "adulterous proceedings" at night, Rice advocated the segregation of sleeping men and women and the appointment of elders to patrol the grounds. But in spite of closer supervision, critics still condemned the carnal atmosphere of camp meetings, which they charged led to more souls being made than saved.[26]

Regulatory measures could not address what Rice considered the fallacies propounded by untutored evangelists. Camp meeting crusaders, complained Rice, preached a "strange heterogeneous mixture" of competing tenets and venerated revelation over reason. A Princeton graduate and a stalwart Calvinist, Rice ridiculed the rantings of Baptist and Methodist preachers. For Rice and like-minded Presbyterian clergymen, the ecumenism of camp meetings exposed people, especially impressionable young people, to a reign of error; there could be no compromise with those sects that licensed men devoid of understanding of ancient "creeds and confessions" to mislead worshippers. These stands—for well-ordered worship, an educated priesthood, and a strict interpretation of the doctrine of election—ruptured the spirit of Christian unity that prevailed at the outset of the revival. The passions James McGready unleashed divided fellow Presbyterian ministers. In the decade after Cane Ridge, debate over the credentials of the priesthood, the modification of predestinarian convictions, and the proper expression of piety split western Presbyterianism.[27]

In the Bluegrass, defenders of orthodoxy contended first with Barton Stone, pastor at Cane Ridge, who unapologetically espoused spontaneous enthusiasm in worship. Rejecting "cold" Calvinism for "the true new gospel" which offered an immediate pardon to converted sinners, Stone rebuffed attempts by synod authorities to dim his "New Light" views. Along with fellow ministers Richard McNemar, Robert Marshall, John Dunlavy, and John Thompson, Stone broke with the Transylvania Presbytery in 1803. At first the dissident clergymen formed their own Presbytery, but in the summer of 1804, they dissolved this organization as an unnecessary impediment to Christian liberty. Thus was born the "Christian

Church," without an ecclesiastical hierarchy and with a priesthood whose sole credential was their personal faith in the Bible.[28]

In the Green River Country, too, Presbyterian clergymen strayed from the old light. In 1802, ministers in southern Kentucky and Tennessee organized themselves into the Cumberland Presbytery and soon deviated from established policies and principles. Sent in 1805 to investigate, John Lyle found the Cumberland Presbytery chiefly filled with "illiterate exhorters and licentiates who are chiefly Arminians in sentiment and who ride in circuits after the manner of the Methodists." Confronted by Lyle, some of the novitiates lamented their lack of formal training, but none agreed to stop preaching. Their faith, they insisted, was a suitable credential, their success in winning converts sufficient proof of their methods and their New Light precepts. When Lyle protested that "success in converting people to error" was not "success in the cause of God," they denied the principle of election. "God," explained John Rankin, a convert to New Light doctrine, "had given to every man a sufficiency of grace, which if he would improve, he would get more &c until he would arrive at true conversion or a living faith." As in the Bluegrass, the attempt to discipline wayward ministers resulted in the breakup of the Presbyterian church in southern Kentucky and Tennessee.[29]

In both Bluegrass and Green River Country, some Presbyterians defected twice: first to the New Light and then to the United Society of Believers, better known as the Shakers. The most prominent examples of this progress (or descent) from orthodoxy to the extremes of millenarian enthusiasm were Richard McNemar and John Rankin. Both ministers had avidly promoted the revival, and both had quickly renounced Calvinist predestination for the Arminian New Light. But when Shaker missionaries came to Kentucky in 1805, McNemar parted with Barton Stone. While Stone vehemently censured the unorthodox arrangements of Shaker society, McNemar converted. In 1806, he helped to found the first Shaker community in Kentucky at Pleasant Hill, a site twenty miles southwest of Lexington. Acting as a Shaker missionary in the Green River Country the following year, McNemar was received warmly at Gasper River; minister John Rankin and twenty members of the Gasper River congregation were soon persuaded to join the Society of Believers. Not far from where James McGready had ten years earlier detected the first signs of an awakening, the Shakers established South Union, their second Kentucky community.[30]

Whereas Presbyterianism split apart, Baptists and Methodists surged ahead. Before the Great Revival, the number of professing Presbyterians nearly equaled the combined total of Baptists and Methodists. But a decade after Cane Ridge, about half of the Presbyterian laity in Kentucky had quit. So had a like proportion of clergymen. Touring the Green River Country in 1813, the Reverend Joseph Howe found Presbyterians thinly scattered and vastly outnumbered by Methodists and Baptists. In parts of Logan County, the place where the revival began, Howe encountered no Presbyterians at all. In the meantime, Baptists and Methodists garnered the largest share of converts from the revival of 1800–1801. Their Kentucky ranks grew tenfold during the first two decades of the nineteenth century. (The overall population of the state, in contrast, increased by only about 150 percent.) [31]

Calvinist dogma was the most often cited reason for Presbyterian defections. The idea that "the salvation of the non-elect must remain as it ever was, an impossibility" convinced David Purviance to reject his Presbyterian upbringing and follow Barton Stone into the Christian Church. Like Purviance, James Finley was from a Presbyterian family, but he could not reconcile his experiences with the doctrine of unconditional election, and so he became a Methodist. According to James McGready, Methodist societies in the Green River Country grew in particular at the expense of the Presbyterians, as itinerant preachers "cunningly" lured crowds with the promise of salvation for the faithful and the righteous. Meanwhile, reported John Lyle, few came to hear the local Presbyterian minister, who was "counted as an enemy to the revival & treated with neglect, partly on account of his doctrine, & partly owing to his opposition to what he deems the extravagance of the times." [32]

Doctrine, as Lyle acknowledged, only *partially* explained Presbyterian schisms and the gains of sectarian competitors. After all, Baptists and Methodists gained most despite profound differences in theology and organization. During the 1780s and 1790s, Kentucky Baptists were split into "Regular" and "Separate" factions. The former adhered to the rigidly Calvinistic Philadelphia Confession of Faith; the latter, among other differences, did not. But the Great Revival, which divided the Presbyterian Church, united Separates and Regulars. The principle of congregational independence made it easier for Baptists as a group to reach a compromise between Arminian and Calvinist tenets and as individuals to follow their consciences. While Presbyterian clergymen feuded about a single standard and fought for or against centralized authority, Baptist preachers answered only to their own congregants. In contrast, Methodists maintained a more centralized hierarchy and an unambiguous Arminian theology.[33]

Yet a common evangelical culture overshadowed the doctrinal and ecclesiastical differences between Methodists and Baptists, and it linked these sects with Stone's Christians, Cumberland New Lights, and even Shakers. This persuasion—what Lyle derogated "the extravagance of the times"—coupled exuberant worship with empowerment of the laity. Evangelical enthusiasm afforded believers an immediate link to the supernatural, a connection that was unmediated by clerical and worldly authorities. By designating individuals as the judges of their personal conversion experiences, appointing laypeople as the overseers of congregational government, and accrediting preachers on the basis of their emotional (as opposed to educational) commitment, evangelicals democratized their churches.

Shakers took the implications of Christian equality to an extreme. Their pacifism, their abolition of private property, their promotion of equal, if generally separate, status of women, and their celibacy went too far for fellow evangelicals. Thus, Baptists and Methodists joined Barton Stone in condemning the "unnatural" arrangements of Shaker communities. But Shaker "families" were not so different from the familial ideal of other evangelicals—especially when compared to the patriarchal model associated with the worlds of Boone and Clay. While backcountry and gentry patriarchs ruled over dependent wives and children, evangelicals addressed one another as "brother" and "sister" and aspired to love one another as spiritual equals. For people enmeshed in webs of deference, the affective bonds of evangelical churches were liberating indeed. Gone were ceremonies designed to confer honor and connote rank; in were rituals that celebrated Christian fellowship, without regard to age, sex, and sometimes even race. Gone were elderly clergymen of aristocratic bearing and ornate language; in were young lay preachers of humble manner and ardent voice.[34]

The message and the messengers naturally appealed to those in positions of worldly dependence—to young men, to women of all ages, to slaves of both sexes. Evangelicalism gave these people control of their destiny in the next world and a greater say in this world as well. It gave dependents the chance to speak for themselves and to hear people like themselves speak. Young men in particular seized the platform offered by evangelical churches. Even more revolutionary were the public voices raised by female lay preachers. Coming across one such preaching woman in the Green River Country, a male evangelist for the Christian Church was "astonished at her flow of speech and consistency of ideas." Another follower of Barton Stone remembered that at meetings in the Bluegrass women "sometimes exhorted with great warmth."[35]

For most evangelical women, public speaking was more limited, though no less significant. The simple act of professing faith, of relating an experience of conversion that was independent of a father or husband, was itself a radical step out of the patriarchal shadow. Evangelicalism offered Kentucky women immediate as well as eternal rewards. Camp meetings granted an escape from lives of rural isolation. Men had other occasions to meet—and play. Women did not. Emotionally cathartic as camp meetings could be, they did not satisfy women's longings for a more consistent, female-centered community. Church-going, though, afforded women the chance to gather regularly outside of homes. As historian Donald Mathews has conjectured, "the intimate bonds of the religious community must have provided some women with the care, sense of worth, and companionship they did not receive from husbands."[36]

All this deeply disconcerted old light Presbyterian clergymen. "Time was when christian pastors were looked up to as *revered fathers, as safe counsellors, as wakeful guardians* of the morals, the peace, and the safety of their congregations," grieved John Campbell, a Presbyterian minister, in 1812. "But, alas! these comfortable days have passed away," for "the people have usurped the station of consequence over the pastor. . . . His person is no longer sacred, his office no longer revered, his instruction . . . without influence, without rule." More disturbing to Campbell, the decline of clerical stature exemplified a general deterioration of patriarchal authority. It was useless, he concluded, to "complain of the want of subordination in families, or in general society, while there is none in the church."[37]

III

The spread of evangelical culture altered the ways of tens of thousands of Kentuckians, but Campbell's fear of a world without subordination, in families or society, was greatly exaggerated. The Kentucky Revival that peaked in 1800–1801 became in the next few years a great revival across the southeastern United States. In Kentucky, however, the anticipated greater revival of 1802 did not come about. Instead, enthusiasm sputtered. For nearly ten years evangelical momentum slowed, its progress continually retarded by apostates and by stubborn opposition from various quarters. Perhaps the most significant source of antievangelicalism were patriarchs who felt themselves imperiled. Yet this, too, was overstated. With the exception of Shakers, few evangelicals ever contemplated a truly egalitarian community. Indeed, during the early nineteenth century, most evangelicals recanted their opposition to the most notorious subordination—that of slave to master.

The associational tables compiled by Baptist churches record the ebbing of enthusiasm after Cane Ridge. At the Mt. Tabor Baptist Church in Barren County, the number of adult baptisms, 31 in 1800 and 58 in 1801, dropped to just 9 in 1802 and 1803 and to 8 in 1804. In the Bluegrass region, the slide was steeper still. At the Great Crossings Church where 259 people were baptized in 1800 and 1801, only three new converts joined in the five years between 1802 and 1806. For the Elkhorn Association as a whole, baptisms plummeted from 3,011 in 1801, to 488 in 1802, to 64 in 1803, to 22 in 1804.[38]

Backsliding also became more prevalent. As revival converts lost fervor and resumed sinful behavior, disciplinary actions against reprobate members proliferated. In the five years prior to 1801, the Elkhorn Baptist Association had averaged only 23 "exclusions" per year. That number doubled in 1801, though the increase was eclipsed by the more than three thousand new conversions registered that year. In 1802, exclusions rose again to 143, but the effects were still offset by the baptism of 488 persons. From 1803 to 1805, however, excommunications continued to exceed 140 per year, and over that span, backsliders outnumbered baptized by four to one.[39]

Enthusiasm slumped for the rest of the decade, until a flood of converts in 1810 announced a new (or revived) revival. From 1802 to 1809, the Mt. Tabor church registered a total of 72 new baptisms. In 1810 alone, 85 were recorded. If the gains that year across the Green River Country were not as dramatic as during the boom of 1800, the enthusiasm to get "real religion" seemed again infectious. When this wave spread to other parts of Kentucky in 1811, the effects were even more startling. For eight straight years, the North District Association of Bluegrass Baptist churches reported more exclusions than baptisms (by an average margin of 53 to 34). But in 1811, a stunning reversal occurred: 510 new baptisms against only 29 exclusions. The following year, the revival continued on its crest: 568 new professors of religion versus a mere 44 disciplinary expulsions.[40]

This renewal of religious enthusiasm was in part a by-product of a series of powerful earthquakes that shook the trans-Appalachian country in 1811 and 1812. The revival (re)commenced in the Green River Country in 1810, before the first tremors shook the Ohio and Mississippi Valleys, but it took off in the wake of the first great quake. After the first tremor and its aftershocks hit on December 17, 1811, terrified Kentuckians gathered together, convinced that the end of the world was imminent. Abandoning secular concerns, "the people relinquished all kinds of labour for a time," recalled Jacob Bower. "Men, Women, and children, everywhere" prayed for salvation in the world to come. Bower joined a Baptist church and awaited the millennium.[41]

Skeptics claimed the "Baptists are all *shakers*, that when the Earth is don[e] shaking, they will all turn back, and be as they were before." Sure enough, with the end of the temblors, some of these "earthquake Christians" slid back into sinful ways and new baptisms dropped sharply. In 1813, the North District Association of Baptists expelled 118 members, while baptizing only 22 new professors. Over the next two years, exclusions for absence from church, betting, dancing, drinking, defrauding, swearing, fighting, fornicating, and the catch-all "immoral conduct" outnumbered baptisms by a three to one margin.[42]

Some of these transgressions obviously involved both men and women, yet exclusions most often pertained to modes of conduct— gambling, drinking, fighting, and swearing—that were distinguishing attributes of rough manhood. Consequently, disciplinary actions involved far more men than women. At the South Elkhorn Christian Church, nearly one of eight members was expelled during the first fifteen years of the nineteenth century. Among women, the proportion was only about one in twenty; by contrast, almost one-quarter of men were excommunicated. At the nearby Great Crossings Baptist Church, the gendered breakdown was even more unequal. In the five years after Cane Ridge, fourteen men were ousted against only one woman. That imbalance attested to the difficulties of men in adapting to an evangelical culture that exalted tenderness over toughness. It also left evangelical churches with a predominantly female membership. Though men and women joined in roughly equal numbers during the revival of 1800–1801, the backsliding of men left women in the majority at most evangelical churches.[43]

Backsliding and resistance to evangelical ways was particularly robust among the heads of patriarchal households. Noting a generation gap in the reception of Methodism in Woodford County, circuit rider Benjamin Lakin allowed that "the work among us appears to be among the young men and Boys." Meanwhile, "the more aged and heads of families seem yet unconcerned about religion." Actually, husbands and fathers were quite concerned by the conversions of their wives, daughters, and sons. When, for example, sixteen year old Peter Cartwright told his parents that he had been reborn and would no longer indulge in horse racing and card playing, his mother was happy. Not his father, though, who felt betrayed by the independence of his dependent. Taking leave from his father's household, Cartwright began itinerating across the Green River countryside. But he did not escape the wrath of free white patriarchs. After Cartwright shepherded the conversion of a woman and her two daughters, "the husband and father of these interesting females" threatened to whip the evangelist for meddling with the order of his household. Perhaps the rage of this husband-father derived from a recognition that a patriarchal house divided against itself could not long endure half saved and half free.[44]

Although evangelists encountered menacing men in all corners of Kentucky, they thought the concentration of heathens greatest at the center, in Lexington. As the revival of 1801 gained momentum in the surrounding Bluegrass countryside, "poor L[exingto]n" remained "this Sodom," its inhabitants scornful of evangelical entreaties. The events at Cane Ridge did become the talk of the town in late summer, though it did not make evangelists any more welcome. In October, an evangelical meeting drew about four thousand people (twice the size of Lexington's population). But the carnivalesque appeal of revival meetings seemed in this instance a primary attraction. The crowd, according to John Lyle, was "very disorderly." Rowdy men taunted the few who fell and drunkenly mocked the gesticulations of preachers. Afterwards, life continued as before. Touring Lexington in 1806, the Englishman Thomas Ashe found profane customs the order of the day—including on the Sabbath, which men treated as a day to give "loose to their dispositions and exhibit many traits that should exclusively belong to savages."[45]

In Lexington, according to harassed evangelicals, infidelity also wore a more genteel face. The Inner Bluegrass gentry entered the nineteenth century with a reputation as deists and unbelievers, as opponents not simply of evangelicals but of Christianity in any form. They greeted the revival with a mixture of apathy and antipathy. Lexington newspapers made no mention of the goings-on at Cane Ridge, and whereas local events were rarely reported, the Cane Ridge meeting was not just local news. The apparent indifference covered more hostile sentiments, which emerged into the open when revivalists brought their act into Lexington. At one revival meeting in 1801, James Bradford, the son of the publisher of the *Kentucky Gazette* and the editor of a newspaper of his own, led the disruption of the service, taking as his responsibility to watch over the ladies in attendance. Asked his name and why he interfered with the worship service, Bradford "drew his fist & said he was a man." Asked again, the scion of one of Lexington's most prominent families offered the same reply and vowed to "hurt" the inquisitive clergyman.[46]

After Cane Ridge, it became commonplace to contrast the enthusiasm of the countryside with the still irreligious character of Lexington, and particularly with the rationalism of the Lexington gentry. The "better informed people" did not "share" the "state of ecstasy," was how François Michaux described the division in Kentucky society in 1802. Evangelists, too, assumed that urban men were unfriendly to them, that merchants, mechanics, and lawyers stood opposed to religious enthusiasm. Especially lawyers. As Robert McAfee explained, it was thought that one could not be religious and a lawyer at the same time. Indeed, McAfee claimed that only one member of the Kentucky bar had "ventured to profess Religion and he was looked upon with jeers and derision" by his peers.[47]

While lawyers jeered evangelicals, evangelicals scorned lawyers—and tried within church circles to maintain order without lawyers. The constitutions adopted by Baptist churches required members to treat one another as brothers and sisters and prohibited siblings from suing one another. Church hearings did away with legal counsel; in Baptist "courts," complainants represented themselves. The assembled brethren acted first as arbitrators. But when reconciliation failed, the brethren became jurors with the power to excommunicate offenders. And unlike "secular" cases, Baptist convictions required only a two-thirds vote or sometimes only a simple majority.[48]

This system generally worked well before the Great Revival. During the 1790s, Baptist congregations typically contained few members, and these were from close-knit families. A number of Kentucky's pioneer Baptist churches had been founded by congregations of Virginia Baptists who had migrated to the western country together. Their ties cemented by intermarriages, Baptist brothers and sisters kept most disputes between members out of court and in the church family. Compared with a court system clogged by land litigation and governed by greed, Baptist justice appeared a perfect alternative. Swift, simple, and seemingly democratic, it was everything disheartened Kentuckians wished their legal system to be.

But enlarged memberships made Baptist justice more cumbersome and less impartial. After the revival of 1800–1801, "accusations in the Church became very common, and for very trivial things," lamented preacher John Taylor. Because neophytes frequently backslid, disciplinary hearings came to dominate church minutes. Lacking long-standing attachments to fellow congregants, newcomers were also more prone to irreconcilable quarrels. To Taylor's chagrin, "personal bickering" replaced evangelical fervor as the cause of "great excitement" among Kentucky Baptists. Secular disagreements more and more intruded on church business and distorted church justice. The rule of simple majorities, Taylor conceded, resulted in a number of incorrect verdicts.[49]

Not all, it seemed to Taylor, were equal in the eyes of Baptist justice, a judgment confirmed by the work of historian Fred Hood. Analyzing the social composition of four Bluegrass Baptist churches, Hood discovered that prior to the Great Revival the laity tended to be from wealthier households than the norm in Inner Bluegrass counties. Preachers, contrary to their humble image, were better off than the laity. However, the revival of 1800–1801 shifted downward the socioeconomic profile of Baptist churches as men and women from what Hood termed the "dependent classes" were baptized. These poorer newcomers also became the focus of church discipline. After 1800, the majority of excluded persons were men from poorer than average households, even though they made up only about a third of the total membership. In cases pitting poorer persons against the wealthiest members, church justice appeared not very different from secular courts. In ecclesiastical, as in civil tribunals, winning and wealth correlated.[50]

The disciplinary ax fell most heavily and most inequitably on the poorest of the poor, on African American slaves. In the Bluegrass churches studied by Hood, over a third of the slaves baptized during the revival of 1800–1801 had been excluded by 1810. Some of these expulsions traced to the usual infractions committed by (mostly male) revelers. But there were also cases such as Sister Esther Boulwares' "Winney." She was tried in the winter of 1807 "for saying she once thought it her duty to serve her Master & Mistress[,] but since the lord had converted her, she had never believed that any Christian kept Negroes or Slaves." Proclaiming that slavery was immoral conduct, Winney affirmed that "Thousands of white people [were] Wallowing in Hell for their treatment of Negroes." For speaking her heart, Winney was excluded from the fellowship of the Forks of Elkhorn Church.[51]

In the years after the Great Revival, no issue was as divisive for Kentucky Baptists as slavery. Just a month before Winney's trial, the members of the Forks of Elkhorn Church had split over an invitation extended by Brother William Hickman to Carter Tarrant, a preacher who had been excommunicated by a sister church for creating disorder. Both Hickman, the founder and longtime pastor of the Forks of Elkhorn Church, and Tarrant had spent many years condemning slavery. In December 1806, three-fourths of the white brethren agreed that Hickman had done nothing improper, but the majority of voting members did not share his anti-slavery sentiments. Nine months later, Hickman, no longer able to abide the continuing toleration of slavery, withdrew from the Forks of Elkhorn Church and from the Elkhorn Baptist Association with which it was affiliated.[52]

The muffling of antislavery voices was an inglorious retreat from the founding principles of the Forks of Elkhorn Church and the Elkhorn Association. Back in 1792 the Elkhorn Association of Baptist churches had with Hickman's support adopted a resolution declaring slavery inconsistent with the principles of Christianity. Because this proclamation sparked protests from several of the associated churches, it never became an official tenet of Kentucky Baptists. But as individuals, preachers and laypersons were free to take a strong stand against slavery, which Hickman and many other Baptists did. During the Great Revival, Baptist preachings in favor of emancipation and spiritual equality brought a full harvest of African American converts.[53]

True, this equality was meant more for the next world than for this one. In their rules, Baptist churches usually disenfranchised slave members and rarely allowed even free blacks to vote on church business, including on exclusions of one of their own. Yet slaves like Winney still insisted on speaking out as equals, and in so doing sent a shudder through slaveholding Baptists. In 1805, the mounting backlash against antislavery agitation was reflected in the Elkhorn Association's advice to affiliated ministers not "to meddle with emancipation from slavery or any other political subject" that has "nothing to do" with "their religious capacities." The warning did not stop a number of principled preachers. When they did not withdraw voluntarily, they were expelled.[54]

Contention over slavery and retreat from emancipationist stands were not unique to Baptists. In Kentucky, and across the slaveholding states, the evangelical path led away from biracial congregation. Of all evangelists, Methodist circuit riders had most aggressively courted slaves and free blacks during the late eighteenth century and through the Great Revival. Early in the nineteenth century, however, Methodists, like fellow evangelicals, accommodated to slavery and to segregation of worshippers. By 1816, the Methodist General Conference, while still damning slavery as "contrary to the principles of moral justice," conceded that "little can be done to abolish the practice."[55]

Only Shakers stood firm behind emancipation. At their inception, Shaker societies in Kentucky included slaveowners and slaves. Yet while other evangelicals were obliging masters and disciplining slaves and free blacks, Kentucky Shakers moved the other way. Putting humanitarian principles into practice, the societies at Pleasant Hill and South Union abolished slavery within their communities. Still, even Shakers stopped short of full racial integration. At South Union, African Americans were organized into a racially distinct "family" and were housed separately from white members. A concession to the intolerance of Logan County neighbors, the decision to segregate showed that "the world" was not as far away as Shakers might have wished.[56]

That explained as well the too frequent defections from Shaker societies at Pleasant Hill and South Union. Once the novelty of communal living wore off and the reality of celibate living wore in, desertions followed. Some backsliders like Henly Jennings decided there must be "an easier way to heaven" than Shakerism offered. Others like Joseph Dunn bounced in and out of the Shaker community at South Union. Four times from June to October of 1812, Dunn departed and returned. At each of his reinstatements, he professed penitence. Alas, "Poor Jo.," wrote the society's journal keeper after Dunn's fourth application for readmission, "the spirit is indeed willing but the flesh is strong." Dunn stayed through the winter, but the next May he was "again fixing for his trinity: world, flesh, & Devil." Two days later, he disappeared for good, or as the journal keeper punned, "Dunn has done it."[57]

WHAT DUNN DID DEMONSTRATED (again and again) the tug of the secular. Across Kentucky, people pursued an easier way to heaven. They also sought an easier way on earth. For the majority of converts, and particularly for women, evangelicalism fulfilled both needs. But the backsliding of individuals, particularly men, affirmed the persisting tension between the way of the world and the otherworld of evangelicalism.

Some backsliding was collective, though. In the late eighteenth century, by word and by example, evangelicals censured slaveholding and reproached gentry lifestyles. But after the Great Revival, evangelicals in Kentucky—and across the slaveholding South—backed off from their antislavery commitments. That disavowal made evangelicalism safe for masters, and it made the Bluegrass System safe from evangelicals.

Conclusion

WHEN DANIEL BOONE DIED in Missouri in the autumn of 1820, he left behind a world in upheaval. Earlier that year Henry Clay, Speaker of the United States House of Representatives, had engineered the compromise that brought the slave state of Missouri into the union. But the conflict over slavery that preceded the political consolidation of Missouri rang the fire bell in Thomas Jefferson's night. At the same time that the Missouri controversy sparked fears of disunion, a nationwide depression rekindled doubts about the economic consolidation of the western country.

In Kentucky, the "Panic of 1819" began earlier, lasted longer, and hit harder than almost anywhere in the country. Economic travails inspired a renewal of religious revivalism. The depth and persistence of hard times also stoked secular fires against the rule of law and the inequities of the Bluegrass System. During the 1820s, debtor relief legislation triggered a political and constitutional crisis that once again imperiled the independence of the judiciary.[1]

But even as the world of Henry Clay trembled, there was no resurrection for that of Daniel Boone. If the economic and political consolidation of the western country remained incomplete, the conquest and colonization of the Ohio Valley were irreversible. By 1820 it was clear that neither Bluegrass nor Green River Country were destined to be good poor man's countries. By then, too, Kentucky's transformation from Boone to Clay had set the westward expansion of the United States on its way.

I

A good poor man's country. The phrase was ubiquitous among the contemporaries of Daniel Boone. Its meaning, however, was ambiguous. Indeed, that ambiguity helps explain why Kentucky did not become one. In its most common usage, the trope referred to a territory where men and the households they headed could *get ahead*. From the founding of British North America, promoters of settlement recommended various colonies as places where cheap land and high wages allowed Europeans of low stations and slim prospects to advance up social and economic ladders. In the era of the American Revolution, Kentucky became the latest and the most renowned land of opportunity. Tens of thousands of poor men and their families joined Boone in the conquest and colonization of trans-Appalachia, propelled by what Michel-Guillaume-Jean de Crèvecoeur described as "the happy restlessness . . . which is constantly urging us all to become better off than we now are."[2]

East and west of the Appalachians in the eighteenth century, poor men asked more of a good country than material prosperity. What drove pioneers across the mountains in the last quarter of the century was a hunger for lands that would allow families to *get by* with greater security and less effort. Fertile soil, ample range, and game-filled woods might not produce riches, but they captivated poor men who dreamed of achieving personal independence *and* providing more easily for dependents and descendants. While men in the backcountry from Pennsylvania to the Carolinas habitually testified to the hardships of border life, they also spoke often of the satisfactions of their simple, yet liberating, ways. Instead of "sigh[ing] for what was out of reach," remembered one son of the Greater Pennsylvania backcountry, we were "happy and contented with such living, had fewer aches and pains . . . and slept more soundly." Limiting wants and lending hands to neighbors in need held the key to a good poor man's country in which how well people got along counted for more than how frequently or how far they got ahead.[3]

That formula Ohio Indians well understood. Indian orators did not employ the metaphor of a good poor man's country, and colonial writers did not attach the phrase to the Indian country beyond the Appalachians. Yet judged by the security and ease with which people got by and fellow villagers got along, the best poor man's country belonged to unconquered Indian peoples. Judged by almost any standard, Ohio Indian country was a better poor woman's country than the adjacent backcountry.

The quality of Ohio Indian life deteriorated, however, once backcountry hunters began appearing in the Cumberland, Green, and Kentucky River valleys. Because they competed for the same animal skins and because their ideas about wildlife and other natural resources were different, contacts in the 1760s often precipitated conflict. But through the 1770s and 1780s, some Ohio Indians also sought to accommodate backcountry poachers with whom they recognized a certain kinship. Building on cultural congruences and going beyond mere coexistence, Ohio Indians endeavored to make pioneer adversaries live amongst them and adopt their ways. A few pioneers welcomed the offer; others, including Daniel

Boone, wavered. Ultimately, though, Boone and most pioneers declined the Indians' invitation and set about monopolizing Kentucky's resources. Into the 1790s, confederated Ohio Indians fought a long, losing struggle to maintain control over the fauna of Kentucky. Denied access to Kentucky wildlife, Ohio Indian peoples never got along as well again.

Nor, ironically, did many of their conquerors. Pioneer men, like their Indian counterparts, drew sustenance and gained influence from their success in hunting. Yet backcountry men resisted convergence and undermined coexistence. By the mid-1790s, they had dislodged Indians from the borders of the Bluegrass and had depleted the wildlife of the region. Their aspirations to make money (by selling more skins) and to gain prestige (by giving away meat and killing the most beasts) conflated to deprive hunters of the resource upon which their livelihood and their sense of manhood had depended.

Manly independence became first and foremost a matter of land ownership, but here even more the contradiction between ambition and tradition interfered with homesteaders' dreams. Advocating a system that granted adult white men fee-simple title to family-sized farmsteads, occupying claimants protested distribution policies that rewarded nonresident speculators. The most disheartened, as well as the most demagogic, preached armed resistance. Nevertheless, no rebellion erupted during the 1780s, because too many occupant-improvers had too much to lose from a general redistribution. For Kentucky pioneers in affairs of land, the tradition about what homesteaders needed to get by too often yielded to their ambition to get more.

From the acquisition of "excessive" private landholdings to the defense of privatized rights was a relatively short step. It was at least a shorter step than back across a closing frontier to a receding Indian country. And yet the contradiction between getting ahead and getting along left the colony of Kentucky a long way from a good poor man's country.

II

The separation of Kentucky from Virginia and its admission into the United States transformed a colony into a state. Still, the act of political consolidation was not the same as the fact. After statehood, leading men continued to plot the alienation of Kentucky from the republic. Effective incorporation awaited the stabilization of property rights and the commercial integration of the western country with the rest of the nation.

Everything awaited the clarification of land titles. When Kentucky became independent of Virginia in 1792, only a third of adult white males

owned any land, and most of these titles were contested. Where litigation entangled every tract, only lawyers thrived, or so thought financially
strapped plaintiffs and defendants. The majority of Kentucky's citizenry
concluded that where lawyers ruled, "the people" suffered.

During the 1790s, "the people," which here referred to adult white
men, demanded the simplification of law and the reapportionment of
land. These attacks on the rule of lawyers broadened into a more general
assault on "aristocratic privileges," especially the ownership of slaves. In
constitutional conventions, legislative elections, and extra legal demonstrations, the vox populi shouted for greater democracy and no slavery.

The clamor scared lawyers and alarmed the minority of men who
aspired to reassemble the hierarchies of colonial Virginia in Kentucky.
Quieting the din from below was a top priority for those men whose immense land and slaveholdings put them atop the new state's oligarchic
power structure. Because the rulers were less self-confident and the citizenry more self-assertive, republican Kentucky did not replicate colonial
Virginia. Still, the compromises and concessions worked out by legislators
and jurists muffled the noisiest discontent without sacrificing the land or
slaveholdings of resident gentry.

In legislative and judicial arenas, the maldistribution of land overshadowed other issues, but it was the privatization of property rights that
directed the economic development of Kentucky. Even as radicals noisily
struggled to secure and spread ownership of land, lawmakers quietly
altered the rules of property and the rights of landowners. By curtailing
those "rights in the woods" that had established uncultivated lands as a
hunting and herding common, legislators wrought the demise of Daniel
Boone's Kentucky and the rise of Henry Clay's.

Across the Ohio River, in what remained of Indian country, the
transformation of property regimes and the infiltration of foreign values
ignited unrest that only armed force could put down; in Kentucky, by
contrast, the challenge to backcountry traditions did not provoke "custom's last stand." Whereas Ohio Indians drew enthusiasm from prophetic
visions of a world restored, "the people" of central Kentucky submitted
peacefully to that privatization that promised to increase the commercial
potential of real estate.[4]

Enhancing the productivity of property and effecting the economic
consolidation of Kentucky were the cornerstones of the "Bluegrass System." That political economy was extolled by Henry Clay as a benefit to
all Kentuckians. "The spirit of commercial enterprise," declared Clay in
1812, was a universal "passion as unconquerable as any with which nature

has endowed us." The Bluegrass System encouraged this profit-minded spirit and promoted Kentucky's thorough integration into the national and international market world. But the operation of the Bluegrass System served primarily to make the state government a more effective instrument for owners of slaves and capital. Putting wage and slave labor in competition, the Bluegrass System was no boon for poor men, free or unfree. In the early-nineteenth-century Bluegrass, those who did not get ahead had increasing trouble getting along.[5]

During the first decade of the nineteenth century, the political economy of Henry Clay faced stiff opposition from agrarians and evangelicals. Both movements emerged from the Green River Country at the turn of the century. But though agrarianism and evangelicalism sprang from the same soil at the same moment, they posed largely separate challenges to the supremacy of the Bluegrass System.

Agrarianism had its roots in liberal homesteading laws that turned the Green River Country into a region of 200-acre family farms. The elected representatives of the Green River Country banded in defense of small farmers and, under the leadership of Felix Grundy, combated the hegemony of Bluegrass elites over the government of Kentucky. Grundy was not opposed to the "spirit of commercial enterprise," but he was an articulate foe of any development that promoted concentration of landholdings and "paper aristocracies. His "band," though, was less devoted to the agrarian cause. Instead of getting rid of the Bluegrass System, Green River legislators voted to get in on it. Internal improvements and banks came to the Southside. So also came speculation and slavery, undermining forever the egalitarian character of the Green River countryside.

The spiritual equality idealized by evangelicals was beyond the imagination of the wildest agrarians. Whereas Felix Grundy's political economy sought to protect adult white men from landless dependency and to preserve the essential equality among landowners, evangelicalism tampered with hierarchies inside patriarchal households. For dependents, evangelicalism offered station and solace in a world removed from Boone's, Clay's, and Grundy's too.

It was once commonplace to ascribe the Kentucky revival to the uncertainty and emotional impoverishment of "pioneer life," but that view misleadingly describes Cane Ridge as a "frontier phenomenon." In 1801, the Bluegrass was no longer a perimeter of Anglo-American settlement, nor an intersection with Indian country. Even the more recently colonized Green River Country did not fit either bill. For revivalism to have originated on the frontier, it should have commenced in Daniel Boone's Kentucky, not Henry Clay's.[6]

Though not a product of the frontier, the Great Revival did spread into Ohio Indian country. After Cane Ridge, Christian missionaries redoubled their efforts among Indians. Although evangelicals did not convert many Ohio Indians during the first decade of the nineteenth century, the preoccupation of Indian prophets with the moral reformation of sinners and their revelations of hell showed the influence of Christianity on nativist thinking. Yet there were sharp contrasts between Indian and Christian revivals. The former summoned men back to the ways of fathers and grandfathers; the latter envisioned the erasure of vestigial pioneer manhood.[7]

Even though evangelicals made headway in the reformation of manners and manhood, backsliding reversed some of these gains. Much as the affluence of the Bluegrass captivated Green River agrarians, the temptations of the world enticed individuals from evangelical ways. And like Green River legislators, white evangelicals dropped their challenge to slavery and left the Bluegrass System intact.

III

What, finally, was the legacy of this conquest, colonization, and unfinished consolidation? For Frederick Jackson Turner, the passage of Kentucky from Boone to Clay prefigured the essentials of American expansion from the Appalachians to the Pacific. "Stand at Cumberland Gap," observed Turner, "and watch the procession of civilization, marching single file—the buffalo following the trail to the salt spring, the Indian, the fur trader and hunter, the cattle-raiser, the pioneer farmer—and the frontier has passed by. Stand at South Pass in the Rockies a century later and see the same procession with wider intervals between." For good reason, historians have dismissed much of what Frederick Jackson Turner and his disciples wrote. But Turner's positioning of Kentucky at the head of the history of the Great West still holds. Synchronous with the birth and initial development of the United States, the conquest, colonization, and consolidation of Kentucky established patterns—albeit not those imagined by Turner—for successive American "Wests."[8]

For American national expansion, the conquest of Kentucky and the Ohio Valley was the first and greatest hurdle. Never again would Indians and white Americans meet on such equal terms as they did in the Ohio Valley during the Revolution. Never again would Indians inflict such damage on armies of the United States as the Indian confederacy did in 1790 and 1791. In hindsight, the Indians' last best chance to stem the tide of American expansion vanished at Fallen Timbers in 1794. Thereafter, the balance of power shifted decisively in favor of the United States, for Indians were never again as united.

The conquest of Indian countries was never a matter of military force alone. In the Ohio Valley as elsewhere, Indian resistance was broken less on the battlefield than by the trading that occurred between battles. Commercial relations, which had determined only a fraction of the exchanges between Ohio Indians and Europeans, came to dominate intersocietal transactions. As the market gained a larger place, Ohio Indians modified customs of gifting. The expansion of commercial hunting also indebted Indians and eroded the environmental basis of their mixed subsistence system. One territorial cession after another followed, until there were no more Indian countries to be sold.

The Ohio Indians' mixed subsistence system and their separate rules for exchanging meat and skins resembled that of Kentucky pioneers — with one crucial difference. Indian men and women did not purchase land with profits from the fur trade. While Indian peoples commodified animal pelts, they resisted the commodification of land. For pioneers, by contrast, long hunting and land hunting were ever entwined.

The land hunting of long hunters commenced the colonization of Kentucky, a process that profoundly influenced the subsequent distribution of frontier lands. Pivoting the colonial and national eras, the allocation of Kentucky lands initiated a significant expansion of settlement and preemption rights. The sympathetic rhetoric of pamphleteer Thomas Jefferson gradually evolved into the distribution policy of the United States. What started in Kentucky as a nod to the homestead ethic eventually translated into the Homestead Act. Liberalization of land laws, together with more orderly procedures for surveying tracts, reduced the insurrectionary fury of westering pioneers.[9]

And yet in other respects the passage through the Cumberland Gap and to republican government did not create so sharp a break with the colonial past. The independence of the United States did not mean independence for most Kentuckians or for pioneer successors to the west. As in Kentucky, good lands invited competition among great speculators. As in Kentucky, too, the defense of squatting rights incorporated a formidable critique of market relations. But while pioneers across the continent professed allegiance to simple agrarian principles, they continued to treat land as something more than the guarantor of independence. Liberalized distribution policies made only a limited difference as long as homesteaders' actions negated agrarian ideals.[10]

Henry Clay decried the trend of federal land legislation. In 1838, he was the lone senator from a trans-Appalachian state to vote against bills reducing the minimum price of land and allowing squatters on federal land preference in buying the tracts that they occupied. To Clay, lowering the price "induced" buyers "to purchase more than they actually want." Here Clay sounded an antispeculative note that accorded with homesteader rhetoric. But the defender of the Bluegrass System and the author of the "American System" was no radical. He "considered the preemptioner a trespasser" and detested the rewarding of squatters on the basis of their illegal occupancy. At bottom, Clay feared that too liberal land policies invited haphazard expansion and subverted consolidation of the republic.[11]

Economic development and political integration were the twin goals of Clay's American System, but these did not mesh as easily as Clay envisioned. At the national level, Jacksonians thwarted Clay's ambitious plans for federally financed internal improvements and for protective tariffs to encourage domestic industries. Western state governments nevertheless implemented parts of Clay's agenda. Canal and turnpike projects, along with new rules of privatized property, spread across the trans-Appalachian West. However, these improvements did not complete the consolidation of the western country, and they would not during Henry Clay's lifetime—not as long as slavery split the West and the nation.

Already by the time Daniel Boone died, Green River agrarians and (white) evangelicals, like backcountry hunters and Bluegrass gentlemen before them, had made their bargains with the devil of slavery. Because unfree labor produced Kentucky's most marketable commodities, it abetted the state's economic consolidation. But for the rest of Clay's life, slavery haunted the political consolidation of the United States.

AT THE END OF HENRY CLAY'S LIFE, it was said the ghost of Daniel Boone haunted him too. That, at any rate, was the story that ran in the Louisville *Courier Journal* on August 31, 1884. According to the tale, which was attributed to Clay's daughter-in-law, the author of the American System was sitting in his library at Ashland shortly "before his last and fatal visit to Washington." On this night, a violent thunderstorm raged outside. Suddenly a "grizzled and weather beaten" man appeared out of the rain. Clad in buckskin shirt and coonskin cap, the "unbidden guest" carried a six-foot rifle and powder horn. Entering the library, the drenched figure silently sat down in a large chair across from the desk at which Clay had been writing.

At first, Clay thought "the strange visitant" a "wanderer from the mountains, . . . but this did not seem a sufficient explanation, for the house was known to be carefully closed, and such costumes had become extinct even in the neighboring hill country twenty-five or thirty years before." Uneasily attempting to begin a conversation, Clay inquired why his visitor was out on such a wet night. "But the man in buckskin answered never a word, and continued to stare mournfully at his unwilling host for some seconds, after which he shouldered his rifle and departed as he had come." The doors remained bolted and padlocked, yet the visitor disappeared into the night. "Even more remarkable, the dripping rifle "had left not a trace of moisture on the floor where it stood, neither was the thickly upholstered chair in which the figure rested the least bit dampened by contact with the steaming clothes of the visitor." It was then that Clay recognized the mysterious caller to be "his old friend Daniel Boone," whose return Clay regarded "as a warning of impending death." [12]

As a conclusion to this book, the story of Clay's haunting by Boone is too good to be true, and, of course, it was not true. Daniel Boone and Henry Clay were not old pals. Though their lives overlapped for more than four decades, the two most famous Kentuckians never met (or at least there is no record of a meeting). In fact, Clay's arrival in Kentucky nearly coincided with Boone's departure for Missouri. Far from friends, Boone and Clay were adversaries when their paths almost crossed. In the proceedings of Nathaniel Hart's heirs vs. Daniel Boone, Henry Clay failed to win a settlement against the defendant. But Boone was not present to enjoy his acquittal, and his victory was a case of too little too late. His lands were already lost, and so was his Kentucky.

APPENDIX: TABLES

TABLE A.I. Land Acquisition of Boonesborough Petitioners, 1779

	Number
Recipients of S + P Warrants (1,400 acres)	12
Received no grant	3
Received grants for less than 1,400 acres	5
Received grants for 1,400 acres	1
Received grants for more than 1,400 acres	3
Recipients of P Warrant Only (1,000 acres)	3
Received no grant	0
Received grants for less than 1,000 acres	0
Received grants for 1,000 acres	1
Received grants for more than 1,000 acres	2
Recipients of S Warrant Only (400 acres)	14
Received no grant	6
Received grants for less than 400 acres	0
Received grants for 400 acres	3
Received grants for more than 400 acres	4
Petition Signers Receiving No Warrant	17

Sources: Katherine Phelps, comp., "A Partial List of Those at Fort Boonesborough," *RKHS* 23 (May 1925): 155; "Certificate Book of the Virginia Land Commission," ibid. 21 (1923); Joan E. Brookes-Smith, *Master Index Virginia Surveys and Grants, 1774–1791* (Frankfort, 1976).

TABLE A.2. Land Acquisition of Pioneers, 1773–1775

	Number	Percentage
Recipients of S + P Warrants (1,400 acres)	176	
Received no grant	80	45.5
Received grants for less than 1,400 acres	24	13.6
Received grants for 1,400 acres	16	9.1
Received grants for more than 1,400 acres	56	31.8
Recipients of P Warrant Only (1,000 acres)	138	
Received no grant	63	45.7
Received grants for less than 1,000 acres	9	6.5
Received grants for 1,000 acres	23	16.7
Received grants for more than 1,000 acres	43	31.2

Sources: Neal O. Hammon, comp., "Pioneers in Kentucky, 1773–1775," *FCHQ* 55 (July 1981): 275–83; "Certificate Book of the Virginia Land Commission," *RKHS* 21 (1923); Joan E. Brookes-Smith, *Master Index Virginia Surveys and Grants, 1774–1791* (Frankfort, 1976).

TABLE A.3. Land Acquisition of 1774 Harrod Party

	Number
Members of Company	36
Recipients of S + P Warrant (1,400 acres)	14
Received no grant	2
Received grants for less than 1,400 acres	0
Received grants for 1,400 acres	3
Received grants for more than 1,400 acres	9
Recipients of P Warrant Only (1,000 acres)	10
Received no grant	5
Received grants for less than 1,000 acres	1
Received grants for 1,000 acres	1
Received grants for more than 1,000 acres	3
Recipients of S Warrant Only (400 acres)	1
Received no grant	1
Recipients of No Warrant	11

Sources: Neal O. Hammon, comp., "Pioneers in Kentucky, 1773–1775," *FCHQ* 55 (July 1981): 271; "Certificate Book of the Virginia Land Commission," *RKHS* 21 (1923); Joan E. Brookes-Smith, *Master Index Virginia Surveys and Grants, 1774–1791* (Frankfort, 1976).

TABLE A.4. Nelson County Tobacco Petitions

	Petitioners	Nonpetitioners
0 acres	36 (23.8%)	706 (51%)
1–199 acres	51 (33.8%)	401 (28.9%)
200-999 acres	52 (34.5%)	247 (17.8%)
1,000+ acres	12 (7.9%)	30 (2.1%)
Number on 1792 tax list	151	1,384
Slaveowners	57 (37.8%)	174 (12.6%)
With 10 or more slaves	6 (4%)	15 (1.1%)

Sources: John Frederick Dorman, comp., *Petitions from Kentucky to the Virginia Legislature, 1776–1791: A Supplement to Petitions of the Early Inhabitants of Kentucky to the General Assembly of Virginia, 1769–1792* (Easley, S.C., 1981), 273–79; Nelson County Tax Lists, 1792, microfilm (KHS).

TABLE A.5. Woodford County Land Distribution

	Acres held, 1796			
	0	1–499	500–999	1,000+
Number	451	301	44	69
Percentage	52.1	34.8	5.1	8.0

	Acres held, 1810			
	0	1–499	500–999	1,000+
Number	598	449	56	52
Percentage	51.8	38.9	4.8	4.5

	Acres held, 1825			
	0	1–499	500–999	1,000+
Number	673	610	39	33
Percentage	49.7	45.0	2.9	2.4

Source: Kentucky County Tax Lists, microfilm (KHS).

TABLE A.6. Woodford County Slaveholding

	1796	1810	1825
Total households	865	1155	1355
Nonslaveholders	548	629	633
(% of households)	(63.4)	(54.5)	(46.7)
Holders of 1–4 slaves	198	280	365
(% of households)	(22.9)	(24.2)	(26.9)
(% of slaveowners)	(62.5)	(53.2)	(50.6)
Holders of 5–9 slaves	71	143	200
(% of households)	(8.2)	(12.4)	(14.8)
(% of slaveowners)	(22.4)	(27.2)	(27.7)
Holders of 10–19 slaves	42	86	115
(% of households)	(4.9)	(7.4)	(8.5)
(% of slaveowners)	(13.2)	(16.3)	(15.9)
Holders of 20+ slaves	6	17	42
(% of households)	(0.7)	(1.5)	(3.1)
(% of slaveowners)	(1.9)	(3.2)	(5.8)

Source: Kentucky County Tax Lists, microfilm (KHS).

TABLE A.7. Resident Land Distribution in the Green River Country, 1800–1801

	Acres					
	0	1–199	200	201–299	300–999	1,000+
Logan County, 1800						
Number	246	163	232	18	93	13
Percentage	32.2	21.3	30.3	2.4	12.1	1.7
Barren County, 1800						
Number	151	54	139	7	47	3
Percentage	37.7	13.5	34.7	1.7	11.7	0.7
Muhlenberg County, 1800						
Number	112	20	80	2	34	4
Percentage	44.4	7.9	31.7	0.8	13.5	1.6
Wayne County, 1801						
Number	204	23	72	18	3	0
Percentage	63.8	6.9	22.5	5.6	0.9	0

Source: Kentucky Tax Lists, microfilm (KHS).

TABLE A.8. Resident Land Distribution in the Green River Country, 1792–1825

	Acres				
	0	1–199	200–299	300–999	1,000+
Logan County, 1792					
Number	93	21	11	8	2
Percentage	68.9	15.6	8.1	5.9	1.5
Percentage Owners Only		50.0	26.2	19.1	4.8
Logan County, 1800					
Number	246	163	250	93	13
Percentage	32.2	21.3	32.7	12.1	1.7
Percentage Owners Only		45.3	48.2	17.9	2.5
Logan County, 1810					
Number	412	241	174	254	77
Percentage	35.6	21.0	15.0	22.0	6.6
Percentage Owners Only		32.3	23.3	34.0	10.3
Logan County, 1825					
Number	534	433	180	224	51
Percentage	37.6	30.4	12.7	17.7	3.5
Percentage Owners Only		48.8	20.3	25.3	5.7
Barren County, 1800					
Number	151	54	146	47	3
Percentage	37.7	13.5	36.4	11.7	0.7
Percentage Owners Only		21.6	58.4	18.8	1.2
Barren County, 1825					
Number	695	552	233	211	31
Percentage	40.4	32.1	13.5	12.3	1.8
Percentage Owners Only		53.8	22.7	20.5	3.0
Muhlenberg County, 1800					
Number	112	20	82	34	4
Percentage	44.4	7.9	32.5	13.5	1.6
Percentage Owners Only		14.2	58.5	24.3	2.9
Muhlenberg County, 1825					
Number	296	212	135	162	30
Percentage	35.4	25.4	16.2	19.4	3.6
Percentage Owners Only		39.3	25.0	30.1	5.6
Wayne County, 1801					
Number	204	23	90	3	0
Percentage	63.8	6.9	28.1	0.9	0.0
Percentage Owners Only		19.8	62.1	2.6	0.0
Wayne County, 1810					
Number	473	217	121	94	5
Percentage	52.0	23.9	13.3	10.3	0.5
Percentage Owners Only		49.6	27.7	21.5	1.1

TABLE A.8. continued

	Acres				
	0	1–199	200–299	300–999	1,000+
Wayne County, 1825					
Number	550	491	133	145	5
Percentage	41.6	37.1	10.1	11.0	0.4
Percentage Owners Only		63.6	17.2	18.7	0.6

Sources: Kentucky Tax Lists, microfilm, KHS.

TABLE A.9. Resident Slaveownership

Logan County

	1792	1800	1810	1825
Total households	135	765	1,158	1,422
Slaveholders	21	156	358	622
Percentage of slaveowners	15.6	20.4	30.9	43.7
Distribution of slaves				
Holders of 1–4 slaves	17	114	206	348
Holders of 5–9 slaves	1	32	90	156
Holders of 10–19 slaves	2	10	49	96
Holders of 20+ slaves	1	0	13	22

Barren County

	1800	1825
Total households	706	1,722
Slaveholders	144	560
Percentage of slaveowners	20.4	32.5
Distribution of slaves		
Holders of 1–4 slaves	115	354
Holders of 5–9 slaves	29	132
Holders of 10–19 slaves	4	63
Holders of 20+ slaves	1	9

Muhlenberg County

	1800	1825
Total households	252	835
Slaveholders	23	164
Percentage of slaveowners	9.1	19.6
Distribution of slaves		
Holders of 1–4 slaves	19	101
Holders of 5–9 slaves	3	45
Holders of 10–19 slaves	1	15
Holders of 20+ slaves	0	3

TABLE A.9. continued

Wayne County

	1801	1810	1825
Total households	320	910	1,322
Slaveholders	46	100	167
Percentage of slaveowners	14.4	11.0	12.6
Distribution of slaves			
Holders of 1–4 slaves	37	74	122
Holders of 5–9 slaves	8	20	36
Holders of 10–19 slaves	1	6	8
Holders of 20+ slaves	0	0	1

Source: Kentucky Tax Lists, microfilm, KHS.

TABLE A.10. Account Settlements

James Weir (Greenville, Muhlenberg County), 1813–1814

	Number	Percentage
Total number of accounts	306	—
Settled by cash only	95	31.0
Settled by work/trade only	106	34.6
Settled by combination	105	34.3

Robert Renick (Smith Grove, Barren County), 1816–1821

	Number	Percentage
Total number of accounts	56	—
Settled by cash only	6	10.7
Settled by work/trade only	17	30.4
Settled by combination	33	58.9

Sources: James Weir, Account Book, 1813–1815 (FC); Robert Renick, Account Books, 1816–1821 (WKU).

ABBREVIATIONS

Acts   *Acts Passed at the Session of the General Assembly for the Commonwealth of Kentucky* (Frankfort, 1792–   )

AHR   *American Historical Review*

CVSP   William P. Palmer, ed., *Calendar of Virginia State Papers and Other Manuscripts*, 11 vols. (Richmond, 1875–93)

Draper MSS   Lyman Draper Manuscripts, University of Wisconsin, Madison, Wisconsin

Durrett   Reuben Durrett Collection, University of Chicago, Chicago, Illinois

EKU   Special Collections, Eastern Kentucky University Library, Richmond, Kentucky

FC   Manuscripts, Filson Club, Louisville, Kentucky

FCHQ   *Filson Club History Quarterly*

HCP   James F. Hopkins et al., eds., *The Papers of Henry Clay*, 10 vols. (Lexington, 1959–91)

HL   Manuscripts, Huntington Library, San Marino, California

House   *Journal of the House of Representatives of the Commonwealth of Kentucky* (Frankfort, 1792–   )

KHS   Manuscripts, Kentucky Historical Society, Frankfort, Kentucky

LC   Manuscripts division, Library of Congress, Washington, D.C.

Law   William Littell, ed., *The Statute Laws of Kentucky*, 3 vols. (Frankfort, 1811–19)

MVHR   *Mississippi Valley Historical Review*

NCR   William L. Saunders, ed., *The Colonial Records of North Carolina*, 25 vols. (Raleigh, 1886–1905)

Petitions   James Rood Robertson, ed., *Petitions of the Early Inhabitants of Kentucky to the General Assembly of Virginia, 1769–1792* (Louisville, 1914)

RKHS   *Register of the Kentucky Historical Society*

Senate   *Journal of the Senate of the Commmonwealth of Kentucky* (Frankfort, 1792–   )

Transy   Special Collections, Transylvania University, Lexington, Kentucky

UK   Special Collections, Margaret I. King Library, University of Kentucky, Lexington, Kentucky

VHS   Manuscripts, Virginia Historical Society, Richmond, Virginia

VMHB   *Virginia Magazine of History and Biography*

WKU   Manuscripts, Kentucky Library, Western Kentucky University, Bowling Green, Kentucky

WL   Manuscripts, Washington and Lee Library, Washington and Lee University, Lexington, Virginia

WMQ   William and Mary Quarterly, third series

1 Hughes   James Hughes, comp., *A Report of the Causes Determined by the Late Supreme Court for the District of Kentucky, and by the Court of Appeals, in which Titles to Land Were in Dispute* (Cincinnati, 1869)

1 Sneed   Achilles Sneed, comp., *Decisions of the Court of Appeals of the State of Kentucky from March 1, 1801 to January 18, 1805* (Louisville, 1898)

1 Hardin   Martin D. Hardin, comp., *Reports of Cases Argued and Adjudged in the Court of Appeals of Kentucky from Spring Term 1805 to Spring Term 1808* (Louisville, 1899)

1 Bibb   George M. Bibb, comp., *Reports of Cases at Common Law and in Chancery, Argued and Decided in the Court of Appeals of the Commonwealth of Kentucky, from Fall Term 1808 to Spring and Fall Terms 1809* (Cincinnati, 1910)

4 Bibb   George M. Bibb, comp., *Reports of Cases at Common Law and in Chancery, Argued and Decided in the Court of Appeals of the Commonwealth of Kentucky, from Spring Term 1815 to Spring Term 1817* (Frankfort, 1817)

1 Marshall   Alex K. Marshall, comp., *Decisions of the Court of Appeals of Kentucky, Commencing with the Fall Term 1817 and Ending with the Spring Term 1819* (Washington, Ky., 1819)

3 Marshall   Alex K. Marshall, comp., *Decisions of the Court of Appeals of Kentucky, Commencing with the Fall Term 1820 and Ending with the Fall Term 1821* (Washington, Ky., 1823)

2 Littell   William Littell, comp., *Reports of Cases at Common Law and in Chancery, Decided by the Court of Appeals of the Commonwealth of Kentucky* (Frankfort, 1823)

NOTES

Introduction

1. No dual biography of Daniel Boone and Henry Clay has been written, but individually each has been the subject of a number of fine (and even stirring) biographies. For Boone, start with John Bakeless, *Daniel Boone: Master of the Wilderness* (New York, 1939), which for many decades stood as the definitive treatment. It has only recently been superseded by John Mack Faragher, *Daniel Boone: The Life and Legend of an American Pioneer* (New York, 1992). As for Clay, the New Deal era renewed scholarly interest in his activist vision of state-aided economic development and resulted in a number of still valuable life studies. See Glydon G. Van Deusen, *The Life of Henry Clay* (Boston, 1937); George R. Poage, *Henry Clay and the Whig Party* (Chapel Hill, 1936); Bernard Mayo, *Henry Clay: Spokesman of the New West* (Boston, 1937). More recent biographies include Clement Eaton, *Henry Clay and the Art of American Politics* (Boston, 1957); Merrill D. Peterson, *The Great Triumvirate: Webster, Clay, and Calhoun* (New York, 1987); and Robert V. Remini, *Henry Clay: Statesman for the Union* (New York, 1991). For the period of Clay's life under study here, Mayo's book, the first of a projected but unfortunately unfinished three-volume biography, remains unsurpassed.

2. William Darby, *The Emigrant's Guide to the Western and Southwestern States and Territories* (New York, 1818), 206.

3. Frederick Jackson Turner, "The Significance of the Frontier in American History," in *The Frontier in American History* (New York, 1920), quotation on 12. On the particular importance of Kentucky to Turner's thesis, see Stephen Aron, "The Significance of the Kentucky Frontier," *RKHS* 91 (Summer 1993): 298–323.

4. Turner-bashing has a long history. For a survey of the voluminous literature inspired by Turner's frontier paradigm, see Ray A. Billington, *The American Frontier Thesis: Attack and Defense* (Washington, 1958). For an introduction to a gloomier "new Western history," see Patricia Limerick, *The Legacy of Conquest: The Unbroken Past of the American West* (New York, 1987); Richard White, *"It's Your Misfortune and None of My Own": A New History of the American West* (Norman, 1991). For my critique of the regionalist history of the American West advocated by Limerick and White, see Stephen Aron, "Lessons in Conquest: Towards a Greater Western History," *Pacific Historical Review* 63 (May 1994): 125–47.

5. On the pervasiveness in western American history of claims by miscast "injured innocents," see Limerick, *The Legacy of Conquest*, 35–54.

6. My understanding of the shifting meanings of the word *frontier* follows Lucien Febvre, *"Frontière"*: The Word and the Concept," in Peter Burke, ed., *A*

New Kind of History: From the Writings of Febvre (London, 1973), 208–18; John T. Juricek, "American Usage of the Word 'Frontier' from Colonial Times to Frederick Jackson Turner," American Philosophical Society, *Proceedings* 110 (Feb. 18, 1966): 10–34; Fulmer Mood, "Notes on the History of the Word 'Frontier,' " *Agricultural History* 22 (Apr. 1948): 78–83; John Mack Faragher, "A Nation Thrown Back Upon Itself: Turner and the Frontier," *Culturefront* 2 (Summer 1993): 5–9, 75. The construction of frontiers as cultural-political intersections is succinctly distilled in Howard Lamar and Leonard Thompson, "Comparative Frontier History," in idem, eds., *The Frontier in History: North America and Southern Africa Compared* (New Haven, 1981), 7–8. See also William Cronon, George Miles, and Jay Gitlin, "Becoming West: Toward a New Meaning for Western History," in idem, eds., *Under an Open Sky: Rethinking America's Western Past* (New York, 1992), 3–27; Aron, "Lessons in Conquest," 142–46, for attempts to delineate the processes which take place across cultural-political intersections. Defining eighteenth-century American frontiers exclusively as intersections risks losing the global dimension, however. What were "hinterlands" from the perspective of European empires were, after all, "heartlands" from the perspective of Indian peoples.

Chapter One. The Meeting of Hunters
   1. Carl Bridenbaugh, *Myths and Realities: Societies of the Colonial South* (Baton Rouge, 1952), 127, coined the term "Greater Pennsylvania," but the notion that southeastern Pennsylvania served as the demographic and cultural wellspring for much of the eighteenth-century southern and trans-Appalachian backcountry emerged earlier and has been a subject of continuing controversy. See Russell R. Menard, "Was There a 'Middle Colonies Demographic Regime'?," *Proceedings of the American Philosophical Society* 133 (June 1989): 215–18; Terry G. Jordan and Matti Kaups, *The American Backwoods Frontier: An Ethnic and Ecological Interpretation* (Baltimore, 1989), 7–12; D. W. Meinig, *The Shaping of America: A Geographical Perspective on 500 Years of History*, vol. 1, *Atlantic America, 1492–1800* (New Haven, 1986), 244–54; Robert D. Mitchell, "The Formation of Early American Cultural Regions: An Interpretation," in James R. Gibson, ed., *European Settlement and Development in North America: Essays on Geographical Change in Honour and Memory of Andrew Hill Clark* (Toronto, 1978), 66–90. Not as controversial but still mysterious are the Indian origins of the name Kentucky. Early settlers, like Peter Cartwright, *Autobiography of Peter Cartwright: The Backwoods Preacher*, ed. W. P. Strickland (New York, 1858), 21, assumed that the name derived from an Indian word meaning a land of "cane and turkeys." More recent historians have rejected such literal translations, but the issue has not been settled. Several historians have claimed that the name signified "land of tomorrow," attributing it to various tribes—the Cherokees, the Iroquois, and the Wyandots—which intended to inhabit Kentucky at some point in the future. See Edward Coffman, *The Story of Logan County* (Nashville, 1962), 15–16; George M. Chinn, *Kentucky: Settlement and Statehood, 1750–1800* (Frankfort, 1975), 7; Steven A. Channing, *Kentucky: A Bicentennial History* (New York, 1977), 4. John Mason Brown, *The Political Beginnings of Kentucky* (Louisville, 1889), 10, repeated the view that Kentucky was a Shawnee word signifying "at the head of the river."

Brown, however, along with Robert S. Cotterill, *History of Pioneer Kentucky* (Cincinnati, 1917), 15, and Lucien Beckner, "John Findley: The First Pathfinder of Kentucky," *FCHQ* 43 (July 1969): 209, agreed that the term was Iroquois in origin, and that it was synonymous with meadow land.

2. J. Stoddard Johnson, ed., *First Explorations of Kentucky: Journals of Dr. Thomas Walker, 1750, and Christopher Gist, 1751* (Louisville, 1898), quotation on 75; Butricke to Burnsley, Sept. 25, 1768, in Clarence Alvord and Clarence Carter, eds., *Trade and Politics, 1767–1769* (Springfield, 1921), quotation on 409; "Sketches from Border Life," Draper MSS, 27CC33; Felix Walker's Narrative of His Trip with Daniel Boone from Long Island to Boonesborough, in George W. Ranck, ed., *Boonesborough: Its Founding, Pioneer Struggles, Indian Experience, Transylvania Days, and Revolutionary Annals* (Louisville, 1901), quotation on 163–64.

3. A. Gwynn Henderson, ed., *Fort Ancient Cultural Dynamics in the Middle Ohio Valley* (Madison, 1992); A. Gwynn Henderson, "Dispelling the Myth: Seventeenth- and Eighteenth-Century Indian Life in Kentucky," *RKHS* 40 (1992): 1–25; "1736: Census of Indian Tribes," in R. G. Thwaites, ed., *Collections of the State Historical Society of Wisconsin*, 31 vols. (Madison, 1855–1931), 17:250; Lucien Beckner, "Eskippakithiki: The Last Indian Town in Kentucky," *FCHQ* 6 (Oct. 1932): 355–82.

4. Daniel K. Richter, *The Ordeal of the Long-House: The Peoples of the Iroquois League in the Era of European Colonization* (Chapel Hill, 1992), 144–49; Charles Callender, "Shawnee," in Bruce G. Trigger, ed., *Handbook of North American Indians*, 20 vols. (Washington, D.C., 1978), 15:630–34; A. Gwynn Henderson, Cynthia E. Jobe, and Christopher A. Turnbow, *Indian Occupation and Use in Northern and Eastern Kentucky during the Contact Period (1540–1795): An Initial Investigation* (Frankfort, 1986).

5. Will Emery exemplified the mixing of ethnicities in Ohio Indian country. Although Emery lived among and was often identified as a member of the Shawnees, he was at other times labeled a Cherokee or part Cherokee. (See Richard Henderson to Partners, July 18, 1775, Draper MSS, 4B34–36. I am grateful to John Mack Faragher for this reference.) For contemporary discussions of Shawnee relocation, see "1718: Memoir on the Savages of Canada as far as the Mississippi River, Describing Their Customs and Trade," in Thwaites, ed., *Collections of the State Historical Society of Wisconsin*, 16:364; Conrad Weiser, "Conrad Weiser's Journal of a Tour to the Ohio, August 11–October 2, 1748," in R. G. Thwaites, ed., *Early Western Travels, 1748–1846*, 32 vols. (Cleveland, 1904), 1:31; David Jones, *A Journal of Two Visits Made to Some Nations of Indians on the West Side of the River Ohio in the Years 1772 and 1773* (Burlington, 1774), 37. For general discussions of Shawnee migrations and the repeopling of the Ohio Valley, see Michael N. McConnell, "Peoples 'in Between': The Iroquois and the Ohio Indians, 1720–1768," in Daniel K. Richter and James H. Merrell, eds., *Beyond the Covenant Chain: The Iroquois and Their Neighbors in Indian North America, 1600–1800* (Syracuse, 1987), 93–112; Peter H. Wood, "The Changing Population of the Colonial South: An Overview by Race and Region, 1685–1790," in Peter H. Wood, Gregory A. Waselkov, and M. Thomas Hatley, eds., *Powhatan's Mantle: Indians in the Colonial Southeast* (Lincoln, 1989), 85–87; Jerry Clark, *The Shawnee* (Lexington, 1977), 5–27.

6. Franklin B. Dexter, ed., *Diary of David McClure, Doctor of Divinity, 1748–1820* (New York, 1899), quotation on 68; William A. Galloway, *Old Chillicothe: Shawnee and Pioneer History* (Xenia, Ohio, 1934), 44–45; Helen Hornbeck Tanner, "The Glaize in 1792: A Composite Indian Community," *Ethnohistory* 25 (Winter 1978): 15–39; Michael N. McConnell, *A Country Between: The Upper Ohio Valley and Its Peoples, 1724–1774* (Lincoln, 1992), 210–20.

7. Wood, "The Changing Population of the Colonial South," 85; Clark, *The Shawnee*, 66–67.

8. Orley E. Brown, ed., *The Captivity of Jonathan Alder and His Life with the Indians* (Alliance, Ohio, 1965), 29–30; John Heckewelder, *History, Manners, and Customs of the Indian Nations, Who Once Inhabited Pennsylvania and the Neighbouring States* (1818), ed. William C. Reichel, *Memoirs of the Historical Society of Pennsylvania* 12 (Philadelphia, 1871), 163–69; Galloway, *Old Chillicothe*, 194–95.

9. Brown, ed., *The Captivity of Jonathan Alder*, 22, 29–30; Dexter, ed., *Diary of David McClure*, 89–90; Morgan to Baynton and Wharton, December 11, 1767, in Alvord and Carter, eds., *Trade and Politics*, 135; Henry Harvey, *History of the Shawnee Indians, from the Year 1681 to 1854, Inclusive* (Cincinnati, 1855), 146–51; James Smith, *An Account of the Remarkable Occurrences in the Life and Travels of Col. James Smith*, ed. William Darlington (Cincinnati, 1870), 44–45; James H. Howard, *Shawnee!: The Ceremonialism of a Native American Indian Tribe and Its Cultural Background* (Athens, Ohio, 1981), 43.

10. Mary Kinnan, *True Narrative of the Sufferings of Mary Kinnan, Who Was Taken Prisoner by the Shawanee Nation of Indians on the Thirteenth Day of May, 1791, and Remained with Them Until the Sixteenth of August, 1794* (Elizabethtown, 1795), quotation on 8; Milo Milton Quaife, ed., *The Indian Captivity of O. M. Spencer* (Chicago, 1917), quotation on 75; Brown, ed., *The Captivity of Jonathan Alder*, 29–30; Jones, *A Journal of Two Visits*, 55–58; Dexter, ed., *Diary of David McClure*, 68; Smith, *An Account of the Remarkable Occurrences in the Life and Travels of Col. James Smith*, 44–45, John Brickell, "Narrative of John Brickell's Captivity among the Delawares," *American Pioneer* 1 (Feb. 1842): 47.

11. Heckewelder, *History, Manners, and Customs of the Indian Nations*, quotation on 193.

12. Edwin Erle Sparks, ed., *Incidents Attending the Capture, Detention, and Ransom of Charles Johnston of Virginia* (1827; Cleveland, 1905), 56–57; Smith, *An Account of the Remarkable Occurrences in the Life and Travels of Col. James Smith*, 50; Jones, *A Journal of Two Visits*, 58; Samuel Cole Williams, ed., *Adair's History of the American Indians* (1775; Johnson City, Tenn., 1930), 462–63. Further protection from a life of slavery was provided by the control that women exercised over the beginning and ending of marriages. The forwardness of Indian women in courting stunned European onlookers. The ease with which Indian men and women divorced, simply by separating, also saved females from unfair treatment. (See John H. Moore, ed., "A Captive of the Shawnees, 1779–1784," *West Virginia History* 23 (July 1962): 293; Brown, ed., *The Captivity of Jonathan Alder*, 63; Smith, *An Account of the Remarkable Occurrences in the Life and Travels of Col. James Smith*, 140–41.)

13. Smith, *An Account of the Remarkable Occurrences in the Life and Travels of Col. James Smith*, 45.

14. For a general discussion of this issue, see Wilcomb E. Washburn, "The Moral and Legal Justifications for Dispossessing the Indians," in James Morton Smith, ed., *Seventeenth-Century America: Essays in Colonial History* (Chapel Hill, 1959), 15–32.

15. Delf Norona, ed., "Joshua Fry's Report on the Back Settlements of Virginia, May 8, 1751," *VMHB* 56 (Jan. 1948): 35; Cotterill, *History of Pioneer Kentucky*, 10–15; Steven J. Pyne, *Fire in America: A Cultural History of Wildland and Rural Fire* (Princeton, 1982), 71–83; Mary E. Wharton and Roger W. Barbour, *Bluegrass Land and Life: Land Character, Plants, and Animals of the Inner Bluegrass Region of Kentucky* (Lexington, 1992), 33–39; Samuel N. Dicken, "The Kentucky Barrens," *Bulletin of the Geographical Society of Philadelphia* 33 (Apr. 1935): 42–51.

16. Smith, *An Account of the Remarkable Occurrences in the Life and Travels of Col. James Smith*, 90–91; Brown, ed., *The Captivity of Jonathan Alder*, 56; Frederick Drimmer, ed., *Captured by the Indians: Fifteen Firsthand Accounts, 1750–1870* (New York, 1985), 93–94; Galloway, *Old Chillicothe*, 303–11; James A. Clifton, *Star Woman and Other Shawnee Tales* (Latham, Md., 1984), 1–21, 37–48; Gregory Dowd, *A Spirited Resistance: The North American Indian Struggle for Unity, 1745–1815* (Baltimore, 1992), 4–6; William G. McLoughlin, *Cherokees and Missionaries, 1789–1839* (New Haven, 1984), 18–19; Charles Hudson, *The Southeastern Indians* (Knoxville, 1976), 272–81, 340.

17. Thomas Wildcat Alford, *Civilization* (Norman, 1936), quotation on 53; Heckewelder, *History, Manners, and Customs*, 100–106, 310–11; Dexter, ed., *Diary of David McClure*, 89–90; Harvey, *History of the Shawnee Indians*, 151; Howard, *Shawnee!*, 43–48, 195–96.

18. Ebenezer Denny, *Military Journal of Major Ebenezer Denny, an Officer in the Revolutionary and Indian Wars* (Philadelphia, 1859), 68.

19. Smith, *An Account of the Remarkable Occurrences in the Life and Travels of Col. James Smith*, quotation on 49; Brown, ed., *The Captivity of Jonathan Alder*, quotations on 28, 39; Heckewelder, *History, Manners, and Customs*, 100–106.

20. Richard White, *The Middle Ground: Indians, Empires, and Republics in the Great Lakes Region, 1650–1815* (New York, 1991), esp. 186–222.

21. "Letter from the French minister to Beauharnois, March 24, 1744," in Thwaites, ed., *Collections of the State Historical Society of Wisconsin*, quotation on 18:4; "Letter from the French minister to La Jonquiere, May 4, 1749," ibid., 18:20; White, *The Middle Ground*, 223–68; McConnell, *A Country Between*, 142–206.

22. Beverly W. Bond Jr., ed., "Notes on Proposed Settlements in the West, 1755–1757," Historical and Philosophical Society of Ohio, *Publications* (Cincinnati, 1925), quotation on 42; Williams, ed., *Adair's History of the American Indians*, 305–6; Wilbur R. Jacobs, ed., *Indians of the Southern Colonial Frontier: The Edmond Atkin Report and Plan of 1755* (Columbia, S.C., 1954), 7–13; idem, *Dispossessing the American Indian: Indians and Whites on the Colonial Frontier* (New York, 1972), 50–57, 75–82.

23. Richard J. Hooker, ed., *The Carolina Backcountry on the Eve of the Revolution: The Journal and Other Writings of Charles Woodmason, Anglican Itinerant* (Chapel Hill, 1953), quotation on 6; Lieut.-General Thomas Gage to Earl of Hillsborough, Oct. 7, 1772, in K. G. Davies, ed., *Documents of the American Revolution, 1770–1783*, 21 vols. (Shannon, 1972–81), quotation on 5:203; Sir William

Johnson to Earl of Dartmouth, Nov. 4, 1772, ibid., quotation on 6:225; William J. Hinke and Charles E. Kemper, eds., "Moravian Diaries of Travels through Virginia," *VMHB* 11 (Oct. 1903): 123; Nicholas Cresswell, *The Journal of Nicholas Cresswell, 1774–1777* (New York, 1924), 50.

24. "William Logan's Journal of a Journey to Georgia, 1745," *Pennsylvania Magazine of History and Biography* 36 (Jan. 1912), quotation on 7; Hooker, ed., *The Carolina Backcountry*, quotation on 52.

25. Sir William Johnson to Earl of Dartmouth, Sept. 22, 1773, in Davies, ed., *Documents of the American Revolution*, 6:225; Governor Earl of Dunmore to Earl of Dartmouth, Dec. 24, 1774, ibid., 8:258; Dexter, ed. *Diary of David McClure*, 93. On the late-eighteenth-century elites' understanding of social progress and decay see Drew McCoy, *The Elusive Republic: Political Economy in Jeffersonian America* (Chapel Hill, 1980), 13–47.

26. William Byrd, *Histories of the Dividing Line Betwixt Virginia and North Carolina*, ed. William K. Boyd (New York, 1967), 90, 92. On English game laws, labor, and society, see E. P. Thompson, *Whigs and Hunters: The Origins of the Black Act* (New York, 1975); Douglas Hay, "Poaching and the Game Laws on Cannock Chase," in Hay et al., *Albion's Fatal Tree: Crime and Society in Eighteenth-Century England* (New York, 1975), 189–253; P. B. Munsche, *Gentlemen and Poachers: The English Game Laws, 1671–1831* (Cambridge, 1981).

27. Byrd, *Histories of the Dividing Line Betwixt Virginia and North Carolina*, 92.

28. James Hall, *Sketches of History, Life, and Manners in the West*, 2 vols. (Philadelphia, 1835), 2:69; Michael Zuckerman, "Identity in British America: Unease in Eden," in Nicholas Canny and Anthony Pagden, eds., *Colonial Identity in the Atlantic World, 1500–1800* (Princeton, 1987), 123–25; Harry Roy Merrens, *Colonial North Carolina in the Eighteenth Century: A Study in Historical Geography* (Chapel Hill, 1964), 48–49; Stephen Innes, "Fulfilling John Smith's Vision: Work and Labor in Early America," in Stephen Innes, ed., *Work and Labor in Early America* (Chapel Hill, 1988), 14–15.

29. J. Hector St. John de Crèvecoeur, *Letters from an American Farmer*, ed. Warren Barton Blake (New York, 1957), quotation on 215.

30. William Littell, ed., *The Statute Laws of Kentucky*, 3 vols. (Frankfort, 1811–19), 2:548–61, recapitulates the history of hunting laws in Virginia. On the evolution of colonial game laws and their enforcement, see James A. Tober, *Who Owns the Wildlife?: The Political Economy of Conservation in Nineteenth-Century America* (Westport, Conn., 1981), 23–28; Thomas A. Lund, *American Wildlife Law* (Berkeley, 1980), 19–34.

31. *NCR*, 4:745; ibid., 23:218–19, 656, 775–76, 801–3, 916, 955–56; ibid., 25:503–4; Stuart A. Marks, *Southern Hunting in Black and White: Nature, History, and Ritual in a Carolina Community* (Princeton, 1991), 28–33.

32. Its goals already achieved through vigilantism, the vagrancy statute passed by South Carolina lawmakers in 1787 was something of an afterthought. (See Rachel N. Klein, *Unification of a Slave State: The Rise of the Planter Class in the South Carolina Backcountry, 1760–1808* [Chapel Hill, 1990], 47–64.)

33. John Haywood, *The Civil and Political History of the State of Tennessee from Its Earliest Settlement up to the Year 1796* (Nashville, 1891), 38–39, 44–49,

88–92; Ruth Paull Burdette and Nancy Montgomery Berley, *The Long Hunters of Skin House Branch* (Columbia, Ky., 1970); Otis K. Rice, *Frontier Kentucky* (Lexington, 1975), 20–22.

34. Sir William Johnson to Earl of Dartmouth, Sept. 22, 1773, in Davies, ed., *Documents of the American Revolution*, quotation on 6:225. On the negotiations that culminated in the 1768 Treaty of Fort Stanwix, see Dorothy V. Jones, *License for Empire: Colonialism by Treaty in Early America* (Chicago, 1982), 58–92. For minutes of the treaty, see Edmund B. O'Callaghan and Berthold Fernow, eds., *Documents Relative to the Colonial History of the State of New York*, 15 vols. (Albany, 1856–87), 8:111–37.

35. George Croghan to Lieut.-General Thomas Gage, Jan. 1, 1770, in Davies, ed., *Documents of the American Revolution*, 2:21–22; John Stuart to Governor Lord Botetourt, Jan. 13, 1770, ibid., 27–29.

36. Lieut.-General Thomas Gage to Earl of Hillsborough, Aug. 18, 1770, ibid., quotation on 169; Gage to John Stuart, Oct. 16, 1770, ibid., quotation on 204.

37. Sir William Johnson to Earl of Dartmouth, Sept. 22, 1773, in Davies, ed., *Documents of the American Revolution*, 6:225; Dunmore to Dartmouth, Dec. 24, 1774, in Reuben G. Thwaites and Louise P. Kellogg, eds., *Documentary History of Dunmore's War, 1774* (Madison, 1905), 371; John Johnston, "Recollections of Sixty Years," in Leonard U. Hill, *John Johnston and the Indians in the Land of the Three Miamis* (Piqua, Ohio, 1957), 189; Tom Hatley, *The Dividing Paths: Cherokees and South Carolinians through the Era of Revolution* (New York, 1993), 212–13; Louis De Vorsey Jr., *The Indian Boundary in the Southern Colonies, 1763–1775* (Chapel Hill, 1961), 76–79.

38. For reports of violence perpetrated by Indians against white hunters, see Morgan to Baynton and Wharton, July 20, 1768, in Alvord and Carter, eds., *Trade and Politics*, 354–55; Forbes to Gage, July 28, 1768, ibid., 367; McConnell, *A Country Between*, 245, 256–57.

39. John D. Shane interview with Daniel Boone Bryan, Draper MSS, 22C14; Lyman C. Draper interview with Nathan and Olive Boone, ibid., 6S46–52.

40. James Knox, "Report on a Hunting Trip, 1769 (UK) (quotation); Draper, "Life of Boone," Draper MSS, 3B47–60.

41. John D. Shane interview with Daniel Boone Bryan, Draper MSS, 22C14 (quotation). Fifteen years after the meeting between Boone and Emery, John Filson appended an account of it to his book *The Discovery, Settlement, and Present State of Kentucke*. The appendix, "The Adventures of Col. Daniel Boon; containing a Narrative of the Wars of Kentucke," made Filson's book an international bestseller, and it made Boone a legend in his own time. Although Boone endorsed the accuracy of the narrative, Filson's version altered or deleted several key details of the encounter. Readers of Filson's book did not, for example, learn the name of Will Emery. Of his capture in December 1769, Filson's Boone recalled only that he and Stewart had been treated "with common savage usage" and "plundered of what we had." See John Filson, *The Discovery, Settlement, and Present State of Kentucke*, ed. William H. Masterson (New York, 1962), 50–53.

42. Robert B. McAfee, "The Life and Times of Robert B. McAfee and His Family and Connections," *Register of the Kentucky Historical Society*, 25 (Jan.

1927): 15–16 (quotations); Alexander McKee, "Report on Indian Speech, Pittsburgh, June 20, 1773," in Katherine Wagner Seineke, ed., *The George Rogers Clark Adventure in the Illinois and Selected Documents of the American Revolution at Frontier Posts* (New Orleans, 1981), 136; Shawnese Deputies to Keashuta and Alexander McKee, June 28, 1773, in Davies, ed., *Documents of the American Revolution*, 6:166–67; Sir William Johnson to Earl of Dartmouth, Sept. 22, 1773, ibid., 224–25.

43. James McAfee Journal, 1773, Draper MSS, 4CC1–12; Thomas Hanson, "Journal on the River Ohio," Draper MSS, 24CC1–40; Virginius C. Hall, ed., "Journal of Isaac Hite, 1773," *Bulletin of the Historical and Philosophical Society of Ohio* 12 (Oct. 1954): 262–81.

44. "Terms of Our Reconciliation," in William J. Van Schreevan, ed., *Revolutionary Virginia: The Road to Independence*, 7 vols. (Charlottesville, 1973–83), 3:150n; Thwaites and Kellogg, eds., *Documentary History of Dunmore's War, 1774*, esp. 253–97, 368–95.

45. Governor Earl of Dunmore to Earl of Dartmouth, Dec. 24, 1774, in Davies, ed., *Documents of the American Revolution*, 8:258.

46. On changing notions of manhood and masculinity, see Rupert Wilkinson, *American Tough: The Tough-Guy Tradition and American Character* (Westport, Conn., 1984); Peter Filene, "Between a Rock and a Soft Place: A Century of American Manhood," *South Atlantic Quarterly*, 84 (Autumn 1985): 339–55; Mark C. Carnes and Clyde Griffen, eds., *Meanings for Manhood: Constructions of Masculinity in Victorian America* (Chicago, 1990); David D. Gilmore, *Manhood in the Making: Cultural Concepts of Masculinity* (New Haven, 1990); Nicole Etcheson, "Manliness and the Political Culture of the Old Northwest, 1790–1860," *Journal of the Early Republic* 15 (Spring 1995): 59–77.

47. As was true for the vast majority of colonists on the North Carolina piedmont, the southwestern migration of the family of Daniel Boone to the backcountry of Virginia or North Carolina had occurred in stages over several generations. See Robert W. Ramsey, *Carolina Cradle: Settlement of the Northwest Carolina Frontier, 1747–1762* (Chapel Hill, 1964).

48. John F. D. Smyth, *A Tour in the United States of America*, 2 vols. (London, 1784), (quotation) on 1:292; Nicholas P. Hardeman, *Shucks, Shocks, and Hominy Blocks: Corn as a Way of Life in Pioneer America* (Baton Rouge, 1981), 34–55; Lewis Cecil Gray, *History of Agriculture in the Southern United States to 1860*, 2 vols. (New York, 1941; reprint ed.), 1:448–49.

49. William Dodd Brown, ed., "A Visit to Boonesborough in 1779: The Recollections of Pioneer George M. Bedinger," *RKHS* 86 (Autumn 1988): 324 (quotation); Smyth, *A Tour in the United States of America*, quotation on 1:144. For further discussion of the expansion and diminution of customary "rights in the woods," see chapter 5 below.

50. Henry J. Kaufman, *The Pennsylvania Kentucky Rifle* (Harrisburg, 1960).

51. John D. Shane interview with Samuel Treble, Draper MSS, 12CC43 (quotation); Joseph Doddridge, *Notes on the Settlement and Indian Wars of the Western Parts of Virginia and Pennsylvania from 1763 to 1783 inclusive, Together with a Review of the State of Society and Manners of the First Settlers of the Western Country* (1824; Pittsburgh, 1912), quotation on 101; Lucien Beckner, ed., "Rev-

erend John D. Shane's Interview with Pioneer William Clinkenbeard," *FCHQ* 2 (Apr. 1928): 106 (quotation); Elizabeth Thatcher Clough, ed., "Abraham Thomas: 'This Small Legacy of Experience'," *Kentucky Ancestors* 26 (Autumn 1990): 77 (quotation). For a treatise on the art of hunting, see José Ortéga Y Gasset, *Meditations on Hunting*, trans. Howard Westcott (New York, 1972).

52. Doddridge, *Notes on the Settlement and Indian Wars*, 91–93; Smyth, *A Tour in the United States of America*, 1:179–83; Jordan and Kaups, *The American Backwoods Frontier*, 211–32; John Mack Faragher, *Daniel Boone: The Life and Legend of an American Pioneer* (New York, 1992), 17–23; Harriette S. Arnow, *Seedtime on the Cumberland* (New York, 1960), 76–109.

53. John D. Shane interview with Major Black, Draper MSS, 12CC151 (quotation); Doddridge, *Notes on the Settlement*, quotation on 98; Spencer Records' Narrative, Draper MSS, 23CC5; [?] to Lyman C. Draper, Mar. 27, 1849, ibid., 5C60; William Preston (Smithfield) to Arthur Campbell and William Campbell, Dec. 6, 1780, Preston Family Papers—Gray Collection (FC).

54. On militia traditions, see Albert Tillson, "The Militia and Popular Political Culture in the Upper Valley of Virginia, 1740–1775," *VMHB* 94 (July 1986): 285–306.

55. Various traditions exist on leadership of long hunting expeditions. On the biggest long hunt of 1770 and 1771, James Knox has often been accorded the commanding position. (See Brent Altsheler, "The Long Hunters and James Knox Their Leader," *FCHQ* 5 (Oct. 1931): 169–85.) Such a claim, however, was probably based on Knox's later prominence as a landowner and a legislator in Kentucky. Interviews and correspondence with descendants of long hunters conducted by Lyman C. Draper tell a different story, emphasizing the consensual nature of decision making and assigning leadership to the more experienced Henry Skaggs and Joseph Drake. (John B. Dysart to Lyman C. Draper, June 19, 1849, Draper MSS, 5C61; Draper, "Life of Boone," ibid., 3B64–65.) The system of leadership by consent fell apart when serious differences of opinion split the long hunting company. Jealousy of the leadership of Henry Skaggs led to the defection of two dozen men from a long hunting party in the winter of 1771. Lingering resentments from a trip in 1769 resulted in the filing of several lawsuits between long hunters. Draper, "Life," Draper MSS, 3B60–65. For examples of litigation, see Obediah Terrill vs. Uriah Stone, Casper Masker vs. Uriah Stone, John Baker vs. Humphrey Hogan, in Lewis Preston Summers, ed., *Annals of Southwestern Virginia, 1769–1800* (1929; Baltimore, 1970), 610, 611, 620, 639.

56. Thomas Anburey, *Travels through the Interior Parts of America*, 2 vols. (1789; Boston, 1923), 2:240; John Redd, "Reminiscences of Western Virginia, 1770–1790," *VMHB* 7 (1900): 248; John B. Dysart to Lyman C. Draper, Mar. 27, 1849, Draper MSS, 5C60; Draper, "Life of Boone," ibid., 3B52. On the rough play of backcountry men and its meanings, see Elliott J. Gorn, " 'Gouge and Bite, Pull Hair and Scratch': The Social Significance of Fighting in the Southern Backcountry," *AHR* 90 (Feb. 1985): 18–32.

57. Arnow, *Seedtime on the Cumberland*, 153.

58. Doddridge, *Notes on the Settlement and Indian Wars*, 24; Mann Butler, "Details of Frontier Life," *RKHS* 62 (July 1964): 224; Daniel Linsey Thomas and Lucy Blayney Thomas, *Kentucky Superstitions* (Princeton, 1920), 241; David

Hackett Fischer, *Albion's Seed: Four British Folkways in America* (New York, 1989), 708–15.

59. Johnson, ed., *First Explorations of Kentucky*, quotation on 37; General William Hall to Lyman C. Draper, July 21, 1845, Draper MSS, 6XX82–85; Draper, "Life of Boone," ibid., 3B65.

60. I have pieced together biographical information on forty-four men known to have participated in one or more trans-Appalachian long hunt between 1761 and 1771 from Draper MSS, 5C60–76; 5S62; 10DD80–83; 3XX18, 40; 6XX8, 74–77; John Redd, "Reminiscences of Western Virginia, 1770–1790," *VMHB* 6 (Apr. 1899): 338–40; ibid., 7 (Jan. 1800): 249; Haywood, *The Civil and Political History of the State of Tennessee*, 45–48, 88–92; Lyman Chalkley, ed., *Chronicles of the Scotch-Irish Settlement in Virginia, Extracted from the Original Court Records of Augusta County, 1745–1800*, 3 vols. (Rosslyn, Va., 1912); Lewis Preston Summers, ed., *Annals of Southwest Virginia, 1769–1800* (1929; Baltimore, 1970); Altsheler, "The Long Hunters and James Knox Their Leader," 169–85; Burdette and Berley, *The Long Hunters of Skin House Branch*, 22–35.

61. Redd, "Reminiscences of Western Virginia," quotation on 6:338; "Incidents in the life of Henry Skaggs and Brothers," Draper MSS, 5C76 (quotation).

62. This and the following two paragraphs lean heavily on Faragher, *Daniel Boone*; James William Hagy, "The First Attempt to Settle Kentucky: Boone in Virginia," *FCHQ* 44 (July 1970): 232–33; Annette Kolodny, *The Land before Her: Fantasy and Experience of the American Frontiers, 1630–1860* (Chapel Hill, 1984), 81–89; Harriette S. Arnow, *Flowering of the Cumberland* (New York, 1963), 58–81; idem, *Seedtime on the Cumberland*, 30–57; Helen Deiss Irvin, *Women in Kentucky* (Lexington, 1979), 1–17.

63. James B. Finley, *Autobiography of Rev. James Finley or, Pioneer Life in the West* (Cincinnati, 1853), 149–51.

64. Redd, "Reminiscences of Western Virginia," quotation on 7:250; Levi Purviance, *The Biography of Elder David Purviance, with His Memoirs: Containing His Views on Baptism, the Divinity of Christ, and the Atonement. Written by Himself* (Dayton, 1848), quotation on 204; Albert H. Tillson Jr., *Gentry and Common Folk: Political Culture on a Virginia Frontier, 1740–1789* (Lexington, 1991), 54–55, 73. Supposedly Skaggs returned from a two-year hunt in southern Kentucky to discover that his wife had taken up with another man, with whom she had had a daughter. Skaggs reacted calmly, and after driving off the understudy, "took his wife into favor again." ("Incidents in the life of Henry Skaggs," Draper MSS, 5C76); similar rumors circulated about the paternity of James Harrod's daughter Margaret (Kathryn Harrod Mason, *James Harrod of Kentucky* (Baton Rouge, 1951), 215–17) and about Daniel Boone's daughter Jemima. For a thorough investigation of the facts and folklore surrounding "Boone's surprise," see Faragher, *Daniel Boone*, 58–62.

Chapter Two. The Parting of Hunters

1. For Boone's recollections of his capture and reintroduction to Will Emery as recounted by his son, see Lyman Draper interview with Nathan and Olive Boone, Draper MSS, 6S106–107.

2. "Felix Walker's Narrative of His Trip with Boone from Long Island to

Boonesborough in March, 1775," in George W. Ranck, ed., *Boonesborough: Its Founding, Pioneer Struggles, Indian Experiences, Transylvania Days, and Revolutionary Annals* (Louisville, 1901), quotations on 163, 165; "Judge Richard Henderson's Journal of a Trip to 'Cantuckey' and of Events at Boonesborough in 1775," ibid., quotation on 177; Daniel Boone to Richard Henderson, Apr. 1, 1775, Draper MSS, 17CC166–167; Lewis H. Kirkpatrick, ed., "The Journal of William Calk, Kentucky Pioneer," *MVHR* 7 (Mar. 1921): 369; "Statement of Felix Walker, 1826, when 91 Years of Age," in Katherine Phelps, comp., "A Partial List of Those at Fort Boonesborough," *RKHS* 23 (May 1925): 148–49; John F. D. Smyth, *A Tour in the United States of America*, 2 vols. (London, 1784), 1:329.

3. *Petitions*, quotation on 43–44; Lucien Beckner, ed., "Reverend John D. Shane's Interview with Pioneer William Clinkenbeard," *FCHQ* 2 (Jan. 1928): 115 (quotation). On the importance of hunting to migrant parties, see Samuel and Jean Shannon (English Station) to Thomas Shannon, Nov. 24, 1784, Shannon Family Letters, typescript (WKU); Marquis François Jean de Chastellux, *Travels in North America in the Years 1780, 1781, and 1782*, 2 vols. (London, 1787), 2:96–104; Spencer Records' Narrative, Draper MSS, 23CC1–5; John Rowan, "Unfinished Autobiography of John Rowan, Written in 1841 at Federal Hill, Kentucky," typescript, 3–8 (WKU); Chester Raymond Young, ed., *Westward into Kentucky: The Narrative of Daniel Trabue* (Lexington, 1981), 44–46; Lucien Beckner, ed., "A Sketch of the Early Adventures of William Sudduth in Kentucky," *FCHQ* 2 (Jan. 1928), 43–45. For hunting and the prolific consumption and waste of wild meat by pioneer Kentuckians, see also Spencer Records' Narrative, Draper MSS, 23CC35; "Col. William Fleming's Journal," in Newton Mereness, ed., *Travels in the American Colonies* (New York, 1916), 619; Robert B. McAfee, "The Life and Times of Robert B. McAfee and His Family and Connections," *RKHS* 25 (1927): 33; Nicholas Cresswell, *The Journal of Nicholas Cresswell, 1774–1777* (New York, 1924), 75–76; Elizabeth Thatcher Clough, ed., "Abraham Thomas: 'This Small Legacy of Experience'," *Kentucky Ancestors* 26 (Autumn 1990): 77.

4. Jacob Young, *Autobiography of a Pioneer: or the Nativity, Experience, Travels, and Ministerial Labors of Rev. Jacob Young, with Incidents, Observations, and Reflections* (Cincinnati, 1857), 34; John D. Shane interview with John Graves, Draper MSS, 11CC22; McAfee, "The Life and Times of Robert B. McAfee," 111; Lucien Beckner, ed., "John D. Shane's Interview with Benjamin Allen, Clark County," *FCHQ* 5 (Apr. 1931): 69; idem, "Reverend John Dabney Shane's Interview with Mrs. Sarah Graham of Bath County," *FCHQ* 9 (Oct. 1935): 240; Journal of the House of Delegates of the Transylvania Colony, in Ranck, ed., *Boonesborough*, 206; John D. Shane interview with James Wade, Draper MSS, 12CC28; Beckner, ed., "Reverend John D. Shane's Interview with Pioneer William Clinkenbeard," 104; Col. John Bowman to Gen. Edward Hand, Dec. 12, 1777, in R. G. Thwaites and Louise P. Kellogg, eds., *Frontier Defense on the Upper Ohio, 1777–1778* (Madison, 1912), 182.

5. Kirkpatrick, ed., "The Journal of William Calk," quotation on 367; "Letter of Judge Henderson (June 12, 1775) to Proprietors Remaining in North Carolina," in Ranck, ed., *Boonesborough*, 184; *Petitions*, 48–52; Phelps, comp., "A Partial List of Those at Fort Boonesborough," 155–56.

6. "Letter of Judge Henderson (June 12, 1775) to Proprietors Remaining

in North Carolina," in Ranck, ed., *Boonesborough*, quotation on 189; Abraham Thomas, "Sketches from Border Life," Draper MSS, 27CC31 (quotation); William Hickman, *A Short Account of My Life and Travels* (1828; Louisville, 1969), quotation on 5; Beckner, ed., "A Sketch of the Early Adventures of William Sudduth," 46–47; idem, "Reverend John D. Shane's Interview with Pioneer William Clinkenbeard," 95–98; Ellen Eslinger, "Migration and Kinship on the Trans-Appalachian Frontier: Strode's Station, Kentucky," *FCHQ* 62 (Jan. 1988): 52–66; "Captain John Cowan's Journal," in Willard R. Jillson, ed., *Tales of the Dark and Bloody Ground: A Group of Fifteen Original Papers on the Early History of Kentucky* (Louisville, 1930), 64; Abraham Chapline, "An account of the life of Abraham Chapline," Draper MSS, 4CC33–36.

7. Nathaniel Hart Jr. to Lyman C. Draper, Draper MSS, 2CC26 (quotation); William Dodd Brown, ed., "A Visit to Boonesborough in 1779: The Recollections of Pioneer George M. Bedinger," *RKHS* 86 (Autumn 1988): 321 (quotation); Spencer Records' Narrative, Draper MSS, 23CC38–39; Hugh F. Bell Statement, ibid., 30S264; "Sketches from Border Life," ibid., 27CC35. On fire hunting, see John D. Shane interview with William Moseby, Draper MSS, 11CC273; John J. Audubon, *Delineations of American Scenery and Character* (1835; New York, 1926), 68–75; James B. Finley, *Autobiography of James B. Finley, or, Pioneer Life in the West*, ed. W. P. Strickland (Cincinnati, 1853), 88, 94–95; [Emmanuel Hatfield], *Stories of Hatfield, the Pioneer* (New Albany, Ind., 1889), 81.

8. John Brady Statement, Draper MSS, 16S248 (quotation). John Taylor, *A History of Ten Baptist Churches, of which the author has been alternately a member: in which will be seen something of a journal of the author's life for more than fifty years* (Bloomfield, Ky., 1827), quotation on 44; Mereness, ed., *Travels in the American Colonies*, 636–37; Young, ed., *Westward into Kentucky*, 75–77; James Nourse, "Journey to Kentucky in 1775," *The Journal of American History* 19 (1925): 254, 364; John D. Shane interview with Daniel Bryant, Draper MSS, 22C14; Shane with Mrs. John Morrison, ibid., 11CC152; Spencer Records' Narrative, ibid., 23CC37–38; Finley, *Autobiography*, 96.

9. To an unprecedented extent, husbandry became a collective enterprise. Clearing, cultivating, and harvesting fields were operations that at least into the early 1780s no individual farmer risked alone. Instead, neighbors compacted to work and watch a common plot, with men alternating between working the land and watching out for Indians. Signers further pledged to do their duty for each other, or face forfeiture of their share in the harvest. See "Corn Growing Compact," Apr. 15, 1779, Draper MSS, 1CC206–207; Young, ed., *Westward into Kentucky*, 75–77; Nourse, "Journey to Kentucky in 1775," 254, 364; John D. Shane interview with Daniel Bryant, Draper MSS, 22C14; Shane with Mrs. John Morrison, ibid., 11CC152; Spencer Records' Narrative, ibid., 23CC37–38; Finley, *Autobiography*, 96; Lucien Beckner, ed., "Reverend John D. Shane's Interview with Pioneer William Clinkenbeard," 98, 107; McAfee, "The Life and Times of Robert B. McAfee," 31.

10. "Felix Walker's Narrative," quotation on 163; Beckner, ed., "Reverend John D. Shane's interview with Pioneer William Clinkenbeard," quotation on 116; Smyth, *A Tour in the United States*, quotation on 1:330.

11. C. C. Trowbridge, *Shawnese Traditions*, eds. Vernon Kinietz and E. W.

Voegelin, Occasional Contributions from the Museum of Anthropology, University of Michigan, no. 9 (Ann Arbor, 1939), 11–12; David Jones, *A Journal of Two Visits Made to Some Nations of Indians on the West Side of the River Ohio in the Years 1772 and 1773* (Burlington, 1774?), 54–55; William Wells, "Indian Manners and Customs," *Hunt's Western Magazine* 2 (Feb. 1820): 45; James H. Howard, *Shawnee! The Ceremonialism of a Native American Tribe and Its Cultural Background* (Athens, Ohio, 1981), 106–28.

12. Trowbridge, *Shawnese Traditions*, 12–13.

13. Beckner, ed., "Reverend John D. Shane's Interview with Pioneer William Clinkenbeard," 98.

14. Thomas D. Clark, ed., *The Voice of the Frontier: John Bradford's Notes on Kentucky* (Lexington, 1993), 15; Beckner, ed., "Rev. John Dabney Shane's Interview with Mrs. Sarah Graham," 239; Lucien Beckner, ed., "John D. Shane's Notes on an Interview with Jeptha Kemper of Montgomery County," ibid., 12 (July 1938): 157; Draper's notes of interview with William Whitley Jr., Draper MSS, 12C62(1); Finley, *Autobiography*, 73; Helen Deiss Irvin, *Women in Kentucky* (Lexington, 1979), 1–17.

15. William A. Galloway, ed., *Old Chillicothe: Shawnee and Pioneer History* (Xenia, Ohio, 1934), quotation on 195; John Heckewelder, *History, Manners, and Customs of the Indians, Who Once Inhabited Pennsylvania and the Neighbouring States*, ed. William C. Reichel, Historical Society of Pennsylvania, *Memoirs* 12 (1876), 163–69; Orley E. Brown, ed., *The Captivity of Jonathan Alder and His Life with the Indians* (Alliance, Ohio, 1965), 63. On "open country neighborhoods," see John Mack Faragher, *Sugar Creek: Life on the Illinois Prairie* (New Haven, 1986), esp. 143–55.

16. This and the following paragraphs on Cherokee factionalism draw heavily on Harriette Simpson Arnow, *Seedtime on the Cumberland* (New York, 1960), 172–202; Tom Hatley, *The Dividing Paths: Cherokees and South Carolinians through the Era of Revolution* (New York, 1993), 217–18; Gregory Dowd, *A Spirited Resistance: The North American Indian Struggle for Unity, 1745–1815* (Baltimore, 1992), 51–56.

17. Oconestoto to the Delegates in Convention, June 24, 1775, in William J. Van Schreevan, ed., *Revolutionary Virginia: The Road to Independence*, 7 vols. (Charlottesville, 1973–83), 3:219 (quotation).

18. Henry Stuart to John Stuart, Aug. 25, 1776, in K. G. Davies, ed., *Documents of the American Revolution, 1770–1783*, 21 vols. (Shannon, Ireland, 1972–81), 12:202 (quotation).

19. Colin G. Calloway, " 'We Have Always Been the Frontier': The American Revolution in Shawnee Country," *American Indian Quarterly* 16 (Winter 1992): 39–40; Richard White, *The Middle Ground: Indians, Empires, and Republics in the Great Lakes Region, 1650–1815* (New York, 1991), 191, 355–56; Charles Callender, "Shawnee," in Bruce G. Trigger, ed., *Handbook of North American Indians*, 20 vols. (Washington, D.C., 1978), 15:623–24.

20. "A Speech delivered in writing by the Shawanese dated Shawanese Towns July 26th. 1775," in Van Schreevan, ed., *Revolutionary Virginia*, 7:770; Calloway, " 'We Have Always Been the Frontier'," 41–42.

21. "Continuation of Treaty Negotiations, July 18, 1775," in Van Schreevan,

ed., *Revolutionary Virginia*, quotation on 7:770; "Treaty at Pittsburgh, 1775" in R. G. Thwaites and Louise P. Kellogg, eds., *The Revolution on the Upper Ohio, 1775–1777* (Madison, 1908), quotation on 111.

22. "Report of Indian Commissioners on Speeches and Messages, Oct. 12, 1775," in Van Schreevan, ed., *Revolutionary Virginia*, quotation on 4:199.

23. Dowd, *A Spirited Resistance*, 52; John Mack Faragher, *Daniel Boone: The Life and Legend of an American Pioneer* (New York, 1992), 131–40.

24. Guy Johnson to Lord George Germain, Mar. 12, 1778, in Davies, ed., *Documents of the American Revolution*, quotation on 15:69.

25. Col. John Bowman to Gen. Edward Hand, Dec. 12, 1777, in Thwaites and Kellogg, eds., *Frontier Defense on the Upper Ohio*, 181–83; R. S. Cotterill, *History of Pioneer Kentucky* (Cincinnati, 1917), 111–18.

26. "Report of Indian Commissioners on Speeches and Messages, October 12, 1775," in Van Schreevan, ed., *Revolutionary Virginia*, quotation on 4:201; Henry Stuart to John Stuart, Aug. 25, 1776, in Davies, ed., *Documents of the American Revolution*, quotation on 12:205.

27. General Edward Hand to Jasper Yeates, Dec. 24, 1777, in Thwaites and Kellogg, eds., *Frontier Defense on the Upper Ohio*, quotation on 188; see also ibid., 19–20, 157–63, 168–69, 175–77; James H. O'Donnell III, ed., "Captain Pipe's Speech: A Commentary on the Delaware Experience, 1775–1781," *Northwest Ohio Quarterly* 64 (Autumn 1992): 126–33.

28. Guy Johnson to Lord George Germain, Mar. 12, 1778, in Davies, ed., *Documents of the American Revolution*, 15:68; Gov. Henry Hamilton to Sir Guy Carleton, Apr. 25, 1778, in Thwaites and Kellogg, eds., *Frontier Defense on the Upper Ohio*, 283.

29. William Smith, *An Historical Account of the Expedition Against the Ohio Indians in the Year 1764* (Philadelphia, 1765), quotation on 27; Col. Henry Bouquet to Gen. Thomas Gage, Nov. 15, 1764, in "Bouquet Papers," *Michigan Pioneer Collections* 19 (1892): 281; John Slover, "The Narrative of John Slover," in Samuel L. Metcalf, ed., *A Collection of Some of the Most Interesting Narratives of Indian Warfare in the West* (1821; New York, 1977), 58.

30. Boone's speech quoted in Draper's interview with Joseph Jackson, Draper MSS, 11C62(8); Deposition of Ansel Goodman, Oct. 29, 1832, ibid., 11C28.

31. Draper with Joseph Jackson, Draper MSS, 11C62. Boone was provided with a running translation of the Indians' speeches by Pompey, a former Virginia slave who had lived among the Shawnees for some time and often served as an interpreter. For a translation of common metaphorical expressions, see Heckewelder, *History, Manners, and Customs of the Indian Nations*, 137–40; Thomas Hughes, *A Journal by Thomas Hughes, For his Amusement, & Designed only for his Perusal by the time he attains the Age of 50 if he lives so long. (1778–1789)* (Cambridge, 1947), 179. The significance of execution rituals was even less understood. Most of the saltmakers heard stories of excruciating tortures involving cannibalism and coerced self-devourment, of prisoners burned alive, their flesh stripped away and consumed in front of them or stuffed down their own throats. Of course, pioneer men knew more about butchery than they liked to admit, having

on occasion mutilated the bodies of live and dead Indian victims. Some appreciated that Indians cannibalized condemned men not "from a like to human flesh, but out of a kind of bravado." Backcountry men, after all, were well versed in the art of bravado. Few if any of the saltmakers, however, understood that Indians ingested the flesh of their more courageous enemies because they think "it will make them bolder," that it allowed them to capture the physical and spiritual strength of their victim. In that sense, the alternatives debated by Shawnee warriors, ingestion or adoption, were different means of incorporation. The distinction, needless to say, was not lost on the captives, whose life or death rested on the verdict of a 120-man jury. See Hughes, *A Journal by Thomas Hughes*, quotation on 180; Beverley Bond Jr., ed., "The Captivity of Charles Stuart, 1755–1757," *MVHR* 13 (June 1926): 61–62; Otto Rothert, ed., "John D. Shane's Interview with Pioneer John Hedge, Bourbon County," *FCHQ* 14 (July 1940): 181; Paul A. Wallace, ed., *Thirty Thousand Miles with John Heckewelder* (Pittsburgh, 1958), 318.

32. Draper with Joseph Jackson, Draper MSS, 11C62(9).

33. Draper with Joseph Jackson, Draper MSS, 11C62(9); Statement of Boone Hays, ibid., 23C36(3–4); Draper interview with Nathan and Olive Boone, ibid., 6S109–110.

34. Heckewelder, *History, Manners, and Customs of the Indian Nations*, quotation on 136. For details of the saltmakers' travails, see Ted Franklin Belue, "Terror in the Canelands: The Fate of Daniel Boone's Salt Boilers," *FCHQ* 68 (Jan. 1994), 3–34; William Dodd Brown, ed., "The Capture of Daniel Boone's Saltmakers: Fresh Perspectives from Primary Sources," *RKHS* 83 (Winter 1985): 1–18.

35. John Wade to Draper, Dec. 28, 1859, Draper MSS, 24C135(2) (quotation); Gov. Henry Hamilton to Sir Guy Carleton, Apr. 25, 1778, in Thwaites and Kellogg, eds., *Frontier Defense on the Upper Ohio*, quotation on 283. For a recap of the hard treatment, escapes, and releases of saltmakers ransomed by Hamilton, see Belue, "Terror in the Canelands," 3–34. On Hamilton's reputation, see Bernard W. Sheehan, "'The Famous Hair Buyer General': Henry Hamilton, George Rogers Clark, and the American Indian," *Indiana Magazine of History* 79 (Mar. 1983): 1–28.

36. Gov. Henry Hamilton to Sir Guy Carleton, Apr. 25, 1778, in Thwaites and Kellogg, eds., *Frontier Defense on the Upper Ohio*, 283.

37. Brown, ed., *The Captivity of Jonathan Alder*, quotation on 14. For descriptions of the gauntlet and of the rites of adoption among Ohio Indians, see Edwin Erle Sparks, ed., *Incidents Attending the Capture, Detention, and Ransom of Charles Johnston of Virginia* (Cleveland, 1905), 79, 87–88; Smith, *An Account of the Remarkable Occurrences*, 8, 14–16; Beckner, ed., "John D. Shane's Interview with Benjamin Allen," 74–77; Mary Kinnan, *True Narrative of the Sufferings of Mary Kinnan, Who Was Taken Prisoner by the Shawanee Nation of Indians on the Thirteenth Day of May, 1791, and Remained with Them Until the Sixteenth of August, 1794* (Elizabethtown, 1795), 7–8; Milo Miton Quaife, ed., *The Indian Captivity of O. M. Spencer* (Chicago, 1917), 100; Bond, ed., "The Captivity of Charles Stuart," 66. The adoption of Boone figures prominently in all biographies of him, and nowhere can historiographic shifts during the twentieth century be more easily discerned. Compare, for example, the treatment of Boone's adoption

in Reuben G. Thwaites, *Daniel Boone* (1902; Williamstown, Mass., 1985), 150–57; John Bakeless, *Daniel Boone: Master of the Wilderness* (1939; Harrisburg, 1965), 165–77; Faragher, *Daniel Boone*, 162–76.

38. Nathan Boone Statement, Draper MSS, 6S118 (quotation); John Filson, *The Discovery, Settlement, and Present State of Kentucke*, ed. William H. Masterson (New York, 1962), quotations on 65; Draper, "Life of Boone," Draper MSS, 4B194 (quotation).

39. Young, ed., *Westward into Kentucky*, 56–57; Shane with Daniel Bryan, Draper MSS, 22C14(12); Deposition of William Hancock, July 17, 1778, in Louise P. Kellogg, ed., *Frontier Advance on the Upper Ohio, 1778–1779* (Madison, 1916), 114; Lyman C. Draper interview with Josiah Collins, Draper MSS, 12CC74–75.

40. Young, ed., *Westward into Kentucky*, quotation on 57; "Deposition of Stephen Hancock," in Charles Staples, ed., "History in Circuit Court Records," *RKHS* 32 (Jan. 1934): 8; John Bowman to George Rogers Clark, Oct. 14, 1778, in James Alton James, ed., *George Rogers Clark Papers, 1771–1781* (Springfield, Ill., 1912), 69–70. Whatever the wisdom of its timing, Boone's plan was being forwarded by other backcountry leaders at about the same time. Just weeks before Boone led his raiding party, Colonel Arthur Campbell had struck on the same idea. "Would it not be an opportunity for an enterprizing officer from Greenbrier or the point [Pleasant] . . . to make an incursion over the Ohio[?]" wrote Campbell to a fellow leader in Virginia's frontier militia. (Colonel Arthur Campbell to Colonel William Fleming, July 31, 1778, Draper MSS, 4C78).

41. Young, ed., *Westward into Kentucky*, quotation on 58; Lyman Draper interview with Josiah Collins, Draper MSS, 12CC74–75; John D. Shane interview with John Gass, Draper MSS, 11CC12; [William B. Smith], "Attack Upon Boonesborough by the Indians in 1778," *Hunt's Western Magazine* 3 (Jan. 1821): 362–66.

42. Young, ed., *Westward into Kentucky*, quotation on 58.

43. Clark, ed., *The Voice of the Frontier*, 17–20. On the hunting season's interference with war plans, see Guy Johnson to Lord George Germain, Mar. 12, 1778, in Davies, ed., *Documents of the American Revolution*, 15:68.

44. On the seven saltmakers who in addition to Boone attempted to escape in 1778 or 1779, see Belue, "Terror in the Canelands," 3–34.

45. Statement of Joseph Jackson, Apr. 1844, Draper MSS, 11C62(11), 11C63; Leonard Bliss to Lyman Draper, Dec. 18, 1850, ibid., 24C119(1); Draper's notes to interview with Ezekiel Lewis, ibid., 30J80.

46. Hamilton to Haldimand, Oct. 14, 1778, in H. W. Beckwith, ed., "Letters from Canadian Archives," *Collections of the Illinois State Historical Library* (Springfield, 1903), 1:357.

47. Lieut.-Governor Henry Hamilton to General Frederick Haldimand, Jan. 24, 1779, in Davies, ed., *Documents of the American Revolution*, quotation on 17:50; Daniel Brodhead to George Rogers Clark, May 20, 1780, in James, ed., *George Rogers Clark Papers*, quotation on 419; Col. Daniel Brodhead to Indian Penn, Dec. 2, 1780, in Louise P. Kellogg, ed., *Frontier Retreat on the Upper Ohio, 1779–1781* (Madison, 1917), quotation on 299; Galloway, *Old Chillicothe*, 13; Alexander Cameron to Lord George Germain, July 18, 1780, in Davies, ed.,

Documents of the American Revolution, 18:121; Col. Daniel Brodhead to Shawnee Chiefs, Apr. 8, 1779, in Kellogg, ed., *Frontier Advance on the Upper Ohio*, 279–80; Col. Daniel Brodhead to Gen. George Washington, May 29, 1779, ibid., 350; Governor Thomas Jefferson to George R. Clark, Jan. 29, 1780, in Clarence V. Alvord, ed., *Kaskaskia Records, 1778–1790*, Collections of the Illinois State Historical Society Library, vol. 5, Virginia Series, vol. 2 (Springfield, 1909), 147.

48. John Floyd (Jefferson County) to Thomas Jefferson, Apr. 16, 1781, in *CVSP*, 2:48; John Floyd (Jefferson County) to Thomas Nelson, Oct. 6, 1781, ibid., 529–31; Andrew Steel (Fayette County) to the Governor of Virginia, Sept. 12, 1782, ibid., 3:303–4; Clark, ed., *The Voice of the Frontier*, 34–58; Indian Council at Detroit, Apr. 5, 1781, in "Haldimand Papers," *Michigan Pioneer and Historical Collections*, 40 vols. (Lansing, 1877–1929), 10:463–65.

49. O'Donnell, ed., "Captain Pipe's Speech," quotation on 131. See also "The Haldimand Papers," 10:364–65, 420–21; 19:614–15; 20:37–38.

50. Harry Innes (Danville) to Major General Knox, July 7, 1790, Harry Innes Papers (LC) (quotation); William Lytle, "Personal Narrative of William Lytle," Historical and Philosophical Society of Ohio, *Quarterly Publications* 1 (Jan.–March, 1806): 14–15; Galloway, *Old Chillicothe*, 90–92.

51. For a transcript of Logan's speech to the Shawnees, see Clark, ed., *The Voice of the Frontier*, 119. See also Ebenezer Denny, *Military Journal of Major Ebenezer Denny, An Officer in the Revolutionary and Indian Wars* (Philadelphia, 1859), 72–73; "Journal of General Butler," in Neville B. Craig, ed., *The Olden Time*, 2 vols. (Pittsburgh, 1846–48), 2:522; Samuel Montgomery, "A Journey through the Indian Country Beyond the Ohio, 1785," ed. David I. Bushnell Jr., *MVHR* 2 (Sept. 1915): 261–73; Colin G. Calloway, "Beyond the Vortex of Violence: Indian-White Relations in the Ohio Country, 1783–1815," *Northwest Ohio Quarterly* 64 (Winter 1992): 16–26.

52. Harry Innes (Danville) to John Brown, Dec. 7, 1787, in G. Glenn Clift, ed., "The District of Kentucky, 1783–1787, As Pictured by Harry Innes in a Letter to John Brown," *RKHS* 54 (Oct. 1956): 369; John Cleves Symmes to Jonathan Dayton, Oct. 12, 1788, in Beverly W. Bond Jr., ed., *The Correspondence of John Cleves Symmes: Founder of the Miami Purchase* (New York, 1926), 47; Samuel McDowell (Danville) to the Governor of Virginia, July 26, 1789, in *CVSP*, 5:7–8; Harry Innes (Danville) to Major General Knox, July 7, 1790, Harry Innes Papers (LC); James Taylor, "Autobiography of General James Taylor of Newport, Ky.," 15–16 (microfilm typescript at FC, original at University of Chicago Library); Isaac Shelby to Major General Knox, Secretary of War, Jan. 10, 1794, Isaac Shelby Papers (FC); Roseann R. Hogan, ed., "Buffaloes in the Corn: James Wade's Account of Pioneer Kentucky," *RKHS* 89 (Winter 1991): 29.

53. Rufus Putnam (Fort Washington) to General Knox, July 8, 1792, in William Henry Smith, ed., *The St. Clair Papers: The Life and Public Services of Arthur St. Clair: Soldier of the Revolutionary War; President of the Continental Congress; and Governor of the North-Western Territory, with His Correspondence and Other Papers*, 2 vols. (Cincinnati, 1882), 1:303–4; Rowena Buell, ed., *The Memoirs of Rufus Putnam and Certain Official Papers and Correspondence* (Boston, 1903), 116, 257–67, 269–71; Dwight L. Smith, ed., "William Wells and the Indian Council of 1793," *Indiana Magazine of History* 56 (Sept. 1960): 217–26; John

Heckewelder, "Narrative of John Heckewelder's Journey to the Wabash in 1792," *Pennsylvania Magazine of History and Biography* 12 (1888): 50; R. David Edmunds, "'Nothing Has Been Effected': The Vincennes Treaty of 1792," *Indiana Magazine of History* 74 (Mar. 1978): 23–35; Wiley Sword, *President Washington's Indian War: The Struggle for the Old Northwest, 1790–1795* (Norman, 1985).

54. For changing population estimates of Ohio Indian groups from the 1760s to the 1790s, see [Anthony Benezet], "Some Account of the Behaviour & Sentiments of a Number of well-disposed Indians mostly of the Minusing Tribe," HM824 (HL); George Croghan, "Croghan's Journal, 1765," in R. G. Thwaites, ed., *Early Western Travels, 1748–1846,* 32 vols. (Cleveland, 1904), 1:167–69; Dexter, ed., *Diary of David McClure,* 93; Jones, *A Journal of Two Visits,* 56; David I. Bushnell Jr., "The Virginia Frontier in History—1778," *VMHB* 23 (Oct. 1915): 345–46; Gilbert Imlay, *A Topographical Description of the Western Territory of North America* (London, 1793), 290. For the effects of invasion on Indian hunting patterns and increasing reliance on the British, see Brown, ed., *The Captivity of Jonathan Alder,* 36; John H. Moore, ed., "A Captive of the Shawnees, 1779–1784," *West Virginia History* 23 (July 1962): 291; M. M. Quaife, ed., "A Narrative of Life on the Old Frontier: Henry Hay's Journal from Detroit to the Miami River," *Proceedings of the State Historical Society of Wisconsin* 62 (1915): 255.

55. Franklin B. Dexter, ed., *Diary of David McClure: Doctor of Divinity, 1748–1820* (New York, 1899), quotation on 89–90; Brown, ed., *The Captivity of Jonathan Alder,* quotation on 62; Heckewelder, *History, Manners, and Customs,* 191–92; Beckner, ed., "John D. Shane's Interview with Benjamin Allen," 85.

56. Pennsylvania Council, [Minutes of meetings with a delegation of] Minisink, 2 Nantocokes, & 3 Delawares from an Indian Town . . . above Wyoming on the Susquehannah, Philadelphia, July 11–16, 1760, HM 8249 (HL), quotation on 3; Dexter, ed., *Diary of David McClure,* quotation on 75; Sparks, ed., *Incidents Attending the Capture . . . of Charles Johnston,* quotation on 97; Milo Milton Quaife, ed., *The Indian Captivity of O. M. Spencer* (Chicago, 1917), 109–10; Thomas Ridout, "The Narrative of the Captivity among the Shawanese Indians, in 1788, of Thos. Ridout, Afterwards Surveyor-General of Upper Canada," in Matilda Edgar, ed., *Ten Years of Upper Canada in Peace and War, 1805–1815; Being the Ridout Letters* (Toronto, 1890), 349–50; Smith, ed., *The St. Clair Papers,* 1:83; Denny, *Military Journal of Major Ebenezer Denny,* 63.

57. John D. Shane interview with John Gass, Draper MSS, 11CC12–14; Young, ed., *Westward into Kentucky,* 58; John D. Shane interview with Nathaniel Hart Jr., Draper MSS, 17CC198; John D. Shane interview with Jesse Daniel, ibid., 11CC94. Boone's humiliation was such that John Filson's "autobiography" of Daniel Boone, the first word on the subject, omits the court-martial as "nothing worthy of a place in this account." (See Filson, *The Discovery, Settlement, and Present State of Kentucke,* 70.)

58. No transcript of the trial has ever surfaced. The only firsthand account of Callaway's charges, Boone's answers, and the trial's outcome was set down by Daniel Trabue some forty-nine years after the fact. Callaway and Boone never spoke after the court-martial, the results of which did not sit well with Callaway. See Young, ed., *Westward into Kentucky,* 63–64; Draper, "Life," Draper MSS,

4B253–256; William E. Ellis, H. E. Everman, and Richard D. Sears, *Madison County: 200 Years in Retrospect* (Richmond, Ky., 1985), 19.

59. *Petitions*, quotation on 45–46; Young, ed., *Westward into Kentucky*, quotation on 75–76; Col. William Fleming (St. Asaph's) to Mrs. Anne Fleming, Dec. 15, 1779, William Fleming Collection (WL); Neal O. Hammon, ed., "The Journal of James Nourse, Jr., 1779–1780," *FCHQ* 47 (July 1973): 265; Beckner, ed., "Reverend John D. Shane's Interview with Pioneer William Clinkenbeard," 112; "Col. William Fleming's Journal," 636–37; James R. Bentley, ed., "A Letter from Harrodsburg, 1780," *FCHQ* 50 (Oct. 1976): 369–71; John May (Kentucky County) to Samuel Beall, Apr. 15, 1780, Beall-Booth Family Papers (FC).

60. Smyth, *A Tour in the United States of America*, 1:291; John Haywood, *The Civil and Political History of the State of Tennessee from its Earliest Settlement up to the Year 1796, Including the Boundaries of the State* (1823; Nashville, 1891), 26; Chastellux, *Travels in North America in the Years 1780, 1781, and 1782*, 2:38–40; Joseph Doddridge, *Notes on the Settlement and Indian Wars of the Western Parts of Virginia and Pennsylvania from 1763 to 1783* (1824; Pittsburgh, 1912), 96–97.

61. Morgan to Baynton and Wharton, Dec. 10, 1767, in Clarence W. Alvord and Clarence E. Carter, eds., *Trade and Politics, 1767–1769* (Springfield, Ill., 1921), quotation on 132; Bakeless, *Daniel Boone*, 37; Arnow, *Seedtime on the Cumberland*, 155–56. To increase their packing capacity, hunters sometimes borrowed neighbors' horses. In exchange, horse owners received one-half the load of game. See Beckner, ed., "Rev. John Dabney Shane's Interview with Mrs. Sarah Graham," 228. For similar interpretations of the compartmentalization of exchange relations, see Alan Taylor, *Liberty Men and Great Proprietors: The Revolutionary Settlement on the Maine Frontier, 1760–1820* (Chapel Hill, 1990), 77–85; Christopher Clark, *The Roots of Rural Capitalism: Western Massachusetts, 1780–1860* (Ithaca, 1990).

62. John Shane interview with James Wade, Draper MSS, 12CC39 (quotation); Finley, *Autobiography*, 96.

63. "Judge Richard Henderson Journal," quotation on 176; John D. Shane interview with Joshua McQueen, Draper MSS, quotation on 13CC21; Rothert, ed., "John D. Shane's Interview with Pioneer John Hedge," 179; Beckner, ed., "A Sketch of the Early Adventures of William Sudduth," 47; Clough, ed., "Abraham Thomas," 77.

64. Journal of the House of Delegates of the Transylvania Colony, in Ranck, ed., *Boonesborough*, 206; Hogan, ed., "Buffaloes in the Corn," 5; Spencer Records' Narrative, Draper MSS, 23CC35; Beckner, ed., "Reverend John D. Shane's Interview with Pioneer William Clinkenbeard," 104; Lucien Beckner, ed., "John D. Shane's Interview with Jesse Graddy of Woodford County," *FCHQ* 20 (Jan. 1946): 13; "Some Particulars Relative to the Soil, Situation, Production, &c of Kentucky: Extracted from the Manuscript Journal of a Gentleman Not Long Since Returned from Those Parts," in Eugene L. Schwaab, ed., *Travels in the Old South, Selected from Periodicals of the Time*, 2 vols. (Lexington, 1973), 1:60.

65. Young, ed., *Westward into Kentucky*, quotation on 136; Rothert, ed., "John D. Shane's Interview with Pioneer John Hedge," 180; Hogan, ed., "Buffaloes in the Corn," 30; Levi Todd, Narrative, Draper MSS, 15CC159; Beck-

ner, ed., "A Sketch of the Early Adventures of William Sudduth," 45; Spencer Records' Narrative, Draper MSS, 23CC24; Shane interview with Mrs. Morrison, ibid., 11CC152; Beckner, ed., "John D. Shane's Interview with Jesse Graddy," 11; John D. Shane interview with John Hedges, Draper MSS, 11CC19; Shane with David Crouch, ibid., 12CC23; Nathaniel Hart Jr. to Lyman C. Draper, ibid., 2CC26; J. S. McHargue, "Canebrakes in Prehistoric and Pioneer Times in Kentucky," *Annals of Kentucky Natural History* 1 (Sept. 27, 1941): 1–13.

66. Finley, *Autobiography*, 39; Paul Woehrmann, ed., "The Autobiography of Abraham Snethen, Frontier Preacher," *FCHQ* 51 (Oct. 1977): 316; Beckner, ed., "Reverend John D. Shane's Interview with Pioneer William Clinkenbeard," 115; David Meade (Lexington) to Ann Randolph, Sept. 1, 1796, in Bayrd Still, ed., "The Westward Migration of a Planter Pioneer in 1796," *William and Mary Quarterly*, 2d ser., 21 (Oct. 1941): 335; Beckner, ed., "Rev. John Dabney Shane's Interview with Mrs. Sarah Graham," 228.

67. G. Hubert Smith, ed., "A Letter from Kentucky," *MVHR* 19 (June 1932): quotations on 93.

Chapter Three. Land Hunting

1. The meaning and importance of "independence" in Revolutionary America is assayed in Jack P. Greene, "Independence, Improvement, and Authority: Toward a Framework for Understanding the Histories of the Southern Backcountry during the Era of the American Revolution," in Ronald Hoffman, Thad Tate, and Peter Albert, eds., *An Uncivil War: The Southern Backcountry during the American Revolution* (Charlottesville, 1985), 3–36; Richard Bushman, " 'This New Man': Dependence and Independence, 1776," in Richard Bushman et al., eds., *Uprooted Americans: Essays in Honor of Oscar Handlin* (Boston, 1979), 77–96.

2. Richard Maxwell Brown, "Backcountry Rebellions and the Homestead Ethic in America, 1740–1799," in Richard Maxwell Brown and Don E. Fehrenbacher, eds., *Tradition, Conflict, and Modernization: Perspectives on the American Revolution* (New York, 1977), 73–99. Among the more notable studies of various backcountries in rebellion and revolution are James P. Whittenburg, "Planters, Merchants, and Lawyers: Social Change and the Origins of the North Carolina Regulation," *WMQ* 34 (Apr. 1977): 215–38; Thomas Slaughter, *The Whiskey Rebellion: Frontier Epilogue to the American Revolution* (New York, 1986); Alan Taylor, *Liberty Men and Great Proprietors: The Revolutionary Settlement on the Maine Frontier, 1760–1820* (Chapel Hill, 1990); Rachel N. Klein, *Unification of a Slave State: The Rise of the Planter Class in the South Carolina Backcountry, 1760–1808* (Chapel Hill, 1990). For reviews of recent literature, see Gregory Nobles, "Breaking into the Backcountry: New Approaches to the Early American Frontier, 1750–1800," *WMQ* 46 (Oct. 1989): 641–70; Albert H. Tillson Jr., "The Southern Backcountry: A Survey of Current Research," *VMHB* 98 (July 1990): 387–422.

3. H. H. McDowell to Lyman C. Draper, Aug. 10, 1887, Draper MSS, 20C39 (quotation).

4. Washington quoted in Bernard Bailyn, *Voyagers to the West: A Passage in the Peopling of America on the Eve of the Revolution* (New York, 1986), 23. On the various aborted, half-baked, and nearly successful land companies that vied

to acquire grants and establish colonies west of the Appalachians, see Thomas Perkins Abernethy, *Western Lands and the American Revolution* (New York, 1937); Clarence W. Alvord, *The Mississippi Valley in British Politics: A Study of the Trade, Land Speculation, and Experiments in Imperialism Culminating in the American Revolution*, 2 vols. (New York, 1916).

5. Archibald Henderson, "Richard Henderson and the Occupation of Kentucky, 1775," *MVHR* 1 (Dec. 1914): 342–43; William Stewart Lester, *The Transylvania Colony* (Spencer, Ind., 1935), 1–3.

6. James Murray to William Ellison, Feb. 14, 1736, in Nina Moore Tiffany, ed., *Letters of James Murray, Loyalist* (Boston, 1901), 26.

7. Hermon Husband, "An Impartial Relation of the First Rise and Cause of the Present Differences in Publick Affairs in the Province of North Carolina," in William K. Boyd, ed., *Some Eighteenth-Century Tracts Concerning North Carolina* (Raleigh, 1927), quotations on 309, 312.

8. Governor William Tryon to the Earl of Shelburne, Mar. 14, 1768, in *NCR*, 7:697–98.

9. Archibald Henderson, ed., "Hermon Husband's Continuation of the Impartial Relation," *North Carolina Historical Review* 18 (Jan. 1941): 62–63 (quotation); Husband, "An Impartial Relation," quotations on 302, 291; Richard Henderson to Governor Tryon, Sept. 29, 1770, in Hugh Talmage Lefler, ed., *North Carolina History Told by Contemporaries* (Chapel Hill, 1948), quotation on 91; Council Journals, in *NCR*, 8:258–59 (quotation).

10. John Mack Faragher, *Daniel Boone: The Life and Legend of an American Pioneer* (New York, 1992), 73–76, provides the most thorough and convincing evaluation of the connections between Boone and Henderson, concluding that the employment commenced only in 1774. That does not rule out, however, Henderson's employment of other long hunters as land hunters.

11. John May (Batterseathe) to Samuel Beall, Aug. 30, 1779, Beall-Booth Family Papers (FC) (quotation); Washington quoted in Archibald Henderson, "The Creative Forces in Westward Expansion: Henderson and Boone," *AHR* 20 (Oct. 1914): 100.

12. Louisa Company Articles of Agreement, Draper MSS, 1CC2; Proposals for the Encouragement of settling the Lands purchased by Richard Henderson & Co. on the Branches of the Mississippi River from the Cherokee tribe of Indians, Dec. 25, 1774, in *NCR*, 9:1129–31. On the intertwining familial histories and anti-regulator connections between partners, see Durward T. Stokes, "Thomas Hart in North Carolina," *North Carolina Historical Review* 41 (Summer 1964): 324–37; Archibald Henderson, "The Transylvania Company: A Study in Personnel," *FCHQ* 21 (1947): 3–21, 228–42, 327–49.

13. Deposition of James Robinson, Apr. 16, 1777, in *CVSP*, 1:285–87; Treaty of Watauga, in George W. Ranck, ed., *Boonesborough: Its Founding, Pioneer Struggles, Indian Experiences, Transylvania Days, and Revolutionary Annals* (Louisville, 1901), 151–56; Lester, *The Transylvania Colony*, 29–47; Gregory E. Dowd, *A Spirited Resistance: The North American Indian Struggle for Unity, 1745–1815* (Baltimore, 1992), 48–49, 52.

14. Washington quoted in Lester, *The Transylvania Colony*, 41; A Proclamation by Governor Martin against Richard Henderson and the Transylvania Pur-

chase, Feb. 10, 1775, in *NCR*, 9:1124 (quotation); Governor Martin to the Earl of Dartmouth, Nov. 12, 1775, ibid., 10:324 (quotation); Proclamation of Lord Dunmore against "Richard Henderson and His Abettors," Mar. 21, 1775, in Ranck, ed., *Boonesborough*, quotation on 181–82; Governor Dunmore to William Preston, Mar. 21, 1775, Draper MSS, 4QQ9 (quotation); Colonel William Preston to Governor Earl of Dunmore, Jan. 23, 1775, in K. G. Davies, ed., *Documents of the American Revolution, 1770–1783*, 21 vols. (Shannon, Ireland, 1972–81), 9:33–34.

15. The depositions of witnesses affirming the honesty of dealings between Henderson and the Cherokees appear in *CVSP*, 1:282–92.

16. Deposition of John Floyd, Oct. 28, 1778, in *CVSP*, 1:310 (quotation); Letter to Patrick Henry from Henderson and Co., Apr. 26, 1775, in Ranck, ed., *Boonesborough*, quotation on 195; James Alves Statement, Draper MSS, 2CC34 (quotation); Deposition of Arthur Campbell, Oct. 21, 1778, in *CVSP*, 1:303–4; William Christian (Richmond) to Nathaniel Hart, July 25, 1775, in "Shane Collection of Documents: The Hart Papers," *Journal of the Presbyterian Historical Society* 14 (Sept. 1931): 319. Patrick Henry claimed that he never solicited the proprietors directly or indirectly and that he "uniformly refused & plainly Declared his Strongest Disappropation" of the "Distant though plain Hint" made in the letter of April 1775. On the efforts of Henderson and partners to obtain compensation, see Report from James Hogg to Col. Richard Henderson, Jan. 1776, in *NCR*, 10:373–76; A Memorial of Richard Henderson, Thomas Hart, Nathaniel Hart, John Williams, William Johnson, John Luttrell, James Hogg, David Hart, and Leonard Hendly Bullock, in Peter Force, ed., *American Archives*, 4th ser. (Washington, D.C., 1846), 6:1574; Richard Henderson to Judge John Williams, Oct. 29, 1778, in *NCR*, 13:491.

17. Colonel Williams to Proprietors, Jan. 3, 1776, in *NCR*, 10:383–84; Minutes of a Meeting of the Proprietors of Transylvania, Sept. 25, 1775, ibid., 256–61; Deposition of James Douglas, Oct. 28, 1778, in *CVSP*, 1:307–9.

18. Richard Henderson to Judge John Williams, Oct. 29, 1778, in *NCR*, 13:491; Report from James Hogg to Col. Richard Henderson, Jan. 1776, ibid., 10:373–76.

19. Joseph Doddridge, *Notes on the Settlement and Indian Wars of the Western Parts of Virginia and Pennsylvania from 1763 to 1783* (1824; Pittsburgh, 1912), quotation on 85; William Christian to William Preston, July 12, 1774, Draper MSS, 3QQ63 (quotation).

20. James McAfee Journal, 1773, Draper MSS, 4CC1–12; Virginius C. Hall, ed., "Journal of Isaac Hite, 1773," *Bulletin of the Historical and Philosophical Society of Ohio* 12 (Oct. 1954): 262–81; James William Hagy, "The First Attempt to Settle Kentucky: Boone in Virginia," *FCHQ* 44 (July 1970): 227–34; Neal O. Hammon, "Land Acquisition on the Kentucky Frontier," *RKHS* 78 (Autumn 1980): 297–301; idem, "Captain Harrod's Company, 1774: A Reappraisal," ibid., 72 (July 1974): 224–42.

21. H. H. Brackenridge, "Thoughts on the present Indian War," in Thomas D. Clark, ed., *The Voice of the Frontier: John Bradford's Notes on Kentucky* (Lexington, 1993), quotation on 177. For additional insights (and debate) about woodland Indians' conceptions of female-controlled fields and familial use rights, see John Phillip Reid, *A Law of Blood: The Primitive Law of the Cherokee Nation*

(New York, 1970), 136–40; William Cronon, *Changes in the Land: Indians, Colonists, and the Ecology of New England* (New York, 1983), 61–68; Elisabeth Tooker, "Women in Iroquois Society," in Michael K. Foster, Jack Campisi, and Marianne Mithun, eds., *Extending the Rafters: Interdisciplinary Approaches to Iroquoian Studies* (Albany, N.Y., 1984), 109–23; Robert S. Grumet, "Sunksquaws, Shamans, and Tradeswomen: Middle Atlantic Coastal Algonkian Women during the 17th and 18th Centuries," in Mona Etienne and Eleanor Leacock, eds., *Women and Colonization: Anthropological Perspectives* (New York, 1980), 43–62.

22. Judge Richard Henderson's Journal of a Trip to 'Cantuckey' and of Events at Boonesborough in 1775, in Ranck, ed., *Boonesborough*, quotations on 177, 173; Lewis H. Kirkpatrick, ed., "The Journal of William Calk, Kentucky Pioneer," *MVHR* 7 (Mar. 1921): 369; Daniel Boone Letter to Richard Henderson, Apr. 1, 1775, in Ranck, ed., *Boonesborough*, 169; Letter of Judge Henderson (June 12, 1775) to Proprietors Remaining in North Carolina, ibid., 184–93; Deposition of William Cocke, Oct. 1, 1796, William Cocke versus Henderson and Company Papers (UK).

23. John Floyd to William Preston, Apr. 21, 1775, in Neal O. Hammon and James R. Harris, " 'In a dangerous situation': Letters of Col. John Floyd, 1774–1783," *RKHS* 83 (Summer 1985): 210 (quotation); Henderson quoted in George Morgan Chinn, *Kentucky: Settlement and Statehood, 1750–1800* (Frankfort, 1975), 112; Robert B. McAfee, "The Life and Times of Robert B. McAfee and His Family and Connections," *RKHS* 25 (1927): 24–26.

24. Journal of the Proceedings of the House of Delegates or Representatives of the Colony of Transylvania, in Ranck, ed., *Boonesborough*, 196–210.

25. Richard Henderson's Journal, in Ranck, ed., *Boonesborough*, quotation on 178; John Floyd to William Preston, May 30, 1775, Draper MSS, 17CC180 (quotation); Letter of Judge Henderson (June 12, 1775) to Proprietors Remaining in North Carolina, in Ranck, ed., *Boonesborough*, 190.

26. Henderson's Journal, quotations on 174; John Floyd to William Preston, Aug. 10, 1775, Draper MSS, 33S279–282.

27. Letter of Judge Henderson (June 12, 1775) to Proprietors Remaining in North Carolina, quotation on 193.

28. Minutes of a Meeting of the Proprietors, in *NCR*, 10:256–61; Advertisement of John Williams, Agent for Proprietors of Transylvania, Dec. 1, 1775, in William J. Van Schreevan, ed., *Revolutionary Virginia: The Road to Independence*, 7 vols. (Charlottesville, 1973–83), 7:776.

29. George Rogers Clark to Jonathan Clark, July 6, 1775, in John Alton James, ed., *George Rogers Clark Papers, 1771–1781* (Springfield, Ill., 1912), quotation on 9–10; Colonel Williams (Boonesborough) to Proprietors, Jan. 3, 1776, in *NCR*, 10:383 (quotation); John Williams to the Gentlemen Inhabitants in & about Harrodsburg, Jan. 1, 1776, in Van Schreevan, ed., *Revolutionary Virginia*, 7:778–79; Deposition of Abraham Hite, Oct. 23, 1778, in *CVSP*, 1:304–5.

30. George Rogers Clark to John Brown, in James, ed., *George Rogers Clark Papers*, 209; William Hickman, *A Short Account of My Life and Travels* (1828; Louisville, 1969), 5.

31. Petition of Aggrieved Transylvania Settlers, Mar. 15, 1776, in Schreevan, ed., *Revolutionary Virginia*, 7:781 (quotation); *Petitions*, quotations on 36–37.

32. Johann David Schoepf, *Travels in the Confederation, 1783–1784*, 2 vols., ed. and trans. Alfred J. Morrison (Philadelphia, 1911), 2:36 (quotation); Levi Todd to J. McColloh, Feb. 15, 1784, in Richard J. Cox, ed., "'A touch of Kentucky News & State of Politicks': Two Letters of Levi Todd, 1784 and 1788," *RKHS* 76 (July 1978): 219–20 (quotation); Hickman, *A Short Account of My Life and Travels*," 5; McAfee, "The Life and Time of Robert B. McAfee," 220–21; John Taylor, *A History of Ten Baptist Churches, of which the author has been alternately a member: in which will be seen something of a journal of the author's life for more than fifty years* (Bloomfield, Ky., 1827), 13; James R. Bentley, ed., "A Letter from Harrodsburg, 1780," *FCHQ* 50 (Oct. 1976): 369–71. The foremost explanation of this concern with land for subsistence and familial continuity is drawn in James Henretta, "Families and Farms: *Mentalité* in Pre-Industrial America," *WMQ* 35 (Jan. 1978): 3–32.

33. Susannah Johnson, *Recollections of the Rev. John Johnson and His Home: An Autobiography*, ed. Rev. Adam C. Johnson (Nashville, 1869), 16–17.

34. Mary Adair to Mary McCalla, Mar. 16, 1797, Adair-Hemphill Family Papers (FC) (quotation); Hickman, *A Short Account of My Life and Travels*, 12; Thomas Hart (Paradise) to Nathaniel Hart, Oct. 4, 1781, in "Documents from the Shane Collection: The Hart Papers," 352; Rebecca Gratz to Benjamin Gratz, Mar. 7, 1819, in Rabbi David Philipson, ed., *Letters of Rebecca Gratz* (Philadelphia, 1929), 16. On the different attitudes of men and women regarding westward migrations, see John Mack Faragher, *Women and Men on the Overland Trail* (New Haven, 1979); Joan E. Cashin, *A Family Venture: Men and Women on the Southern Frontier* (New York, 1991), 32–52; Hazel Dicken-Garcia, *To Western Woods: The Breckinridge Family Moves to Kentucky in 1793* (Rutherford, N.J., 1991), 129–32, 145.

35. Thomas Jefferson, "A Summary View of the Rights of British America," in Paul L. Ford, ed., *The Writings of Thomas Jefferson*, 12 vols. (New York, 1892), quotation on 1:445. For a fuller discussion of Jefferson's evolving view of the derivation of titles on western lands, see Anthony Marc Lewis, "Jefferson and Virginia's Pioneers, 1774–1781," *MVHR* 34 (Mar. 1948): 551–88; Stanley N. Katz, "Thomas Jefferson and the Right to Property in Revolutionary America," *Journal of Law and Economics* 19 (Oct. 1976): 467–88.

36. William W. Hening, ed., *The Statutes at Large: Being a Collection of All the Laws of Virginia*, 13 vols. (New York, 1809–23), 10:39–41.

37. Joan E. Brookes-Smith, comp., *Master Index Virginia Surveys and Grants, 1774–1791* (Frankfort, 1976); Samuel M. Wilson, *The First Land Court of Kentucky, 1779–1780* (Lexington, 1923), 43; Abernethy, *Western Lands and the American Revolution*, 224–25; Patricia Watlington, *The Partisan Spirit: Kentucky Politics, 1779–1792* (New York, 1972), 17–23, 35–44.

38. *Petitions*, 47.

39. John Floyd to William Preston, Sept. 1, 1775, in Hammon and Harris, eds., "Letters of Col. John Floyd," quotation on 212; John Floyd to [?], May 27, 1776, ibid., quotation on 215; Floyd to Martin, May 19, 1776, ibid., 214; John D. Shane interview with William Tyler, Draper MSS, 11CC130; Deposition of Evangelist Hardin and Patrick Jordan, Aug. 2, 1800, HM995, Huntington Library, San Marino; Deposition of John Ray, Feb. 7, 1816, in Walter Brashear vs. Henry Crist,

Bullitt Circuit Court, Robert Emmett McDowell Collection, vol. 13, 51 (FC); Deposition of John Bently, May 25, 1805, ibid., vol. 3B, 17; John D. Shane interview with Wymore, Draper MSS, 11CC130; John Floyd to Martin [?], May 19, 1776, in Hammon and Harris, eds., "Letters of Col. John Floyd," 213–14.

40. "The Certificate Book of the Virginia Land Commission, 1779–1780," *RKHS* 21 (1923): 82 (quotation); Wilson, *The First Land Court of Kentucky*, 1–13, 32–45; William Ayres, "Land Titles in Kentucky," *Proceedings of the Eighth Annual Meeting of the Kentucky State Bar Association* (Louisville, 1909), 160–91.

41. "Some particulars relative to Kentucky; Extracted from the Manuscript Journal of a Gentleman not long since returned from those parts," *National Gazette* 1 (Nov. 1791), reprinted in Eugene L. Schwaab, ed., *Travels in the Old South: Selections from Periodicals of the Times* (Lexington, 1973), quotation on 58; Rev. John Brown to Col. William Preston, May 5, 1775, Draper MSS, 4QQ15 (quotation); G. Hubert Smith, ed., "A Letter from Kentucky," *MVHR* 19 (June 1932): 93 (quotation); Samuel Rogers, *Autobiography of Elder Samuel Rogers*, ed. Elder John Rogers (Cincinnati, 1880), 3 (quotation); Timothy Flint, *Recollections of the Last Ten Years, Passed in Occasional Residences and Journeyings in the Valley of the Mississippi* (Boston, 1826), quotation on 64. The pervasiveness of Edenic metaphors in the early literature about Kentucky, much of it written by those with heavy financial interests in land, is ably pursued in Arthur K. Moore, *The Frontier Mind* (Lexington, 1957).

42. Jonathan Ball Nichols (Danville) to William Nichols, Nov. 6, 1808, Jonathan Ball Nichols Papers, microfilm (UK) (quotation); Lucien Beckner, ed., "Reverend John D. Shane's Notes on Interviews, in 1844, with Mrs. Hinds and Patrick Scott of Bourbon County," *FCHQ* 10 (July 1936): 169; idem, "John D. Shane's Interview with Jesse Graddy of Woodford County," ibid, 20 (Jan. 1946): 13–14; idem, "Rev. John Dabney Shane's Interview with Mrs. Sarah Graham of Bath County," ibid., 9 (Oct. 1935): 228; Josiah Morrow, ed., "Tours into Kentucky and the Northwest Territory: Three Journals by the Rev. James Smith of Powhatan County, Va., 1783, 1795, 1797," *Ohio Archaeological and Historical Publications* 16 (1907): 359; John Filson, *The Discovery, Settlement, and Present State of Kentucke*, ed. William Masterson (New York, 1962), 20–28; "Extract from a Letter from a Gentleman Living in Kentucky to His Friend in Chester County, Pennsylvania," Dec. 8, 1786, Samuel Wilson Collection (UK); Gilbert Imlay, *A Topographical Description of the Western Territory of North America* (London, 1793), 98–99, 143–44, 168–69; Harry Toulmin, *The Western Country in 1793: Reports on Kentucky and Virginia*, ed. Marion Tinling and Godfrey Davies (San Marino, Calif., 1948), 74–77, 80–82.

43. "Colonel William Fleming's Journal of Travels in Kentucky, 1779–1780," in Newton D. Mereness, ed., *Travels in the American Colonies* (New York, 1916), quotation on 644; James Ray to Levi Todd, Aug. 26, 1806, Draper MSS, 16CC43 (quotation); Caleb Wallace to William Fleming, Mar. 30, 1784, Hugh Blair Grigsby Papers (VHS); Caleb Wallace (Lincoln County) to James Madison, July 12, 1785, Caleb Wallace Letters (KHS).

44. "Letter from a 'gentleman of veracity,' June 24, 1780," quoted in George Morgan to William Trent, Sept. 12, 1780, Draper MSS, 46J59 (quotation); *Maryland Journal*, Dec. 9, 1783, Draper MSS, 3JJ114 (quotation); Thomas P. Abernethy,

ed., "Journal of the First Kentucky Convention, December 27, 1784–January 5, 1785," *Journal of Southern History* 1 (Feb. 1935): 75–76 (quotation); "The Deposition of Captain John Cox, July 16, 1779," *VMHB* 36 (Oct. 1918): 373; Major Arent S. Depeyster (Detroit) to Lt. Col. Mason Bolton, May 16, 1780, in "Haldimand Papers," *Michigan Pioneer and Historical Collections*, 40 vols. (Lansing, 1877–1929), 19:519; James Speed (Lincoln) to Governor Harrison, May 22, 1784, in *CVSP*, 3:588–89; Walker Daniel to Governor Harrison, Jan. 19, May 21, 1784, ibid., 555–56, 584–88; "A Real Friend to the People," *Kentucky Gazette*, Apr. 25, 1789, Aug. 15, 1789. The fullest discussion of disaffection in Revolutionary Kentucky can be found in Patricia Watlington, "Discontent in Frontier Kentucky," *RKHS* 65 (Apr. 1967): 77–93.

45. *Petitions*, quotation on 36. For the "ancient cultivation" precedents in Virginia, see Hening, ed., *The Statutes at Large*, 3:204, 206–7, 313. On the meaning of a "competence," see Daniel Vickers, "Competency and Competition: Economic Culture in Early America," *WMQ* 47 (Jan. 1990): 3–29.

46. Doddridge, *Notes on the Settlement and Indian Wars*, 84.

47. Hickman, *A Short Account of My Life and Travels*, 5. For private estimations, presumably uninflated by real estate boosterism, of crop yields in frontier Kentucky, see William Christian (Beargrass) to Elizabeth Christian, Aug. 17, 1785, Hugh Blair Grigsby Papers; "Personal Narrative of William Lytle," Historical and Philosophical Society of Ohio, *Quarterly Publications* 1 (Jan.–Mar. 1806): 6; Daniel Drake, *Pioneer Life in Kentucky*, ed. Emmet Field Horine (New York, 1948), 49.

48. *Petitions*, 47.

49. John Floyd to William Preston, Oct. 30, 1779, Draper MSS, 17CC184–185; Letter from Harrodsburg, 1780 (FC); Neal O. Hammon, "Settlers, Land Jobbers, and Outlyers: A Quantitative Analysis of Land Acquisition on the Kentucky Frontier," *RKHS* 78 (Autumn 1980): 241–62.

50. John May to Samuel Beall, Mar. [?], 1780 (quotation), May 18, 1780 (quotation), May 28, 1780 (quotation), Apr. 15, 1780, Beall-Booth Family Papers (FC).

51. Daniel Bryan to Lyman C. Draper, Feb. 27, 1843, Draper MSS, 22C5(7); Nathan Boone Statement, ibid., 6S79–83; Statement of M. B. Wood, in Ranck, ed., *Boonesborough*, 146–47; Hagy, "The First Attempt to Settle Kentucky," 227–34.

52. Daniel Boone to Thomas Hart, Aug. 11, 1785, Daniel Boone Papers (UK); Daniel Boone Agreement, Sept. 6, 1788, Daniel Boone Papers (FC). It should be noted that at least some of the Transylvania partners appreciated Boone's loyalty. Although they did not make good on their promises of land, partner Thomas Hart maintained a paternalistic concern for Boone. Two years after the court-martial, when Boone's character was impugned again for allowing the money of other settlers, including Hart, to be stolen from him, Thomas Hart immediately excused Boone of any culpability or liability. (Thomas Hart (Grayfields) to Nathaniel Hart, Aug. 3, 1780, "Documents from the Shane Collection: The Hart Papers," 343.) It was probably this "past favor" that Boone insisted on repaying.

53. Daniel Boone, Receipt, Dec. 24, 1781, Miscellaneous Manuscripts Collection (LC) (quotation); Daniel Boone Deed, July 20, 1786, Samuel Wilson

Collection (UK) (quotation); Deposition of Daniel Boone, Mar. 18, 1799, Draper MSS, 15C25(12); John Floyd to William Preston, Dec. 19, 1779, Draper MSS, 17CC122; Thomas Marshall to Michael Gratz, Apr. 23, 1783, in William Vincent Byars, ed., *B. and M. Gratz Merchants in Philadelphia, 1754–1798: Papers of Interest to Their Posterity and the Posterity of Their Associates* (Jefferson City, Mo., 1916), 212. Thomas Marshall, Account Book, 1782–83, Thomas Marshall Papers (FC), contains the details of Boone's surveying work in Fayette County between November 29, 1782 and February 24, 1783. The account indicates that although his commission varied, Boone received a basic fee of 2s 6d Virginia currency, as well as an off-the-books land bonus for executing a survey. See also Thomas Hart to [?], Sept. 30, 1784, Thomas Hart Papers (UK); Daniel Boone to William Christian, Aug. 23, 1785, Daniel Boone Papers (FC); Willard R. Jillson, comp., "Land Surveys of Daniel Boone," *RKHS* 44 (Apr. 1946): 86–100; idem, *With Compass and Chain: A Brief Narration of the Activities of Col. Daniel Boone as a Land Surveyor in Kentucky* (Frankfort, 1954).

54. Boone's personal surveys and sales tallied from Brookes-Smith, comp., *Master Index Virginia Surveys and Grants*, 17, 88.

55. John May to Samuel Beall, Jan. 20, 1781, Jan. 25, 1785, Beall-Booth Family Papers.

56. Moses Austin, "A Memorandum of M. Austin's Journey from the Lead Mines in the County of Wythe in the State of Virginia to the Province of Louisiana West of the Mississippi, 1796–1797," *AHR* 5 (Apr. 1900): 526 (quotation); Otto Rothert, ed., "John D. Shane's Interview with Pioneer John Hedge, Bourbon County," *FCHQ* 14 (July 1940): 177 (quotation). For land distribution figures, see Fredrika J. Teute, "Land, Liberty, and Labor in the Post-Revolutionary Era: Kentucky as the Promised Land" (Ph.D. diss., Johns Hopkins University, 1988), 185, 404–11; Joan Wells Coward, *Kentucky in the New Republic: The Process of Constitution Making* (Lexington, 1979), 55.

57. Rothert, ed., "John D. Shane's Interview with Pioneer John Hedge," quotation on 177. On tenancy in Kentucky in the 1780s, see Teute, "Land, Liberty, and Labor in the Post-Revolutionary Era," 313–47.

58. For an example of how an Ohio speculator appealed to disappointed Kentuckians with the promise of better management, less engrossment, and greater security, see John Cleves Symmes (Beargrass) to the People of Kentucky, May 29, 1787, in Beverly W. Bond Jr., ed., *The Correspondence of John Cleves Symmes: Founder of the Miami Purchase* (New York, 1926), 280; John D. Barnhart, "The Migration of Kentuckians Across the Ohio River," *FCHQ* 25 (Jan. 1951): 24–32.

59. Robert H. Bishop, ed. *An Outline of the History of the Church in the State of Kentucky, During a Period of Forty Years: Containing the Memoirs of Rev. David Rice, and Sketches of the Origin and Present State of Particular Churches, and of the Lives and Labours of a Number of Men Who Were Eminent and Useful in Their Day* (Lexington, 1824), 36.

Chapter Four. The Rules of Law

1. Otto, Chargé d'Affaires (New York) to Monseigneur [?], Mar. 11, 1786, Otto Letter (KHS).

2. Extract from a letter from a gentleman living in Kentucky to his friend in Chester County, Pennsylvania, Dec. 8, 1786, Samuel Wilson Collection (UK).

3. John D. Shane interview with Asa Farrar, Draper MSS, 13CC3.

4. Humphrey Marshall, *The History of Kentucky: Exhibiting an Account of the Modern Discovery, Settlement, Progressive Improvement, Civil and Military Transactions, and the Present State of the Country*, 2 vols. (Frankfort, 1824), 1:150 (quotation); Frankfort *Commentator*, Mar. 6, 1822 (quotation); Thomas Perkins Abernethy, *Western Lands and the American Revolution* (New York, 1937), 228.

5. Lee Soltow, "Kentucky Wealth at the End of the Eighteenth Century," *Journal of Economic History* 43 (Sept. 1983): 620–26; and Joan Wells Coward, *Kentucky in the New Republic: The Process of Constitution Making* (Lexington, 1979), 55, provide quantitative summaries of the county tax lists for 1800. Even these numbers underestimated the divergence from the principles of the homestead ethic. Tax lists counted as a landholder everyone who had taken the first step toward obtaining a title, though many small property owners had yet to establish clear deeds. For comparative figures in other trans-Appalachian states, see Lee Soltow, "Inequality Amidst Abundance: Land Ownership in Early Nineteenth Century Ohio," *Ohio History* 88 (1979): 133–51; idem, "Land Inequality on the Frontier: The Distribution of Land in East Tennessee at the Beginning of the Nineteenth Century," *Social Science History* 5 (1981): 275–92.

6. For the list and location of Boone's post-1792 surveys and grants, see Joan Brookes-Smith, ed., *Index for Old Kentucky Surveys and Grants* (Frankfort, 1975), 14. For an example in which half a dozen other claims overlapped with one of Boone's, see the map in Mary E. Wharton and Roger W. Barbour, *Bluegrass Land and Life: Land Character, Plants, and Animals of the Inner Bluegrass Region of Kentucky: Past, Present, and Future* (Lexington, 1992), 44.

7. Bourbon County Court, Order Book A, 1786–1793, 133, 139, 161, 243 (microfilm at UK); Michael L. Cook, ed., *Virginia Supreme Court District of Kentucky: Order Books, 1783–1792* (Evansville, 1988), 108, 110, 130, 187, 215, 218, 242, 255, 259, 274, 300, 347, 410, 417, 525; Thomas Todd Statement, Draper MSS, 6S309–310; Nathaniel Hart (Lexington) to Uncle, Jan. 10, 1791, Nathaniel Hart Letter (FC); William P. Hart Statement, Draper MSS, 16CC158; John D. Shane interview with William Risk, ibid., 11CC87; Deposition of Daniel Boone, Apr. 24, 1794, in Michael L. Cook and Bettie A. Cummings Cook, eds., *Fayette County Kentucky Records*, 5 vols. (Evansville, Ind., 1985), 1:178–79. According to Henry Clay, the "chimney corner surveys," for which Boone was denounced, were "frequently practiced." See Henry Clay (Lexington) to Robert Smith, Aug. 7, 1805, in *HCP*, 1:194. Another accusation leveled at Boone and other surveyors was that through incompetence or malfeasance they surveyed land "off its Ground." That is, they ran their survey lines on different ground than the location specified in a prior entry. (See John Allen [Shelbyville] to Archibald Stuart, Aug. 7, 1800, Allen-Butler Family Papers [UK].)

8. Deposition of Squire Boone, May 18, 1804, in Cook and Cook, eds., *Fayette County Kentucky Records*, 1:259 (quotation); Notice to Sheriff of Mason County, Nov. 29, 1798, Daniel Boone Papers (FC); Draper MSS, 16C4–5, 54.

9. *Petitions*, 76.

10. Lexington *Independent Gazetteer*, Oct. 19, 1804 (quotation); A. Shoe-

maker, comp., *Charles's Kentucky, Tennessee, & Ohio Almanac for the Year of Our Lord 1805* (Lexington, 1805), November (quotation).

11. Russellville *Mirror*, June 23, 1808 (quotation); Meeting of Farmers and Planters of County of Fayette, Apr. 28, 1798, Broadside Collection (UK) (quotation); William Littell, "To the People of Kentucky," in Lexington *Independent Gazetteer*, Nov. 2, 1804 (quotation); *Petitions*, 77; John Bradford, comp., *The New Clerk's Magazine and Farmer's Safe Guide, Containing Precedents, or Forms of Writing, Suited to All Kinds of Business; by Which Every Farmer as Well as Others May Execute Any Writing That May Be Needed, Without the Assistance of a Lawyer* (Lexington, 1821). On the politics of constitution making and the movement to simplify the laws and reduce the role of lawyers, see Coward, *Kentucky in the New Republic*, and Richard E. Ellis, *The Jeffersonian Crisis: Courts and Politics in the Young Republic* (New York, 1971), 111–56.

12. Lexington *Reporter*, Apr. 22, 1809 (quotation); Robert Triplett, *Roland Trevor, or, The Pilot of Human Life, Being an Autobiography of the Author, Showing How to Make and Lose a Fortune, and Then to Make Another* (Philadelphia, 1853), quotation on 20; Micah Taul, "Memoirs of Micah Taul," *RKHS* 27 (Jan. 1929): 362, 367 (quotations); John Brown to William Preston, July 6, 1780, Draper MSS, 5QQ39; Henry Clay (Washington) to William Prentiss, Feb. 13, 1807, in *HCP* 1:281; Henry Clay (Washington) to Caesar A. Rodney, Dec. 29, 1812, ibid., 1:751; George Robertson, *An Outline of the Life of George Robertson. Written by Himself* (Lexington, 1876), 37–38; Lucius P. Little, *Ben Hardin: His Times and Contemporaries, with Selections from His Speeches* (Louisville, 1887), 32–34.

13. Amos Kendall, *Autobiography of Amos Kendall*, ed. William Stickney (Washington, D.C., 1872), 126.

14. William S. Bryan, "Daniel Boone in Missouri," *Missouri Historical Review* 3 (Jan. 1909): 96–97; W. C. Caywood Jr., "Boone in Missouri: 1800–1820," *FCHQ* 38 (Apr. 1964): 115–18.

15. Swope and Smith Agreement in "District Court Deed Book C," in Cook and Cook, eds., *Fayette County Kentucky Records*, 2:216 (quotation); Providence Church, Clark County, "Transcript of the First Record Book, 1780–1833," quotation on 165 (KHS); Alfred Tischendorf and E. Taylor Parks, eds., *The Diary and Journal of Richard Clough Anderson, Jr., 1814–1826* (Durham, N.C., 1964), 17; James B. Finley, *Autobiography of Rev. James Finley, or, Pioneer Life in the West*, ed. W. P. Strickland (Cincinnati, 1853), 99–100; Neal O. Hammon, "Land Acquisition on the Kentucky Frontier," *RKHS* 78 (Autumn 1980): 315–16.

16. François André Michaux, *Travels to the West of the Alleghany Mountains, in the States of Ohio, Kentucky, and Tennessee, and Back to Charleston, by the Upper Carolines*, in R. G. Thwaites, ed., *Early Western Travels, 1748–1846*, 32 vols. (Cleveland, 1904), 3:227 (quotation); Lexington *Stewart's Kentucky Herald*, July 4, 1797 (quotation).

17. Harry Innes to Thomas Jefferson, Aug. 27, 1791, in Charles T. Cullen, ed., *The Papers of Thomas Jefferson* (Princeton, 1986), 22:86.

18. *Acts* (1795), quotation on 4; ibid. (1793), 19–22. Beginning with the first session of the legislature, lawmakers offered some relief to land claimants by passing a series of annual extensions for filing the necessary plats and surveys and pay the required fees. Lawmakers also suspended sheriffs' sales of lands for tax

penalties and allowed residents to redeem forfeited tracts. See ibid. (1792), 3; ibid. (1793), 22–23; ibid. (1794), 46; ibid. (1795), 84–85; ibid. (1796), 10–11, 43; ibid. (1797), 182–83; ibid. (1798), 48; ibid. (1799), 49–50; ibid. (1800), 18; ibid. (1801), 51–52; *Law*, 3:118–19, 168, 228–32, 309, 335–36, 404; ibid., 4:5–6, 117–18, 246–48, 333–36.

19. Walter Alves to Thomas Hart, Jan. 6, 1795, Dec. 8, 1794, Thomas Hart Papers (UK).

20. *Acts* (1797), quotations on 143. For an excellent discussion of the background and evolution of Kentucky's occupying claimant laws, see Paul W. Gates, "Tenants of the Log Cabin," *MVHR* 49 (June 1962): 3–31.

21. Lexington *Stewart's Kentucky Herald*, Jan. 14, 1795 (quotation); *House* (1794), 49, 64, 67, 81–82; James Hughes, *A Report of the Causes Determined by the Late Supreme Court for the District of Kentucky, and by the Court of Appeals, in which Titles to Land Were in Dispute*, ed. Harvey Meyers (Cincinnati, 1869), 251–322. (Hereafter, I cite judicial cases in the form used in legal works. Thus, this case, which was finally settled in 1799, would appear as Kenton v. McConnell, 1 Hughes 251 [Ky. Ct. App., 1799].) George Muter and Benjamin Sebastian, *The Address of George Muter and Benjamin Sebastian, Two Judges of the Court of Appeals, to the Free Men of Kentucky* (Lexington, 1795), 24; Humphrey Marshall, *A Reply to the Address of the Hon. George Muter and Benjamin Sebastian* (n.p., 1795); Coward, *Kentucky in the New Republic*, 82–83; Ellis, *The Jeffersonian Crisis*, 134–37; Edna Kenton, *Simon Kenton: His Life and Period, 1755–1836* (Garden City, N.Y., 1930), 241–42.

22. *Acts* (1795), 21–38, 47–49; ibid. (1796), 68–72, 137–40. While radicals focused on the independence of the judges on the court of appeals, the day-to-day lives of Kentuckians were much more directly affected by decisions of the county courts. Copying Virginia, Kentucky's first constitution lodged significant power in the county courts, whose magistrates comprised a self-perpetuating oligarchy safe from democratic influence. See Robert M. Ireland, *The County Courts in Antebellum Kentucky* (Lexington, 1972).

23. Benjamin Howard (Frankfort) to Major William Preston, Nov. 17, 1802, Preston-Joyes Collection (FC) (quotation); Lexington *Reporter*, Apr. 22, 1809 (quotation); *Acts* (1802), 7–34; Ellis, *The Jeffersonian Crisis*, 154–56; Lynn L. Marshall, "The Early Career of Amos Kendall: The Making of a Jacksonian" (Ph.D. diss., University of California, Berkeley, 1962), 180–81.

24. Henry Clay (Lexington) to John Breckinridge, Dec. 18, 1800, in *HCP*, 1:45.

25. Vernon F. Martin, "Father Rice, the Preacher Who Followed the Frontier," *FCHQ* 29 (Oct. 1955): 324–30.

26. David Rice, *Slavery Inconsistent with Justice and Good Policy; Proved by a Speech Delivered in the Convention, Held at Danville, Kentucky* (Philadelphia, 1792), 24.

27. The text of the 1792 constitution is printed in Lowell Harrison, *Kentucky's Road to Statehood* (Lexington, 1992), 152–68, quotations on 163, 162; Patricia Watlington, *The Partisan Spirit: Kentucky Politics, 1779–1792* (New York, 1972), 220–22; Coward, *Kentucky in the New Republic*, 12–47.

28. On Nicholas's handiwork, see Fredrika Johanna Teute, "Land, Liberty,

and Labor in the Post-Revolutionary Era: Kentucky as the Promised Land" (Ph.D. diss., Johns Hopkins University, 1988), 101–38.

29. Harrison, *Kentucky's Road to Statehood*, quotations on 163–64; Coward, *Kentucky in the New Republic*, 37.

30. Teute, "Land, Liberty, and Labor in the Post-Revolutionary Era," 207–12.

31. Thomas Hart (Grayfields) to Nathaniel Hart, Aug. 3, 1780, in "Shane Collection of Documents: The Hart Papers," *Journal of the Presbyterian Historical Society* 14 (Dec. 1931): 343–44.

32. John May (Falls of Ohio) to Samuel Beall, Dec. 9, 1780, Beall-Booth Family Papers (FC); Breckinridge quoted in Hazel Dicken-Garcia, *To Western Woods: The Breckinridge Family Moves to Kentucky in 1793* (Rutherford, N.J., 1991), 171.

33. "A Political Creed," Apr. 1798, Broadsides Collection (UK) (quotation); Coward, *Kentucky in the New Republic*, quotation on 108; Asa Earl Martin, *The Anti-Slavery Movement in Kentucky Prior to 1850* (Louisville, 1918), quotation on 27.

34. [Franklin], "To the People of Kentucky," Apr. 1798, Broadsides Collection (UK).

35. [Scaevola], "To the Electors of Fayette County," Apr. 16, 1798, in *HCP*, 1:7; Bernard Mayo, *Henry Clay: Spokesman of the New West* (Boston, 1937), 1–86.

36. [Scaevola], "To the Citizens of Fayette," Feb. 1799, in *HCP*, quotations on 1:12.

37. Merrill D. Peterson, *The Great Triumvirate: Webster, Clay, and Calhoun* (New York, 1987), quotation on 12; Timothy Flint, *Recollections of the Last Ten Years, Passed in Occasional Residences and Journeyings in the Valley of the Mississippi*, ed. George R. Brooks (1826; Carbondale, Ill., 1968), quotation on 58.

38. Coward, *Kentucky in the New Republic*, quotation on 112.

39. George Nicholas to John Brown, Nov. 12, 1789, George Nicholas Papers (KHS) (quotation); Coward, *Kentucky in the New Republic*, 115–17.

40. Teute, "Land, Liberty, and Labor in the Post-Revolutionary Era," quotation on 4–5; *Kentucky Gazette*, Jan. 31, 1799 (quotation); Huntley Dupre, "The Political Ideas of George Nicholas," *RKHS* 39 (July 1941): 201–23.

41. Coward, *Kentucky in the New Republic*, 123–61.

42. Lowell Harrison, *John Breckinridge: Jeffersonian Republican* (Louisville, 1969), 103–9.

43. John Mack Faragher, *Daniel Boone: The Life and Legend of an American Pioneer* (New York, 1992), 273. A complete list of clients can be found in Henry Clay, Account Book, 1797–1814 (UK); Durward T. Stokes, "Thomas Hart in North Carolina," *North Carolina Historical Review* 41 (Summer 1964): 335.

44. Fayette County Tax Lists, 1799–1808, microfilm (KHS); Agreement with Cuthbert Banks, Sept. 13, 1804, in *HCP*, 1:148–49; Richard L. Troutman, "Henry Clay and His 'Ashland' Estate," *FCHQ* 30 (Apr. 1956): 159–74.

45. Lexington *Reporter*, June 13, 1809; Henry Clay (Lexington) to Adam Beatty, July 8, 1809, in *HCP*, Supplement: 12; Mayo, *Henry Clay*, 94, 180–84.

46. Speech to the Virginia General Assembly, Feb. 7, 1822, in *HCP*, 3:164 (quotation); Lexington *Kentucky Gazette*, Mar. 28, 1822; F. A. Michaux, *Travels*

to the West of the Alleghany Mountains, 3:227–28. Additional refinements in the occupying claimants laws followed in 1812, 1819, and 1820, which tilted the law even more in favor of occupants. See *Law*, 4:55–57, 345–49; *Acts* (1819), 761; ibid. (1820), 148–51.

47. Carrol v. Moss' Heirs, 4 Bibb 395 (Ky. Ct. App., 1816); see also Johnson v. Rowland, 1 Sneed 77 (Ky. Ct. App., 1801); Whitledge v. Wait's Heir, 1 Sneed 335 (Ky. Ct. App., 1804); Hart's Heir v. Baylor, 1 Hardin 606 (Ky. Ct. App., 1808); Fowler v. Halbert, 4 Bibb 52 (Ky. Ct. App., 1815); White v. Ogden, 1 Marshall 42 (Ky. Ct. App., 1817); Barlow v. Bell, 1 Marshall 246 (Ky. Ct. App., 1818); Chiles v. Patterson, 1 Marshall 444 (Ky. Ct. App., 1819); Parker v. Stephens, 3 Marshall 197 (Ky. Ct. App., 1820); Smith's Heirs v. Nowell, 2 Littell 165 (Ky. Ct. App., 1822). During the tenure of Judge Harry Innes, which stretched from 1789 to 1816, the Federal Court of Kentucky also sustained the occupying claimant statutes and respected state court precedents. See Mary K. Bonsteel Tachau, *Federal Courts in the Early Republic: Kentucky, 1789–1816* (Princeton, 1978), 183–85.

48. George M. Bibb, "Introduction," in idem, *Reports of Cases at Common Law and in Chancery, Argued and Decided in the Court of Appeals of the Commonwealth of Kentucky, from Fall Term 1808 to Spring and Fall Terms 1809* (Cincinnati, 1910), quotation on 19. On the standardization of the shape of tracts, see Swearingen v. Higgins, 1 Hughes 7 (Ky. Ct. App., 1787); Hite v. Harrison, 1 Hughes 29 (Ky. Ct. App., 1789); Walker v. Orr, 1 Hughes 38 (Ky. Ct. App., 1790); Frye v. Essry, 1 Hughes 103 (Ky. Ct. App., 1795); Cleland v. Thorp, 1 Hughes 192 (Ky. Ct. App., 1798). For specific cases setting precedents for the rules of identity and the definition of notoriety, see Ammons v. Spears, 1 Hughes 10 (Ky. Ct. App., 1787); Pawling v. Merewether Heirs, 1 Hughes 26 (Ky. Ct. App., 1789); Smith v. Evans, 1 Hughes 169 (Ky. Ct. App., 1795); McClanahan v. Berry, 1 Hughes 323 (Ky. Ct. App., 1799).

49. Bodley and Hughes v. Taylor, 5 Cranch 191 (U.S. Sup. Ct., 1809).

50. George Nicholas to John Brown, Nov. 12, 1789, in Humphrey Dupre, ed., "Three Letters of George Nicholas to John Brown," *RKHS* 41 (Jan. 1943): 3; Matthew Scott (Lexington) to Mssrs. Prevost and Company, Jan. 4, 1817, Matthew T. Scott Letterbook, 1816–1821, Scott Family Papers (UK); Robert Wickliffe (Lexington) to James D. Wolf, Jan. 26, 1819, Robert Wickliffe Letterbook, 1817–1835, microfilm (UK).

51. Harry Innes (Danville) to John Brown, Feb. 20, 1788, Harry Innes Papers (LC).

52. Tachau, *Federal Courts in the Early Republic*, esp. 180–82. Tachau concludes that "the court records provide no evidence that the Kentucky federal courts had any bias toward non-residents or toward residents" (quotation on 182).

53. Carter Tarrant, *The Substance of a Discourse Delivered in the Town of Versailles, Woodford County, State of Kentucky, April 20, 1806* (Lexington, 1806); Martin, *The Anti-Slavery Movement in Kentucky Prior to 1850*, 33–48.

54. For Clay's public denunciations of slavery and his advocacy of gradual emancipation followed by deportation, see Speech at Organization of American Colonization Society, Dec. 21, 1816, in *HCP* 2:263–64; Speech to Kentucky Colonization Society, Aug. 26, 1836, ibid., Supplement: 265–66; Speech in Senate, Feb. 7, 1839, ibid., 9:283.

55. For statistical evidence of the decline of landlessness across Kentucky, see Teute, "Land, Liberty, and Labor in the Post-Revolutionary Era," 254.

56. Coward, *Kentucky in the New Republic*, 63; Marion B. Lucas, *A History of Blacks in Kentucky: Volume 1: From Slavery to Segregation, 1760–1891* (Frankfort, 1992), xv–xvi, 101–7; Ellen Eslinger, "The Shape of Slavery on the Kentucky Frontier, 1775–1800," *RKHS* 92 (Winter 1994): 1–23.

57. Daniel Drake, *Pioneer Life in Kentucky, 1785–1800*, ed. Emmet Field Horine (New York, 1948), quotation on 93.

58. E. P. Thompson, *Whigs and Hunters: The Origins of the Black Act* (New York, 1975), 258–69; idem, "The Moral Economy of the English Crowd in the Eighteenth Century," *Past & Present* 50 (Feb. 1971): 76–136.

Chapter Five. Rights in the Woods

1. For the reference to "right in the woods," see Thomas Anburey, *Travels through the Interior Parts of America*, 2 vols. (1789; Boston, 1923), 2:190.

2. The criminalization of custom and the defense of common rights have been the themes of a number of important studies in eighteenth-century British history. See especially Douglas Hay et al., *Albion's Fatal Tree: Crime and Society in Eighteenth-Century England* (New York, 1975); E. P. Thompson, *Whigs and Hunters: The Origin of the Black Act* (New York, 1975); and most recently E. P. Thompson, *Customs in Common* (London, 1991), esp. 97–184. On this side of the Atlantic, the conflicts between semiprivate and fully privatized property regimes are taken up in Gary Kulik, "Dams, Fish, and Farmers: Defense of Public Rights in Eighteenth-Century Rhode Island," in Steven Hahn and Jonathan Prude, eds., *The Countryside in the Age of Capitalist Transformation: Essays in the Social History of Rural America* (Chapel Hill, 1985), 25–50; Steven Hahn, *The Roots of Southern Populism: Yeoman Farmers and the Transformation of the Georgia Upcountry, 1850–1890* (New York, 1993), 239–53.

3. For a similar argument about backcountry attitudes about private property and community rights, see Andrew R. L. Cayton, "Marietta and the Ohio Company," in Robert D. Mitchell, ed., *Appalachian Frontiers: Settlement, Society, and Development in the Preindustrial Era* (Lexington, 1991), 193–95.

4. *Petitions*, 43–44.

5. William W. Hening, ed., *The Statutes at Large: Being a Collection of All the Laws of Virginia*, 13 vols. (New York, 1809–23), 9:122, 310; James R. Bentley, ed., "Letters of Thomas Perkins to Gen. Joseph Palmer, Lincoln County, Kentucky, 1785," *FCHQ* 49 (Apr. 1975): 145–46; Thomas D. Clark, "Salt, A Factor in the Settlement of Kentucky," ibid., 12 (Jan. 1938): 42–52.

6. Chester Raymond Young, ed., *Westward into Kentucky: The Narrative of Daniel Trabue* (Lexington, 1981), quotation on 42; Nathan Boone Statement, Draper MSS, 6S103; Joseph Jackson Statement, ibid., 11C62.

7. Lexington *Kentucky Gazette*, July 24, 1815, Jan. 27, 1817. On the practice of taking timber from private lands and efforts to combat it, see W. Croghan (near Louisville) to Edmund Rogers, Feb. 7, 1804, Rogers-Underwood Family Papers (FC); Fanney Slaughter (Louisville) to Polly Campbell, May 18, 1809, Slaughter Family Papers (FC).

8. Lewis H. Kirkpatrick, ed., "The Journal of William Calk, Kentucky Pio-

neer," *MVHR* 7 (Mar. 1921): 375; Richard Laverne Troutman, "Plantation Life in the Antebellum Bluegrass Region of Kentucky" (M.A. thesis, University of Kentucky, 1955), 20; John Bradford, *The General Instructor: or the office duty and authority of Justices of the Peace, Sheriffs, Coroners, and Constables in the State of Kentucky* (Lexington, 1800), 72–74; *Law*, 2:548–49, 554–61; ibid., 3:655–61.

9. *Law*, 2:27–28. The act stipulated that the first time another man's cattle or pigs intruded the victim was entitled to reparations. A second offense merited double damages plus court costs. A third infraction brought the same penalties, and it afforded the aggrieved party liberty to exterminate trespassing stock.

10. Henry Clay (Washington) to John T. Mason, Mar. 9, 1826, in *HCP*, 5:155; Agreement with John Watkins, Oct. 27, 1815, ibid., 2:87; Lexington *Kentucky Gazette*, Mar. 21, 1822; *Acts* (1818), 552.

11. *Acts* (1820), 114–16.

12. For examples of Ohio Indians' refusal to treat land as a commodity, see "Journal of General Butler," in Neville B. Craig, ed., *The Olden Time*, 2 vols. (Pittsburgh, 1846–48), 2:522; "A Journal of the Proceedings at a Council Held with The Indians of the Wabash and Illinois at Post Vincents, by Brigadier General Putnam," in Rowena Buell, ed., *The Memoirs of Rufus Putnam and Certain Official Papers and Correspondence* (Boston, 1903), 343; "Address of the General Indian Council to the United States Commissioners, August 13, 1793," in U.S. Congress, *American State Papers: Documents, Legislative and Executive, of the Congress of the United States*, 38 vols. (Washington, 1832–61), *Class II: Indian Affairs*, 1:356–57.

13. Franklin B. Dexter, ed., *Diary of David McClure: Doctor of Divinity, 1748–1820* (New York, 1899), quotation on 85.

14. John W. Jordan, ed., "Journal of James Kenny, 1761–1763," *Pennsylvania Magazine of History and Biography* 37 (1913): 22; Paul A. W. Wallace, ed., *Thirty Thousand Miles with John Heckewelder* (Pittsburgh, 1958), 41, 44; Rev. David Jones, *A Journal of Two Visits Made to Some Nations of Indians on the West Side of the River Ohio in the Years 1772 and 1773* (Burlington, 1774), 65, 67; Thomas Ridout, "The Narrative of the Captivity among the Shawanese Indians, in 1788, of Thos. Ridout, Afterwards Surveyor-General of Upper Canada," in Matilda Edgar, ed., *Ten Years of Upper Canada in Peace and War, 1805–1815; Being the Ridout Letters* (Toronto, 1890), 361, 366; Governor St. Clair (Fort Harmar) to Secretary of War, Aug. 17, 1788, in William Henry Smith, ed., *The St. Clair Papers: The Life and Public Services of Arthur St. Clair: Soldier of the Revolutionary War; President of the Continental Congress; and Governor of the North-Western Territory, with His Correspondence and Other Papers*, 2 vols. (Cincinnati, 1882), 2:82; O. M. Spencer, *The Indian Captivity of O. M. Spencer*, ed. Milo M. Quaife (Chicago, 1917), 96; Joseph E. Walker, ed., "Plowshares and Pruning Hooks for the Miami and Potawatomi: The Journal of Gerard T. Hopkins, 1804," *Ohio History* 88 (Autumn 1979): 396. The introduction of livestock did not simply undermine traditional beliefs. As with other imports from Europe, Ohio Indians successfully integrated domesticated animals into existing ritual systems. Ceremonies connected with hunting expanded to pay respect for slaughtered livestock. See Michael N. McConnell, *A Country Between: The Upper Ohio Valley and Its Peoples, 1724–1774* (Lincoln, 1992), 218–19. For a case study of New England Indians and

the adoption of livestock, see Virginia Dejohn Anderson, "King Philip's Herds: Indians, Colonists, and the Problem of Livestock in Early New England," *WMQ* 51 (Oct. 1994): 601–24.

15. Lawrence Henry Gipson, ed., "The Moravian Indian Mission on White River: Diaries and Letters, May 5, 1799, to Nov. 12, 1806," *Indiana Historical Collections* 23 (1938): 297, 338–39; Walker, ed., "Plowshares and Pruning Hooks for the Miami and Potawatomi," 389–93, 402–3; John Johnston, "Recollections of Sixty Years," in Leonard U. Hill, *John Johnston and the Indians in the Land of the Three Miamis* (Piqua, Ohio, 1957), 188–89; Helen Hornbeck Tanner, "The Glaize in 1792: A Composite Indian Community," *Ethnohistory* 25 (Winter 1978): 15–39; R. David Edmunds, " 'Unacquainted with the Laws of the Civilized World': American Attitudes toward the Métis Communities in the Old Northwest," in Jacqueline Peterson and Jennifer S. H. Brown, eds., *The New Peoples: Being and Becoming Métis in North America* (Lincoln, 1985), 185–93; Joseph A. Parsons Jr., "Civilizing the Indians of the Old Northwest, 1800–1810," *Indiana Magazine of History* 56 (Sept. 1960): 195–216.

16. Dexter, ed., *Diary of David McClure*, 51; Jones, *A Journal of Two Visits*, 98; Gipson, ed., "Mission on White River," 68; John Heckewelder, *A Narrative of the Mission of the United Brethren among the Delaware and Mohegan Indians, From Its Commencement, in the Year 1740, to the Close of the Year 1808* (Philadelphia, 1820), 103–4, 157.

17. Gipson, ed., "Mission on White River," quotation on 36; Heckewelder, *A Narrative of the Mission*, 122–24.

18. Earl P. Olmstead, *Blackcoats among the Delaware: David Zeisberger on the Ohio Frontier* (Kent, Ohio, 1991), 79, 127–30; Heckewelder, *A Narrative of the Mission*, 123; Gipson, ed., "Mission on White River," 226–27.

19. Eugene F. Bliss, ed., *Diary of David Zeisberger: A Moravian Missionary among the Indians of Ohio*, 2 vols. (Cincinnati, 1885), quotation on 2:65; Heckewelder, *A Narrative of the Mission*, 126–27; Gipson, ed., "Mission on White River," 168.

20. Gipson, ed., "Mission on White River," quotation on 254. For the fluctuation of Christian Indian populations at Moravian settlements, see Bliss, ed., *Diary of David Zeisberger*, 1:253, 316, 386, 464; 2:74, 147, 240, 294, 337, 389, 433, 469, 509.

21. Gipson, ed., "Mission on White River," quotations on 497, 496. For John and Catherine Thomas, see ibid., 254, 260–61, 266–67, 303–4, 349, 497.

22. Gipson, ed., "Mission on White River," quotations on 450, 427.

23. On the gendered character of livestock-raising, see McConnell, *A Country Between*, 218–19; Thomas Hatley, Cherokee Women Farmers Hold Their Ground," in Mitchell, ed., *Appalachian Frontiers*, 43–45; Anderson, "King Philip's Herds," 607.

24. Gipson, ed., "Mission on White River," quotations on 340, 262.

25. Ibid., 262, 339–40, 364, 392, 451–53, 573; Gregory Dowd, *A Spirited Resistance: The North American Indian Struggle for Unity, 1745–1815* (Baltimore, 1992), 123–47; Bil Gilbert, *God Gave Us This Country: Tekamthi and the First American Civil War* (New York, 1989), 184–262.

26. Gipson, ed., "Mission on White River," quotations on 364, 452.

27. Draper MSS, 16C4–5, 54. For an eloquent rhapsody on the essence of hunting and manhood in a cross-cultural perspective, see José Ortega y Gasset, *Meditations on Hunting*, trans. Howard B. Westcott (New York, 1972).

28. Roseann R. Hogan, ed., "Buffaloes in the Corn: James Wade's Account of Pioneer Kentucky," *RKHS* 89 (Winter 1991): 31 (quotation); David Barrow, Journal and Some Notes, Draper MSS, 12CC192–193; John D. Shane interview with David Crouch, ibid., 12CC226.

29. Paul Woehrmann, ed., "The Autobiography of Abraham Snethen, Frontier Preacher," *FCHQ* 51 (Oct. 1977): 316; Shane interview with David Crouch, Draper MSS, 12CC225, 229; François André Michaux, *Travels to the West of the Alleghany Mountains, in the States of Ohio, Kentucky, and Tennessee, and Back to Charleston, by the Upper Carolines*, in R. G. Thwaites, ed., *Early Western Travels, 1748–1846*, 32 vols. (Cleveland, 1904): 3:192; Hogan, ed., "Buffaloes in the Corn," 31. John D. Shane with James Wade, Draper MSS, 12CC39 (this passage is omitted from the published account edited by Hogan). See also Charles G. Talbert, ed., "Looking Backward through One Hundred Years: Personal Recollections of James B. Ireland," *RKHS* 57 (Apr. 1959): 106–7; Josiah Morrow, ed., "Tours into Kentucky and the Northwest Territory: Three Journals by the Rev. James Smith of Powhatan County, Va., 1783, 1795, 1797," *Ohio Archaeological and Historical Publications* 16 (1907): 384; John Cox to Russel Cox, Jan. 6, 1806, John Cox Letter (UK); William Newnham Blane, *Travels through the United States and Canada* (London, 1828), 106.

30. Christian Schultz Jr., *Travels in an Inland Voyage through the States of New York, Pennsylvania, Virginia, Ohio, Kentucky, and Tennessee, and through the Territories of Indiana, Louisiana, Mississippi, and New Orleans*, 2 vols. (New York, 1810), 2:21. Elizabeth A. Perkins, "The Consumer Frontier: Household Consumption in Early Kentucky," *Journal of American History* 78 (Sept. 1991): 491, 500, provides a quantitative assessment of the declining place of hunting in Kentucky life. Her survey of inventories revealed in the early 1780s, 68 percent of households included hunting equipment. Twenty years later, only 41 percent of households contained this species of property.

31. David Meriwether, "Memoirs of David Meriwether," typescript, 6–7 (FC).

32. New York *Spirit of the Times*, Aug. 25, 1832; John J. Audubon, "Pitting of Wolves," in Clarence Gohdes, ed., *Hunting in the Old South: Original Narratives of the Hunters* (Baton Rouge, 1967), 80–86; *Acts* (1795), 57–58, 64–65; *Law*, 1:336; ibid., 3:101–2; ibid., 4:30, 142–43; ibid., 5:101–2; Receipt for Squirrel Scalps, Aug. 22, 1796, George F. Doyle Papers (UK); John D. Shane interview with Isaac Howard, Draper MSS, 11CC253; Anderson, "The Story of Soldier's Retreat," part 3, pp. 1–3 (FC); F. A. Michaux, *Travels to the West*, 3:228–37; Frances L. S. Dugan and Jacqueline P. Bull, eds., *Bluegrass Craftsman: Being the Reminiscences of Ebenezer Hiram Stedman Papermaker, 1808–1885* (Lexington, 1959), 29, 35, 54–64; Daniel Drake, *Pioneer Life in Kentucky*, ed. Emmet Field Horine (New York, 1948), 129–31, 93; Meriwether, "Memoirs," 1–2 (FC); Talbert, ed., "Looking Backward through One Hundred Years," 109–17; Lexington *Kentucky Gazette*, May 17, 1796; ibid., Apr. 16, 1805; John Brown, Diary, Mar. 16, 1822, typescript, 41 (FC).

33. Blane, *Travels through the United States*, quotation on 302; Audubon, *De-*

lineations of American Scenery, 60–67; Paris *Western Citizen*, Dec. 11, 1824; Dugan and Bull, eds., *Bluegrass Craftsman*, 119–20; Talbert, ed., "Looking Backward through One Hundred Years," 108–9; Drake, *Pioneer Life in Kentucky*, 130, 187; Lexington *Kentucky Gazette*, May 14, 1796; ibid., May 18, 1801, ibid., Feb. 12, 1816.

34. Joseph Doddridge, *Notes on the Settlement and Indian Wars of the Western Parts of Virginia and Pennsylvania from 1763 to 1783* (1824; Pittsburgh, 1912), 101; Blane, *Travels through the United States and Canada*, 106.

35. New York *Spirit of the Times*, Aug. 25, 1832; Dugan and Bull, eds., *Bluegrass Craftsman*, 28–30; James B. Finley, *Autobiography of Rev. James Finley or, Pioneer Life in the West*, ed. W. P. Strickland (Cincinnati, 1853), 72–73; [Hatfield], *Stories of Hatfield*, 115–17, 162; [John Rogers Underwood], "The Life of John Rogers Underwood as dictated to his daughter Elizabeth," Underwood Collection (WKU); John Cox to Russel Cox, Jan. 6, 1806, John Cox Letter (UK).

36. Warner L. Underwood, Diary, typescript, quotation on 34, Underwood Collection (WKU); Dugan and Bull, eds., *Bluegrass Craftsman*, quotations on 192, 30.

37. Dugan and Bull, eds., *Bluegrass Craftsman*, 185–94, quotation on 185.

38. Maria R. Audubon, ed., *Audubon and His Journals* (New York, 1897), 245.

39. John Palmer, *Journal of Travels in the United States of North America, and Lower Canada, Performed in the Year 1817* (London, 1818), 114–15; John Shane, "Henderson Company Ledger," *FCHQ* 21 (Jan. 1947): 42.

40. For a case involving timber theft in which the jury acquitted all but one defendant and assessed only a token fine against the single convicted person, see Benjamin Stansberry vs. John Dickerson, James Cochren, and Peter Bonta, May 1797, Abstract from Bullitt Circuit Court Records, Robert Emmett McDowell Collection (FC).

41. John May (Kentucky County) to Samuel Beall, Apr. 15, 1780 (FC) (quotation); David W. Meriwether (Bear Grass) to Father, Sept. 14, 1785, David Meriwether Letter (FC); Bentley, ed., "Letters of Thomas Perkins to Gen. Joseph Palmer," 148; Harry Innes (Danville) to John Brown, Dec. 7, 1787, in G. Glenn Clift, ed., "The District of Kentucky, 1783–1787, as Pictured by Harry Innes in a Letter to John Brown," *RKHS* 54 (Oct. 1956): 370; Broadsheets & Circulars, box 1, folder 2 (Durrett); Broadsides Collection (UK); George Rogers Taylor, "Agrarian Discontent in the Mississippi Valley Preceding the War of 1812," in Harry N. Scheiber, ed., *The Old Northwest: Studies in Regional History, 1787–1910* (Lincoln, Neb., 1969), 28–29. On the secret dealings of Kentucky gentry and Spanish officials, and the controversies that raged over the "Spanish Conspiracy," see John Mason Brown, *The Political Beginnings of Kentucky: A Narrative of Public Events Bearing on the History of that State up to the Time of Its Admission into the American Union* (Louisville, 1889); Thomas Marshall Green, *The Spanish Conspiracy: A Review of Early Spanish Movements in the South-West* (Cincinnati, 1891); Patricia Watlington, "John Brown and the Spanish Conspiracy," *VMHB* 75 (1967): 52–68.

42. Bourbon County Court, Order Book A, 36, 54–55, 162–67, 180–82, 188–89, 254 (microfilm at UK); H. E. Everman, *The History of Bourbon County, 1785–1865* (Paris, Ky., 1977), 9–11; Robert M. Ireland, *The County Courts in Antebellum Kentucky* (Lexington, 1972), 27–29.

43. Bourbon County Court, Order Book A, 258–59; *Petitions*, 144–53.

44. *Petitions*, 148–49.

45. *Petitions*, quotation on 146–47. For the various memorials and remonstrances to the Virginia General Assembly, see *Petitions*, 144–53. On the tobacco warehouse, see ibid., 120; Hening, ed., *The Statutes at Large*, 12:677.

46. Ellen T. Eslinger, "The Great Revival in Bourbon County, Kentucky" (Ph.D. diss., University of Chicago, 1988), 117–29. The petition tally showed 166 men in favor and 366 opposed. See also Finley, *Autobiography of Rev. James Finley*, 73, 93; Drake, *Pioneer Life in Kentucky*, 57–58.

47. William J. Rorabaugh, *The Alcoholic Republic: An American Tradition* (New York, 1979), 76–78; *Petitions*, 102–3, 105; Hening, ed., *The Statutes at Large*, 12:258.

48. Bourbon County Court, Order Book A, 245, 288–89.

49. *Acts* (1792), 38; ibid. (1793), 46; *Law*, 3:193–95; *Acts* (1802), 184–87.

50. *Acts* (1793), 46; ibid. (1801), 32–33; *Law*, 3:354; ibid., 4:222–23, 331.

51. John Roche, Journal, July 21, 1825, Draper MSS, 17CC90.

52. Thomas D. Clark, *A History of Kentucky* (1937; Lexington, 1960), 169; Rorabaugh, *The Alcoholic Republic*, 78–80; Mary K. Bonsteel Tachau, "The Whiskey Rebellion in Kentucky: A Forgotten Episode of Civil Disobedience," *Journal of the Early Republic* 2 (Fall 1982): 241–42.

53. Tachau, "The Whiskey Rebellion in Kentucky," 257; idem, *Federal Courts in the Early Republic: Kentucky, 1789–1816* (Princeton, 1978), 99–101; Thomas P. Slaughter, *The Whiskey Rebellion: Frontier Epilogue to the American Revolution* (New York, 1986), 117–20.

54. George Nicholas, *To the Citizens of Kentucky* (Lexington, 1798), quotation on 3; "At a meeting of sundry inhabitants of the State of Kentucky in Lexington, the 8th of July 1793," in Thomas D. Clark, ed., *The Voice of the Frontier: John Bradford's Notes on Kentucky* (Lexington, 1993), 196; Tachau, "The Whiskey Rebellion in Kentucky," 252–57. For a general discussion of the composition and character of grand and petit juries, see Christopher Waldrep, "Egalitarianism in the Oligarchy: The Grand Jury and Criminal Justice in Livingston County, 1799–1808," *FCHQ* 55 (July 1981): 253–67, and Robert M. Ireland, "Law and Disorder in Nineteenth-Century Kentucky," *Vanderbilt Law Review* 32 (Jan. 1979), 289–92. On Judge Innes's scrupulous attention to legal procedures as a part of the evasion of the whiskey tax in Kentucky, see Tachau, *Federal Courts in the Early Republic*, 95–126.

Chapter Six. The Bluegrass System

1. *Niles' Weekly Register*, Jan. 28, 1815.

2. John Filson, *The Discovery, Settlement, and Present State of Kentucke*, ed. William H. Masterson (New York, 1962), quotation on 51; Joseph Thomas, *The Life of the Pilgrim, Joseph Thomas, Containing an Accurate Account of His Trials, Travels and Gospel Labours to the Present* (Winchester, Va., 1817), quotation on 137; D. B. Warden, *A Statistical, Political, and Historical Account of the United States of North America; from the Period of Their First Colonization to the Present Day*, 3 vols. (Edinburgh, 1819), 2:314 (quotation); Samuel R. Brown, *The Western Gazetteer; or Emigrants' Directory* (Auburn, N.Y., 1817), quotation on 81; "Some particulars relative to the Soil, Situation, Productions, &c. of Kentucky: Extracted from the

Manuscript Journal of a Gentleman not long since returned from those parts,"
National Gazette 1 (Nov. 1791), reprinted in Eugene L. Schwaab, ed., *Travels in
the Old South: Selected from Periodicals of the Times*, 2 vols. (Lexington, 1973),
1:56; Gilbert Imlay, *A Topographical Description of the Western Territory of North
America* (London, 1793), 35–42, 48; "Report of Lexington Emigration Society,"
in Paris *Rights of Man, or the Kentucky Mercury*, Sept. 27, 1797; Josiah Morrow,
ed., "Tours into Kentucky and the Northwest Territory: Three Journals by the
Rev. James Smith of Powhatan County, Va., 1783, 1795, 1797," *Ohio Archaeological and Historical Publications* 16 (1907): 375; Henry Bradshaw Fearon, *Sketches
of America: A Narrative of a Journey of Five Thousand Miles through the Eastern
and Western States of America* (London, 1819), 235–36; William Newnham Blane,
Travels through the United States and Canada (London, 1828), 106–7; François
André Michaux, *Travels to the West of the Alleghany Mountains, in the States of
Ohio, Kentucky, and Tennessee, and Back to Charleston, by the Upper Carolines*, in
R. G. Thwaites, ed., *Early Western Travels, 1748–1846*, 32 vols. (Cleveland, 1904),
3:238.

    3. Thomas Ashe, *Travels in America, Performed in 1806, for the Purpose of Ex-
ploring the Rivers Alleghany, Monongahela, Ohio, and Mississippi, and Ascertaining
the Produce and Condition of Their Banks and Vicinity* (London, 1808), 170–72,
188, quotation on 170; Howard L. Applegate and Martin H. Bush, eds., *A Tour to
the South: Travel Diary of Moses Dewitt Burnet, 1815–1816* (Syracuse, 1965), 18; John
Breathitt, "Commencement of a Journal from Kentucky to the State of Pennsylvania," *RKHS* 52 (Jan. 1954): 8; John Melish, *Travels in the United States of America
in the Years 1806 & 1807, and 1809, 1810, & 1811*, 2 vols. (Philadelphia, 1812), 2:196–
201. Twentieth-century geographers have confirmed the intraregional distinctions
deduced by earlier travelers. Geographers draw the Bluegrass region as a roughly
circular area of some eight thousand square miles of north central Kentucky. The
region as a whole boasts certain characteristics: a growing season of approximately
one hundred eighty days, rainfall averaging between forty-two and sixty inches
per year, and limestone-impregnated soils which, as any thoroughbred breeder
will tell you, make the area ideal for raising fast racehorses. But as the comments
of early travelers and the current concentration of horse farms around Lexington
divulge, the grass was and still is greener in some parts of the Bluegrass than in
others. Indeed, geographers divide the region into an especially fertile inner circle
and a relatively poorer outer belt. Encompassing roughly two thousand four hundred square miles, the Inner Bluegrass contained the rich lands around Lexington, including all of the present counties of Fayette, Woodford, and Jessamine,
as well as portions of Anderson, Franklin, Scott, Harrison, Nicholas, Bourbon,
Clark, Madison, Garrard, Boyle, and Mercer. See Darrell Haug Davis, *The Geography of the Blue Grass Region of Kentucky* (Frankfort, 1927); Mary E. Wharton and
Roger W. Barbour, *Bluegrass Land and Life: Land Character, Plants, and Animals
of the Inner Bluegrass Region of Kentucky* (Lexington, 1992), 1–18.

    4. Josiah Murdoch Espy, *Memorandums of a Tour Made by Josiah Espy in the
States of Ohio and Kentucky and Indiana Territory in 1805* (Cincinnati, 1871), quotation on 8; Amos Kendall (Lexington) to Mr. Flugel, May 14, 1814, Amos Kendall Letters (FC) (quotation); Amos Kendall, *Autobiography of Amos Kendall*, ed.
William Stickney (Washington, D.C., 1872), quotation on 109; Robert Triplett,

Roland Trevor, or, The Pilot of Human Life. Being an Autobiography of the Author Showing How to Make and Lose a Fortune, and Then to Make Another (Philadelphia, 1853), quotation on 264.

5. F. A. Michaux, *Travels to the West of the Alleghany Mountains*, quotation on 3:212; Thomas R. Joynes, "Memoranda Made by Thomas R. Joynes on a Journey to the States of Ohio and Kentucky, 1810," ed. Edward S. Joynes, *William and Mary Quarterly*, 1st ser., 10 (Apr. 1902): 225; James McBride, "Journey to Lexington, Kentucky by James McBride of Hamilton, Ohio, Related in Letter to Margaret Poe, 1810," *Quarterly Publication of the Historical and Philosophical Society of Ohio* 5 (Jan.–Mar. 1910): 26; Earl Gregg Swem, ed., *Letters on the Condition of Kentucky in 1825* (New York, 1916), 171; Mary Cronan Oppel, "Paradise Lost: The Story of *Chaumiere des Prairies*," *FCHQ* 56 (Apr. 1982): 206.

6. Margaretta Brown (Frankfort) to Orlando Brown, July 7, 1819, Brown Family Papers (FC); Thomas Chapman, "Journal of a Journey through the United States, 1795–1796," in Schwaab, ed., *Travels in the Old South*, 1:28–30; James Preston (Lexington) to William Preston, Sept. 7, 1793, Preston Family Papers, Joyes Collection (FC); Harry Innes to James Innes, Aug. 23, 1795, Randolph Family Papers (VHS); M. A. Crosby (Louisville) to Elizabeth Bullock, Mar. 1804, Shelby Family Papers, Samuel Wilson Collection (UK); Elias Pym Fordham, *Personal Narrative of Travels in Virginia, Maryland, Pennsylvania, Ohio, Indiana, Kentucky, and of a Residence in the Illinois Territory: 1817–1818*, ed. Frederic Austin Ogg (Cleveland, 1906), 223; William A. Leavy, "A Memoir of Lexington and Its Vicinity," *RKHS* 41 (July 1943): 251; Amos Kendall (Lexington) to Mr. Flugel, Mar. 10, 1815, Amos Kendall Letters; James B. Finley, *Autobiography of James B. Finley or, Pioneer Life in the West*, ed. W. P. Strickland (Cincinnati, 1853), 97.

7. Charles F. Mercer (Loudon County, Va.) to Robert Wickliffe, July 5, 1807, Robert Wickliffe Letterbook, microfilm (UK) (quotation); Charles Anderson, "The Story of Soldier's Retreat: A Memoir," part 1, quotation on 11, typescript (FC); Alex Edmiston (Lexington) to Margaret M. Edmiston, Feb. 28, 1807, Alexander M. Edmiston Letters (FC) (quotation); Joseph Hornsby Diary, Jan. 26, 1803, Jan. 18, 1804, May 12, 1804, typescript (FC); Lexington *Kentucky Gazette*, Mar. 19, 1788; ibid., June 6, 1789; J. Winston Coleman Jr., *The Squire's Sketches of Lexington* (Lexington, 1972), 30; Rhys Isaac, *The Transformation of Virginia, 1740–1790* (Chapel Hill, 1982), 80–87.

8. F. A. Michaux, *Travels to the West of the Alleghany Mountains*, 3:247 (quotation); Harry Toulmin, "Comments on America and Kentucky, 1793–1802," *RKHS* 47 (Apr. 1949): 112; Lee Soltow, "Horse Owners in Kentucky in 1800," *RKHS* 79 (Summer 1981): 203–10; Brown, *The Western Gazetteer*, 109; Warden, *A Statistical, Political, and Historical Account of the United States*, 2:339; James A. Ramage, *John Wesley Hunt: Pioneer Merchant, Manufacturer, and Financier* (Lexington, 1974), 41–53. On the importance of horse racing to gentry status in colonial Virginia, see T. H. Breen, "Horses and Gentlemen: The Cultural Significance of Gambling among the Gentry of Virginia," in idem, *Puritans and Adventurers: Change and Persistence in Early America* (New York, 1980), 148–63.

9. Fordham, *Personal Narrative*, quotation on 169; J. Winston Coleman Jr., "The Code Duello in Ante-Bellum Kentucky," *FCHQ* 30 (Apr. 1956): 125–40;

Charles S. Sydnor, "The Southerner and the Laws," *Journal of Southern History* 6 (Feb. 1940): 3–23; Bertram Wyatt-Brown, *Southern Honor: Ethics and Behavior in the Old South* (New York, 1982); Kenneth S. Greenberg, "The Nose, the Lie, and the Duel in the Antebellum South," *AHR* 95 (Feb. 1990): 57–74.

10. For additional statistics on the extent and expansion of slavery in Kentucky, see Ivan E. McDougle, *Slavery in Kentucky, 1792–1865* (1918; Westport, Conn., 1970), 8–9; Joan Wells Coward, *Kentucky in the New Republic: The Process of Constitution Making* (Lexington, 1979), 37, 63; Lewis Cecil Gray, *History of Agriculture in the Southern United States to 1860*, 2 vols. (New York, 1941), 2:656; Davis, *The Geography of the Blue Grass Region of Kentucky*, 195.

11. On the powerful hold of tobacco on the worldview of eighteenth-century Virginia gentlemen, see T. H. Breen, *Tobacco Culture: The Mentality of the Great Tidewater Planters on the Eve of the Revolution* (Princeton, 1985).

12. Thomas Cooper, *Some Information Respecting North America* (London, 1794), 29–33; Paul C. Henlein, *Cattle Kingdom in the Ohio Valley, 1783–1860* (Lexington, 1959), 1–20; Gray, *History of Agriculture in the Southern United States*, 2:833; Richard Laverne Troutman, "Plantation Life in the Antebellum Bluegrass Region of Kentucky" (M.A. thesis, University of Kentucky, 1955), 55–59, 71; Elizabeth L. Parr, "Kentucky's Overland Trade with the Ante-Bellum South," *FCHQ* 2 (Jan. 1928): 71–81.

13. Henry Clay (Lexington) to Langdon Cheves, Oct. 30, 1820, in *HCP*, quotation on 2:896; James Franklin Hopkins, "A History of the Hemp Industry in Kentucky" (M.A. thesis, University of Kentucky, 1938), 1–56; George Rogers Taylor, "Prices in the Mississippi Valley Preceding the War of 1812," *Journal of Economic and Business History* 3 (Nov. 1930): 154–61.

14. Hopkins, "A History of the Hemp Industry," 1–25; J. Winston Coleman Jr., *Slavery Times in Kentucky* (Chapel Hill, 1940), 42–47; Troutman, "Plantation Life in the Antebellum Bluegrass Region," 81–88; Marion B. Lucas, *A History of Blacks in Kentucky: Volume 1: From Slavery to Segregation, 1760–1891* (Frankfort, 1992), 4; Charles S. Sydnor, *The Development of Southern Sectionalism, 1819–1848* (Baton Rouge, 1948), 8–9.

15. Chapman, "Journal of a Journey through the United States," 1:31; Nedham Parry, Diary, 1794, Draper MSS, 14CC2; Bayrd Still, ed., "The Westward Migration of a Planter Pioneer in 1796," *William and Mary Quarterly*, 2d ser., 21 (Oct. 1941): 343; Lewis Condict, "Journal of a Trip to Kentucky in 1795," *Proceedings of the New Jersey Historical Society*, new ser., 4 (1919): 120; John Shane interview with John Coons, Draper MSS, 12CC130; Melish, *Travels in the United States of America*, 2:185; Espy, *Memorandums of a Tour*, 8; Breathitt, "Commencement of a Journal from Kentucky to the State of Pennsylvania," 7–8; Fortescue Cuming, *Sketches of a Tour to the Western Country, through the States of Ohio and Kentucky*, in Thwaites, ed., *Early Western Travels*, 4:183–88; McBride, "Journey to Lexington, Kentucky," 20–25; Joynes, "Memoranda Made by Thomas R. Joynes," 225; "Kentucky Manufactures, Extract of a letter from a gentleman in Lexington, Ken. to his friend in Charleston, S.C., dated May 1, 1810," in Schwaab, ed., *Travels in the Old South*, 1:66–67. For more on the settlement and early economic development of Lexington, see Lee Shai Weissbach, "The Peopling of Lexington, Kentucky: Growth and Mobility in a Frontier Town," *RKHS* 82 (Spring 1983):

115–33; Charles R. Staples, *The History of Pioneer Lexington, 1779–1806* (Lexington, 1939).

16. Blane, *Travels through the United States and Canada*, quotation on 104. On the Kentucky River, see John G. Stuart, "A Journal Remarks or Observations in a Voyage Down the Kentucky, Ohio, Mississippi Rivers &c," *RKHS* 50 (Jan. 1952): 5–14; Mary Verhoeff, *The Kentucky River Navigation* (Louisville, 1917). On the Lexington to Limestone Road, see John Shane interview with Ned and Mrs. Darnaby, Draper MSS, 11CC164–165; Adam Beatty (Washington, D.C.) to Valentine Peers, Dec. 14, 1818, Valentine Peers Papers (KHS); William Henry Perrin, ed., *History of Bourbon, Scott, Harrison, and Nicholas Counties* (Chicago, 1882), 56; Theodore G. Gronert, "Trade in the Blue-Grass Region, 1810–1820," *MVHR* 5 (Dec. 1918): 317.

17. Thomas Perkins (Lincoln County) to Joseph Palmer, July 24, 1785, in James A. Bentley, ed., "Letters of Thomas Perkins to Gen. Joseph Palmer, Lincoln County, Kentucky, 1785," *FCHQ* 59 (Apr. 1975): 147; "Some particulars relative to the Soil, Situation, Productions, &C. of Kentucky," in Schwaab, ed., *Travels in the Old South*, 1:60; Hazel Dicken Garcia, "'A Great Deal of Money . . .': Notes on Kentucky Costs, 1786–1792," *RKHS* 77 (Summer 1979): 186–200; Toulmin, "Comments on America and Kentucky," 114; Eneas MacKenzie, *An Historical, Topographical, and Descriptive View of the United States of America, and of Upper and Lower Canada* (Newcastle upon Tyne, 1819), 233; Swem, ed., *Letters on the Condition of Kentucky in 1825*, 68; W. W. Lewis (Natchez) to Gabriel Lewis, Jan. 8, 1806, box 1, folder 16, Lewis Family Papers (Durrett); Craig T. Friend, "Inheriting Eden: The Creation of Society and Community in Early Kentucky, 1792–1812" (Ph.D. diss., University of Kentucky, 1995).

18. Nathaniel Hart (Lexington) to Uncle, Jan. 10, 1791, Nathaniel Hart Letter (FC); Richard Major (Madison County) to Brother, Sept. 26, 1797, Samuel I. M. Major Papers (EKU); William Barry (Lexington) to John Barry, Mar. 19, 1806, William Taylor Barry Letters, typescript (FC); John Bradford, "Letters to patrons of *Kentucky Gazette*," Jan. 4, 1797, codex 25 (Durrett); Shane with John Coons, Draper MSS, 12CC130; Lucien Beckner, ed., "John D. Shane's Notes on an Interview with Jeptha Kemper of Montgomery County," *FCHQ* 12 (July 1938): 156; Elizabeth A. Perkins, "The Consumer Frontier: Household Consumption in Early Kentucky," *Journal of American History* 77 (Sept. 1991): 506.

19. B. Tardiveau (Danville) to H. St. John de Crèvecoeur, Oct. 7, 1789, in Howard C. Rice, *Barthelemi Tardiveau: A French Trader in the West* (Baltimore, 1938), quotation on 36; D. Maccoun (Philadelphia) to James Maccoun, Mar. 14, 1813, in "Documents from the Shane Collection," *Journal of the Presbyterian Historical Society* 14 (1930–1931): 222; J. C. Owings, Account Book, 1790–1791 (UK). Owings recorded 114 accounts, of which 6 (5.3 percent) were settled in cash, 13 (11.4 percent) in cash and kind, and 95 (83.3 percent) entirely by bartering of goods and labor. A triangle trade was involved in the settlement of 29 (25.9 percent) accounts.

20. Lexington *Kentucky Gazette*, Jan. 20, 1817; Paris *Rights of Man*, Jan. 10, 1798; Charles William Janson, *The Stranger in America* (London, 1807), 440.

21. "Some particulars relative to the Soil, Productions, &c. of Kentucky," in Schwaab, ed., *Travels in the Old South*, 1: 60; Thomas Todd (Frankfort) to

Charles S. Todd, May 16, 1812, Todd Collection (FC). For evidence of discrimination and renunciation of credit and barter arrangements, see the advertisements of Samuel and George Trotter, Lexington *Kentucky Gazette*, Jan. 15, 1801; Lewis Sanders and Company, ibid., July 20, 1801; and Alexander Parker and Company, ibid., May 14, 1802. For protests, see Lexington *Kentucky Gazette*, Oct. 11, 1803; William Barry (Lexington) to John Barry, Jan. 2, 1807, William Taylor Barry Letters; F. A. Michaux, *Travels to the West*, 3:203–4; Lexington *Reporter*, Feb. 5, 1809.

22. Abraham Hunt (Trenton) to John Wesley Hunt, Mar. 20, 1796, Hunt-Morgan Papers (UK) (quotation); Abajiah Hunt (Philadelphia) to John W. Hunt, Apr. 30, 1795, John Wesley Hunt Papers (FC); Leavy, "A Memoir of Lexington," 259–60.

23. Hart quoted in "Lucretia Hart Clay: A Portrait by Her Contemporaries, written by her granddaughter," Clay-Russell Family Papers, typescript on microfilm (UK); Leavy, "A Memoir of Lexington," 117–18; Ashe, *Travels in America*, 193; Richard Flower, *Letters from Lexington and the Illinois*, in Thwaites, ed., *Early Western Travels*, 10:95; Lexington *Kentucky Gazette*, Sept. 29, 1803; Cuming, *Sketches of a Tour*, 4:187–88; Brown, *The Western Gazetteer*, 94; Richard C. Wade, *The Urban Frontier: The Rise of Western Cities, 1790–1830* (Cambridge, Mass., 1959), 109–10; George W. Ranck, *History of Lexington, Kentucky: Its Early Annals and Recent Progress Including Biographical Sketches and Personal Reminiscences of the Pioneering Settlers, Notes of Prominent Citizens, Etc., Etc.* (Cincinnati, 1872), 240.

24. Lexington *Kentucky Gazette*, Apr. 12, 1794; ibid., Sept. 18, 1810; ibid., Feb. 9, 1811; Leavy, "A Memoir of Lexington and Its Vicinity," 118–19, 259–60, 374; Tench Coxe, comp., *A Statement of the Arts and Manufactures of the United States of America for the Year 1810* (Philadelphia, 1814), 121–28; Ramage, *John Wesley Hunt*, 54–71; Hopkins, "A History of the Hemp Industry," 57–70.

25. William Darby, *The Emigrant's Guide to the Western and Southwestern States and Territories* (New York, 1818), 207.

26. Henry Clay (Washington D.C.) to John Randolph, Mar. 31, 1826, in *HCP*, 5:208 (quotation); Henry Clay (Lexington) to John M. Clayton, Aug. 8, 1842, ibid., 9:754 (quotation); Agreement with John Hart, Jan. 29, 1816, ibid., 2:159–60; Peter Irving (Liverpool) to Henry Clay, Feb. 12, 1817, ibid., 2:314–15; "Inventory of Livestock and Farming Implements at 'Ashland', February 25, 1825," ibid., 4:7–8; Henry Clay (Washington, D.C.) to Thomas Todd, Jan. 24, 1807, ibid., 1:272; Lexington *Kentucky Gazette*, June 14, 1808; Thomas Hulme, *Journal of a Tour in the Western Countries of America — September 30, 1818–August 8, 1819*, in Thwaites, ed., *Early Western Travels*, 10:65–66; Triplett, *Roland Trevor*, 217–18; Alfred Tischendorf and E. Taylor Parks, eds., *The Diary and Journal of Richard Clough Anderson, Jr., 1814–1826* (Durham, N.C., 1964), 52–53; James F. Hopkins, ed., "Henry Clay, Farmer and Stockman," *Journal of Southern History* 15 (Feb. 1949): 89–96; Richard L. Troutman, "Henry Clay and His 'Ashland' Estate," *FCHQ* 30 (Apr. 1956): 159–74.

27. Speech on Domestic Manufactures, Mar. 26, 1810, in *HCP*, 1:459–63.

28. Resolution to Encourage Use of American Manufactures, in *HCP*, 1:396 (quotation); Speech on Domestic Manufactures, Mar. 26, 1810, ibid., 1:460 (quotation); Speech on the Tariff, Apr. 26, 1820, ibid., 2:834 (quotation); Henry

Clay (Lexington) to Francis T. Brooke, Aug. 28, 1823, ibid., 3:479 (quotation); *The Memorial of the Mechanics and Manufacturers of Lexington, Kentucky, to Congress* (Lexington, 1810); Drew R. McCoy, "An Unfinished Revolution: The Quest for Economic Independence in the Early Republic," in Jack P. Greene, ed., *The American Revolution: Its Character and Limits* (New York, 1987), 131–48; E. Merton Coulter, "The Genesis of Henry Clay's American System," *South Atlantic Quarterly* 25 (Jan. 1926): 45–54.

29. Henry Clay to John M. Clayton, Aug. 8, 1842, in *HCP*, 9:754 (quotation); George Rogers Taylor, "Agrarian Discontent in the Mississippi Valley Preceding the War of 1812," in Harry N. Scheiber, ed., *The Old Northwest: Studies in Regional History, 1787–1910* (Lincoln, 1969), 28–61.

30. Speech on Increase in the Naval Establishment, Jan. 22, 1812, in *HCP*, 1:626; *Acts* (1793), 35–36; ibid. (1794), 32–33; ibid. (1795), 54–55; ibid. (1798), 35–36; Verhoeff, *The Kentucky River Navigation*, 19–24; James C. Klotter, "Two Centuries of the Lottery in Kentucky," *RKHS* 87 (Autumn 1989): 405–25.

31. Lexington *Kentucky Gazette*, Nov. 29, 1817; ibid., Mar. 19, 1819; ibid., Mar. 26, 1819; Lexington *Reporter*, Mar. 24, 1819; *Law*, 4:279–80; ibid., 5:519–38; *Acts* (1818), 435; Cecil Harp and J. Winston Coleman, "The Old Lexington and Maysville Turnpike," *Kentucky Engineer* 4 (Dec. 1941): 13.

32. Adam Beatty (Washington, D.C.) to Valentine Peers, Dec. 7, 1818, Valentine Peers Papers (quotation); Lewis Vincent (Millersburgh) to Valentine Peers, Nov. 28, 1826, Maysville Turnpike Papers (KHS) (quotation); R. Higgins (Lexington) to Valentine Peers, Nov. 30, 1826, Valentine Peers Papers (quotation); Robert N. Richardson, *Valentine Peers* (Hamilton, Ohio, 1976), 111–12.

33. Speech on Internal Improvements, Mar. 7, 1818, in *HCP*, 2:448; Speech on Internal Improvements, Mar. 13, 1818, ibid., 2:480 (quotation).

34. Speech on Surveys for Roads and Canals, July 30, 1824, ibid., 3:620; Speech on the Bank of the United States, June 3, 1816, ibid., 2:199–205; Speech on the Bill to Recharter the Bank of the United States, Feb. 15, 1811, ibid., 1:527–40; Campaign Speech at Sandersville, July 25, 1816, ibid., 2:216–22.

35. For a more extended discussion of the debates and maneuverings of Clay and the opponents of the Kentucky Insurance Company, see below, chapter 7.

36. Royalty, "Banking, Politics, and the Commonwealth," 138–39.

37. Melish, *Travels in the United States*, 2:188 (quotation) and 2:181; *Niles' Weekly Register*, Jan. 28, 1815 (quotation); F. A. Michaux, *Travels to the West*, 3:201 (quotation); Ida Earle Fowler, ed., "Kentucky 150 Years Ago as Seen through the Eyes of an English Emigrant Told in Two Letters Written by Henry Alderson, Dated September 10, 1801," *RKHS* 49 (Jan. 1951): 56; *Niles' Weekly Register*, June 11, 1814; Margaret M. Bridwell, "Kentucky Silversmiths before 1850," *FCHQ* 16 (Apr. 1942): 114; Frances L. S. Dugan and Jacqueline P. Bull, eds., *Bluegrass Craftsman: Being the Reminiscences of Ebenezer Hiram Stedman, Papermaker, 1808–1885* (Lexington, 1959), 20–21. A comparison of rates of pay in Lexington can be made from the list of wages broken down by craft in Paris *Rights of Man or the Kentucky Mercury*, Sept. 27, 1797; and Hulme, *Journal of a Tour in the Western Countries of America*, 10:68.

38. Dugan and Bull, eds., *Bluegrass Craftsman*, quotations on 14 and 23.

39. Of 267 taxpayers in 1797, 65 (24.3 percent) owned land. The median

holding was 1,093 acres. In 1805, tax lists showed 415 taxpayers in Lexington, of which 77 (18.6 percent) owned land. The acreage owned by Lexington taxpayers totaled 257,274 acres. The 6 largest landowners, all of whom possessed at least 10,000 acres, paid taxes on 164,564 acres. The 42 taxpayers with the largest land holdings owned over 250,000 acres. Figures calculated from Fayette County Tax List, 1797, 1805, microfilm (KHS). One hundred five craftsmen listed in *Lexington Directory, Taken for Charles's Almanac for 1806*, typescript (UK), also appeared in the Fayette County Tax List for 1805, microfilm (KHS). Of these 105 artisans, 10 owned land. Except for one silversmith with holdings of 1,499 acres, all of the other land owners claimed less than 300 acres. The persistence figure was calculated by comparing the names on the 1806 directory with those in *Directory for 1818 of the Town of Lexington, Kentucky, from Worsley and Smith's Almanac*, typescript (UK).

40. Dugan and Bull, eds., *Bluegrass Craftsman*, 41–45, 103–4.

41. John Robert Shaw, *A Narrative of the Life and Travels of John Robert Shaw, the Well-Digger, Now Resident in Lexington, Kentucky* (Lexington, 1807), quotation on 168; see also Shaw's advertisements in Lexington newspapers, especially Lexington *Kentucky Gazette*, June 20, 1798; Lexington *Independent Gazetteer*, Feb. 15, 1805. For a similar story of an alcoholic downfall, see Dugan and Bull, eds., *Bluegrass Craftsman*, 22–26.

42. Lexington *Kentucky Gazette*, Mar. 26, 1796; ibid., Aug. 21, 1810; ibid., Feb. 26, 1811; ibid., Mar. 5, 1811.

43. John Brown (Frankfort) to Margaretta Brown, Mar. 10, 1811, John Mason Brown Family Papers (UK); Leavy, "A Memoir of Lexington," 317–18; William Barry (Washington, D.C.) to Catherine A. Barry, Feb. 20, 1815, William Taylor Barry Letters; James Weir (Lexington) to John Henderson, Oct. 28, 1814, Draper MSS, 21CC113; James Weir (Lexington) to Bartlett and Cox, Dec. 22, 1814, ibid., 21CC118; James Weir (Lexington) to Adams, Knox, and Nixon, June 1, 1815, ibid., 21CC126; James Weir (Lexington) to John Henderson, July 25, 1816, ibid., 22CC2–3; James Weir (Lexington) to John P. Pleasants, Feb. 2, 1817, ibid., 22CC19; James Weir (Lexington) to John Henderson, Dec. 6, 1817, ibid., 22CC248; Lexington *Kentucky Gazette*, May 7, 1819; *Digest of Accounts of Manufacturing Establishment in the United States and of Their Manufactures* (Washington, 1823), 24–25.

44. Lexington *Kentucky Gazette*, Aug. 23, 1817; ibid., Oct. 11, 1817; ibid., Apr. 30, 1818; Bernard Mayo, "Lexington: Frontier Metropolis," in Eric F. Goldman, ed., *Historiography and Urbanization: Essays in Honor of W. Stull Holt* (Port Washington, N.Y., 1968), 21–42; Richard Wade, *The Urban Frontier: The Rise of Western Cities* (Cambridge, Mass., 1959), 169.

45. John Brand (Lexington) to Father and Mother, Jan. 24, 1820, John Brand Letterbooks, microfilm (UK) (quotation); John Brown (Frankfort) to Orlando Brown, Mar. 14, 1820, Brown Family Papers (UK); John Palmer, *Journal of Travels in the United States of North America, and in Lower Canada, Performed in the Year 1817* (London, 1818), 105–8; Leavy, "A Memoir of Lexington," 126–27, 318; Brown, *The Western Gazetteer*, 94; Stuart Seely Sprague, "Town Making in the Era of Good Feelings: Kentucky, 1814–1820," *RKHS* 72 (Oct. 1974): 337–41; Wade, *The Urban Frontier*, 170.

46. Lexington *Kentucky Gazette*, May 7, 1819; Dale Maurice Royalty, "Banking, Politics, and the Commonwealth, Kentucky, 1800–1825" (Ph.D. diss., University of Kentucky, 1971), 203–4.

47. George Lockebie (Lexington) to the Directors of the Sanders Manufacturing Company, Feb. 14, 1818, Sanders Family Papers (FC).

48. Lucas, *A History of Blacks in Kentucky*, xv–xviii; Coward, *Kentucky in the New Republic*, 37, 63.

49. Louisville *Daily Journal*, Nov. 29, 1830, typescript (FC); McBride, "Journey to Lexington, Kentucky," 24–25; Agreement between John Wesley Hunt and John Brand, Jan. 5, 1803, John Wesley Hunt Papers (Transy); Ramage, *John Wesley Hunt*, 61; *Digest of Accounts of Manufacturing Establishments*, 24–25; Lucas, *A History of Blacks in Kentucky*, 8–11.

50. Speech on Tariff, Mar. 30–31, 1824, in *HCP*, 3:718–19 (quotation); Henry Clay (Lexington) to John Sloane, Aug. 12, 1823, ibid., Supplement: 149 (quotation); see also Robert Seager II, "Henry Clay and the Politics of Compromise and Non-Compromise," *RKHS* 85 (Winter 1987): 18.

51. Susan Yandell (Lexington) to Sarah Wendell, Apr. 8, 1834, Yandell Family Papers (FC) (quotation); Melish, *Travels in the United States of America*, 2:206–7 (quotation); Henry Clay (Richmond) to Joseph Gales Jr., Oct. 14, 1817, in *HCP*, 2:391 (quotation); Amos Kendall (Frankfort) to Henry Clay, July 8, 1826, ibid., 5:534; John Bradford (Lexington) to Henry Clay, Oct. 3, 1816, ibid., Supplement: 56–57; Fordham, *Personal Narrative of Travels*, 180; Anderson, "The Story of Soldier's Retreat," part 2, p. 22; part 3, pp. 23–26; part 4, pp. 17–19, 44–51; James Flint, *Letters from America, Containing Observations on the Climate and Agriculture of the Western States, the Manners of the People, the Prospects of Emigrants, &c., &c.* (Edinburgh, 1822), 117; Lucius P. Little, *Ben Hardin: His Life and Contemporaries, with Selections from His Speeches* (Louisville, 1887), 544; Alice Allison Dunnigan, *The Fascinating Story of Black Kentuckians: Their Heritage and Traditions* (Washington, 1982), 14; Coleman, *Slavery Times in Kentucky*, 15–16; McDougle, *Slavery in Kentucky*, 71–92.

52. John Breckinridge (Fayette County) to James Breckinridge, July 20, 1801, John Breckinridge Letters (FC) (quotation); *Law*, 5:368–69 (quotation).

53. Lewis Clarke, "Leaves from a Slave's Journal of Life," in John W. Blassingame, ed., *Slave Testimony: Two Centuries of Letters, Speeches, Interviews, and Autobiographies* (Baton Rouge, 1977), quotation on 152; Louisville *Daily Journal*, Nov. 29, 1830, typescript (FC) (quotation); J. Winston Coleman Jr., "John W. Coleman: Early Kentucky Hemp Manufacturer," *FCHQ* 24 (Jan. 1950): 40–42; Clement Eaton, "Slave-Hiring in the Upper South: A Step Toward Freedom," *MVHR* 46 (Mar. 1960): 663–78. On slaves' purchasing their freedom, see for example the interviews with Tab Gross, Lewis Smith, Washington Spradling, and Mrs. Lewis Bibb in Blassingame, ed., *Slave Testimony*, 346–53, 385–86, 446. See also the manumission agreements in Michael L. Cook and Bettie A. Cook, eds., *Fayette County Kentucky Records*, 5 vols. (Evansville, Ind., 1985), 2:19–20, 118, 302, 349, 368. For the exceptional biography of one Kentucky slave who managed to purchase the freedom of sixteen family members, see Juliet E. K. Walker, *Free Frank: A Black Pioneer on the Antebellum Frontier* (Lexington, 1983).

54. Address to Gentlemen of the Colonization Society of Kentucky, Dec. 17, 1829, in *HCP*, 8:147 (quotation); Juliet E. K. Walker, "The Legal Status of Free Blacks in Early Kentucky, 1792–1825," *FCHQ* 57 (Oct. 1983): 382–95; Lucas, *A History of Blacks in Kentucky*, 107–17.

55. Anderson, "The Story of Soldier's Retreat," part 4, pp. 41–42. For examples of rescinded promises of emancipation see Blassingame, ed., *Slave Testimony*, 185–89, 250–54, 446; Harding Negroes v. Harding Heirs, Mar. 6, 1820, in Montgomery Vanderpool, ed., *Logan County, Kentucky: Abstract of Equity Cases*, 2 vols. (Russellville, 1986–87), 2:31–39; Lucas, *A History of Blacks in Kentucky*, 52–57.

56. "Speech of Lewis Richardson," Mar. 13, 1846, in Blassingame, ed., *Slave Testimony*, quotation on 164–65; Robert Anderson, *From Slavery to Affluence: Memoirs of Robert Anderson, Ex-slave, by Daisy Anderson Leonard* (Steamboat Springs, Colo., 1967), quotation on 26; Clarke, "Leaves from a Slave's Journal of Life," 151–64; [Martha Griffith Browne], *Autobiography of a Female Slave* (New York, 1857), 9; Clement Eaton, *Henry Clay and the Art of American Politics* (Boston, 1957), 66.

57. Wilson Yandell (Craggy Bluff) to Lundsford Yandell, Jan. 2, 1825, Yandell Family Papers (quotation); Clement Eaton, "A Law Student at Transylvania University in 1810–1812," *FCHQ* 31 (July 1957): 270 (quotation); Clarke, "Leaves from a Slave's Journal of Life," quotation on 160; Buckner Thruston (Jefferson County) to Charles Thruston, Nov. 2, 1800, Charles William Thruston Papers (FC); Will S. Gree (Retreat) to John C. Green, July 25, 1823, Green Family Papers (FC); John Daveiss to Joseph H. Daveiss, July 21, 1810, Joseph Hamilton Daveiss Papers (FC); Lucas, *A History of Blacks in Kentucky*, 84–100.

58. Coleman, *Slavery Times in Kentucky*, 142–72.

59. James Taylor, "Autobiography of General James Taylor of Newport, Ky." (microfilm at FC), 25–26.

60. Lewis Clarke, *Narrative of the Sufferings of Lewis Clarke* (Boston, 1845), quotation on 25–26; Henry Bibb, *Narrative of the Life and Adventures of Henry Bibb* (New York, 1849), quotation on 166; John Brand (Lexington) to John Wesley Hunt, Sept. 2, 1810, Hunt-Morgan Papers; Thomas H. Burbridge (Lexington) to John Wesley Hunt, June 29, 1813, John Wesley Hunt Papers (FC).

61. Lexington *Kentucky Gazette*, Feb. 25, 1812; ibid., Jan. 14, 1812; ibid., Jan. 21, 1812; John Brown (Frankfort) to Margaretta Brown, Feb. 17, 1811, John Mason Brown Papers; Joseph Underwood (Lexington) to Edmund Rogers, Feb. 13, 1812, Underwood Collection (WKU); Ramage, *John Wesley Hunt*, 64–65.

62. Joseph Underwood (Lexington) to Edmund Rogers, Dec. 26, 1810, Underwood Collection; John Brown (Frankfort) to Margaretta Brown, Jan. 20, 1811, John Mason Brown Papers; Harry M. Ward, *Charles Scott and the "Spirit of '76"* (Charlottesville, 1988), 154; Eaton, "A Law Student at Transylvania University in 1810–1812," 270.

63. Lexington *Kentucky Gazette*, Jan. 16, 1823 (quotation); for Shaw advertisement, see ibid., Feb. 12, 1811.

64. Margaretta Brown (New York) to John Brown, Feb. 27, 1811, Brown Family Papers (FC).

Chapter Seven. The Blueing of the Green River Country

1. Thomas Ashe, *Travels in America, Performed in 1806, for the Purpose of Exploring the Rivers Alleghany, Monongahela, Ohio, and Mississsippi, and Ascertaining the Produce and Condition of Their Banks and Vicinity* (London, 1808), 171; John L. Blair, ed., "A Baptist Minister Visits Kentucky: The Journal of Andrew Broaddus I," *RKHS* 71 (Oct. 1973): 412; Robert Davidson, *An Excursion to Mammoth Cave and the Barrens of Kentucky. With Some Notices of the Early Settlement of the State* (Philadelphia, 1840), 32; Jacob Young, *Autobiography of a Pioneer: or the Nativity, Experience, Travels, and Ministerial Labors of Rev. Jacob Young, with Incidents, Observations, and Reflections* (Cincinnati, 1857), 86.

2. Samuel N. Dicken, "The Big Barrens: A Morphologic Study in the Kentucky Karst" (Ph.D. diss., University of California, Berkeley, 1930), 116–26; idem, "The Kentucky Barrens," *Bulletin of the Geographical Society of Philadelphia* 33 (Apr. 1935): 42–47; Carl O. Sauer, *Geography of the Pennyroyal* (Frankfort, 1927), 123–30, provide extensive discussion of the various theories of the origin of the prairies of southwestern Kentucky. Deposition of John Helm, Aug. 23, 1823 (FC); Neal Hammon, "Land Acquisition on the Kentucky Frontier," *RKHS* 78 (Autumn 1980): 297–321; Thomas Perkins Abernethy, *Western Lands and the American Revolution* (New York, 1937), 336; James A. Ramage, "The Green River Pioneers: Squatters, Soldiers, and Speculators," *RKHS* 75 (July 1977): 177–78; see also the advertisements offering to buy and sell military land warrants in the Lexington *Kentucky Gazette*, Apr. 21, 1792.

3. The Bluegrass planter was John Breckinridge, whose view of the Green River Country is quoted in Richard E. Ellis, *The Jeffersonian Crisis: Courts and Politics in the Young Republic* (New York, 1971), 148. On the lawlessness of the Green River Country, see Peter Cartwright, *The Backwoods Preacher: An Autobiography of Peter Cartwright* (London, 1958), 4–6; André Michaux, *Journal of Travels into Kentucky; July 15, 1793-April 11, 1796*, in R. G. Thwaites, ed., *Early Western Travels, 1748-1846*, 32 vols. (Cleveland, 1904), 3:64, 88; François André Michaux, *Travels to the West of the Allegany Mountains, in the States of Ohio, Kentucky, and Tennessee, and Back to Charleston, by the Upper Carolines*, ibid., 215–16; Chester Raymond Young, ed., *Westward into Kentucky: The Narrative of Daniel Trabue* (Lexington, 1981), 146–53; Robert Herndon Statement, Draper MSS, 30S117; Samuel Hopkins (Henderson) to W. Alves, May 15, 1800, Samuel Hopkins Papers (KHS); John James Audubon, *Delineations of American Scenery and Character* (1835; New York, 1926), 19–22; James B. Finley, *Autobiography of Rev. James Finley, or, Pioneer Life in the West*, ed. W. P. Strickland (Cincinnati, 1853), 346; James Hall, *Letters from the West; Containing Sketches of Scenery, Manners, and Customs; And Anecdotes Connected with the First Settlements of the Western Sections of the United States* (London, 1828), 291–92.

4. W. L. Underwood (Bowling Green) to Malvina and Jane Underwood, Mar. 29, 1827, Underwood Collection (WKU) (quotation); Blair, ed., "A Baptist Minister Visits Kentucky," 412, 414–15; James J. W. H. Lewis (Breckinridge County) to William Quinitchet, Sept. 14, 1835, James Lewis Letter (FC); Thomas Joynes, "Memoranda Made by Thomas R. Joynes on a Journey to the States of Ohio and Kentucky, 1810," ed. Edward S. Joynes, *William and Mary Quarterly*,

1st ser., 10 (Jan. and Apr. 1902): 157–58; George M. Bibb (Frankfort) to Gabriel Lewis, Nov. 12, 1808, Lewis-Starling Papers (WKU); Gilbert Imlay, *A Topographical Description of the Western Territory of North America* (London, 1793), 57; Samuel R. Brown, *The Western Gazetteer; or Emigrants Directory* (Auburn, N.Y., 1817), 84; D. B. Warden, *A Statistical, Political, and Historical Account of the United States of North America; from the Period of Their First Colonization to the Present Day*, 3 vols. (Edinburgh, 1819), 2:315, 338; Edmund Dana, *Geographical Sketches of the Western Country: Designed for Emigrants and Settlers* (Cincinnati, 1819), 90; Terry G. Jordan, "Between the Forest and the Prairie," *Agricultural History* 38 (Oct. 1964): 205–16; Dicken, "The Kentucky Barrens," 50–51; John A. Jakle, *Images of the Ohio Valley: A Historical Geography of Travel, 1740 to 1860* (New York, 1977), 55; James A. Ramage, "The Green River Pioneers," 175–76.

5. Ramage, "The Green River Pioneers," 177–79; *House* (1793), 35; ibid. (1794), 20, 37.

6. *House* (1794), 83–84, 130–32; ibid. (1795), 105–6, 129–30; *Senate* (1794), 44, 49, 55; ibid. (1795), 23–24, 32; John Smith (Lexington) to Capt. John Preston, Dec. 3, 1793, Preston Family Papers—Joyes Collection (FC); Ramage, "The Green River Pioneers," 179–81; William Garrard Leger, "The Public Life of John Adair" (Ph.D. diss., University of Kentucky, 1953), 60–61.

7. *Acts* (1795), 79–81. By fixing certain guidelines on the shapes of surveys, however, the Kentucky act improved on Virginia's, which had permitted the most irregular and confusing lines.

8. *Acts* (1795), 81; ibid. (1797), 184–87. While the 1797 act specified that failure by new claimants to survey and return plats, as well as pay all accompanying fees, would result in forfeiture, it permitted earlier settlers further time to November 1, 1798, to make their payments and enter their various certificates.

9. Continued migration combined with healthy rates of natural increase to more than double the Southside census count in 1810, so that one in five white Kentuckians then resided in the Green River Country. A decade later, the district's population numbered nearly 150,000, more than one-fourth of Kentucky's white inhabitants. Population growth in the Green River Country derived from county figures given in *Second Census of the United States* (Washington, D.C., 1801), 2P; *Aggregate Amount of Persons within the United States in the Year 1810* (Washington, D.C., 1811), 71–74; *United States Census for 1820* (Washington, D.C., 1821), 33. Christopher Waldrep, "Immigration and Opportunity along the Cumberland River in Western Kentucky," *RKHS* 80 (Autumn 1982): 398. In 1792, at the time of its creation, nearly a third of Logan County householders (31.1 percent) owned land. As the county's population tripled with an influx of squatters over the next three years, however, the proportion of landholders fell to about one in eight (66 out of 545); see Logan County Tax Lists, 1792, 1795, microfilm (KHS). A table by county of Kentucky landownership in 1800 can be found in Joan Wells Coward, *Kentucky in the New Republic: The Process of Constitution Making* (Lexington, 1979), 55. In the eleven counties that were located all or in part in the Green River Military District 3,843 of 6,899 householders were landowners (55.7 percent). Outside the district only 12,160 of 25,604 householders owned land (47.5 percent).

10. Coward, *Kentucky in the New Republic*, 55. Of 3,843 landholders, 2,854 (74.3 percent) owned between 1 and 200 acres. Thus only 989 of 6,899 resident householders (14.3 percent) owned more than 200 acres.

11. Paul C. Henlein, *Cattle Kingdom in the Ohio Valley, 1783–1860* (Lexington, 1959), quotation on 66; "James Weir's Journal," in Otto Rothert, *A History of Muhlenberg County* (Louisville, 1913), quotation on 57; Brown, *The Western Gazetteer*, 84; Harriette Simpson Arnow, *Flowering of the Cumberland* (New York, 1963), 265. Coward, *Kentucky in the New Republic*, 63. Overall, according to figures compiled from 1800 tax lists, 25.2 percent of Kentucky households owned slaves. In the richest Inner Bluegrass counties, the proportion rose to 34.8 percent. Of 6,899 household heads south of the Green River, however, only 1,431 owned slaves (20.7 percent). The mean holding for Kentucky slaveowners was 4.39, for the Inner Bluegrass 5.16, and for the Green River Country 3.62. See Coward, *Kentucky in the New Republic*, 63. After investigating the inventories of turn-of-the-century settlers in Livingston County, Christopher Waldrep, "Immigration and Opportunity along the Cumberland River in Western Kentucky," 398, concluded that the value of slaveholders' personal estates was greater only because of the value of their chattel. In general slaveowners possessed no more tools, household items, or livestock than nonslaveholders; my own investigation of inventories of Green County wills between 1798 and 1810 reveals that the value of slaves accounted for about 60 percent of the value of slaveholders' estates. Even without slaves, though, the remaining value of the estates was still on average more than twice that of nonslaveowners.

12. John Rowan, "Unfinished Autobiography of John Rowan Written in 1841 at Federal Hill, Kentucky," quotation on 13–14, typescript (WKU); Henry Fox, "Recollections of Henry Fox," typescript, 6 (WKU); Richard Bibb (Logan County) to Gabriel Lewis, June 2, 1809, Lewis-Starling Papers; Rothert, *A History of Muhlenberg County*, 57; [Emmanuel Hatfield], *Stories of Hatfield, the Pioneer* (New Albany, Ind., 1889), 24–26, 112–13.

13. William McKee (Knox County) to Jacob Van Lear, June 14, 1812, William McKee Letters (UK); Micah Taul, "Memoirs of Micah Taul," *RKHS* 27 (Jan. 1929): 357–59; Eneas MacKenzie, *An Historical, Topographical, and Descriptive View of the United States of America, and Upper and Lower Canada* (Newcastle upon Tyne, 1819), 231; William Newnham Blane, *Travels through the United States and Canada* (London, 1828), 261. On the rough play of southern backcountry-men and its importance to their standing as men, see Elliot J. Gorn, " 'Gouge and Bite, Pull Hair, and Scratch': The Social Significance of Fighting in the Southern Backcountry," *AHR* 90 (Feb. 1985): 18–32.

14. George M. Bibb (Logan County) to Dr. [?], Aug. 26, 1810, George Bibb Letter (UK) (quotation); Joynes, "Memoranda Made by Thomas Joynes," quotations on 223, 222, 221; Blair, ed., "A Baptist Minister Visits Kentucky," 410, 415; Young, *Autobiography of a Pioneer*, 93–95; Harvey Woods, "Memoirs," Calvert-Obenchain-Younglove Collection (WKU).

15. Joynes, "Memoranda Made by Thomas R. Joynes," quotation on 222; Susannah Johnson, *Recollections of the Rev. John Johnson and His Home: An Autobiography*, ed. Rev. Adam C. Johnson (Nashville, 1869), quotations on 25, 167; William McKee (Knox County) to Jacob Van Lear, Apr. 12, 1812, William McKee

Letters. See the account book kept by Mary Lewis from 1802 to 1816 for a detailed record of one woman's marketing, Lewis-Starling Papers.

16. Johnson, *Recollections of the Rev. John Johnson and His Home*, 130; Joseph Thomas, *The Life of the Pilgrim, Joseph Thomas, Containing an Accurate Account of His Trials, Travels and Gospel Labours to the Present* (Winchester, Va., 1817), 131; F. A. Michaux, *Travels to the West*, 3:178–79; A. Michaux, *Journal of Travels into Kentucky*, 3:92; Blair, ed., "A Baptist Minister Visits Kentucky," 412; "The Life of John Rogers Underwood as dictated to his daughter Elizabeth," Underwood Collection; Polly McDowell to Peggy Nixon, Mar. 16, 1802, Adair-Hemphill Family Papers (FC); Cartwright, *The Backwoods Preacher*, 6–7; Blane, *Travels through the United States*, 259.

17. Mary Adair to Sister, Nov. 23, 1799, Adair-Hemphill Papers (quotation). In Montgomery Vanderpool, ed., *Logan County, Kentucky: Abstract of Equity Cases*, 2 vols. (Russellville, 1986–87), I found ten divorce cases. Of these, two involved wives who had deserted their husbands; the other eight actions were initiated by women who had been abandoned. (In one case, the husband contested his wife's accusations, claiming that he had moved to Illinois with his wife's consent to escape creditors and that he had promised to return when he had the money to pay his debts.) For the cases, see reference numbers EC5-58, EC5-74, EC6-83, EC6-85, EC6-95, EC6-108, EC6-110, EC6-112, EC7-131, EC8-139.

18. Charles Lewis quoted in Boynton Merrill Jr., *Jefferson's Nephews: A Frontier Tragedy* (Princeton, 1976), 126; Joynes, "Memoranda Made by Thomas R. Joynes," quotation on 222.

19. Gabriel Lewis to Peter [?], May 25, 1806, Lewis-Starling Papers.

20. Walter Alves to Thomas Hart, Mar. 5, 1796, Thomas Hart Papers (UK); Abraham Hunt (Trenton, N.J.) to John Wesley Hunt, July 25, 1797, Hunt-Morgan Papers (UK); John Brown (Frankfort) to Margaretta Brown, July 20, 1800, John Mason Brown Papers (UK). For the plans of the former Transylvania Company, see Samuel Hopkins Papers.

21. Robert Triplett, *Roland Trevor, or, The Pilot of Human Life. Being an Autobiography of the Author Showing How to Make and Lose a Fortune, and Then to Make Another* (Philadelphia, 1853), 122–29, quotation on 123; Samuel Hopkins (Danville) to Walter Alves, Feb. 17, 1800, Samuel Hopkins Papers; Wilson Hunt (Philadelphia) to Abijah and John Wesley Hunt, Aug. 9, 1796, Hunt-Morgan Papers; Mann Butler, *A History of the Commonwealth of Kentucky* (Cincinnati, 1834), 258–60; Fredrika Johanna Teute, "Land, Liberty, and Labor in the Post-Revolutionary Era: Kentucky as the Promised Land" (Ph.D. diss., Johns Hopkins University, 1988), 299–300; Ramage, "The Green River Pioneers," 185; Joseph Howard Parks, *Felix Grundy: Champion of Democracy* (Baton Rouge, 1940), 7.

22. Quotation from Russellville *Mirror*, July 25, 1807; *Acts* (1798), 156–57; ibid. (1799), 104–6; ibid. (1800), 121–28; *Law*, 3:134–36, 195–96, 306–8; *House* (1823-1824), 37–38. Levi Purviance, ed., *The Biography of Elder David Purviance, with His Memoirs: Containing His Views on Baptism, the Divinity of Christ, and the Atonement. Written by Himself* (Dayton, 1848), 32–38, offers a fascinating account of the parliamentary struggles over Green River relief during the 1796–1799 sessions by a legislator from Bourbon County who initially supported the extensions but subsequently joined his fellow Bluegrass representatives in opposition.

23. Parks, *Felix Grundy*, 19–21.

24. For the text of the act incorporating the Kentucky Insurance Company, see *Law*, 3:25–31.

25. Henry Clay (Lexington) to John Breckinridge, Dec. 22, 1804, in *HCP*, 1:166–67; *House* (1804), 95; Lexington *Kentucky Gazette*, Jan. 29, 1805; ibid., Apr. 30, 1805.

26. [Felix Grundy], "An Address to the People of Kentucky," Lexington *Kentucky Gazette*, Apr. 16, 1805.

27. *Law*, 3:213; Dale Maurice Royalty, "Banking, Politics, and the Commonwealth, Kentucky, 1800–1825" (Ph.D. diss., University of Kentucky, 1971), 12–20, 407–8.

28. *House* (1805), 51, 59, 148; *Senate* (1805), 40, 112; Lexington *Kentucky Gazette*, Dec. 12, 1805; Frankfort *Argus of Western America*, Sept. 16, 1829; Royalty, "Banking, Politics, and the Commonwealth," 22–34; Parks, *Felix Grundy*, 21–31.

29. Orval W. Baylor, "The Career of Felix Grundy, 1777–1840," *FCHQ* 16 (Apr. 1942): 88–110.

30. *Law*, 3:390–401; Tom K. Barton, "Politics and Banking in Republican Kentucky, 1805–1824" (Ph.D. diss., University of Wisconsin, 1968), 94–100; Royalty, "Banking, Politics, and the Commonwealth," 34–38, 62–63, 417–20. In the vote to establish the Bank of Kentucky in the House of Representatives, Green River assemblymen voted eleven to one in favor.

31. James Brown (New Orleans) to Henry Clay, Mar. 12, 1805, in *HCP*, 1:180.

32. Washington County Tax List, 1805, microfilm (KHS); Christopher Tompkins (Barren County) to John J. Crittenden, Jan. 22, 1814, John J. Crittenden Papers, microfilm (LC); Parks, *Felix Grundy*, 1–18; Christopher Waldrep, "Immigration and Opportunity along the Cumberland River in Western Kentucky," 392–407; Barton, "Politics and Banking in Republican Kentucky," 138–39.

33. The line about voting for "him who merits most" is from a poem circulated in Kentucky in the 1780s and is quoted in Patricia Watlington, *The Partisan Spirit: Kentucky Politics, 1779–1792* (New York, 1972), 158. Taul, "Memoirs of Micah Taul," quotations on 364–65; Samuel Hopkins (Henderson) to Thomas Hart, Apr. 8, 1799, Samuel Hopkins Papers; Amos Kendall, *Autobiography of Amos Kendall*, ed. William Stickney (Washington, D.C., 1872), 126; Charles G. Talbert, ed., "Looking Backward through One Hundred Years: Personal Recollections of James B. Ireland," *RKHS* 57 (Apr. 1959): 108–9. William Littell, *Festoons of Fancy: Consisting of Compositions Amatory, Sentimental, and Humorous in Verse and Prose* (1814; Lexington, 1940), 44–49, contains a delicious satire of Kentucky electoral practices in which a fictional candidate's expense account consists entirely of liquor charges. Or as Humphrey Marshall, *The History of Kentucky. Exhibiting an Account of the Modern Discovery, Settlement, Progressive Improvement, Civil and Military Transactions, and the Present State of the Country*, 2 vols. (Frankfort, 1824), 1:244, put it, in Kentucky politics "the way to men's hearts was down their throats."

34. Coward, *Kentucky in the New Republic*, 48–96; Robert Ireland, "Aristocrats All: The Politics of County Government in Antebellum Kentucky," *Review of Politics* 32 (July 1970): 365–83; Christopher Waldrep, "Egalitarianism in the Oligarchy: The Grand Jury and Criminal Justice in Livingston County, 1799–

1808," *FCHQ* 55 (July 1981): 253–67; Alan Taylor, "From Fathers to Friends of the People: Political Personas in the Early Republic," *Journal of the Early Republic* 11 (Winter 1991): 465–91.

35. Royalty, "Banking, Politics, and the Commonwealth," 165–89; Barton, "Politics and Banking in Republican Kentucky," 138–45, 202–35.

36. Lexington *Reporter*, Dec. 18, 1816. Immediately after the war, commercial interests in the Bluegrass began clamoring for a state appropriation to improve the Kentucky River. The promoters insisted that the Kentucky deserved primary consideration because it flowed through the oldest and wealthiest settlements in the state. The promoters claimed that the state's other major river systems would "all in due time become objects of public concern and expenditure" as their surrounding population became more numerous and wealthy, conveniently ignoring the fact that without navigational improvements the other regions would remain commercially retarded and thus undeserving of appropriations. Rejecting this "Catch-22" logic, the legislators from the Southside succeeded in having the $40,000 appropriation divided among the Kentucky, Green, Barren, Cumberland, Licking, and Salt Rivers, with the largest share earmarked for the first two (*Acts* [1817–18], 396–99). Spread around fairly, the money accomplished little in the way of improving navigation and facilitating commerce. (See the article "Internal Improvement," *Western Review and Miscellaneous Magazine* 3 (Jan. 1821): 368–75.)

37. Henry Clay (Washington, D.C.) to Thomas Bodley, Dec. 3, 1817, in *HCP*, 2:406. On Clay's difficult fight for reelection in 1816, see Thomas Smith (Lexington) to William Worsley, June 6, 1816, Draper MSS, 6CC47; [A Voter], "The Case Fairly Stated," ibid., 8CC170; George T. Blakey, "Rendezvous with Republicanism: John Pope vs. Henry Clay in 1816," *Indiana Magazine of History* 62 (Sept. 1966): 233–50.

38. "A Friend to the People," Russellville *Mirror*, Sept. 12, 1807 (quotation); Lexington *Kentucky Gazette*, July 19, 1788 (quotation); John J. Crittenden to Jonathan Smith, Dec. 28, 1806[?], John J. Crittenden Letter (UK); Russellville *Mirror*, June 16, 1808; Taul, "Memoirs of Micah Taul," 348. Business was so slow that Bank of Kentucky officials in the Bluegrass refused the unsound notes of their Green River office. See Royalty, "Banking, Politics, and the Commonwealth," 66–80.

39. *Acts* (1800), 125–28; ibid. (1801), 59–61.

40. Russellville *Mirror*, Nov. 7, 1806; Robert Henry (Rockcastle County) to John Henry, Oct. 9, 1817, Henry Family Papers (FC); Blair, ed., "A Baptist Minister Visits Kentucky," 416. In 1817, the same year that Broaddus reported eight to ten dollars per acre, Brown (*The Western Gazetteer*, 96) advised that improved land near the Tennessee border had reached ten to twenty dollars per acre.

41. Figures compiled from *Second Census of the United States*, 2P; *Aggregate Amount of Persons within the United States in the Year 1810*, 71–74; *United States Census for 1820*, 33.

42. Warner L. Underwood, Diary, Apr. 17, 1833, Dec. 26, 1834, Underwood Collection; Charles W. Short (Christian Court House) to John Cleves Short, Aug. 17, 1817, Short Papers (FC); Robert Henry (Hopkinsville) to John Henry, Aug. 24, 1818, Henry Family Papers.

43. Hopkinsville *Western Eagle*, Feb. 12, 1813; Lexington *Reporter*, July 30, 1814; Warden, *A Statistical, Political, and Historical Account of the United States*, 2:339.

44. Charles W. Short (Christian Court House) to John Cleves Short, Aug. 17, 1817; Charles W. Short (Hopkinsville) to William Short, Dec. 21, 1818, Short Papers; Richard A. Buckner (Greensburgh) to Hubbard Taylor, Mar. 14, 1817, Hubbard Taylor Papers (UK). On the cultivation of tobacco in the Green River Country see Brown, *The Western Gazetteer*, 84–85; Lewis Cecil Gray, *History of Agriculture in the Southern United States to 1860*, 2 vols. (New York, 1941), 2:755; Cecil E. Goode and Woodford L. Gardner Jr., eds., *Barren County Heritage: A Pictorial History of Barren County, Kentucky* (Bowling Green, Ky., 1980), 93; W. F. Axton, *Tobacco and Kentucky* (Lexington, 1975), 50. Southside planters also attempted to cash in on the postwar boom in cotton prices, but their experiments were less profitable than hoped. Only in the southernmost parts of the Southside, near the Tennessee border, did cotton challenge tobacco as a cash crop. See Howard L. Applegate and Martin H. Bush, eds., *A Tour to the South: Travel Diary of Moses Dewitt Burnet, 1815–1816* (Syracuse, 1965), 20.

45. Samuel Hopkins (Henderson) to Walter Alves, May 15, 1800; Samuel Hopkins (Henderson) to Samuel G. Hopkins, Sept. 1, 1801, Samuel Hopkins Papers; Goode and Gardner, eds., *Barren County Heritage*, 258.

46. Davidson, *An Excursion to Mammoth Cave and the Barrens of Kentucky*, quotation on 25. For descriptions of Green River Country towns and town life in the first two decades of the nineteenth century, see Elizabeth Morehead (Russellville) to Polly Campbell, May 19, 1807, Slaughter Family Papers (FC); William Clark, Diary, Oct. 3, 1809 (WKU); Charles W. Short (Hopkinsville) to William Short, Dec. 21, 1818, Short Papers; Robert Henry (Hopkinsville) to John Henry, Feb. 20, 1818, Henry Family Papers; John Brown, Diary, Sept. 26, 1821, typescript (FC); Lexington *Reporter*, Aug. 28, 1813; Lexington *Kentucky Gazette*, Apr. 24, 1815; Blair, ed., "A Baptist Minister Visits Kentucky," 411; R. A. Curd (Russellville) to John Wesley Hunt, May 6, 1822, Hunt-Morgan Papers; Warden, *A Statistical, Political, and Historical Account of the United States*, 2:330–32.

47. The 1820 United States Census showed that for the twenty-one counties situated all or in part in the Green River Country, 32,840 out of 35,462 persons (92.6 percent) reporting an occupation were principally engaged in agriculture, 320 (0.9 percent) in commerce, and 2,302 (6.5 percent) in manufacturing or crafts. These figures roughly corresponded to the proportions in the rest of the state, where overall 132,161 out of 145,557 persons (90.8 percent) reporting a primary employment listed agriculture, 1,617 (1.1 percent) commerce, and 11,779 (8.1 percent) manufacturing or crafts. By contrast, in the Inner Bluegrass counties surrounding Lexington (Bourbon, Fayette, Jessamine, Scott, Woodford), "only" 13,529 (83.7 percent) were engaged in agriculture, while 326 (2.0 percent) were in commerce, and 2,311 (14.3 percent) were in manufacturing or crafts.

48. Charles W. Short (Hopkinsville) to William Short, Apr. 20, 1819, Short Papers; Gabriel Lewis to Peter [?], May 25, 1806, Lewis-Starling Papers. The breakdown of types of settlements between two Green River Country merchants and their customers furnishes evidence of the looseness. As shown in Table A.10, James Weir of Muhlenberg County conducted less than a third of his business

exclusively on a cash basis. In the remainder of his dealings, Weir collected part or all of his debts with a payment in work or produce. The account book of Robert Renick, a storekeeper in the Barren County village of Smith Grove, confirms the prevalence of barter. More often than not, Renick received some cash, but the majority of these and other settlements were accounted by work or trade.

49. Ja. H. & A. Rice (Glasgow) to Messrs. J. & D. Maccoun, Jan. 12, 1809, "Documents from the Shane Collection," *Journal of the Presbyterian Historical Society* 14 (Mar. 1931): 212. The letters in this collection between Rice and Maccoun catalog the problems that Green River Country merchants had in securing payment from their customers and satisfying their creditors.

50. Russellville *Farmer's Friend*, Oct. 2, 1809; Russellville *Weekly Messenger*, Jan. 26, 1819; Russellville *Mirror*, Feb. 22, 1807. Nearly any issue of any Southside newspaper will furnish numerous examples of the preferences discussed in the above paragraph. But no example better illustrated the trend toward commercialism in the Green River Country of Kentucky than a stud fee advertisement that appeared in the Russellville *Mirror*, Feb. 27, 1807. The owner of the horse in question asked ten dollars in "merchantable cotton, pork, beef, wheat, rye, corn, flour, whiskey, tallow, beeswax, [or] country linen" for the services of his stallion, if any of the above items were delivered by Christmas Day. If payment was made at the time of "leap," the stallion owner offered a discounted rate of seven dollars. In this case, one man's 30 percent discount was another man's 40 percent interest penalty. Prompt payment in cash or notes entitled the mare owner to the lowest fee of four dollars for a season. These interest rates violated the spirit if not the letter of antiusury acts that set a 6 percent maximum annual interest rate on contracts, loans, and wares. See *Law*, 2:45; *Acts* (1819), 707–8.

51. See for example the advertisements of William Whitaker, Russellville *Mirror*, Mar. 24, 1808; Reavill E. T. Fords, ibid., Nov. 10, 1808; Richard Bibb Jr. and Company, Russellville *Farmer's Friend*, Dec. 14, 1810.

Chapter Eight. Worlds Away

1. Daniel Boone to Sarah Boone, Oct. 19, 1816, Draper MSS, 27C88.

2. Henry Clay to Fernando C. Putnam, Oct. 9, 1844, in *HCP*, 10:131–32 (quotation); Henry Clay to Unknown Recipient [1844], ibid., 10:1 (quotation); Henry Clay to James Madison Pendleton, Nov. 29, 1844, ibid., 10:165; Robert V. Remini, *Henry Clay: Statesman for the Union* (New York, 1991), 649–50.

3. Paul K. Conkin, *Cane Ridge: America's Pentecost* (Madison, 1990), 3.

4. John Rankin, "Autobiography of John Rankin, Sen., Written at South Union, KY. 1845," in Harvey L. Eades, ed., "History of the South Union Shaker Colony from 1804–1836," 2 vols. (typescript, 1870, at WKU), 1:16 (quotations); Peter Cartwright, *Autobiography of Peter Cartwright: The Backwoods Preacher*, ed. W. P. Strickland (New York, 1858), quotation on 25.

5. David Barrow, "Diary of David Barrow, 1795," typescript, quotation on 26 (WKU).

6. Josiah Morrow, ed., "Tours into Kentucky and the Northwest Territory: Three Journals by the Rev. James Smith of Powhatan County, Va., 1783, 1795, 1797," *Ohio Archaeological and Historical Publications* 16 (1907): 374; John Taylor, *A History of Ten Baptist Churches, of which the author has been alternately a mem-*

ber: in which will be seen something of a journal of the author's life for more than fifty years (Bloomfield, Ky., 1827), 45; Walter B. Posey, "Kentucky, 1790–1815: As Seen by Bishop Francis Asbury," *FCHQ* 21 (Oct. 1957): 335, 339; James S. Dalton, "The Kentucky Camp Meeting Revivals of 1797–1805 as Rites of Initiation" (Ph.D. diss., University of Chicago, 1973), 180–81.

7. Charles G. Talbert, ed., "Looking Backward through One Hundred Years: Personal Recollections of James B. Ireland," *RKHS* 57 (Apr. 1959): 105 (quotation); Lucien Beckner, ed., "Reverend John D. Shane's Notes on Interviews, in 1844, with Mrs. Hinds and Patrick Scott of Bourbon County," *FCHQ* 10 (July 1936): 174; William M. Darlington, ed., *Journal and Letters of Col. John May, of Boston: Relative to Two Journeys to the Ohio Country in 1788 and '89* (Cincinnati, 1873), 40–41; Roderick Nash, *Wilderness and the American Mind* (New Haven, 1967), 8–43; Timothy Silver, *A New Face on the Countryside: Indians, Colonists, and Slaves in the South Atlantic Forests, 1500–1800* (New York, 1990), 104; Jon Butler, *Awash in a Sea of Faith: Christianizing the American People* (Cambridge, Mass., 1990), 7–36, 67–97; Alan Taylor, "The Early Republic's Supernatural Economy: Treasure Seeking in the American Northeast, 1780–1830," *American Quarterly* 38 (Spring 1986): 6–34.

8. Robert H. Bishop, *An Outline of the History of the Church in the State of Kentucky, during a Period of Forty Years: Containing the Memoirs of Rev. David Rice* (Lexington, 1824), quotation on 68. For estimates of pre-Revival church membership, see John Asplund, *The Annual Register of the Baptist Denomination in North America; to the First of November, 1790* (n.p., 1792); Fred J. Hood, "The Restoration of Community: The Great Revival in Four Baptist Churches in Central Kentucky," *Quarterly Review* 39 (1978): 75; Niels Henry Sonne, *Liberal Kentucky, 1780–1828* (New York, 1939 [1968]), 13; Conkin, *Cane Ridge*, 64.

9. For good secondary treatments of McGready and the Green River awakening, see Conkin, *Cane Ridge*, 26–63; John D. Boles, *The Great Revival, 1787–1805: The Origins of the Southern Evangelical Mind* (Lexington, 1972), 36–63; John Opie Jr., "James McGready: Theologian of Frontier Revivalism," *Church History* 24 (Dec. 1965): 445–56; Thomas Whitaker, "The Gasper River Meeting House," *FCHQ* 56 (Jan. 1982): 30–61.

10. James McGready, "A Short Narrative of the Revival of Religion in Logan County in the State of Kentucky, and the adjacent settlements in the State of Tennessee, from May 1797, until September 1800," *New York Missionary Magazine, and Repository of Religious Intelligence* 4 (1803): 74 (quotations).

11. Rankin, "Autobiography of John Rankin," quotations on 18.

12. McGready, "A Short Narrative of the Revival of Religion in Logan County," 192–95; Rankin, "Autobiography of John Rankin," 19–20.

13. "Extract of a Letter from a Gentleman to his Friend at the City of Washington, dated Lexington, Kentucky, March 8, 1801," in William W. Sweet, ed., *Religion on the American Frontier: The Baptists* (New York, 1931), quotation on 609. A sample of nine Southside churches disclosed a gain from 361 members in 1800 to 733 in 1801. The nine churches included in this sample were Mt. Tabor, Dripping Springs, Blue Springs, Pitman's Creek, Trammel's Creek, Brush Creek, Mt. Gilead, Sinking Creek, and Mill Creek. The "associational tables" for these churches appear in C. P. Cawthorn and N. L. Warnell, eds., *Pioneer Baptist*

Church Records of South-Central Kentucky and the Upper Cumberland of Tennessee,
1799–1899 (n.p., 1985), 74, 125, 128–29, 209–10, 218–19, 236–37, 241, 250–51, 429.
For the Bluegrass surge, see Louis M. Applegate, comp., *Membership Great Cross-*
ings Baptist Church, 1785–1806 (typescript, FC); "Minutes of the Elkhorn Baptist
Association, Kentucky, 1785–1805," in Sweet, ed., *Religion on the American Fron-*
tier: The Baptists, 484–88; Ward Russell, *Church Life in the Bluegrass, 1783–1933*
(Lexington, 1933), 44.

14. "Extract of a Letter from a Gentleman to his Friend at the City of Wash-
ington, dated Lexington, Kentucky, March 9, 1801," in Sweet, ed., *Religion on the*
American Frontier: The Baptists, 610; Taylor, *A History of Ten Baptist Churches,* 90;
Fred J. Hood, "Restoration of Community: The Great Revival in Four Baptist
Churches in Central Kentucky," *Quarterly Review* 39 (1978): 78.

15. "Extract of a Letter from Gentleman to his Sister in Philadelphia, dated
Lexington, Kentucky, August 10, 1801," in Sweet, ed., *Religion on the American*
Frontier: The Baptists, 610–11; "Copy of a letter from a Minister of the Presby-
terian denomination, in Kentucky, to his friend in Northumberland County,
Pennsylvania, dated September 20, 1801," in *New York Missionary Magazine,*
and Repository of Religious Intelligence 3 (1802): 82–83; "Extract of a Letter from
Colonel Robert Paterson of Lexington (Ken.) to the Rev. Doctor John King of
Pennsylvania," Sept. 23, 1801, ibid., 121; Charles A. Johnson, *The Frontier Camp*
Meeting: Religion's Harvest Time (Dallas, 1955), 67.

16. Firsthand accounts of the Cane Ridge meeting include "Copy of a letter from a Minister of the Presbyterian denomination, in Kentucky, to his friend
in Northumberland County, Pennsylvania," 82–83; John Lyle, "Rev. John Lyle's
Diary, 1801," typescript, 21–35 (KHS); Cartwright, *Autobiography of Peter Cart-*
wright, 45–46; Richard McNemar, *The Kentucky Revival, or, A Short History of*
the Late Extraordinary Out-Pouring of the Spirit of God, in the Western States of
America, Aggreeably to the Scripture-Promises, and Prophecies Concerning the Latter
Day (1846; Cincinnati, 1807), 26–27; Levi Purviance, *Biography of David Pur-*
viance, with His Memoirs: Containing His Views on Baptism, the Divinity of Christ,
and the Atonement. Written by Himself (Dayton, 1848), 247–50; "Extract of a Letter from a Gentleman to his Sister in Philadelphia, dated Lexington, Kentucky,
August 10, 1801," 611.

17. James B. Finley, *Autobiography of Rev. James Finley or, Pioneer Life in the*
West, ed. W. P. Strickland (Cincinnati, 1853), quotation on 166–67; Lyle, "Diary,"
quotations on 34, 2.

18. McNemar, *The Kentucky Revival,* 26; John Lyle, "A Narrative of J. Lyle's
Mission in the Bounds of the Cumberland Presbytery, during the Year 1805,"
typescript, 6 (KHS); Ida Earle Fowler, ed., "Kentucky 150 Years Ago as Seen
Through the Eyes of an English Emigrant Told in Two Letters Written by Henry
Alderson, Dated September 10, 1801," *RKHS* 49 (Jan. 1951): 55; Conkin, *Cane*
Ridge, 92; Ellen T. Eslinger, "The Great Revival in Bourbon County, Kentucky"
(Ph.D. diss., University of Chicago, 1988), 362–63.

19. Finley, *Autobiography of a Pioneer,* quotations on 168, 96, 168, 169; Lyle,
"Diary," quotation on 31; see also ibid., 4; Fowler, ed., "Kentucky 150 Years Ago,"
55; Cartwright, *Autobiography,* 37–38.

20. Fowler, ed., "Kentucky 150 Years Ago," quotation on 55; Lyle, "Diary,"

quotation on 34; François André Michaux, *Travels to the West of the Alleghany Mountains, in the States of Ohio, Kentucky, and Tennessee, and Back to Charleston, by the Upper Carolines*, in R. G. Thwaites, ed., *Early Western Travels, 1748–1846*, 32 vols. (Cleveland, 1904), 3:249; "Membership List, Mt. Tabor Baptist Church, 1798–1820," in Cawthorn and Warnell, eds., *Pioneer Baptist Church Records of South-Central Kentucky and the Upper Cumberland of Tennessee*, 74; Applegate, *Membership Great Crossings Baptist Church*.

21. Finley, *Autobiography*, quotation on 168; Jacob Young, *Autobiography of a Pioneer: Or, The Nativity, Experience, Travels, and Ministerial Labors of Rev. Jacob Young, with Incidents, Observations, and Reflections* (Cincinnati, 1857), quotation on 41; McGready quoted in Christopher Waldrep, "The Making of a Border State Society: James McGready, the Great Revival, and the Prosecution of Profanity in Kentucky," *AHR* 99 (June 1994): 769; Cartwright, *Autobiography*, 34–39; Paul Woehrmann, ed., "The Autobiography of Abraham Snethen, Frontier Preacher," *FCHQ* 51 (Oct. 1977): 321–22.

22. McGready, "A Short Narrative of the Revival of Religion in Logan County," quotations on 195, 234, 153.

23. Fowler, ed., "Kentucky 150 Years Ago," 55; Boles, *The Great Revival*, 45, 57. Still, revivalists recognized more than demographics at work in the conversions of children and teenagers. Prior to the first signs of awakening, it tormented McGready and other clergymen to see churches occupied by only a handful of older women and men. The indifference of boys and girls to their fate in the next world consumed revivalists. To witness young people tortured, prostrated, and reborn as God-fearing Christians was a revelation for revival preachers. Nothing encouraged McGready more than the sight of children getting what he called "real religion." McGready, "A Short Narrative of the Revival of Religion in Logan County," quotation on 196.

24. Baxter quoted in Conkin, *Cane Ridge*, 116; Polly McDowell to Peggy Nixon, Mar. 16, 1802, Adair-Hemphill Family Papers (FC).

25. Lyle, "Diary," quotations on 58, 4, 93; Finley, *Autobiography*, 173.

26. Ibid., quotations on 1, 30, 25, 45.

27. David Rice, *An Epistle, To the Citizens of Kentucky, Professing Christianity; Especially Those That Are, Or Have Been Denominated Presbyterians* (Lexington, 1805), quotation on 9; Bishop, *An Outline of the History of the Church in the State of Kentucky*, quotation on 367; "Copy of a letter from a Minister of the Presbyterian denomination, in Kentucky, to his friend in Northumberland County, Pennsylvania, dated September 20, 1801," 82–83; Benjamin Lakin, "The Journal of Benjamin Lakin, 1794–1802," in William Warren Sweet, ed., *Religion on the American Frontier, 1783–1840: Vol. IV: The Methodists: A Collection of Source Materials* (Chicago, 1946), 224.

28. Lyle, "Diary," quotation on 21; Barton W. Stone, *Biography of Barton W. Stone, Written by Himself with Additions and Reflections*, ed. John Rodgers (Cincinnati, 1847), 44–45; Purviance, *The Biography of Elder David Purviance*, 110; Joseph Thomas, *The Life, Travels, and Gospel Labors of Eld Joseph Thomas, More Widely Known as the "White Pilgrim"; To Which Are Added His Poems* (New York, 1861), 23; Richard T. Hughes and C. Leonard Allen, *Illusions of Innocence: Protestant Primitivism in America, 1630–1875* (Chicago, 1988), 103–4.

29. John Lyle, "A Narrative of J. Lyle's Mission in the Bounds of the Cumberland Presbytery, during the Year 1805," quotations on 3, 4.

30. Beckner, ed., "Reverend John D. Shane's Notes on Interviews, in 1844, with Mrs. Hinds and Patrick Scott of Bourbon County," 175; McNemar, *The Kentucky Revival*, 93, 95; James McGready (Henderson County) to Archibald Cameron, Dec. 11, 1807, James McGready Letters (photostats at WKU, originals at Presbyterian Historical Society, Philadelphia); Robert Stuart, "Journals of Robert Stuart," *Journal of the Presbyterian Historical Society* 23 (Sept. 1945): 156; Finley, *Autobiography*, 373.

31. Rice, *An Epistle*, 3; Thomas C. Pears, ed., "A Journal of Two Missionary Tours Made in Kentucky and Tennessee by the Rev. Joseph P. Howe in the Years 1813 and 1814," *Journal of Presbyterian Historical Society* 16 (Dec. 1935): 377, 382; James McGready (Henderson County) to Archibald Cameron, Nov. 6, 1811, James McGready Letters; Robert Stuart, "Reminiscences, Respecting the Establishment and Progress of the Presbyterian Church in Kentucky," *Journal of Presbyterian Historical Society* 23 (Sept. 1945): 165–79; Herman R. Friis, "The Great Revival, the West, and the Crisis of the Church," in John Francis McDermott, ed., *The Frontier Re-examined* (Urbana, 1967), 78; Conkin, *Cane Ridge*, 118; Catharine C. Cleveland, *The Great Revival in the West, 1797–1805* (Chicago, 1916), 131, 148.

32. Purviance, *The Biography of Elder David Purviance*, quotation on 109; Lyle, "A Narrative of J. Lyle's Mission in the Bounds of the Cumberland Presbytery," quotations on 7, 10; Finley, *Autobiography*, 172; Stuart, "Reminiscences, Respecting the Establishment and Progress of the Presbyterian Church in Kentucky," 177.

33. Sweet, ed., *Religion on the American Frontier: The Baptists*, 22–24.

34. For a study of a Shaker community, see Julia Neal, *By Their Fruits: The Story of Shakerism in South Union, Kentucky* (Chapel Hill, 1947). On the affective community of evangelicals, see A. Gregory Schneider, "From Democratization to Domestication: The Transitional Orality of the American Methodist Circuit Rider," in Leonard I. Sweet, ed., *Communication and Change in American Religious History* (Grand Rapids, 1993), 141–64; idem, *The Way of the Cross Leads Home: The Domestication of American Methodism* (Bloomington, 1993).

35. Joseph Thomas, *The Life of the Pilgrim Joseph Thomas, Containing an Accurate Account of his Trials, Travels, and Gospel Labors, up to the Present Date* (Winchester, Va., 1817), quotation on 132; Samuel Rogers, *Autobiography of Elder Samuel Rogers*, ed. John Rogers (Cincinnati, 1880), quotation on 22.

36. Donald Mathews, *Religion in the Old South* (Chicago, 1977), quotation on 105.

37. John P. Campbell, *A Portrait of the Times; or, The Church's Duty* (Lexington, 1812), quotations on 29, 30; Robert H. Bishop, *The Glory of the Latter Days, A Sermon, Delivered at the Annual Meeting of the Bible Society of Kentucky, Sept. 1815* (Lexington, 1815), 16–18.

38. Baptist figures tallied from Cawthorn and Warnell, eds., *Pioneer Baptist Church Records of South-Central Kentucky*, 74; Applegate, comp., *Membership Great Crossings Baptist Church, 1785–1806*; "Minutes of the Elkhorn Baptist Association, Kentucky, 1785–1805," 417–509.

39. "Minutes of the Elkhorn Baptist Association, Kentucky, 1785–1805," 417–

509. For a similar pattern, see George F. Doyle, ed., *Transcript of the Minutes of the South Kentucky Association of Baptists 1787–1803 and the Minutes of the North District Association of Baptists from 1803 to 1823* (typescript, FC); Hood, "Restoration of Community," 78–83. The disequilibrium at least temporarily reversed the expansion of Baptist church rolls. Mt. Tabor, for example, grew from 37 members in 1800 to 89 in 1801. But by 1804, membership was down to 75. At nearby Blue Springs Church, the congregation swelled from 22 in 1800 to 63 in 1801, before rolling back to 52 in 1803. Cawthorn and Warnell, eds., *Pioneer Baptist Church Records of South-Central Kentucky*, 74, 128–29.

40. "Membership List, Mt. Tabor Baptist Church, 1798–1820" (Barren Co.), 74; Doyle, ed., *Transcript of the Minutes*.

41. Jacob Bower, "The Autobiography of Jacob Bower: A Frontier Baptist Preacher and Missionary," in Sweet, ed., *Religion on the American Frontier: The Baptists*, quotation on 192; Woehrmann, ed., "The Autobiography of Abraham Snethen," 319–20.

42. Bower, "The Autobiography of Jacob Bower," quotation on 200; Doyle, ed., *Transcript of the Minutes*; Cartwright, *Autobiography of Peter Cartwright*, 181; Johnson, *The Frontier Camp Meeting*, 105.

43. At the South Elkhorn Church, a record of members to 1817 showed that 25 of 105 men (23.8 percent) and 8 of 164 women (4.9 percent) were excluded. See Mary Florence Jones, ed., *The South Elkhorn Christian Church (Disciples of Christ): Minutes Book I, 1792–1874* (typescript, FC). For Great Crossings, see Applegate, comp., *Membership Great Crossings Baptist Church, 1785–1806*.

44. "The Journal of Benjamin Lakin," in Sweet, ed., *The Methodists*, quotation on 259; Cartwright, *Autobiography of Peter Cartwright*, quotation on 144; see also ibid., 35, 49–50, 90–92, 144–47; Young, *Autobiography*, 42–44.

45. "Extract of a Letter from a Gentleman to his Friend at the City of Washington, dated Lexington, Kentucky, March 9, 1801," quotation on 610; Lyle, "Diary," quotation on 51; Thomas Ashe, *Travels in America, Performed in 1806, for the Purpose of Exploring the Rivers Alleghany, Monongahela, Ohio, and Mississippi, and Ascertaining the Produce and Condition of Their Banks and Vicinity* (London, 1808), quotation on 191. See also Lyle, "Diary," 4; Joshua L. Wilson (Lexington) to Mrs. Sally Wilson, Mar. 14, 1808, Joshua L. Wilson Papers (Durrett).

46. Lyle, "Diary," quotation on 12; Fowler, "Kentucky 150 Years Ago," 55. Lyle also noted the opposition of gentlewomen. At the same meeting that James Bradford disrupted, "Mrs. Nicholas relic of the late Colonel Nicholas came with vinegar & bread" and whenever her friends seemed ready to succumb to the revivalist's fervor, she "rub'd their faces & noses & put it in their mouths." See Lyle, "Diary," 10.

47. F. A. Michaux, *Travels to the West of the Alleghany Mountains*, quotation on 249; Robert B. McAfee, "The Life and Times of Robert B. McAfee and His Family and Connections," *RKHS* 25 (1927): 222 (quotation); Josiah Murdoch Espy, *Memorandums of a Tour, Made by Josiah Espy in the States of Ohio and Kentucky in 1805* (Cincinnati, 1871), 24; Pears, ed., "A Journal of Two Missionary Tours Made in Kentucky and Tennessee," 383.

48. William Warren Sweet, "The Churches as Moral Courts of the Frontier," *Church History* 2 (Jan. 1933): 3–21.

49. Taylor, *A History of Ten Baptist Churches*, quotations on 77. On the migration of Baptist congregations, see George W. Ranck, *The Travelling Church, an Account of the Baptist Exodus from Virginia to Kentucky under the Leadership of Rev. Lewis Craig and Captain William Ellis* (Louisville, 1910).

50. Hood, "The Restoration of Community," 73–83. In 1800, according to Hood's examination of the memberships at Providence Church (Clark County), Bryan's Station Church (Fayette County), Forks of Elkhorn Church (Franklin County), and Stamping Ground (Scott County), about one-quarter of members came from the wealthiest 10 percent of households (as measured by tax payments), while fully two-thirds of members were in the upper 40 percent of taxable wealth. By contrast, only about one of nine members were from the lowest 40 percent. After 1800, "50 percent of the exclusions came to people in the lowest 40 percent of wealth, although they comprised only 30 percent of the membership" (ibid., 81).

51. "Records of the Forks of Elkhorn Baptist Church, Kentucky, 1800–1820," in Sweet, ed., *Religion on the American Frontier: The Baptists*, quotation on 328–29; Hood, "The Restoration of Community," 80; Marion B. Lucas, *A History of Blacks in Kentucky: Volume 1: From Slavery to Segregation, 1760–1891* (Frankfort, 1992), 119.

52. "Records of the Forks of Elkhorn Baptist Church," 328, 338; William Hickman, *A Short Account of My Life and Travels. For more than fifty years; A Professed Servant of Jesus Christ* (Louisville, 1969, orig., 1828), 19–20; Carter Tarrant, *The Substance of a Discourse Delivered in the Town of Versailles, Woodford County, State of Kentucky, April 20, 1806* (Lexington, 1806).

53. A. E. Martin, *Anti-Slavery Movement in Kentucky Prior to 1850* (Louisville, 1918), 19–20; Jeffrey Brooke Allen, "Were Southern White Critics of Slavery Racists?: Kentucky and the Upper South, 1791–1824," *Journal of Southern History* 44 (May 1978): 169–90.

54. "Minutes of the Elkhorn Baptist Association," quotation on 508.

55. Donald Matthews, *Slavery and Methodism: A Chapter in American Morality, 1780–1845* (Princeton, 1965), quotation on 28.

56. Neal, *By Their Fruits*, 59–61, 39.

57. Eades, ed., "History of the South Union Shaker Colony from 1804–1836," quotations on 218, 117, 122; "Journal kept by a member of the United Society of Believers, called Shakers, at Pleasant Hill, Mercer Co., Ky., January 3, 1815 to August 17, 1816" (FC).

Conclusion

1. On the Panic of 1819 and the economic and political crises of the 1820s, see Samuel Rezneck, "The Depression of 1819–1822: A Social History," *AHR* 39 (Oct. 1933): 28–47; Murray Rothbard, "The Frankfort Resolutions and the Panic of 1819," *RKHS* 61 (July 1963): 214–19; Arndt Stickles, *The Critical Court Struggle in Kentucky, 1819–1829* (Bloomington, Ind., 1929); Stephen Fackler, "John Rowan and the Demise of Jeffersonian Republicanism in Kentucky, 1819–1831," *RKHS* 78 (Winter 1980): 1–26; Lynn Marshall, "The Genesis of Grass-Roots Democracy in Kentucky," *Mid-America* 47 (Oct. 1965): 269–87; Frank F. Mathias, "The Relief and Court Struggle: Half-Way House to Populism," *RKHS* 81 (Apr. 1973): 154–

76; Sandra F. VanBurkleo, "'That Our Pure Republican Principles Might Not Wither': Kentucky's Relief Crisis and the Pursuit of 'Moral Justice,' 1818–1826" (Ph.D. diss., University of Minnesota, 1988).

2. St. John de Crèvecoeur, "Sketch of the River Ohio and of the Country of Kentucky," transcript translation from vol. 3, p. 387, Codex 52-A (Durrett) (quotation). For similar assessments of North American regions, including Kentucky, as good poor man's countries, see R. C. Ballard Thruston, ed., "Letter by Edward Harris, 1797," *FCHQ* 2 (July 1928): 166; Carl Bridenbaugh, ed., "Patrick M'Robert's Tour through Part of the North Provinces of America," *Pennsylvania Magazine of History and Biography* 59 (Apr. 1935): 136; Robert Beverly, *The History and Present State of Virginia* (1705; Chapel Hill, 1947), 275; Bernard Bailyn, *Voyagers to the West: A Passage in the Peopling of America on the Eve of the Revolution* (New York, 1986), 504.

3. Samuel Rogers, *Autobiography of Elder Samuel Rogers*, ed. Elder John Rogers (Cincinnati, 1880), quotation on 4–5; see also Mary Dewees, *Journal of a Trip from Philadephia to Kentucky, 1787–1788* (Crawfordsville, Ind., 1936), 189; Jacques P. Brissot de Warville, *New Travels in the United States of America, Performed in 1788*, ed. Durand Echeverria (Cambridge, Mass., 1964), 361; Joseph Poultney, "A Letter of Joseph Poultney," *Pennsylvania Magazine of History and Biography* 52 (Jan. 1928): 95; Spencer Records' Narrative, Draper MSS, 23CC5; "Sketches from Border Life," ibid., 27CC35; Barton Stone, *The Biography of Eld. Barton Warren Stone, Written by Himself: With Additions and Relections by Elder John Rogers* (Cincinnati, 1847), 1–2; James B. Finley, *Autobiography of Rev. James Finley, or, Pioneer Life in the West*, ed. W. P. Strickland (Cincinnati, 1853), 152–54.

4. I took great pride in coining "custom's last stand," only to discover that Edward Countryman came up with it first. Oh well.

5. Speech on Increase in the Naval Establishment, Jan. 22, 1812, in *HCP*, quotation on 1:626.

6. For "frontier" explanations of the origins of the Great Revival, see Catharine C. Cleveland, *The Great Revival in the West, 1797–1805* (Chicago, 1916); William W. Sweet, *Religion in the Development of American Culture, 1765–1840* (New York, 1952), 91–159, 210–21; idem, *Revivalism in America: Its Origin, Growth and Decline* (New York, 1944); Charles A. Johnson, *The Frontier Camp Meeting: Religion's Harvest Time* (Dallas, 1955). For revisionist view emphasizing old world roots of camp meeting and the "post-frontier" conditions in Kentucky, see Paul Conkin, *Cane Ridge: America's Pentecost* (Madison, 1990); Ellen T. Eslinger, "The Great Revival in Bourbon County, Kentucky" (Ph.D. diss., University of Chicago, 1988).

7. Anthony F. C. Wallace, "Handsome Lake and the Great Revival in the West," *American Quarterly* 4 (Summer 1952): 149–65; Gregory E. Dowd, *A Spirited Resistance: The North American Indian Struggle for Unity, 1745–1815* (Baltimore, 1992), 126–29; Richard White, *The Middle Ground: Indians, Empires, and Republics in the Great Lakes Region, 1650–1815* (New York, 1991), 336–39, 502–7.

8. Frederick Jackson Turner, "The Significance of the Frontier in American History," in *The Frontier in American History* (New York, 1920), quotation on 12. Later in the essay, Turner made explicit the representative character of Daniel Boone and his descendants: "Daniel Boone, the great backwoodsman, who com-

bined the occupations of hunter, trader, cattle-raiser, farmer and surveyor . . .
pioneered the way for the farmers to that region [Kentucky]. Thence he passed
to the frontier of Missouri, where his settlement was long a landmark on the
frontier. Here again he helped to open the way for civilization, finding salt licks,
and trails, and land. His son was among the earliest trappers in the passes of the
Rocky Mountains, and his party are said to have been the first to camp on the
present site of Denver. His grandson, Col. A. J. Boone, of Colorado, was a power
among the Indians of the Rocky Mountains, and was appointed an agent by the
government. Kit Carson's mother was a Boone. Thus his family epitomizes the
backwoodsman's advance across the continent" (quotation on 19).

9. On the importance of Kentucky to the evolution of national land policy,
see Paul W. Gates, "Tenants of the Log Cabin," *MVHR* 49 (June 1962): 25–31.

10. Allan Kulikoff, *The Agrarian Origins of American Capitalism* (Charlottesville, 1992), 77–90; Allan G. Bogue, "The Iowa Claim Clubs: Symbol and Substance," *MVHR* 45 (Sept. 1958): 231–53.

11. Henry Clay to John B. Dillon, July 28, 1838, in *HCP*, 9:214; Robert V.
Remini, *Henry Clay: Statesman for the Union* (New York, 1991), 381, 521–22.

12. The clipping from the Louisville *Courier Journal* can be found in Draper
MSS, 15C73–78.

NOTE ON SOURCES

This book draws on a wide range of published and unpublished materials. The manuscript collections at the Kentucky Historical Society, the Filson Club, the University of Kentucky, and Western Kentucky University provide much of the documentary records upon which this study rests. But the most important source for this (or any) study of the trans-Appalachian frontier are the voluminous notebooks collected by Lyman C. Draper (housed at the State Historical Society in Wisconsin and available on microfilm). Anyone who has examined the Draper manuscripts knows how rich they are and also knows how difficult they can be to read (especially the interviews conducted by the Reverend John D. Shane). Fortunately, many of the memoirs, letters, and interviews collected by Draper have been published. To save the vision of future researchers, I have generally cited the published accounts in the notes that follow. In a few cases, however, where the published version was abridged or differed from my own transcription, I have referenced the original manuscript. In any case, before venturing into the Draper manuscripts, researchers should read the first chapter of Elizabeth A. Perkins, *Border Life: Experience and Perception in the Revolutionary Ohio Valley* (forthcoming).

INDEX

Library of Congress Cataloging-in-Publication Data

Aron, Stephen.
How the West was lost : the transformation of Kentucky from
Daniel Boone to Henry Clay / Stephen Aron.
    p.   cm.
Includes bibliographical references and index.
ISBN 0-8018-5296-x (alk. paper)
    1. Kentucky—History—To 1792.   2. Kentucky—History—
1792–1865.   3. Frontier and pioneer life—Kentucky.   I. Title.
F454.A76   1996
976.9—dc20   95-52620